DAM RUN

MEMOIR OF A BETTER-THAN-AVERAGE RUNNER

Dr. Raymond D. Screws

Author: Raymond Screws
Publisher: Kingdom News Publication Services, LLC.

Printed in the United States of America.
ISBN 978-1-955127349

Dedication

Dedicated to my wife Alice and my son Ryan.

Also dedicated to my track coaches:

- Frank Kennedy
- Stan Coons
- Gary Cagle
- Gary Billions
- Riley Cartwright
- Don Barcus
- Dale Burkholder
- Robert Osburn
- Mark McGarity

Table of Contents

Introduction

This is the story of the ups and downs of life through athletics, and mostly running, and how persistence can pay off through the tribulations. I was born on December 6, 1961, in Los Angeles, California, possibly a descendant of a *Mayflower* passenger, original Massachusetts Bay colonists, New Haven Puritans, French Huguenots, and probably 17th-century English scoundrels. But other than the fact that I was born, the date, location, and heritage have little to do with this story. Although my 5th great-grandfather, Matthew Maddox, was tough. He fought in the Revolutionary War and was severely wounded and left for dead for several days but survived to "run" another day.

A story does require a beginning, and what the hell, why not my beginning? After all, the story is about me as viewed through the prism of running. This sounds a little narcissistic, and I hope I'm not all that. But maybe we're all just a little stuck on ourselves. Some people are completely narcissistic, and I ran against one or two over the years.

When I was 18, a teammate and I were invited to swim at a so-called exclusive pool where his girlfriend was a lifeguard. We ran the 4 miles to the pool, paddled about, and jumped off the diving board with the local elite. A man, maybe in his 50s or 60s, with a large handlebar mustache, perfectly waxed and curled, was drinking a can of light beer. I'm surprised he wasn't working on a glass of finely aged single-malt Bourbon. But maybe most elites in southeast

Kansas hadn't discovered smooth Kentucky spirits. He was certainly stuck on himself – a self-importance, if you will! Finally, after sipping on that fine vintage of water-downed malt beverage for a long while, the mustachioed gentleman entered the swimming pool in the shallow end with a beer in hand, held at head level, and walked through the water that reached midway up his chest with his chin held high at a fixed pompous angle, and exited at the other end. The swimmers in the pool parted for him like the Red Sea. Now that's narcissism. My teammate and I felt the urge to leave at that point, laughing our asses off as we ran the 4 miles back to town. If I saw that scene today, I'd still bust a gut. I've met others like that through the years, but not many in track. These people exist among runners, but few notice, especially those not involved in the sport.

Whether we are narcissistic, most of us like a little adulation. But adulation is rare in track and field unless you are a record-setting world-class athlete or an Olympic champion. At most meets in the United States, the only people to attend are athletes, coaches, some parents, and a few others scattered about. I once received a standing ovation after winning a tightly contested college 800-meter race. I think all 15 or 20 in the small rickety bleachers stood as I won the slow contest on a cinder track with a blistering fast finish! I deserved it – after all, I was missing my cousin's wedding only a few miles away. Thank about it. Adulation is so uncommon that I remember a handful of people standing and cheering on a hot day more than 40 years ago. I can't remember it happening any other time in college. I remember a guy falling on the ice with his feet flying above his head and receiving a standing ovation for his acrobatic misfortune. But then again, he wasn't competing or delivering a speech, and we were already standing. Maybe the adulation was because he didn't hurt himself, but the cheering began before anyone knew his condition.

My first taste of adulation occurred when I was 4 years old at some place in Arizona I can't fully describe. Borrowing a phrase from the

"Beverly Hillbillies," it was some sort of "cement pond" full of rainbow trout. It must have been 1966, and I don't recall much about that trip. I remember my sister getting sick and throwing up on her Raggedy Ann. It was dark outside, and I awoke when my dad pulled the car off the road. He threw the doll out into the desert – I can still see the smooth but cautious swing of my dad's arm as he slung the soiled cloth doll into the darkness. I don't remember what was wrong with my sister, but I do remember that we were stuck in the sand because it was the desert, and my dad parked on the shoulder. We were saved by a contentious truck driver, who pulled us back onto the road with his 18-wheeler.

And the other thing I remember about that trip was that trout-filled cement pond surrounded by a gaggle of retirees sitting in lawn chairs. For some reason, and I'm not sure why, people were allowed to catch fish in the "pond." Now, I don't know if it was just for kids or if anyone could fish for the trout, but I was there to catch my first fish. I don't even know where we were in Arizona and how my dad decided to stop in that location. I can't remember driving up to the place or what the area looked like. I just remember standing at the edge of the pool with a fishing rod in my hands. My dad was an avid trout fisherman and very good at it. He learned from my grandfather when he was a boy on trips to the High Sierras. My grandpa was a great trout fisherman. He used to catch trout with barbless hooks to avoid harming the fish when he released them. I never saw Grandpa catch trout, but I used to talk to him all the time about it. He and my dad would tell stories about going high up in the Sierras in some specific place, up above 9,000 feet, to catch golden trout. I have yet to catch the rare golden, but I dream of the day I will. One time, in the early 1980s, I think, my dad and cousin, Bob Smith, went trout fishing at Big Rock Creek in the Angeles National Forest, where my dad also fished as a youth. My dad out-fished Bob that day, and he asked my dad, "Uncle Billy, how did you out-fish me? Grandpa taught me how to trout fish." My dad replied that Grandpa taught him how to fish for trout as well. Big Rock Creek is also where I caught my first wild trout!

But the year before my Big Rock Creek accomplishment, I stood by that cement pond in Arizona, trying to catch an allusive caged rainbow. Time after time, one would bite, and I missed the catch as the old folks sounded their disappointment. Those senior citizens wanted me to catch a trout so badly – maybe seeing a 4-year-old fishing for his first trout made their day, or possibly it was a break from shuffleboard. But they kept waiting with anticipation as the gentlemen baiting my hook tossed the line in the water. I don't think I put the bait in the water myself, but I could be wrong. It could just as well have been my dad. All I know is I was trying to catch a fish and didn't have a clue what I was doing. I doubt I even knew they were trout – I'm sure I didn't know the difference between a trout and a bass. I'd seen pictures of catfish and even fish that lived in the ocean, and I might have seen trout when my dad caught them but could not have pointed one out.

Finally, after what seemed an eternity, I landed one of the not-so-elusive trout. And when I brought that colorful rainbow "ashore" (and I'll never forget the beauty of that trout), the geriatric audience gave me an ovation and even cheered a little. They were proud of me, and I was proud of myself, as were my mom and dad, but I doubt my 2-year-old sister was old enough to care. Oh, I don't think the hand the retirees gave me was wild and loud, but more of a golf clap. But it was an ovation nonetheless, and it was good! As I think about it, maybe that was the highlight of my life, and the last 58-plus years have all been downhill. Well, probably not. Even without the cheering and recognition, running and track gave me many terrific moments, as did earning a Ph.D., and of course, my marriage and the birth of my son, which was the greatest day of my life.

*

So, I repeat – this is a story about running, competing, and life. And not from the mind of a great runner. I became a very good small-college runner, but certainly not national class. I think this type of story is rarely told in sports, and maybe it's not important, but not everything has to be important. I had a running career, and I still do in the guise of a volunteer track and cross-country coach. I try to use what I learned as an athlete when I coach, as many coaches do, but also in life and career. I think I'm a better coach than I was a runner, but the athletes might disagree! I'm surrounded by men and women I respect and admire in my job. Maybe that's true adulation, done quietly and without fanfare. Those I work and coach with, along with some educators at the school where I coach cross-country, are outstanding people, but I have never given them standing ovations. Nonetheless, they have my respectful adulation. So maybe I'm confusing adulation with simple cheering, but it's my story, so I don't care. At any rate, this might be the work of a relativist, which, in that case, you can make of it as you will.

Chapter 1
Realizing I Was Slow

When I was a little kid, I thought I was fast, I mean really fast, faster than any kid my age in the neighborhood, and maybe even faster than a few boys a little older than me. I'm sure I thought I was faster than kids from other neighborhoods as well. We lived on Victory Boulevard in Burbank, California, but I rarely had the opportunity to display my blazing legs because Victory was a busy street, and my mom wouldn't let me out of her sight. Still, even though I couldn't compare my speed to other kids, I lived on the right street because I was fast enough to beat anyone, at least as I saw it. I know I didn't catch the irony then.

On Victory, our next-door neighbors were a French-speaking family. I believe they were French Canadian. Their home was not part of our duplex, and the yards were separated by a tall chain-link fence covered in ivy. Our duplex and their home were owned by the same man who always wore heavy work boots and walked shuffling his feet. The family consisted of a mother, a father, and a little girl. She was my best friend, unlike her parents, she could not speak English. I think her name was Lynn. When I was allowed outside, I would run to one of the holes in the Ivy and talk with my little friend. Since I was fast, I could make it to the fence lickety-split. After speaking with Lynn for a while, we would sprint to another hole in the ivy and talk some more until it was time to high tail it to another ivy opening.

Now, you might ask: "I thought she only spoke French? Did you also know French?" Well, no, I didn't speak French. But I was told by my mom that by speaking to her through the fence, I actually taught Lynn to speak English. I can't confirm this myself, but it must be true. But I can still remember speaking to her through that fence and racing her to the next opening. Her face is etched in my mind. And most important, these were my first races – and I won! I think. Eventually, the owner of the homes decided to get rid of the chain-link fence and build one out of concrete blocks. But he made sure he created holes in the fence with special blocks so me and my "girlfriend" could still carry on with our joyous communications and race from opening to opening.

When I was 5 years old and before I started kindergarten, we moved to Brighten Street in Burbank. Because Brighten was not busy, my mom allowed me to leave our home, which was a light green triplex, and play on our side of the street. We lived in the back home, and the triplex was in the middle of a long block; at least, it seemed long to a 5-year-old. My new best friend, John, lived across the street. I remember a girl named Robin in my kindergarten class at Washington Elementary School who lived down the street on our side of the road. I had another friend who lived down the street as well, but I don't remember his name. There was a kid in my class who lived on another street who had a cool dad because he always wore white t-shirts with cigarettes rolled up in his short sleeves. His son also wore short-sleeve white t-shirts with a sleeve rolled up – but without the pack of cigarettes, of course.

Living on a quiet street allowed me to run up and down the sidewalk, blazing by people and letting everyone know how fast I was. I just knew I was the fastest kid around. I don't even know if I ever raced John, but I was confident I was faster. The people who owned the triplex were Jack and Joan, who lived in the middle home and liked to drink and have a good time. I remember that in the winter of 1968, my dad was watching TV with Jack, and both of them were laughing so loud that my sister and I couldn't sleep. They were watching a new program called "Laugh-In."

One of the fastest sprints I ever mustered came one day when I walked into Jack and Joan's home without knocking. I used to visit her, and she would read to me, and I know I walked in other times without knocking. But on this day, I think she was drunk or hung over. As soon as I opened the door, she came at me, face to face, growling and screaming at the top of her lungs with a fierce look of anger, ugliness, and meanness, full of popping veins and bulging eyes with yellow knurled teeth and alcohol infested spit flying in every direction…. Not that I even noticed most of this. I was too busy breaking the world record in the 50-yard dash getting my ass out of there, screaming my own tune as I rushed through my own front door. I still have nightmares! Joan called my mom to apologize, and I never entered a home again without knocking.

One September, probably in 1967, my dad and Jack attended a few Dodger games when the team was out of the pennant race. It was easy to get seats when the season was lost, but Jack, a rabid Dodgers fan, saw this as an opportunity to see his beloved team in action. Jack was a tremendous chef, but when he attended these games, he would gorge himself on cheap hotdogs (although I hear that the Dodger Dog is the best ballpark dog there is) and guzzle tons of beer. He would get so drunk he could hardly stand. I still don't know who drove to the games, my dad or Jack, but if it was Jack they were lucky to make it home. At least Jack never vomited from eating too many ballpark dogs. My dad ate too many hotdogs at an Angels game and threw up while driving down the Golden State Freeway. My uncle, Ernie Mercado, tried to jump out while the car was still moving but didn't make it in time. I won't describe the mess.

So, there's Jack, drunk and angry because the Dodgers were losing. It's the late innings, and as is typical of Dodger games, most fans filed out after the 7th. Few people are left at Chavez Ravine, and Jack's drunken, obnoxious voice can be heard throughout the stadium and maybe clear to Chinatown. My dad had to pull Jack away from several drunken fights – there were not enough people left for a brawl. My dad said that happened at several games. But Jack was a nice guy; it's just that he and Joan drank far too much.

I was confined to my side of the street, and except for walking to school, I was not allowed to cross a street without an adult. And even then, there were usually crossing guards to help navigate the dangerous intersections. I used to ask my mom if I could walk to the store with friends or even by myself, but of course, I was told "no." But one day, I decided on the trek anyway and made my way to the store a couple of blocks away with friends. Since I was fast, I could run across the streets without fear of harm – I could outrun any car or vehicle of any description! Plus, my speed allowed me to leave and return without my mom knowing I was gone. When I returned home, I proudly proclaimed to my mom that I had indeed gone to the store without her permission, and I had obviously made it back in one piece. My mom was not amused, but I don't remember the punishment – I'm sure it wasn't pleasant. My mom reminded me until her death about the day I disobeyed her and skipped off to the store that sunny day in Burbank.

Although I was ridiculously fast, it seemed that I could never escape the clutches of the bully down the street. Mike would throw me on my back in the grass and sit on my chest, holding my hands back beside my head, and brag, "I'm in second grade, and I'm bigger than you." True enough. Mike was, let's just say, overweight – it's a nice way of putting it! I should have realized that when fat Mike could catch me and hold me down, I might not be quite as fast as I imagined. But then again, I don't recall ever attempting to run from Mike, and I'm not sure why I continued to matriculate down by Mike's house. Nonetheless, Mike never actually hurt me. I just think the other second graders at Washington School teased him, and he needed a little kindergarten kid to express his frustrations. I know my cousin, also named Mike, and a second grader at Washington School as well didn't care for fat-ass Mike, the bully.

My first cousins, Mike and Phillip Mercado, lived a couple of blocks away on Frederic. They lived on a dead-end street, and it was at the end of their road where I experienced my first "athletic" competition. It was a game we called hot foot, and it might be a name Mike made up, or it could have been universal. It was a game of tag played on the hot asphalt in bare feet. It had to be a scorching day, and the objective was to move your feet all the time to avoid being burned on the bottom of the feet while not being tagged by the one who was "it." Like any game of tag, if you were touched by the "it" person, you became "it." But you were also "it" if you ran onto the grass, which was hard to avoid when your feet were blistering. Those who could not keep their feet moving quickly enough got the hot foot and had to exit the street. Of course, I was fast enough to keep from being tagged and had quick enough feet to keep from being burned. I was blistering fast, and my feet remained blister-free – at least, that's the way I like to remember my skills.

One day, at the end of Frederic Street, I demonstrated my possible lack of speed, or maybe I just didn't pay attention to my peripheral vision. Phillip and I decided to make our way down to the dead-end and cause havoc. At the end of the street, on the other side of a tall chain-link fence, was an on-ramp to the Golden State Freeway. The ramp was from Buena Vista Street, and it crossed the wash before merging into the freeway. Phillip and I decided to throw rocks at the cars entering the freeway, but truth be told, the combination of our ages (6 and 4) and the fact that the ramp was a fair distance from the fence meant we never came remotely close to hitting vehicles with our rocky ammunition. I doubt anyone in the cars and trucks ever knew a couple of young, potential juvenile offenders were "tossing" rocks their way. But we kept trying, and we were having a grand time until Phillip picked up a board and said something like

"I'm Superman" and attempted to heave the battered board over the fence at an unsuspecting car. But instead of flying over the fence, the small piece of lumber traveled about two feet and hit me above my left eye. I never saw it coming. I don't know if the impact alone caused the problem or if there was a nail in the board, but blood spurted everywhere. We made it back to Phillip's house, and my mom took me to our doctor, who decided to give me three stitches. The scar is still perfectly visible in my eyebrow today. My aunt Judy, Phillip's mom, said they should turn the end of her street into a park to prevent these sorts of things, but it wouldn't have stopped me and Phillip from expressing our inner "criminal inclinations."

On April 1, 1968, my dad came home from his job, where he worked as a millwright, and proclaimed we were moving to Kansas. My mom didn't believe him at first because of the timing, but my dad didn't realize it was April Fool's Day. When my mom asked if she could call her mother to tell her the news, my dad said yes, and she knew it was true. My dad wanted out of LA. My parents were born and raised in Los Angeles, and both attended Poly High in San Fernando Valley – LA was all they knew. But from vacations, my dad understood that there was a better life out there...somewhere. I think the kicker was when Dad attempted to get a loan to buy a house that cost $10,000, and the banker essentially laughed at him. He knew there was not much future in the Los Angeles area, and he concluded that we needed to get out of that hell.

We had visited friends who moved to Grants Pass, Oregon, and Dad loved it. But while there, he realized he had hay fever and decided southern Oregon wouldn't be the best place for us despite the beauty of the graceful Rogue River. I, for one, am not sure how I would have liked it, but I think it would have been a terrific place to live. One thing I remember about visiting Grants Pass was attempting to demonstrate to my friends, who were two boys about my age, how tough I was by stepping on a large nail sticking out of a board. That rusty piece of sharp metal went right through my cheap tennis shoes and into the bottom of my young foot at something a little less than an inch. (Or maybe well short of an inch!) It's a wonder I later earned a Ph.D. with the amount of intelligence I mustered that day. Other than that, and my dad's hay fever, it was a great trip, although my sister, Karen, who was three at the time, might disagree when she became petrified by the dune buggy ride, we took on the dunes along the Oregon coast, and had to ride up front with the driver.

On that trip, I saw my first sailboat, viewed whales off the coast in the Pacific, and stayed in the creepiest but quietest hotel I think I've ever seen. We crossed the Columbia River near the mouth at Astoria, Oregon, on what seemed like the longest bridge in the world. And we also visited the Redwoods, and although I haven't been back, the grandeur of those wonders of the world is still branded in my mind.

The other thing about the visit to the Redwoods is that the starter in our car went out. Luckily, our car was a stick shift, so we could get a push and get the car started again. When we were on our way home, we got stuck in a Sacramento traffic jam on the freeway. I remember a man walking between cars and talking to people through their windows, but as a five-year-old, I didn't know what he wanted. But it was hot, and there was the possibility that the car would overheat. But my dad didn't want to turn the motor off because it would be difficult to get the damn thing started again. Air conditioning wasn't an issue because there wasn't an air conditioner in the car. For some reason, the car stalled, and we ended up needing a push anyway, which wasn't easy in a traffic jam!

Besides our friends in Grants Pass, a reason to move to Oregon was that my aunt and uncle, Leila and Edward, lived there. We visited them on the trip, and what I remember is arriving late at night. My sister and I got our pictures taken on a small tractor my uncle owned. Edward built houses and built the house they lived in. From the pictures, it seems like it was a nice ranch-style home, but I don't recall much about it. Leila was my Grandpa LaRue's older sister and was extremely proper and very nice. Leila and Edward moved to Kansas a few years after we did, so they wouldn't have been around us in Oregon for very long.

I wish they'd remained in Oregon because, as it turned out, Edward was the biggest, hateful asshole that ever lived. Other than writing about him here, I mostly choose to forget him. When my dad called me a few years ago to tell me Edward had died, my answer was, "So, I don't care." This was my dad's reaction as well, but he felt he needed to tell me, which was true. I should feel bad about how I reacted and how I still feel about his passing and about him as a man – but I don't. For years, I didn't even know where the bastard was buried, and I didn't care to know. But I accidentally came across his grave while looking for another relative. Nonetheless, Leila was a sweet and wonderful lady, and my memories of her are good.

I sometimes wonder what it would have been like to live in Oregon and become a runner in a state with such a rich running tradition. Would I have become a runner? And if so, would I have become a better runner than I became? But my mom and dad decided to move to Kansas, which wasn't such a bad thing. My Grandma and Grandpa LaRue were born and raised in Kansas. They moved to California in 1941, and my grandpa said Los Angeles, and especially San Fernando Valley, was a paradise. But after the Korean War, in the mid-1950s, Grandpa said it began to change, and it was when he first noticed the smog that would become worse by the time 1968 rolled around. I suspect from the late 1950s on, he thought about leaving LA. I know that, in the late 1960s, he thought about buying a vineyard in the Central California Valley, but he decided he was too old to begin that career. I don't know how he would have liked a career in agriculture – he left the farm in Kansas because he didn't want to be a farmer.

When my mom was growing up, the family vacationed in Kansas almost every summer to visit relatives. Her Grandpa LaRue, my great-grandfather, was still alive, and many other relatives, such as her great-grandmother Foltz, lived there as well, although some had

13

moved to southern California during WWII. My Great Grandma LaRue died in the 1930s, and my mom never knew her. In 1965, we took a vacation to Kansas. To get an idea about the difference in how the information got around then, my parents didn't even know about the Watts Riots, which took place in LA while we were in Kansas, until we returned. Now, I'm not suggesting that communications were in the dark ages and comparing the 1960s to 1815, when the Brits and Americans didn't know the War of 1812 had ended before they fought the Battle of New Orleans, but it wasn't like it is today.

I had the opportunity to see my Kansas relatives for the first time, including my Great Grandma Peterson (her mother, Grandma Foltz, had already died), who scared the tarnation out of me one evening, although not nearly as bad as Joan would do three years later. Great Grandma watched me and my sister while our parents were out with relatives. I was in the kitchen saying "night, day – night, day – night, day," as I switched the light off and on. She screamed bloody murder at me, and I'm lucky I didn't sprint away like I did with Joan, or I would have run smack into a wall – it was a very small kitchen.

On our Kansas vacation, I wanted a gun and holster. I must have mentioned this to my Uncle Tom, who was my Grandpa LaRue's oldest brother by 15 years. Uncle Tom owned a radiator shop, but by the time I came along, he had a small appliance fixit shop in a garage behind his house. He told me that if I wanted a gun and holster, I needed to ask Uncle Pete, who lived on the family farm, because he was rich! My Great-Grandpa and Great-Grandma LaRue lived on the farm, and my grandpa, along with his brothers and sisters, were raised there. I think my great-grandfather was a gentlemen farmer, and in one federal census, he was listed as a butcher. However, my mom didn't think he did much of anything. In 1941, the government bought the farm, along with another few thousand acres of land, to build the Kansas Ordnance Plant in anticipation of America's involvement in World War II. My great-grandfather moved to town, and eventually, Uncle Pete was drafted into the Army when he was in his 30s.

When Uncle Pete returns from the war, he wanted to farm, so he bought some land. But in 1947, the government sold some land that was part of the Ordnance Plant, and because the old family farm was on the edge of the federal property, it was part of the sale. Uncle Pete bought back the family farm as well as adjacent land. The Army had demolished the family homestead, so Uncle Pete, who was single, took a guard shack that stood at the edge of the property and pulled it to a place just a few feet in front of the old home. The shack didn't have running water or electricity. Pete lived there until he died in 1989, although he did manage to get the place wired before I was born. He didn't have barns either, just old railroad boxcars he used to store grain and other agricultural items. In the last few years of his life, Pete's wells became contaminated, and he had to have water trucked in.

When we went to visit Uncle Pete while on vacation, I confidently asked him for a gun and holster and said Uncle Tom told me to do it. I remember visiting Pete that day, but I don't remember asking for the gift. But my mom said that's just how it happened. I think Pete was amused, so he gave me $20 for the gun and holster, which was much more than enough for the toy. We also visited my aunt and uncle and cousins, who consisted of 8 boys and 1 girl. Aunt Betty was my Grandma LaRue's youngest sister. The second youngest of the Cruse family, Billy, is my age, and Brent is the same age as my sister. At that age, I would draw people without arms, and my cousin Keith, who was a few years older than me and who I found out a few years later could really draw well, said that people without arms wouldn't be able to carry things or even run properly – I began to create my people with arms.

When it was known that we were moving to Kansas, I had the opportunity to go to the drag races and witness real speed, even better than what I demonstrated on our neighborhood sidewalks.

Down the street from us on Brighten was a young family with a little boy and a girl who were both younger than me. I used to visit them all the time. The mother's sister, who babysat the kids, took a liking to me and decided a nice going away present was to take me to the drag races – her husband was a driver. And man, she was right! As we got closer to the drag strip, we began to see cool cars, including a few roadsters, driving to the track. I was excited, and what made the day super special was that we didn't sit in the stands but stayed in the pits with her husband and his mechanics.

Her husband drove what was then called a rail – a car with a long, skinny front, big tires on the back, and small bicycle-looking wheels on the front. Today, these fast cars are usually called top-fuel dragsters. Her husband won both his races, but I witnessed all sorts of races with all kinds of cars. The pits were located close to the starting line, and the sound the cars made at the start was so loud you couldn't hear yourself think – it was exhilarating! The only issue was I couldn't tell who won the races because we were at ground level and a quarter mile from the finish. But this inconvenience was outweighed for me because I got to sit in the car between races while the mechanics worked on the engine. It was one of the greatest days in a young boy's life!

Although I had never seen him race, my uncle, Wayne Smith, was a drag racer who had built roadsters when he was young. I have a picture of him beside one of his cars. Wayne got out of drag racing by the mid-1960s because, as he told me years later, it got too expensive. In the 1950s, he built cars with Don Prudhomme in San Fernando. Prudhomme became one of the greatest and most famous drag racers in history and is known as "The Snake."

Wayne belonged to one of the toughest, meanest car clubs or gangs in the Valley during the 1950s, called the Jacks. My dad told me a story of the time 4 or 5 members of a rival club jumped Wayne, and my uncle put them all in the hospital without receiving a scratch. Wayne was not a tall man, but he had wide shoulders and was tough as nails. When I was little, he used to enjoy looking at the kids, scaring the hell out of them, and then laughing at his accomplishments. The last time I saw my uncle was in 1984 in Lancaster, California, and I brought up the incident with the rival gang. Wayne's health had deteriorated by then, and he was physically a shell of his former self. He sat at the kitchen bar with a popsicle in his hand, looked in the other direction with a far-away look in his eyes, and didn't say anything for a few seconds. Then he kind of chuckled and said, "Yeah, I remember that." That was it – no details, no story, just an acknowledgment. Wayne died the next year.

In June 1968, after I was out of school, we moved to Kansas. My Grandma and Grandpa LaRue had decided to move as well, so we went together. My Grandpa bought a truck for the move instead of renting. He took me with him one day to look at the truck he bought, and I assume he finalized the details or signed some forms. I walked beside Grandpa LaRue with a salesperson at the truck dealership as we made our way to a distant corner of the lot. Along the way, we passed all sorts of trucks – Mack trucks, 18-wheelers, 10-wheelers, and some other types as well – and I kept asking him every time we came close to a cool truck if that was the one he bought. But they weren't. Finally, we got to the last truck, an old green thing with wooden side panels on the back and no windows in the doors. But there was a windshield! I was disappointed – I wanted one of those big trucks with a flat front end.

For the move, my dad drove the truck with newly inserted cardboard for the side windows. My uncle Albert, my mom's younger brother, who I think was 14 or 15 at the time, traveled with dad in the truck, while grandpa followed in his car with Albert sometimes with him when he became tired of the rough-riding hunk of machinery. I was supposed to ride with my dad in the truck as well, but Grandpa thought that without real windows, it might not be the best place for a six-year-old to make the trip. My mom drove our 1964 tan Ford

Falcon that my dad bought to take the place of the car we took on the Oregon trip. In that small car, we crammed my grandma, who sat in the front seat, my four-year-old sister, my mom's youngest sister, Mary, who was 10, and me. We also had two cats who didn't get along. Our cat, Rusty, who was huge, was in the back seat with us kids, and my grandparents' cat, Princess (a somewhat mean-spirited black cat with a bobtail), stayed in the front.

We left Burbank in the Falcon late in the day to avoid the desert heat, and my dad, uncle, and grandpa left a few hours later. By the time we arrived in Needles, California, well after dark, my grandmother was sick, so we stopped at a motel for the night. The truck, with my grandpa on its tail, rumbled by us sometime later without knowing we had stopped – this was well before cell phones. The route we took for much of the trip was Highway 66, in the opposite direction the "Okies" traveled to California during the Dust Bowl days of the Depression. It's probably the route my grandparents took when they moved to LA in 1941. Grandma LaRue was sick enough that we had to stay in Needles for more than two days. While we were at the motel, the temperature reached over 120 degrees, and I remember trying to open the car door, which was made of metal, and burning the hell out of my hand. The asphalt was so hot the heat could be felt through the soles of our shoes – it would have been a great day for hot feet. Finally, after two and a half days, we left that God-forsaken place in the middle of the night so as not to be burned. The car didn't have air conditioning!

A few days later, we limped into this town, which didn't appear to be any different from many other towns we had driven through. As we got to the other end, my mom turned onto a back street, and as we drove a few blocks, my grandma said: "Look at all these great trees. Wouldn't you like to live here?" My sister and I said, "Yes." The street was lined with tall oak and elm trees that shaded almost every inch. Then we pulled up and parked in front of a small house with a porch swing – and I recognized the house as my Great

Grandma Peterson's. I was excited but scared, as I had remembered that night three years before. But there was nothing to fear. Great grandma wasn't the bear I remembered. We were in our new hometown – Parsons, Kansas, a town of about 14,000 people stuck in the southeast corner of the state. My dad, uncle, and grandpa arrived a couple of days before us and, of course, didn't know where we were. I don't know if they worried or not or if they just thought we got lost for a few days because, apparently, my mom couldn't read a map. Whether she could or not is irrelevant because she navigated the route just fine, and none of us were the worst for wear and tear – except maybe the cats. With a new town and a new neighborhood, when we found a place to live, I would be able to demonstrate my speed to a new bunch of kids.

We soon found a home on Gabriel Street on the north end of town, about half a block from Highway 59 and a couple of blocks from Labette Creek. One thing that was different from Burbank was the smell – the stockyards were on the other side of the creek, and that terrible odor was especially bad in the winter when the wind blew from the north. I soon had the opportunity to demonstrate my tremendous speed while walking to my new school, Lincoln Elementary, one morning during the fall of 1968. A brown, medium-sized female dog with pups must have decided I was a threat and chased me home with her teeth snarling at my heels. But she never caught me! Nevertheless, I had the wits scared out of me, and my mom took me to school. It's amazing how scared I was as a little kid because as I got older, I feared little.

Later, when I became a pretty good middle-distance runner in college, I wondered where my ability came from. I think my dad was decently fast, but that's not endurance. But I have a clue. When I was little, we were at my Grandma Peterson's house, and two of her sisters, Aunt Lavere, who lived in Cherokee, Kansas, and Aunt Hick of Flint, Michigan, were visiting. The three sisters began to talk, but they didn't listen to each other; they just got louder and louder and went on and on and on and on. Finally, one, red-faced and about to pass out, sucked in that precious life-saving oxygen with a huge breath that thundered with a vicious wheezing sound and continued bellowing words. Another did the same, and then the third, and this cycle continued in a fierce battle for what seemed forever. These three overweight old women had never heard a word from the others. This is where I got my wind.

*

I should have had an inkling that I wasn't as fast as I imagined when I raced my cousin Billy and got smoked. But it seemed all the Cruses were fast, and so it didn't dawn on me that others were faster than me as well. Toward the end of first grade, we moved to the other side of Parsons, and I attended Washington Elementary, where some of the Cruses attended. It was really in second grade when the realization that I was slow was finally embedded in my young, disappointed mind. The class held some races on the playground, and I was buried by a number of kids. At least I beat all the girls and the real big boys. A kid named Roger was devastatingly fast, and I held no illusion that I would ever beat him in a fair race. Hell, Roger could have fallen twice and beat me from one end of the playground to the other!

For some reason, I equated size with speed. A kid who was big or overweight had to be slow. It goes to reason. Well, I found out the hard way that my assumption is not always correct. We moved to Stevens Street in Parsons in 1969. While we lived in Stevens, my aunt and uncle, Judy and Ernie, and cousins Mike and Phillip moved to Parsons and rented a house next to us. Within a few years, they bought a house around the corner north of Stevens, close to the switching yards of the Katy Railroad, and we bought a home around the other corner on Clark, an old street pathed with red bricks. Across the street from us on Clark lived the Kerrs, who had moved there from the other side of town not long before we moved.

Their oldest son, John, was my age and was much bigger than me, and I was not small for my age. One day, and I'm not sure why I decided on stupidity, I called John a fat–so–big mistake! John started to chase me. Because I was smaller and faster, there was no way John Kerr would catch me. I found out two important things that day; first, John was not only faster than me, but he was just plain fast. And second, he was not fat. John was big, there was no question, but he was all muscle. As I made my way through a backyard not far from my house, I ran up a large brick barbecue so I could easily jump the fence into the alley, and that's where John caught me – I didn't make it over the fence. I think John was scared he hurt me, and I remember that it didn't feel too good! Luckily, I learned my lesson, and I must have decided that having a friend who was big, strong, and fast was to my advantage because we became good friends.

As time went on during my elementary school years, it became increasingly apparent that I was not nearly the fastest kid in the neighborhood and at Washington School, but I wasn't the slowest either. When we still lived on Stevens, there was a family that lived next door to us on the opposite side of my cousins. This family was wild. The father didn't live at home and was away much of the time anyway because he was a truck driver. I think he was a good man who attempted to keep his two boys in line. The mother didn't know how to raise kids and sometimes left her second grader and kindergartener sons at home alone all night while she was out with some man. The boys constantly stole from neighbors and even egged our house once, but my mom forced them to clean our screens with soap and water, under protest, of course.

The younger brother, who was actually bigger, just did what his smaller but older brother told him to do. I used to regularly beat up the older brother because of his indiscretions, even though he was a year older than me. My cousin Mike beat the hell out of him, too. Now, I can't say I was actually faster than the kid because I'm not sure he ever attempted to run away from me. I just think he was dumb. For example, his stupidity was on display one day after school, across the street from the Washington playground, when he opened his mouth at the wrong time and received the whopping of his life. The kid doing the beating kept telling his opponent to stay down, but he wouldn't do it – he was bloodied and bruised, but he kept getting up. Eventually, the school principal, Mr. Dove, arrived and broke it up. Otherwise, I think the kid would have ended up in the hospital.

The best pure speed I have ever witnessed from human beings was demonstrated by the brothers' mom. She was at our house with a couple of other mothers, as they "discussed" the "adventures" of her boys as they destroyed our neighborhood. Finally, the boys' mother said something defending her sons, and a mother who lived across the street, Hennie, threatened to beat her ass and chased her out the front door. They both hit that screen door like a bolt of lightning, but Hennie never caught her. The speed, quickness, and agility from both were impressive – any NFL scout would have signed them up on the spot. They didn't live there much longer, and we never saw them again after they moved. I think they left town.

Even though I wasn't fast, and some might even say I was slow, I was still good at some of the playground games, including "last one to the wall." This game usually involved some semblance of speed, and I must have had just enough ability in my legs to do well. Usually, there were several people who were "it." The rest of those playing remained at the wall of the school, touching it with a hand. The objective was to run across the playground to the other wall without being tagged. If you were tagged, you became another "it" person. But the name of the game was to get back to the starting wall, and if you were at the far wall and someone yelled, "last one to the wall," you needed to run back to the first wall. The last one, or the last few, were "it" for the next round. I was rarely "it," so I must have used guile because of my lack of great speed. I was also good at tetherball, but it only required the players to remain in one place so I could overcome the deficiency of my legs.

I was also good at softball and, later, baseball. During the spring of my first-grade year, notices were sent home with the students about summer softball and baseball. I wanted to play and showed the note to my mom when she and my Aunt Betty picked us up from school. My mom was no fan of me playing baseball and feared that I would get hurt, but my cousin, Kevin Cruse, assured her that it was only softball at my age, and no one would get hurt. Kevin and his twin brother, Keith, were both good baseball players, so I wanted to be like them. My dad was fine with me playing and was a great player as a kid, so I signed up!

The team I was assigned to was sponsored by the Eagles Club, and we were called the Trojans. We wore black caps with a yellow "E" on the front, which confused some of our opponents because, to them, we should have had a "T" on the hat. My cousin Brian Scott, one of Keith and Kevin's brothers, was also on the team, but the team picture was taken during the only game he missed. We ended up being a very good team and finished second in the league. Our pitcher, Ricky Clifton, was the son of the head coach. Many times, I have found when the son of the coach is the pitcher, the kid really can't pitch worth a damn – favoritism is still alive and well. But in this case, the usual didn't stand up because Ricky was the best pitcher in the league. We lost two games – one to the first-place team and one to a team that cheated and did so by intimidating and threatening the umpires. Not that our coaches were scared, quite the contrary. I think Mr. Clifton was pretty tough, and if it wasn't for the kids, the other coaches might have been in physical danger.

Mr. Clifton was a fair and very good coach. No matter how good you were, or lack thereof, you got to play. Apparently, I was not a good player that first year. In fact, the only hit I got was when I smacked the ball on the ground to one of the infielders, who had ice in his glove. He had to make a decision – drop the ice and get the ball or keep chewing the ice in his glove – he chose the latter, and I hit the ball through his legs. My Grandma and Grandpa Screws were visiting from Los Angeles, so they got to witness the grandeur of a single by their grandson. The next year, the team I played on was not nearly as good, but I became an outstanding player. I hit over .800 and was one of the best home run hitters in the league.

Being able to run fast was not a prerequisite for being a good baseball player. The third year of playing was my first year in hardball. I was a good player but not the best on the team. I did start, however, and we had a terrific team. My Baptist teammates could really play, and we had a great pitcher. We finished third behind WAME and St. Mary's, both of whom had the most talent and also had great pitchers (and uniforms). During our last league game, I hit a single, a double, and a triple in that order. We were winning big, and while I was on deck waiting for my fourth at-bat, a teammate hit a home run. There wasn't a fence, so if you could hit a line drive over the heads of the outfielders, you had a good chance for a four-bagger. As my teammate crossed home plate, and I wish I could remember his name, I told him I was hitting a home run as well.

I hit the ball hard, hard enough that it would have been an easy homerun for many – not for me, though. But I was determined! I rounded third base with the gait of a worn-out, loaded-down mule. I wasn't going to make it, so I turned back to chug myself back to third as the ball reached the catcher, but my slow churning legs had me trapped as the catcher wheeled and threw to the third baseman. There was no doubt I was about to be tagged out, so I tuned back home and waddled the best I could to the catcher, who caught the ball well before I arrived. So, I turned again and headed back to third. But this time, my tortoise-like reflexes served me well because as soon as the catcher threw back to third, I spun as quickly as I could and was determined not to run back to third again. The catcher didn't run me back, and I was close to home. It was make or break, and I slid into home, feet first, with everything I had as the ball arrived back to the catcher – SAFE! I don't know if there was an error, and it didn't matter to me. This was a home run!

The next game was the first of the end-of-the-season tournament, and we played a team that we had smothered earlier. I was confident because I demonstrated I was a great hitter. I went hitless, and we lost the game. Not to suggest we lost because I couldn't get the bat on the ball. No, we all played lousy, and I wasn't good enough to make a real difference in the outcome. By the next year, I was. I was second in the league in home runs and even hit one against my cousin Billy in an exhibition game – that's what you get for being faster than me! I also had a high batting average and was a good catcher. But I never played for a good baseball team again.

My last year of playing, after 6th grade, was the worst athletic experience of my life. But it's partially my fault because I was recruited and agreed to play for the team. The coach was so bad he took the fun out of the game. I was one of the best hitters on the team, but after he realized his son was a terrible pitcher, one that kept me constantly running to the backstop, he placed him at catcher, which essentially ended my playing time. The only time I got to play again, and the only time we had any fun, was when the coach and his son went on a fishing trip, and his wife and daughter took over the team for two games. We won both games and because we didn't have pitching, we gave up tons of runs. But that made it fun. We just outscored both teams, and I got to play catcher again.

During the last game of the season, the "real" coach put me in right field with a couple of innings left. A low line drive was hit my way, and when it landed about 20 feet in front of me, it bounced in the other direction. I picked up the ball and threw it into the infield and was then promptly taken out of the game. I never even got an at-bat. I left the game before it was over and attempted to walk home. When I got a few blocks away, I was picked up by the coach and his son, along with a couple of other players who were in the car. They asked me why I left early, but I don't think I gave them the satisfaction. I didn't say a word all the way home. John Kerr and I got out of the car and went our separate ways, and I never played organized baseball again. My desire was gone. John continued with baseball and was a very good player.

As for me, I needed to find new sports in which to participate, and I found them in football and track. Luckily, my love for America's pastime returned in adulthood, and I even played and umpired 19th-century vintage base ball [note: this is baseball was spelled in the 19th century] interpretations.

So, is there a purpose to all these stories? Yes, I realized I was slow!

Chapter 2
"I'm Going to Kick Your ..."

I should have known that I was blessed with natural endurance and even strength in my late elementary school days. I actually did know that I could run a fair distance without getting tired, but I didn't equate this with sports, especially track and field. I was really unfamiliar with the sport other than it existed, and I needed to be fast to compete. I just didn't know about all the events that were included in track and field. One evening, while we were at the Cruse's house, my cousin Keith came home all excited because his track team at Parsons High School had just beaten their rival, Labette County High School. Keith had apparently run very well – and that made sense because he was fast. But I didn't understand the events he competed in because I thought of track as the 50-yard and 100-yard dashes – that's it. He was jumping up and down with his twin brother Kevin, who must not have been on the team, and his mom, my Aunt Betty, was excited as well. Truthfully, that scene was beyond me because sports were football, baseball, and basketball.

I followed the three sports like most boys that I grew up around. Since we lived in Kansas, hockey was some odd foreign sport that was played on ice, and there were no ice rinks around our area. But football, baseball, and basketball were different, and truth be told, basketball was a distant third, although we did play it during the winter. And we always followed the pattern – we played football in the fall, basketball during the winter, and baseball when it warmed up in the spring and summer. Most of the kids in my neighborhood followed the Kansas City Chiefs, but my cousin Mike Mercado and I were huge LA Rams fans because that's where we came from. We couldn't stand the Chiefs, and it always caused contention with the other kids we knew. In some ways, it was difficult to see the Chiefs win Super Bowl IV, but in another sense, the one team that Mike and I disliked more than the Chiefs was the Minnesota Vikings because they kept the Rams out of that fourth Super Bowl (and would be the bane of our existence throughout the '70s). The Vikings probably did us a favor because if the Rams had lost to the Chiefs in the Super Bowl, and I suspect that they would have, Mike and I could have never lived that down. At least this way, we only had to deal with one side of a negative. Plus, our favorite player was Roman Gabriel, and I didn't want to see him lose. And I was a huge fan of Merlin Olsen, Deacon Jones, and Jack Snow – these guys couldn't lose the Super Bowl, not to the Chiefs! It was better the way it turned out. And what would we be without "matriculating the ball down the field, boys?"

When we were younger, I think I was in second grade. Mike and I received football uniforms from Santa Claus. But they were Packers uniforms. Santa couldn't find ones for the Rams, but Green Bay was cool as well. In the 1990s, when the Rams left Los Angeles for St. Louis, I lost interest not only in the team but also in the NFL. I think Mike gave up on the NFL long before that. Now that the Rams have relocated back to LA, I have found that I just don't care. As far as college football, it was UCLA and USC. I was probably rare because I liked both the cross-town rivals, but I got that from my dad. However, I always rooted for UCLA over the Trojans. In baseball, I was a huge Angels fan, and I liked the Dodgers as well. In the early 1970s, my favorite player became Nolan Ryan. I got lucky with Ryan because he didn't retire until I was in my 30s! Today, I don't follow the Angels and Dodgers, but instead, and usually, unfortunately, I'm a huge Cubs fan. But they won it all in 2016, so I can rest easy for another 108 years. My second favorite player of all time is former Cubs, Andrea Dawson.

In college basketball, there was no other team than UCLA! When I was growing up, I didn't know that any other team was supposed to win the NCAA championship. Finally, in 1974, when UCLA was defeated in the semifinals of the Final Four by North Carolina State, I was devastated. John Wooden doesn't lose. But he did – how can that be? And I felt so bad for Bill Walton, the best player in the college game at that time (and I think the second-best college player ever), who didn't lead his team to the Promised Land as a senior. But the team righted the ship the next year. Then Coach Wooden retired, and we moved on to a new era of college basketball. My favorite basketball player of all time is Kareem Abdul Jabbar, which is why I followed the Milwaukee Bucks in the first half of the 70s and the Lakers after that. Today, I don't have a favorite pro basketball team – the game bores the hell out of me. In college basketball, I moved away from UCLA in the mid-1980s and started following the Kansas Jayhawks. I'm not sure who my favorite Jayhawk is, but it's probably Danny Manning, although I was a huge fan of Richard Scott, Steve Woodberry, Greg Ostertag, Paul Peirce, Kirk Hinrich, and the entire 2008 roster. Actually, as I think about it, there are too many KU players I have really liked over the years to list them all.

Although I did understand that I had endurance, and I don't believe I knew that word in elementary school, when one of your best friends, who lived directly across the street from you, was John Kerr, you wouldn't know you were strong. It was only later that I realized I was stronger than most boys because the only person I could compare my strength to was John, and he was super strong! When we walked home from school in 7th grade, our first year of junior high, there were almost always older bullies around, but even the 9th graders didn't mess with John. Some might not have wanted to admit it, but they were all scared of John Kerr. And John was not a bully. He was just a nice guy. But he would have kicked the shit out of any of those older boys if they would have messed with him. It made for a safe walk home.

When I was about 10 or 11 years old, there were a bunch of kids over at our house on Clark playing in the backyard. I don't remember the occasion, but I'm sure my cousins, Mike and Phillip, were there, along with John Kerr and his brother Kenny, Mike Heenen, who lived on the other side of the alley on Stevens, and others I don't recall. For some reason, I decided to see how many laps I could run around the inside perimeter of the backyard before I got exhausted and had to stop. I don't know how far one lap was, but we had a fairly big backyard. Although I must confess that the house, until a few years ago, was owned by my aunt, and when I stepped back into the yard, I was stunned at how tiny it was. So, the perception of a kid is not always correct. Nonetheless, regardless of the length of a lap, the importance of my perception in the early 1970s was what I thought about my endurance, or whatever I called it 50 years ago.

So, I began to run, announcing that I would run many, many laps. Some of the kids paid attention to some degree, and others paid me no mind – everyone must have had their own agendas. But I kept running, and the few times my mom snuck a peek out the back door, I told her how many laps I had run. Fifty years have dimmed my full memory, so I'm not sure how many laps I ran, but I know I made at least 50. Whatever it was, no matter if I really didn't run very far, the quest made me confident that I could run a long way without getting tired. In fact, I do remember that I stopped because it was getting dark and not because I had run out of gas. It's possible I ran two miles, but I doubt it. Having the ability to run long distances didn't seem to have practical applications at that time, and I didn't perceive that it would help me in sports. I guess if my aspiration was to be a criminal, running from the police over a long distance might help me escape justice, but stealing and otherwise playing havoc on society didn't meet my standards of a productive life – hell, I wanted to be a truck driver at that age.

Over the next year or two, I must have temporarily forgotten my backyard exploit because when I joined Little League Football as a 12-year-old, I could hardly keep up with the rest of the team when we ran a couple of laps around the field. The first practices were held in the spring, and then we began again in the late summer before we started back to school. When we resumed practice, team members were given quick physicals by local doctors. In small groups, we were told to go below the stadium to get our physicals. The doctor checked for hernias, which I apparently passed with flying colors, although as a first-time physical getter, it seemed awful strange.

Then the doctor checked our hearts. I was one of the last in my group to get the stethoscope treatment. The heart check was quick, with a couple of listens on the chest and on the back, and then on to the next player. But when the doctor checked me out, he kept listening in several places on my chest for a few minutes with a puzzled look on his face, turning his eyes to one side while looking up at nothing in particular. Finally, he called for our head Coach, Mr. Rutter, a tough-as-nails man who loved us kids. Then, at some point, my parents were brought into the discussion. I already knew something smelled bad before Coach was called. The diagnosis was a heart murmur.

Now, I didn't know what a heart murmur was, but Coach Rutter treated me with kid gloves, and the doctors said I needed to take it easy. Whether I was going to be able to play football was still up in the air. Right after the physical, we took a vacation to Colorado and Rocky Mountain National Park. We took the road through the park, which reached an elevation of 12,000 feet, and when I got out to walk, it didn't take long for my chest to begin to hurt pretty severely. I just figured it was the murmur, although it could have been altitude sickness, and it could have been me convincing myself that I had a heart problem. Regardless, it was scary. When we returned from vacation, I was convinced I had real health issues. Another thing that happened was when we left the mountains and quickly changed elevation, my ears popped, and the pain was immediate. I had ringing in my ears for several months.

When I returned to football practice after the Colorado trip, I was given a new physical by the same doctor at his office. He couldn't find anything wrong with my heart and gave me a clean bill of health and permission to participate in football at full strength. That was great news, and I played well. I was an offensive and defensive lineman. During our first game against Baxter Springs, I completely dominated and was awarded defensive player of the game. The opposing coach said I was in their backfield more than their running backs. We did lose, but we would move on to be a great team.

My problem was not playing football – I was great, and I don't mean this as bragging. It was really outstanding. No, my issue was the lap or two we ran around the field after practice. In the back of my mind, I believe I still thought something was wrong with my heart. This had to be psychological, but I didn't have any endurance, and I always fought it out with one kid not to get last. But after a few weeks, I started to finish ahead of more and more teammates. At some point, I must have realized that there was nothing wrong with me, and that was liberating! By the end of the year, I always finished first. Coach Rutter would get on the skilled players for letting the lineman beat them.

I learned to be tough playing Little League football for Coach Rutter and his assistant. These were hard-nosed men, one middle-aged and the other young. One drill that was designed to toughen us up was running at each other and smashing our helmets together. I hated this drill, and it would not only be frowned upon today, but it might be illegal. Two players would stand 20 yards apart (or maybe it was 10) and run toward each other and, before they met, put their heads down and crash into each other head-to-head like two battling rams. There were many times my head would just ring and occasionally knock me silly. If I end up with early dementia, we'll know the reason why. Our assistant, the young and energetic Coach O.J., got so mad at us at halftime against Oswego because we were only ahead 12-0 that he lined us up against a side wall at the stadium, where all the parents could see, made us turn around with our rear-ends facing him as we leaned against the wall, and threatened to stick his foot up our asses with swift hard kicks if we didn't play better. We won 25-0. Now we loved Coach O.J., and we respected him, and one might say that he really wouldn't have put his foot up our asses, but he's now in prison for murder.

One game in which I demonstrated my strength, toughness, and endurance was tackle-the-man-with-the-ball. Many of us played this during the lunch period on the old junior high football field. The other 7th-grade boys knew when I got the round all-purpose ball that they were going to have one hell of a time getting me down. I could carry as many as could jump on me without hitting the ground. Then, I would finally shake them all off and continue to run until I was caught again and start the whole process over – I just would not allow myself to get tackled. I had the strength, endurance, toughness, and even a little meanness to beat them all and keep asking for more. That is, until John Kerr arrived from his lunch, then I was in trouble. One time, after a particularly long session in which no one or groups of kids could get me down, I turned and saw John barreling down on me at full speed. That's all she wrote – I went down in a heap.

The only other kid that I remember tackling me by himself was future track teammate Eric Zink. Eric wasn't big or fast, but he knew how to tackle. He hit me low, right above my left knee, with his shoulder, and I dropped like a rock. Eric later played junior high football but ran cross-country in high School, which was a better sport for him. But I have no doubt that if he had played high school football, Eric would have been the best tackler on the team. Later, in 9th-grade football, our coach, Mr. Strathe, got mad at me for missing some blocks in practice. He told me he was going to demonstrate how running backs felt, so he made me run through the defense by myself without blockers. Well, I just ran through all the defenders several times, and Coach Strathe forgot his anger. We only had one game left, but I started as a running back in that last one.

I actually had a small, almost insignificant, introduction to track and field before I entered the 7th grade. For 5th and 6th graders, the Parsons School District hosted an elementary school meet at the high school. The events consisted of the 50-yard dash, long jump (or broad jump, as it was called), high jump, and softball throw. There might have been a 75-yard dash as well, and a couple of other events, but I really can't remember. What I do remember is the excitement of the track meet day when we got out of school and traveled to the other side of town. I'm not sure the pleasure of the competition or the fact that we were out of school made it a special day. When I was in 6th grade, our teacher, Mr. Duroni, drilled us in our events. We didn't have mats to land on for the high jump or sand for the broad jump, but we did our best, and many of us loved it.

Most of us would have done anything for Mr. Duroni, and I thought he was the best teacher one could ever have – and I haven't changed my mind. He made learning fun and seemed to understand some of the problems kids struggled with. One time, a girl slammed my fingers between our desks, and I picked up my chair and threw it at her, but it sailed over her head, and then I attempted to sling my desk at her, but it fell short of her feet. Then I stormed out of the room, not understanding why I did what I did. Mr. Duroni chased after me and shouted my name a couple of times, at which point I stopped. He calmed me down and indicated that he wouldn't tell my parents, although I suspect he did during conferences. For many of us, he was cool.

Mr. Duroni also made our preparation for the elementary school track meet enjoyable. One of the special events left till the end of the meet, and one that instilled school pride, was the shuttle relay. Each school selected four runners, who would run 50 yards each in a shuttle-style relay. Of course, I wasn't fast enough to make the shuttle team, but I was fine with that because we knew we had the fastest four guys in town. John Kerr was on the relay, and my cousins Bill Cruse and Mike Cloke were also on it. I don't remember the fourth, but it could have been Randy Braun. Well, we were all correct – we smoked the other four, Lincoln, Garfield, McKinley, and Guthridge Elementary Schools. Like President Washington, Washington Elementary was first! President Lincoln was important, but not first, and presidents Garfield and McKinley were not known for much to students other than being assassinated. Guthridge was not even a president but a past superintendent of the school district, although he did have an athletic connection as the father of North Carolina basketball coach Bill Guthridge. I know Coach Strathe and Coach Guthridge were great friends and former teammates.

Winning at the elementary school track meet was not necessarily the objective in some of the events. If you long jumped or threw the softball a certain distance, you received a blue first-place ribbon. There were also second-place distances and heights for the field events, and anything below that was a third-place ribbon. The only event, besides the shuttle, in which you competed against others was the 50-yard dash. We each stood in a line on the six-lane track, and when it was our turn, we raced against the other five who were at the line with us. Mostly, it was pure chance who we raced, although I think there was some gamesmanship about placing ourselves in positions to race those we wanted. I'm not sure, but there might have been a race that pitted the best of each school against each other. In 6th grade, I received first-place ribbons in my events, including the high jump and softball throw, except for the 50, in which I took second. The only thing that might have possibly made the day better is if the two Catholic schools, St. Mary's and St. Patrick's, could have participated – those two schools had good athletes as well.

But when I entered junior high, I was still almost completely naive about what track and field really was. Other than the elementary school track meets, a band performance in 5th grade, and visits to an aunt and uncle, I rarely made it to the area of town where the high school sat. The high school football team played on the other side of town, and it never dawned on me to attend a track meet. So, the real-track world was alien to me. My sport was football, and I understood it, and I was good at it. During the late season of Little League Football, I decided to go out for the 7th-grade basketball team, but after a couple of practices, I realized that it conflicted with football practice. Since I had decided not to play basketball, and it looked as if I had given up on baseball, football was all I had, and I was great with that. When the Little League season was over, I would set my sights on playing 8th-grade football the next fall for Parsons Junior High. Yes, the track was coming in in a few months, but I wouldn't be participating in the spring sport – I just wasn't fast enough. My early revelation of being the fastest kid around had long been dashed.

During the second semester in seventh grade, which began in January, I had Physical Education, or gym class, as most of us called it. Our teacher was Mr. Kennedy, who was a terrific gym teacher and the new track coach. In junior high, Mr. Kennedy coached the 7th, 8th, and 9th grade boys. Coach Kennedy's assistant was going to be a new teacher, Mr. Coons, who started in January as a mid-year hire to teach math. He was young, right out of college, a graduate of Fort Hays State. So, only two coaches for a ton of early to mid-teen boys, something I wouldn't wish on anyone.

Around late February 1975, Mr. Kennedy announced to our 7th-grade gym class that track practice would begin soon, and he encouraged us to go out for the team. I had an interest in this! No, not to go out for the team. Remember, I wasn't fast enough, but to be a team manager. Hey, this would give me a chance to see some of my fast friend's race. Mr. Kennedy agreed to let me be a manager but wondered why I wouldn't just come out for the team. As you might imagine, I told him I wasn't fast enough. I think he knew I was a pretty good athlete, but I don't think he could argue with my logic because I'm sure he understood that I was slow. Finally, maybe a couple of days before the first practice, Coach Kennedy did attempt to challenge my logic when he asked me to come out and run. But he approached it in a unique way. He explained that there were a number of events, but he also indicated that he had one spot left for 7th graders and that I should sign up – he would leave the spot open for me. I thought about it and decided to give track and field a shot. It was a day that changed my life.

Now, let's be clear: I was still completely clueless about what track and field was and what I was getting myself into. And there wasn't a spot left on the team – there were no spots, or to put it another way, the spots were unlimited. He just used that strategy to get me to come out for the team, convincing me that this was a special spot just for me. Coach Kennedy was going to be the new head 8th-grade football coach the next year, and I think he wanted to help get me in shape for that. Nonetheless, I didn't understand any of that then. I was just going out for track.

After school was out, the track kids walked several blocks to the high school to practice on their rubber asphalt track, which was the same track on which we competed during the elementary school meet. We had been given sweats and lockers in the basement of the high school. We were ready to run! Coach Kennedy started the first three weeks of the practice season by having all of us run three miles on the track to get us in general condition. We ran three laps and walked one until we reached 12 running laps. It was a bit intimidating, but I did it. And I remembered that I had run all those laps around my backyard a couple of years before and that I had finished first in our end-of-the-year football runs. I also finally learned that endurance has practical athletic applications. Not only would it help me in long, tiring football games, but I learned that there were these things called distance races. Yes, the track was more than running fast for short distances and jumping high or long. We could run several laps. That was for me! The 8th grade team had a really good distance runner, Brad Burkes, who befriended me and would be my teammate for years to come. Brad tried to teach me what distance running was, but I don't believe I fully comprehended it. It didn't matter because this was what I was going to do.

One day, after the first three weeks of practice, but before any meets, I was standing on the high jump apron when Mr. Hill came over to talk with me. Mr. Hill was a new science teacher, and I had him in the second period. Like Mr. Coons, he was a mid-year replacement and newly graduated from Fort Hays State. Mr. Hill didn't coach track but did come to practice quite often. Mr. Hill asked me what events I was going to compete in, and I told him "Distance," whatever that really meant, because I didn't know how far these races were. He answered back, "So you're going to be a miler." Not as a question but more of a statement. "Yes," I said, even though I wasn't sure what that meant, but it sounded cool, and in the back of my mind, I thought I had heard of the race. Although I didn't know why, being from Kansas, I had actually heard the name Jim Ryun, and I must have known he was in track – but the mile? I guess I didn't know. But Mr. Hill's words resonated with me; yes, I'm going to be a miler! A miler! It did take a number of years before I became a miler, and I even resisted it for several seasons. But Mr. Hill is extremely important to me, even today, because of the course that led me down, even though he never coached me on track. But he would be my assistant football coach the next year. Unfortunately, Mr. Hill died a few years ago after retiring as a principal from a fall. His son is former NFL quarterback Shaun Hill.

I couldn't compete in the mile in 7th grade. The longest race we were allowed to run was the quarter mile, or the 440-yard dash. In other words, one lap. I was disappointed, but I would make the best of the situation. However, as the first 7th-grade track meet approached, I was one of those on the outside looking in. It was perfectly clear that I had not distinguished myself, which is what I feared would happen when I decided to come out for track. At first, it really didn't make much difference to me how well I did. At least, that's what I convinced myself. I suppose that was a way to protect myself from disappointment, although I doubt, I could intellectualize it that way as a 13-year-old. Coach Kennedy could only enter two in each individual event, plus there were two or three relays.

I thought I would have a chance to run the 440, especially because the fast guys wanted nothing to do with the one-lapper, although I found out over the years that followed the race was actually a sprint. But I was one of the slow 7th graders vying for a spot as a quarter-miler. Apparently, I was not one of those clodhoppers who made the grade in the 440. But now I had a strong competitive feeling as I did on the defensive line when I shot through the offensive line to bury the quarterback. I do remember running some 440s against other 7th graders, but I can't recall how I did – but the runs must not have been good. It was nothing as dramatic as Jim Ryun running the 440 in 9th grade in an attempt to make the track team falling short. We all made the team. And we never had a winner-take-all, sudden-death race.

I remember after the first three weeks of practice, Coach Kennedy challenged the entire team, all three grades, for someone to run the quarter mile under 70 seconds in practice. I thought that would be easy, but I must have failed by a significant margin. I was not listed as one of the quarter-milers going to the first meet, and, in fact, I was not on the list to go, period! At this point, only a few days before the meet, I had failed, and I felt terrible. But I wasn't going to quit. Then something interesting happened. Coach Kennedy realized that he had forgotten to fill the 220-yard leg on the medley relay. There was an open slot. The coach was standing inside the track near the starting line for the 100-yard dash, and a few of us were standing with him as he pondered out loud who he could add. My teammates,

John Kerr and Mike Cloke, came to my rescue. Several times, they said, "What about Raymond?" Finally, Coach decided to enter me – I was going to compete in my first real track meet!

I should have stayed home. But that's getting a little ahead of the story. First, I needed track shoes. My image of track shoes was those like the other kids wore, like thin tennis shoes that came in two colors: black and red. Many kids in my neighborhood had worn them, and I wanted a pair to run in my first meet. When my dad and I went up to Bob's Sporting Goods, I found out that those cheap things that were called track shoes were not really track shoes at all. Real track shoes had spikes, and most of the time, they were just called "spikes." I bought the only track shoes Bob carried – white Pumas with a red stripe or something that looked similar along the side. Like the cheap things we called track shoes, these spikes had super thin soles. I thought this is where the term thin clades came from, which our local sports editor, Jack Harris, sometimes used in his *Parsons Sun* articles. But I think the term comes from track guys being thinly clad in tank tops and shorts. What was difficult for me to comprehend was how those half-inch spikes would work on the track. Wouldn't they ruin the surface?

Coach Kennedy explained that we would be running on a cinder track, so the long spikes were needed. On our all-weather track, quarter-inch spikes were used. I didn't know what a cinder track was, but I was about to find out – the hard way. The meet was held in Coffeyville, Kansas, at the junior high and Field Kindley High School. And sure enough, it was a cinder track in piss-poor condition. I couldn't believe people actually ran on dirt and mud with a few of these little black, funny-looking rocks or pebbles. What I would find out as I ran more track meets is that the track at Coffeyville was bad, and I mean really bad. The track was neglected, no matter what they say about it. In fact, the first meet in which I competed was, by far, the worst track I ever raced on. Plus, it must have rained the previous day or two because they had this little tractor out there attempting to smooth out the mud, but all it really accomplished was creating these small ruts, although some looked like crevasses.

Regardless, I just took in the atmosphere of my first track meet. I went over and watched John Kerr compete in the shot put. This was a big track meet with a lot of schools, so there were a ton of kids in the event. Most, if not all, of the competitors utilized the glide technique, except John. Our coaches taught the technique in stages, so John used more of a half glide. I heard a few guys snicker because it looked a little silly, I guess, until John threw the eight-pound ball several feet beyond their capabilities. John won easily. I had the opportunity to see how real races were run, and I saw all the athletes from different schools and the multitude of colors. We were the Parsons Jr. High Lancers, and our singlet was blue with the classic white angled wide stripe on the front.

It was an exciting day, and as my race approached, I became more and more nervous. What if I messed up, or didn't run well, or couldn't figure out where I was supposed to be on the track? I watched our 440 guys get blown off the track by runners from other schools that looked like men. Our quarter-milers looked like little boys compared to those big kids who were already shaving, and I think one already had hair on his chest! Wow, how was I going to do? I know I would have run that one lap better than our two guys, but would I have been creamed as well? And one team had a 6-foot 6-inch 7th grader in the race who towered over our boys. Our sprinters did great, but the 440 was where we put the kids who couldn't make it anywhere else, and I couldn't even make that team. It's like little league baseball, where you put the worst kid in the right field and hope no one hits the ball in that direction.

Finally, it was my turn to race. I didn't know how to warm up, nor what that meant. We did have great coaches, but there were just too many kids on the team to teach everything in a few weeks. The medley relay was not like the 440 for us because we had really good and fast kids on the team, except for me. For high school or college runners, our relay would be considered a short sprint medley. The first two legs ran 110 yards, with the 220 next, and the anchor finished with a 440 leg. Our first leg was probably our best all-around athlete. He was not the fastest or the strongest, but he was still exceptional at whatever he did. Randy Braun started us off well. Most of the races, except for the 100 and 220, started at the midway point of the home stretch. Although I was unfamiliar with staggered starts, it was clear that Randy was in first place as he dug into the curve. When Randy reached the second leg, my cousin Bill Cruse, he gave him a great handoff, and I awaited my turn. Bill came off the curve, burning up that crappy cinder track. I was situated midway down the back stretch in one of the middle lanes. As Bill got closer, I began to wave him in. I don't know why I remember this so clearly, but I can see myself ready to go as Bill quickly barreled down on me. I forgot that I had butterflies, and when Bill was at the appropriate place, I took off and heard him say, "reach!" It was a perfect handoff!

That's where the perfection ended. First, as my teammates cheered me on, two runners in lanes inside me quickly passed. We were in the lead when I took the handoff, but my lack of speed soon won us the third position. Still, I wasn't running too badly. As I reached the curve, I tried to put as much into the race as I could. Off the curve, I stayed in third, so I had run well enough not to lose any more ground over the previous 110. With 50 yards to go, I knew I wasn't going to catch the two who passed me, but if I could only remain in third and not lose too many more yards to the leaders, our anchor might just catch one or both.

As I approached our 440 runners, I was relieved to find that I had kept my third-place position and was still relatively close to the first two teams. Our last leg, Joe Woodworth, waited, and as I just about reached him, I stuck the baton out for the exchange – the next thing I knew, I was sliding headfirst on the beat-up cinder track. For some reason, one of my feet didn't hit the ground when it should have landed. I had partially stepped in one of the damn tractor ruts and fell flat on my face, or more like a base runner sliding headfirst into second. My arm was still extended out in front of me on the ground, and luckily, Joe hadn't run past the exchange zone, so he ran back, snatched the baton out of my hand, and took off.

With the fall, our chance for first or second was squandered. Joe ran a good leg and kept us in third. But I was embarrassed. That old Coffeyville track didn't have a lot of cinders left, but what it did have were now embedded in my knees and elbows. The coaches asked me what happened, but Coach Coons didn't believe me. And others didn't accept my explanation either. I was bleeding, but the only thing that hurt was my pride. Pride is the bane of most of us. It gets in the way of success, and when our pride is injured, it causes more issues. For the remainder of the meet, every time Coach Coons looked at me, he just shook his head and gave me a look of disgust. I know Coach liked me, but I had upset him a few weeks earlier when he took me to practice, and without asking, I jumped in his car when he was leaving to take me home. I just assumed that if he took me to practice, he would take me home as well. He asked me if I had asked if he could take me home, and I said "no." But he took me home anyway, with a lecture. After the Coffeyville meet, I ended up having a great relationship with Coach Coons for the next two years.

When the track meet was over, we all piled into the bus for the 35-mile trip home. But I was not in a good mood or ready to take anyone's shit. I ended up sitting a seat away from Woodworth. He was sitting with one of the girls, and I was just a little (or a lot) shy of girls. Joe was cocky. I remember when I had a paper route in the 5th grade, and the Woodworth's house was my last delivery. During those years, the kids who had *Parsons Sun's* routs had to collect the money for the paper by going from house to house. Some people were notorious for not paying and came up with all kinds of excuses. That was never the issue with the Woolworths. They always paid when I collected, but they always had to give you shit and mess with you. I came to realize that they only did it for fun, and I never had any problems with them. But at this moment on the bus, I was in no mood for Joe's shit. But, of course, he had to show his ass. He turned to look at me while still sitting, put his hands up, clenched into fists, and said, "I'm going to kick your ass." Well, I knew Joe wasn't really going to kick my ass, and I knew he wouldn't have tried. But with him sitting next to a girl and my general state of embarrassment, I didn't respond or just muttered a few things. Good thing Joe didn't attempt anything because with my temper and fragile mood at that moment, I'd have been like a pit bull.

This was not the first time Joe threatened to kick my ass. At practice, before the first meet, he and I were running a 440, and someone stepped out on the track in front of us. I was right behind Joe, and when the person stepped out, Joe stutter-stepped, which caused us to tangle our legs, and we both went down hard. We both walked away in different directions, not saying a word to each other, but later at practice, Joe decided it would be good to let me be aware that he was going to kick my ass. I didn't back down, and Joe didn't kick my ass. So, I knew nothing was going to happen on the bus or anywhere else.

Now, you might think that Joe and I didn't get along and that I really disliked him, but that's not the case at all. I never had issues with Joe, and in fact, I liked him quite well. I thought Joe was hilarious, and he was a terrific football teammate from junior high through high school. Joe had a big mouth, but that's one thing I liked about him. And he was a tough football player. In high school shop class, occasionally, Joe would, but he was handed up and explained that he was about to kick the hell out of me. I just laughed. Of course, it was only a joke to him.

From such an auspicious beginning, I could go nowhere but up in track. For our medley relay exploits, we received white, third-place ribbons. Although I had fallen, my dad explained that we still did well enough to place third and get an award, so he placed the ribbon on my bedroom bulletin board. I also soon took up the shot put. As I viewed it, I should have been the 440 leg, and Joe should have run the 220. Not because I was necessarily faster than Joe in the quarter, but because Joe probably would have run a better 220 than me – and not fallen. But I had not given up on the 440. I don't remember how many 7th-grade meets we had, but I only recall two. Between Coffeyville and our next meet, I somehow managed to make the cut in the 440. There was not a single moment or time trial that put me in the top two, but I had finally distinguished myself as a quarter-miler, although, to some degree, it might have been by default, judging how poorly our 440 guys ran in the Coffeyville Invitational.

Our next competition was a dual meet in Chanute, Kansas. They also had a cinder track, but it was in much better shape than the disaster Coffeyville called a track. I competed in two events. The first of the day was the shot put. I didn't place, but I did fairly well, and it felt good to do alright. And it didn't hurt that John Kerr won, so at least a teammate got us first-place points. We must have been able to enter more than two per event because there were several kids throwing the shot, and in my next event, the 440-yard dash, the lanes were full, so there were probably six competitors. I remember being nervous, but not nearly as bad as I was in Coffeyville. I don't think any of us used starting blocks; at least, I know I didn't.

When the gun sounded, I took off fast, or fast for me. Like most of the meets, we started at the midway point of the front stretch, the 50-yard line of the football field. At the 220-yard mark, I think I was in the lead, although it was difficult to determine because of the stagger. But before I reached the final curve, I was passed on the inside by a Chanute runner. As we came off the curve for the last 50 yards, I was still in second and attempted to catch the leader. I was never able to re-pass the Chanute kid, but I was close to him as we crossed the finish line. I had finished second and had exorcised the Coffeyville demons. Plus, I ran the race in 67 seconds! I had run under 70. I don't know how fast my two teammates ran in Coffeyville, but I doubt they managed to break 80 seconds. Plus, I had beaten at least one of them in Chanute. Now, 67 seconds might not seem fast for a 13-year-old boy, but for me, it was like qualifying for the Olympics. I've coached a couple of 13-year-olds who have run 55 seconds and a little faster, but I don't think they were as happy as I was that afternoon in Chanute, Kansas. I was now a legitimate track and field athlete. I could run a good race and get the team points, and I was not half bad at the shot put either.

The League Meet only consisted of the 9th-grade, or A Division, and the 8th-grade B Division. Seventh graders didn't participate as a division but could compete with the 8th graders. I was not good enough to be included, although several 7th-grade teammates, such as John Kerr, who was in the shot put. The 1975 version of League was held at our home track, the only all-weather track around. The schools competing were Coffeyville, Independence, Chanute, Iola, and Parsons. Although I didn't compete, I did work at the meet. There were some good performances by athletes from all the schools. But about halfway through, a huge storm came rushing in from the west. The sky turned almost completely black, and then two funnels started forming. The would-be tornados never hit the ground, although one funnel went past a third of the way. Then the wind became extremely strong as everyone sprinted to the high school for cover, even the weight guys, as the heavy rain and hail were driven like bullets into our faces. The storm passed quickly, but so much rain had fallen that it would have been difficult to continue, even with the all-weather track. There was standing water everywhere, and it was difficult to get back to the track without walking through several inches of water.

Ultimately, the rest of the meet was postponed, and the teams were to come back to finish several days later. When the meet resumed, several of our athletes decided not to show up, including some in the 8th-grade division. We didn't have enough 8th graders to run our relays, so I told Coach Kennedy that I would gladly compete. Even though I wasn't fast, it would still be better than not running the relays. And after all, I could provide a pretty good 440 leg on the Mile Relay. I knew that I could run 64 or 65 seconds, especially with a running start that I would get as I took the handoff. This wasn't like it is now, in which the coaches must declare their relay participants and alternates if they have any. Coaches usually just entered their teams, and runners were not listed. As long as the kids weren't competing in too many events or running in more than one 440 (open race and relay), they could run a relay. However, Coach Kennedy decided it was best for me not to compete, although I didn't know why. I was there and ready to run!

So, my first track season ended, but it ended in a positive fashion. I was ready for summer and fall football and track the next spring when I would be able to compete in the longest race allowed to 8th-grade kids – the 880-yard run.

Chapter 3
Half Mile

With the end of my first season on track, I can't say I was totally hooked on the sport, but I was excited about the prospects of the 1976 season. One bummer was that my cousin Bill moved with his family to Wisner, Nebraska, during the summer of 1975, so we wouldn't be teammates anymore. But the biggest positive was that 8th-grade football season was fast approaching, and that took precedence over track and any other sport, especially since I no longer played baseball. Nonetheless, I received one of my first subscription issues of *Sports Illustrated* with Brian Oldfield on the cover, wearing a red, white, and blue striped uniform with skimpy shorts that I wouldn't be caught dead wearing. I didn't have a clue who Oldfield was, but I read about him throwing the shot put 75 feet, using a spin technique that I'd never seen. He competed in some pro track organization and wouldn't be able to try out for the '76 Olympics, which was confusing to me. Still, 75 feet with a 16-pound ball – I don't think I'd yet reached 40 feet with an 8-pound shot.

I don't know the order of the *Sports Illustrated* issues I received, but I think the first one had a story about the death of Steve Prefontaine that I believe was written by Kenny Moore. It was a terrific but sad story. I'd heard of Pre but was not sure why. The article mentioned Frank Shorter, and I had heard his name as well, but again, I wasn't sure why. I think the story of Pre inspired me, but I can't quantify how. I just think it did. Although I was not yet hooked on track and field, I was hooked on Kenny Moore's writing, and that couldn't hurt a young athlete attempting to find his niche. I took in other stories about the track, such as Tanzanian Filbert Bayi breaking Jim Ryun's long-standing mile world record with his 3:51.0. And reading about the young Kiwi, John Walker, taking Bayi's record later in the summer with a 3:49.4, the first sub-3:50. I would only later learn of their great 1500m race the year before in the Commonwealth Games. These times seemed fast, but I had nothing to compare them to. How could I relate to a mile in the 3:50 range when the longest race I'd run was a 440 in 67 seconds? I didn't look at multiplying 67 seconds x 4 to come up with a 4:28 mile, which might have given me more perspective, but maybe not. Obviously, a 4:28 mile by a 13-year-old would have been great, but I wouldn't have known that at the time. But these stories kept me interested in track.

For most of the summer, I focused on the coming football season. Regardless of my new interest in track, I was a football guy. I was told by several that I was an elite football player and that I had a great shot at being offered a big-time scholarship when I graduated high school. Of course, this was all based on what I had achieved in little league football as a 12-year-old. Little League had a weight limit, and I came in just under the max. So, I was one of the biggest kids out there. Guys like John Kerr were too big to compete, and he would have dominated. And, although I was the best defensive lineman out there, and we had a couple of other really good ones, I was not the best player on our little league team. That honor went to Derek Hull, who was a fantastic running back, and I think he played linebacker as well.

In 8th-grade football, coached by Mr. Kennedy and assisted by Coach Hill, I played offensive line, and on defense, I played nose-guard. I disliked the offensive line, but it was a necessary evil to get my chance to play defense and hammer running backs and quarterbacks, something I loved to do. I was somewhat dismayed. In Little League, we had brand new, top-notch equipment, but in junior high, our stuff was everywhere. Meaning we didn't have new equipment, and the stuff came from two or three generations. Some of the helmets didn't have padding and only included a strip of leather to hold it to your head. And other helmets, I think, came from the late 1950s. These old, crusty pieces of plastic bulged out around the ears and had several small holes where numerous facemasks had been secured over the years. Nonetheless, we were a well-coached, good team. Coaches Kennedy and Hill knew what they were doing. We had two players who just dominated, John Kerr and Mike Cloke, who were the biggest, strongest, and fastest players we had. I was good, but I noticed one thing that was important – as good as I was, I was not as special as I had been the year before. I had to learn to make some adjustments because I couldn't just do what I wanted as I had done in Little League. The competition was better.

We only played four games and went 3-1. We lost our last game at home to Independence. I have always thought this game was stolen from us. Late in the game, Independence was around our ten-yard line when Cloke, from his linebacker position, blitzed through the line, causing a fumble. He then picked up the ball and sprinted about 85 yards for a touchdown! However, the referees called an offside on Mike, and instead of taking the lead, Independence scored a couple of plays later and won a narrow victory. There is no doubt that it was close, but Cloke blitzed right by me, and he was not offsides – it was one of the last winning football seasons I played in.

I decided not to play basketball in 8th grade, but I did look forward to track so I could run the 880 and throw the shot. One day in gym class, probably in January or February, I shocked myself with an ability I didn't know I had. Several boys were attempting to touch the net of the basketball goal. Some could reach it, and maybe a couple could even reach a few inches above the bottom of the net. I decided to give it a try as well. I was about 5' 5" at the time, and I didn't have any reason to believe I could touch the net, but maybe if a few others could, I might be able to jump that high. I don't recall that I had ever demonstrated the ability to jump, and it's possible I had never really tried. So, I got in line, and when it was my turn, I ran and jumped and attempted to reach the net. Except I didn't touch the net – I placed my fingers above the rim. I was stunned. Had I just jumped high enough to get half my middle finger over the basketball rim? Yes! But it must have been a freak thing because I couldn't jump that high. I tried again, and just like the first time, I touched the rim. Wow! I didn't think about how this might help me in track or even football, but it was a cool thing to be able to do, especially since I was the only one who could do it.

As we did in 7th grade, we spent the first three weeks running three miles on the track. I learned something about track in 8th grade that I hadn't realized the year before – I hated running in practice, but I loved racing at meets! Once the first three weeks were over, I spent most of my time attempting to throw the shot put at practice and not run a single step. And over time, I got really good at it. I'm amazed, as I look back, how much energy I spent trying to get out of running. We had so many kids on the track that it was hard for Coach Kennedy to catch me and make me do some running. Occasionally, though, he would see me, and I'd have to run a 440 or 330. Then I could sneak back to the shot-put ring and hopefully not get caught. Mr. Coons coached the weight events, and sometimes he asked me if I had run, but usually, he didn't say much about it. He did a great job coaching the shot, and so as long as I improved and worked hard at the ring, I could stay most of the practice.

The first track meet was at home. During 8th grade, we moved from Clark to the other side of town on 29th Street, right next to the high school athletic fields. So, the track was about 50 yards away. This was convenient for my parents because they could watch from the backyard. This first competition was a dual meet, but I don't remember who it was against. It could have been Chanute or Iola, but I just don't recall. My first event was the shot put, and I did fairly well, but I didn't come close to winning – John Kerr creamed everyone else. But that was expected, and it was great to have a teammate who could throw the shot as far as he did. Then I waited for the 880. As a rule, the 880-yard run, or today, the 800-meter run, is one of the last events. I can only remember one exception to this in a one-day meet, and I think some uninformed idiots were running the meet. But that was a few years away.

Finally, it was time for the 8th-grade 880 – the half mile. I was nervous. Had I run enough at practice to win or even run well? No! Why hadn't I spent less time at the shot-put ring and more time on the track? After all, I was never going to win the shot put, but I might be able to win an 880-yard run if I'd just work on it. Well, it was too late now, at least for this meet. Why hadn't I prepared more for this race?! From the starting line, I could see my dad sitting in our backyard, waiting to see me race. I wasn't worried about letting him down because he wasn't that kind of father. He just wanted me to do my best. But I couldn't do my best if I was not in shape – I would just have to do my best in the condition I was in at that moment. Then I saw my mom there as well. I didn't have to turn in the opposite direction to see them – I stood in my lane, and they were in my view. I thought I must have blown this opportunity to do well, but I got myself into it. I had no one to blame but me.

I took some breaths and listened nervously to the instructions from the starter. We would have to stay in our lanes for the first curve, 110 yards, and then merge into the first lane, as long as we didn't cut anyone off. Now, I must admit, I don't really remember the starter saying these things; it's just what is said before every half-mile race. I was too nervous to hear. But I had my thin-soled Puma track shoes on, and I was ready to race, or maybe not. It didn't matter if I was ready or not. The starter pistol was about to go off, and I would need to run. Then the gun sounded, and I took off, forgetting, of course, that I had been nervous. I learned over the years that it never mattered how nervous I was before a race because as soon as I started the race, all my nerves were gone. I was in one of the middle lanes. When I cut into the first lane, there was no one there to avoid. I ran down the backstretch about 40 or 50 yards, and I became curious. Where the hell were the other runners? So, I turned around, and there they were, several yards behind me. I must have gone out too fast, but I wasn't tired, and the pace seemed fine, so I kept going. Again, I must make a confession: I didn't know at that time what pace meant, but it's the best word to describe what I felt.

Before I reached the 220-yard mark, or half a lap into the race, I looked back again, but I was further ahead than before. I ran through the curve, and I looked back a couple of more times down the home stretch. But I was even further in front. I reached the end of the first lap. Now, I was in uncharted territory – the 440 was the longest race I'd run. I ran the curve, worried that I would get caught. After all, the first lap was the easy one. I was not in shape, and this is where my lack of conditioning would catch up with me. As I reached the backstretch of that second lap, I looked back two or three times. The other runners were catching me. I just knew it, so could I hang on to the finish line? But when I looked back, they were even further back than before – these guys were not catching me. Was I going to win? I was still not confident. As I reached the final stretch of the race, I couldn't control myself and had to look back a few more times. Then I crossed the finish line – FIRST PLACE!! I had just kept pulling away from the field. My time was 2:30, but I didn't know what that meant either. I asked Coach Kennedy if that was a good time, and he said it might win me a couple of dual meets. He asked me why I kept turning around during the race, and I said I wanted to see where the other runners were. He explained that I didn't need to do that and to stop it. My dad asked me why I turned around so much, and when I told him why, he told me to stop it. So, I rarely turned around again.

I was a winner in my first half mile – I was a half-miler! Never mind that Brad Burkes had run a 2:14 880 the year before as an 8th grader; I was a great runner – I had won. And I learned a good lesson that day. I didn't need to run in practice to prepare for races. I could continue to practice the shot put and then step on the track at any time and win the 880! Some guys might need to work out to be good, but I had proven I didn't need to. And the races I ran after that continued to prove my point. I won in Pittsburg at 2:28 and won easily, and then I ran about 2:27 and won, and we might have had another meet. I can't remember all the meets in 8th grade, but I was undefeated going into the league meet, and I had improved my time each race. Who needs to prepare? Just step out there and blow everyone off the track. League Meet would be no different.

The 1976 League Meet was held in Iola, and I went there with all the confidence a person could have. Plus, I had put in a little running. The week before League, my family took a trip to Wisner, Nebraska, to visit the Cruses, and I had run a few laps on their high school track with my cousin Bill, my teammate in 7th grade. To me, League Meet was kind of like a carnival. There were all sorts of things going on. All these activities, with 8th and 9th grade events, on the track and in the field events. It was exciting, and it got me pumped to run. First, though, was the shot put. I did a good job but didn't finish in the top six to earn the team points. But I wasn't expected to place in the shot, and as usual, John Kerr easily won. At an earlier meet held in Chanute, I tried the discus, but it was horrible, so I was not in that event at League. All I had left was the 880, and I would earn my first blue ribbon. League was the only meet of the year in which awards were included.

When we were called to the line for the half mile, I was nervous, as usual, but I was also ready to run and full of energy. In fact, I was raring to go. Burkes had won the Freshman mile in the 4:40s, I think, and just seeing him win gave me energy, and another Parsons runner, Ron Faulkenberry, took 2nd. My half-inch spikes were tight in my shoes, and the laces were double-knotted. I don't even think I paid attention to my competitors. I had raced against all the teams in the league – Coffeyville, Independence, Chanute, and Iola. No one from those schools had come close to beating me. All I had to do was beat them again, which would be an easy task. I wouldn't even have to run my best to easily win.

It's interesting how lessons are learned, especially when one is over-confident. Although, I don't think it would have made any difference in the world how good my confidence was going into the race. When the gun sounded, I took off fast. I ran with strength and with a purpose. The first lap was a blur, and I didn't feel the least bit tired. But for the first time all season, someone was on my tail. But I wasn't concerned because this runner would soon fall off the pace. I don't know what the first lap was really run in, but I heard 59 seconds. That seems too fast to me. It's hard for me to believe that I could have run the first lap that fast and still finished. But I was also told that it was actually just under 60 seconds. I still don't think so. Whatever it was, it was fast, at least for a 14-year-old. Midway down the backstretch, with 220 yards to go, a kid from Coffeyville, the one that had been shadowing me for 660 yards, passed me like I wasn't even there. The fashion in which he passed demoralized me. Suddenly, I was tired and without energy, and before that point, I felt good. After the race, the girls' coach said it looked like I was painfully jogging, which is exactly what it felt like. When the Coffeyville runner passed me, I recognized him as Mike Lee.

Mike was not as tall as me, but he was bigger and a tremendous athlete. He had never raced in the 880 before; at least, that's what his teammates told me after the race. I was not a small kid, but Mike was like a man to me. He was not as big, strong, and fast as John Kerr, but still physically mature for his age. Just one of those kids who could do almost anything. We had a teammate just like him, Randy Braun, who was a good pole vaulter. I could step on the track and beat most of the guys in the 880 without training, but Randy is the one who could have challenged Lee that day – it certainly wasn't me. Lee had once lived in Parsons when his dad taught in the Parsons School District and was an assistant football coach. I never met him before they moved to Coffeyville, and his father became their high school football coach. For me, it was a devastating loss. I ran a 2:24, which was my best time, but Lee ran a 2:15 and just missed the Burkes meet record. I think Lee could have run under 2:10 that day because he made it look so easy. After the race, I was sitting in the infield, taking off my spikes, and Lee came up to me, not even out of breath, and congratulated me on a good race. That meant a lot to me.

I played football against Mike over the next four years. During that time, I grew bigger and stronger until I was actually bigger than him. But he was still a tremendous athlete. When we were seniors, we played Coffeyville in a home game, and Lee was their quarterback. Late in the first half, Coffeyville was deep in our territory. They called a pass play, and I was able to sprint around the lineman from my defensive tackle position and barrel down on Lee. Just as he released the ball, I leveled him, helmet to helmet, which would be penalized today. The pass was incomplete. Mike stood up, looked at me, and said, "Good hit." The next play, they passed again. The offensive tackle made me go a little wider than the previous play, and when I reached Lee, he stepped up in the pocket, so I grabbed out with my left arm, spun him around, and threw him down over my body. The sack ended the half.

When I got to the locker room, my knee began to stiffen. I played well in the second half, but by the next day, my knee was the size of a football and a mild shade of green. I probably injured my knee on that quarterback sack. It bothered me for the next few weeks, and I didn't play nearly as well as before. I got to know Mike a little after high school when we attended the same college as freshmen. He was there to play football, and I was there to run track. But Mike severely injured his knee before the season began. I found him to be a really nice guy. I can forgive him for beating me in that 880, but not for running back a punt for a touchdown against us when we were juniors!

For my second-place finish at League, I received a red second-place ribbon. But I wanted a blue ribbon. I vowed to win the next year. But for now, I was focused on summer and football the next fall. When school began, my classroom driver's education teacher asked if I was interested in going out for the high school cross-country team. Mr. Wheat was the track and cross-country coach, and because freshmen were technically high school students, although we still went to the junior high, I could run for the high school cross-country team. Because the junior high had a track team, our principal didn't allow us to run for the high school team, not that I would have been good enough. But I wanted to play football, so I declined. Brad Burkes had asked me to run cross-country as well, but my heart was not in fall running; it was football all the way.

For some reason, and I'm not sure why, we were not nearly as good as we had been in 8th grade. We lost a couple of players, but we still had John Kerr, and we gained some good players from St. Patrick's. We were again well-coached. Our head coach was Mr. Strathe, who lived across the street from me, and the assistant was Coach Coons. Coach Strathe was one of the all-time best athletes to come out of Parsons High School, and he once held the high school record in the 880, from back in the 1950s. But for some reason, we just had a tough time winning. I think we only won a single game. But I wasn't discouraged about football because the high school team had played for a state championship the year before and made it to the state semi-finals in 1976. We would be good as well.

One of my goals was to achieve the gold standard on the President's Physical Fitness test in gym class. In order to make that standard, one had to achieve that gold level in every event. My downfall was going to be the 50-yard dash. I could make the standard for all other events, such as setups, pushups, and especially the 600-yard run.

DAM RUN

The Parsons Junior High record for the 600 was 1:32. I knew I could get it. Unfortunately, we were to run the 600 on the same day as a football game. I was lucky that our gym teacher allowed three of us to run another day, which upset the other gym teacher. But I knew how much I was going to put into this run, and I knew it would deaden my legs for the game. A day or two later, Mark Allen, R.C. Schnackenberg, and I lined up for our chance at the record. I had nothing else to run for other than pride because I had not made the gold standard in the 50. I was going to be on the blue level for the second year in a row. The three of us took off fast, and as we reached the first lap around the junior high football field, we were on record pace. As we reached the finish line, Mark and I tied with a 1:32, and R.C. was only a second back. But our teacher decided that we had cut too much off the corners, and we didn't tie the record.

As I look back, and it's something that never entered my mind then, we really didn't run 600 yards, but neither did the kid who ran the 1:32 several years before if he ran on that field. Reese Hughes Field, the old high school football field, was only 95 yards long. It was a legendary field in southeast Kansas. The stadium was built in the 1920s, not long after the high school was constructed, which was now the junior high. The east end zone was up against the backyards of houses, and the west end zone was almost against a street, with only a narrow sidewalk a few feet below the field level. There was no room to expand. Plus, I think the end zones were only 8 yards long. At any rate, we did not run 600 yards; instead, we only ran 580. And that's only if the field was 50 yards wide – who knows?

After football season, I decided to go out for basketball. I wasn't a really good player, but I was now about 5' 10" and could almost dunk. By mid-season, I was 5' 11" and could dunk, but not consistently, and I had to be at the correct angle. I could, however, dunk fairly consistently with a volleyball because I could palm it, something I couldn't do with a basketball. Everyone had to make the team, but after a week or two of practice, it was evident who had done so. I wasn't one of those, and I knew it. There were a couple of slots open, and it would be decided by head-to-head competition. I had to go up against another potential forward who, like me, had not earned a spot during our practices. We had to select a member of the team to play with us for the two-on-two game. Our selection could not shoot or guard against the other attempting to make the team. But they could rebound and pass. Although I don't know why, I was selected to pick first, so I chose Tom Chandler.

Tom had come over from St. Pat's and was a good basketball player. We were about the same height, and I'm sure I could have out-jumped Tom by at least a foot. But Tom was a bulldog. Tom understood how to get position on rebounds, and it didn't matter if you could out-jump him or not; when he had position, you weren't getting the rebound from him. And he could also pass – he just really understood the game. My "opponent" selected John Ozer, another of the St. Pat's boys and a really good player as well. It was close, but somehow, I pulled the game out and earned my position on the team. Another reason I selected Tom was that, although he was friends with the guy I was competing against, I knew he would play fair and do what he could to help me win. The truth is I had mixed feelings. I was elated to make the team but felt bad for the kid I beat out.

I got lucky during my junior high and high school days because I always had good coaches. Coach Wilson was no exception. I know he loved all of us, and I can personally say I loved him, as I think my teammates did as well. In an early season game, we traveled to Coffeyville. When we arrived, some high school guys who were African Americans thought it was odd that our coach was black, and we didn't have a single black player. This was the 1976-77 season, and I don't think anyone would think twice about it today, at least I hope not. But the mid-70s was a different time. Up until that point, I don't believe I had thought about the situation, but maybe it was a bit revolutionary. But if it was, it was only by chance because it just happened to be a year that the 9th-grade team didn't have African Americans. It was certainly not the norm.

In the previous two seasons, beginning in 7th grade, our guys were bad, in a bad way. But with the addition of the St. Pat's guys and Coach Wilson, we were pretty good in our 9th-grade year. We finished second in the league rather than last as they had done the previous two seasons. We battled Independence for a second. The first time we played them; we didn't score a single point in the first quarter – nothing – zilch – zero! At half-time, Coach Wilson laid into us like a rabid bull. He was yelling and spitting and sweating and somewhat miraculously, completely clear considering his unbridled anger. He had never seen a team not score in a quarter. Actually, he was livid. I think it scared the hell out of us. The next game we played, we were kicking the crap out of Iola at halftime. The locker rooms at Iola were next to each other with very thin walls, and their coach was ranting and screaming at his team. Coach Wilson looked at us with a sheepish smile on his face and asked if that's what he sounded like at Independence. "Yeah, coach, it sounds just like you." Coach shook his head, laughed, and then apologized to the team.

And back to the Independence game. We played tough and were close to winning or going into overtime when they hit a half-court shot at the buzzer to beat us. Coach was not upset about it because he knew how hard we fought to get back in the game – there was nothing we could have done to prevent a half-court shot. I'm not sure, but I think the shot was made by Anthony Boggs, a tall blond-haired kid who would become one of the best high school athletes in football, basketball, and track in the state of Kansas during our years. In our last league game, we played Independence at home, and this time, we won behind a great performance by John Kerr. However, in the league tournament after the regular season, Independence drilled us in the rubber match. I had a great time playing basketball that season. Although I might have been the best pure athlete on the team, and that's debatable, I was certainly the worst basketball player we had. I played in every game except one, the victory over Independence, but I only scored three points the entire season. But we were successful, and I learned a lot from Coach Wilson.

As soon as basketball season was over, I set my sights on track. As a 9th grader, I could move up to the mile, but I wanted to remain in the half. I think there were at least three reasons to continue to run the 880. First, I loved the event. Second, I had unfinished business in the half mile because I wanted to win the League in the event. And third, if I moved to the mile, I would have to start working out if I wanted to succeed. In the half, I could continue to hide out around the shot-put ring and still race well, something I was sure I couldn't do in the mile. Plus, the idea of running four laps on a track seemed boring – it might as well have been 20 laps.

To be honest, running 3 miles a day for the first three weeks didn't interest me in the least, but I did it anyway. Many of the guys who ran track in 7th grade were no longer part of the team, and many didn't even make it to the team in 8th. Some, like my cousin Bill, moved away, and others decided that track wasn't for them. But we gained a few from St. Pat's and some other 9th-grade kids who had not participated in track before. Still, we didn't have near the numbers we started with two years before, and that trend continued into high school. I found over the years that a lot of kids who run middle school track discontinue the sport in high school. In Arkansas, where I currently live, I think spring football takes kids away from track.

One of our really good competitors who came over from St. Pat's was Tom Chandler, my basketball teammate. Tom ran the mile, and although he wasn't really fast, he was steady and tough. In our last meet before League, we ran a dual meet in Iola. At the start of the mile, Tom looked good, but it didn't take long to see that something was wrong. Tom had a difficult time running, and his limp was profound. He finished the mile, all on guts. I have to admit, I don't recall what was wrong with him, but I think he had a broken hip or something similar. Whatever it was, Tom should have never finished the race because the injury was severe. I believe it kept him out of sports until our senior year when he played basketball. Of course, John Kerr was our steady shot putter, never losing a meet, and Randy Braun was a record-setting pole vaulter.

Our first meet was a dual at Chanute, and I was entered in the 880 and shot put. I also high jumped that year, but I don't think I was entered at the first meet. I threw well in the shot, but I was nervous as the 880 approached, which was protocol. Chanute didn't have a half-miler who could beat me, at least from my knowledge of the year before. But 1977 was a new year, and one never knew who might line up at the starting line. I should have learned my lesson from League the year before. But I was still not too far removed from the 3-mile runs we had been "forced" to grind out, so I was in decent shape. I took off when the gun sounded on the loose cinder track and never saw a competitor again. Unlike my first race in 1976, I never looked back. The race wasn't very hard, and my only goal, besides winning, was to beat 2:24, my best from 8th grade. Once the first race was over, I could see where I was at and then prepare to beat Mike Lee at League, although not by practicing.

I won going away in 2:16.0, which surprised the hell out of me. It's interesting. I intended to win League, and I knew that to beat Mike, I would probably have to run at least 2:10, yet I didn't expect to run as fast as 2:16 the first meet, and I also didn't intend to work out to improve. What was I thinking? How could I get better without training? I don't know, but for some reason, it made sense at the time. But I was well ahead of schedule, whatever my schedule was. The truth, other than the goal of winning League in the 880, I didn't have a plan, except maybe to hide out at practice near the shot or the high jump. Great strategy to win! Sometimes, maybe once or twice a week, Coach Kennedy would catch me and make me run a 330 or 440, just like the year before. But usually, I was able to slip away to a field event after my one run. In essence, after those three weeks of three-mile runs, I rarely ran again, except in races and possibly my sprints around the track fence to the shot-put ring.

Our second meet was at home against two junior high schools from Pittsburg, Lakeside, and Roosevelt. I enjoyed running at home, not only because my parents could watch from our backyard but also because we had an all-weather track. Honestly, I had no love for cinder tracks. When I first ran on one at Coffeyville in 7th grade, I was surprised that meets could be contested on such crap. But I also learned that there were actually pretty good cinder tracks, although I still didn't like them. Running at home, I felt confident, excited, and nervous. The shot put and high jump were good for me because I could compete in those events without nerves, which also took my mind off the half mile. When I had things to do before my race, I didn't dwell on what I needed to do when I stepped on the track for nearly as long as I would have if I'd just sat in the bleachers waiting my turn.

When the race began, I realized that I had more competition than I had in the Chanute race. This was good, and I welcomed it. Lakeside and Roosevelt each had a good half-miler, but it became a challenging race. I did something I hadn't done before. I came from behind and outkicked those two to win the race. I could hear Mr. Wilson cheer me on as I swept around the two Pittsburg runners, and it gave me energy. It was a much harder race than the previous one, but it felt great to win such a competitive race. All my wins in the 880 through 8th grade and the first 9th-grade race had not been competitive. My time was 2:15.1. This was not too much faster, but I knew I was on to bigger things. Little did I know that this would be my fastest time of the year.

We next traveled back to Chanute for their invitational and our first meet of the year, during which ribbons were awarded. Now, I would get my first blue ribbon, and I knew I would win. I must have been too stubborn or just stupid because I didn't seem to learn my lesson.

Being over-confident was not an endearing trait for me. I should have known earning a blue ribbon would not come easily and without anxiety. I didn't know all the competitors in the 880s. I had not competed against Fort Scott before. They were in our high school league but not in our junior high league. The race began fairly fast, although not excessively so. I took the lead through the first lap. I did like to lead races, and although I didn't do so against the Pittsburg schools, that was not the norm. Regardless, I did have someone right behind me. As with the previous week, the competition was welcome. Through the backstretch, I kept my lead but was shadowed the entire time. Again, this was welcome. But as I reached the midway point of the final curve, about 110 yards from the finish, my shadow was still there, which was unnerving at this point because now there was a threat to "my" blue ribbon.

One thing that should be explained here is that although most of our meets didn't give out ribbons, my main objective was to win awards, not the joy of the competition. Don't get me wrong, I did love the competition, but the goal was to win a first-place ribbon. Yes, I wanted to win the league and redeem myself, but the focus was still on the award more than being the league champion. I think it took me until college to fully remove myself from this mentality. As I came off the curve, I must have run a little wide because a kid began to gain on me from the inside. As we sprinted the last 50 yards, I could feel the blue ribbon slipping away. In desperation, I leaned at the tape with my opponent, which I'm sure exposed every vein in my forehead and arms, with a physically excruciating lunge. Had I won? Had I lost? I couldn't tell. My opponent, from Fort Scott, placed his arms around my shoulders, gave me an exhausting congratulatory hug, and said, "Great race." I was a bite in shock because no one had ever given me a hug in an athletic competition. But this was a pure reaction of joy from a pure, unadulterated, and un-spoiled by fame and money moment of competition – one of those lost moments from several decades ago in the hinterland of America that can make competition great. We can see all the horrible signs of bad sportsmanship from players, coaches, and especially parents in our society, but this small yet significant moment for the two of us was special.

But who won? The judges and timers gathered to confer about the finish as we stood by wondering. Neither of us knew who had won, and it was just too damn close. Finally, we heard the verdict – anticipation over – TIE! A tie? "Who gets the blue ribbon?" is what I thought. Leave it to me to begin to spoil a great moment of competition. They told us they would flip a coin to see who gets the blue and red ribbons. I don't know who called it, but I won and was awarded the blue ribbon. I was overjoyed. I had "earned" my first blue ribbon. I still felt bad for the Fort Scott kid because he had to take home the red ribbon, but I should have learned something from him that day because he didn't seem the least bit disappointed about not getting the blue ribbon. He was thrilled to have been a competitor in such a thrilling race. In other words, he got "it" better than I got "it." Still, I was learning, and I wasn't completely oblivious to the real meaning of our race and great, pure competition.

Our time in the Chanute tie was 2:15.2, only a tenth of a second from my best, and it was the best time for the Fort Scott kid. But on cinders, it was better than the 2:15.1 run on our all-weather track. I wish I could remember the name of the runner from Fort Scott. When I was in high school the next year, I looked for him at meets because I looked forward to racing him over the next three years, but I never saw him again after 9th grade. It's possible he changed events, didn't run track anymore, or even moved away. I'd like to know because it's still an important race to me all these years later. I raced against him one more time at our next meet, the Iola Invitational.

As a 15-year-old, I still needed to learn how to manage my nerves, and I didn't do so well at Iola. With the Fort Scott kid there, plus the two from Pittsburg Lakeside and Roosevelt Junior High Schools, the anticipation of the competition overwhelmed me. And the shot and high jump didn't help me in this meet. I stayed competitive for much of the race, but I wasn't aggressive, and I didn't take the lead from the beginning. I hate to use the word, but I think I feared the moment – I wasn't ready to take it on. Over the last 220 yards, I lost the race. I was tight and worn out. I was worn out from the worry, not so much the running, although, without training at practice, I could have been losing fitness. But my physical condition was not the issue in this race. I finished fourth behind the Fort Scott kid, who won, and the two from Pittsburg. The winning time was 2:15 or 2:16, not any faster than I had run the first three meets. But I ran 2:22. The winner talked with me after the race. I congratulated him, and he told me that I would be back after a poor race. Again, he got "it." He didn't lose respect for me because he knew I was the same guy he raced in Chanute.

After the Iola meet, I needed to regain my confidence. I knew we wouldn't face Fort Scott, Lakeside, and Roosevelt the rest of the season, but I still had to face Mike Lee at League. Then, I severely sprained my ankle. Of course, an ankle sprain wouldn't get in the way of my training since I didn't train, but it would affect my racing. We traveled again to Iola for a dual meet. There were only two of us in the half mile, and I had beaten the Iola kid the week before. But with a sprained ankle, I was unsure what I would do. The Iola kid was a good guy whom I spoke with the week before, and we had a nice conversation at the dual meet. I had raced at Iola twice and had not won either time. But despite the fact that I limped through the race, I won in 2:24. After all, if Tom Chandler could finish a mile on guts and determination with his serious injury, the least I could do was win the 880 against one competitor on a measly sprained ankle, especially since my competitor wasn't Rick Wohlhuter.

Now it was on to League Meet, held on that god-forsaken Coffeyville track. I was a nervous wreck and extremely tight. Not long after we arrived, I found out that Mike Lee had not come out for track. I don't know if I was happy or not. I had anticipated the race against him all

66

season, and now he wasn't there. But, regardless, I still had to race, and his absence didn't seem to stem my nerves. First, though, was the shot and high jump. John Kerr, the overwhelming favorite, had the flu and didn't travel to the meet. But this didn't make the event wide-open because a thrower from Iola had always been second to John since 7th grade. He was now the clear favorite. But something strange happened on the way to the circus. During warm-ups, the Iola kid walked across the sector while one of our 8th graders, Derek Hull, my little league football teammate, was throwing the shot. The shot hit the Iola kid square in the head. I had just turned away and didn't actually see it, but I certainly heard it. When I turned around again, the Iola shot putter was on the ground. He was lucky because something like that can kill someone, and people have been killed when hit by the shot. But this was an eight-pound shot. He had a little time to recover because the 8th graders competed first, but I bet he suffered a concussion. I don't think anyone thought about that kind of injury. He just got his bell rung. It was 1977 – a different era. I had never beaten him before, but I did that day. I had my best all-time throw and took 5th place, earning Parsons a couple of points. It was the last time I competed in the shot until I was 56 years old.

In the high jump, I cleared 5' 4". I'm sure I didn't place, and I was sure I hadn't finished in the top six when I missed three attempts at 5' 6". But after the meet, when we were on the bus, the coach gave me a 6th-place ribbon. I told the coach I didn't get 6th, but he assured me that I did and that I had earned us a point. I don't know – I still have that ribbon, but I'm not so sure I earned the ribbon or the points. Who knows, maybe I did. But I didn't know this when the high jump ended, and I found a place to rest before the 880-yard run. This was the track where I fell two years before, and it didn't look much better that day. The ruts were not there, but it was an atrocious track. As the time came closer, I became tighter and tighter, and the pressure was intense. I attempted to get away from my thoughts about the race by watching Randy Braun win the pole vault with a League record jump. But this was only a temporary reprise. It's a situation in which you hope it hurries up and gets there, and at the same time, you hope it never does.

Then, the race arrived. It's all really a blur today. Some races I can remember clearly, start to finish, but in the 9th grade League Meet, I only remember being at the starting line, the finish, and some vague moments during the race. What I do know is that I was tight, I ran somewhat scared, and I took the lead at the beginning. Being tight and scared is not a good combination when racing, but somehow, I won, and I won easily, in 2:16.0. I was the League champion! All that hard work… in the shot put had helped me win the 880. OK, so I didn't work hard to win the half mile, but I would eventually learn to love the hard work and what it took to be a good runner. For now, I could go home with my second blue ribbon, run an AAU Junior Olympics race or two, and prepare for high school football. After all, that was still my sport, and maybe win some medals in high school track.

A week after school was out for the summer, I traveled to Fredonia, Kansas, with some friends for the area Junior Olympic meet. I was entered in the Intermediate Division 880-yard run, which was for 15 and 16-year-olds. This meant there were some high school kids entering as well. Brad Burkes introduced me to a kid from Girard, Kansas, who had just finished his sophomore year and had run a 2:03 half. Burkes said I would probably have to settle for a second. But I wasn't worried because the top three qualified for the State AAU meet. In fact, I really didn't feel much pressure at all. Yes, I wanted to qualify for the State meet, but my goal for the year had been met. Still, Burkes threw me a challenge. In the end, the Girard kid was never a challenge, and I won fairly easily in 2:15.4 on a decent cinder track. In fact, the Girard kid didn't take second. That was achieved by Steve Gaffney from Coffeyville, who didn't run that event at League. Steve was OK at the half his first time running it, finishing close behind, but he would go on in high school to be a really good 880 runner, along with other events. Steve became an all-purpose guy who could get points in any event he entered on one of the great high school teams in the state.

There are moments that completely alter the way we view the world. That happened to my view of track and competition at the State AAU Junior Olympic Meet at Kansas State University in Manhattan, Kansas, in mid-June 1977. Since I was one of the area champions, I was sure I would do well at the state meet. I really didn't think I would win, and I didn't even believe I would qualify for the Missouri Valley AAU meet – the top four advanced from the state meet – there would be too many 16-year-olds competing. But I was not prepared for what I got myself into. I still didn't train, although Burkes convinced several guys who were going to the meet to do a 10-mile run from town to the swimming area at Parsons Lake. I did it, but one long run in weeks and weeks of non-training wouldn't suddenly make me a great runner. Plus, we did stop a few times, once to try and get lemonade from a kid's stand in the middle of the country. I doubt any of us had money, and I know we didn't get anything to drink.

On the morning of the State Meet, Burkes qualified for the Missouri Valley Meet in the Intermediate two-mile. In the early afternoon, I watched a kid win the Intermediate mile in the 4:20s, and he was impressive. Then, in the late afternoon, the 880 runners were called to the line. There were too many Intermediate half milers for one heat, but they ran us together anyway. Because of the number of competitors, we were lined up in a waterfall start, which I had never heard of. A meet official had a list of names, and not everyone entered was there, including Gaffney. I noticed that the first kid they called was not there, but they didn't give it too much notice. Finally, after all the names were called, and maybe 30 seconds before the start, a kid ran up to the start asking if this was the 880. He was the kid who had been first called, and he was also the kid who won the mile – he was good!

And he was good. I ran around my norm, a 2:16, finishing behind gobs of runners, but Tim Gundy, from a small town in central Kansas, won in 1:59. That seemed otherworldly to me. I didn't know kids my age could run under two minutes in a half mile. As we were about to leave the track, I saw Gundy and asked him if he had won the race because I was so far behind, I didn't know who it was at that moment. He said he had and asked me if I was the one that finished right behind him. I thought, "You mean another kid ran close to the same time?" I explained that I was not that runner. The next year, at the same meeting, Burkes asked Gundy what his best time in the 880 was. He said he ran 1:54 the year before in a meet after the State AAU. A 1:59 was fast to me, but 1:54 at the age of 15 or 16? I thought that was unbelievable. Kansas is a state with its fair share of legendary high school runners, of which I am not one. But Gundy is one of those runners. He ran a 4:12 mile in 1979. I raced against Gundy in an 8-K road race in 1983. He ran poorly, and I ran great – he finished 20 seconds ahead of me.

Chapter 4
2:14s

In the summer of 1977, high school football was on the horizon. I didn't run again for the rest of the summer, but I anticipated football. The team had a new head coach, Don Barcus, who had been an assistant at league-rival Fort Scott. Coach Barcus called a meeting during the summer so we could meet. This caused me to be fired up about football even more. The first half of my summer was busy. Besides track meets, I had Driver's Ed., the driving portion, with Mr. Stathe as the instructor. One of the students I drove with was John Kerr. Toward the end of the summer, right before a family vacation and about two weeks before football practice began, I received a call late one morning about working in the hay fields. I was bored at that point in the summer and said I would do it. I had no clue what I was getting myself into!

A friend, Chris Breneman, worked for a local dairy farmer, Donald Dean, and they needed someone to help for a couple of days. I think I was several names down Chris' list, and I think the others called before me and said, "Are you kidding?" Mrs. Dean came by my house, picked me up, and drove me to their farm about 5 miles north of town. As we headed to the hay field, Mr. Dean asked me if I could drive a truck. Of course, I could until I got in and realized it was a stick shift. One thing I learned quickly by working on the farm was how to drive a stick. We made it to the hay field that was about a mile and a half south on the gravel road, where the hay was already mowed, dried, and raked. Of course, at that point, I didn't know the process; I was just ready to go. We were going to bail prairie hay, whatever that was.

Mr. Dean hooked up the bailer to the tractor and a hay wagon to the bailer and explained what we were to do and how to stack the hay. Then I was handed a hay hook, which I had never heard of, and we jumped up on the wagon, or hay rack, and we started down the field. It was a disaster. We didn't know what we were doing, and we couldn't keep up with the bails as they were pushed out the back end of the bailer up to the edge of the rack. Somehow, we managed to finish the field and stack the hay in a barn. I was exhausted and decided I would never do this again. Of course, I spent the next three summers in the hay fields working for Mr. Dean and became damn good at it. Plus, working in the hay fields was the best preparation for football one could have – it made one tough as hell.

When I entered high school, my cousin Mike, who was a senior, told me there was a good chance that I would get challenged on the first day and that I needed to stand up for myself, or this would go on my entire sophomore year. He was correct. I was challenged by a senior in my second-period class, and I did stand up for myself. Nothing happened at that moment, and I was not picked on for the rest of the year. I was now in my years in which I didn't fear anyone, so I wouldn't have backed down from any challenge, but it was nice not to have to worry about it.

As I transitioned into high school, one good athlete we wouldn't have for track or football was Randy Braun, who moved over the summer. Nonetheless, we believed, at least I did, that we had a number of sophomores who would help make the junior varsity football team a success. I was sure that the majority of us would not make varsity because of how good the high school team had been the previous two years. There were some starters back and some good players who were second-team the year before. The one kid we had that I thought would start as a sophomore was John Kerr. Although John made the traveling squad for varsity for every road game, he never did start. To this day, I believe he should have been a starting linebacker as a 10th grader. Only one other sophomore made the traveling squad in 1977, and he only achieved it once.

The varsity lost a close game to start the season against Fort Scott, who had also made the playoffs the previous two years. In the second game, we beat Iola 20-0, but then it all went downhill, and the varsity team ended up going 3-5. As far as the junior varsity, we went 5-2, and we were confident we would have a great season in 1978. With the combination of returning varsity starters and sophomores and juniors who played on a winning junior varsity, we believed we had a good future. As sophomores, we had to endure the hazing of the upperclassmen. But this wasn't like the stuff that gets bad press today. When it rained and a small ditch filled with water, sophomores were dragged through the mud and not much else. It didn't hurt, and if you didn't fight it, it went quick. If you didn't play as a sophomore but waited until you were a junior, you still got the mud treatment.

We did have one senior who was an asshole who did other things to "Mores," as sophomores were called. One time, when I had raffle tickets to help raise funds to attend a Kansas City Chiefs game after the season, this bastard came up behind me and hit me with his shoulder behind my knees, and I went crashing down and ruined my tickets in the water. I was so pissed I threatened to kick his ass, and I'm sure I would have because he was a squirrely guy. But Coach Barcus and John Kerr settled me down. Another time, this good-for-nothing senior came up behind a sophomore during practice and hit him on the hamstring with his fist. I saw it happen, and the kid just dropped to the ground – his season was over. This senior thought he was cute and a bigtime football player, but he was actually no better at the game than a worm – he was a weasel. Some of the other seniors actually took him aside and told him that was enough.

DAM RUN

When football season ended, I had no intention of playing basketball. But shortly after the season began, our gym teacher, Mr. Turner, who was called "Teach," asked me to come out for the team. Teach was the assistant coach, which meant he was the head coach for the junior varsity team. Teach played college basketball at Philander Smith College in Little Rock, a historically black college. When he graduated in the mid-1960s, I believe he tried out for the Chicago Bulls but didn't make the final cut. I don't know how he made it to southeast Kansas, but most of us liked him. I told Teach I didn't want to play, but he told me that I could run circles around the other guys and would be an asset to the team. It was tempting, but I didn't want to come in a few games into the season. Finally, he told me he would fail me if I didn't play. But I didn't go out for basketball, and Teach didn't fail me, and I knew he wouldn't.

In mid to late February, track practice began. I was excited but nervous because this was my first high school track season, and I was afraid I was going to be made to workout at practice. Although we had one coach for the boys, unlike junior high, in high school, we didn't have an unmanageable number of kids who came out for the team, so I felt I wouldn't be able to hide. Plus, the high school boys had a new coach. I knew the old coach, Mr. Wheat, but the new coach was young and full of energy. It was like the "on" button was continually pressed. The girl's coach was also new, and he was Mr. Barcus, the head football coach. As I look back, it's strange that a medium-size high school didn't provide assistant coaches. I think almost all the teams we competed against had more than one coach.

Our new boy's track coach was Gary Cagle, and he did indeed make me workout. Coach Cagle had only recently graduated from college. I think he was 24 or 25 years old my sophomore season. I remember going to Burkes' house for a surprise birthday party for Coach when he turned 26, but I don't recall whether it was when I was a sophomore or my junior year. He ran track and cross-country at Pittsburg State University, about 35 miles from Parsons. He had come from Topeka, Kansas when he matriculated to attend college in the far southeast corner of the state. Coach Cagle ran the 400, 800, and 400m hurdles in college or the yard equivalents. I think he ran 440 yards in 47 seconds, and I know he ran an 880 on a relay in 1:53. I also know he was a good 600-yard runner during the indoor season. Although he was a good intermediate hurdler, I don't know how fast he ran. So, Coach Cagle was a good small college track athlete. And he could coach all the events, including the field events. I learned a tremendous amount about training from him and about events in which I never competed. Before football practice began the previous summer, Coach called me and asked if I would like to run cross county. I told him thanks, but I was playing football. This didn't upset him.

Coach Cagle's intensity was hard to get used to, and some kids couldn't take it, but I liked Coach. It took me a while before I got used to working out but also to enjoyed it. I think it took the next three years to evolve to that point. My opinion was that Coach was all about motivation in how he treated us, whether he was praising us or being critical. For example, he used to really get on Burkes. At the time, I didn't get it because Burkes was our best runner. But I understand now. I think it was because Coach Cagle knew that Burkes could handle it, and if he got on our best runner, it demonstrated that Coach didn't show favoritism. Burkes wasn't lazy and worked extremely hard, and Coach understood that, but sometimes, he needed a kick in the pants during races to challenge himself.

In most local meets, Burkes' only competition was himself, and Coach attempted to motivate him by yelling criticisms at him while he raced. In one small meet during his senior year, Coach kept calling Burkes a pussy as he ran the 2-miles. He won the race by 220 yards. Although that might get a coach in trouble today, the late 1970s was a different time. As the son of a Four-Square Church pastor, I wondered how Burkes dealt with these things, but I don't think they ever fazed him. I think Brad knew that Coach loved and respected him.

Coach Cagle was the greatest thing that could happen to me in track at that time. I needed someone to not allow me to get away with the shenanigans I got away with in junior high. Coach would give a look that could make you turn away in shame. And if he was pissed at you, his stare would burn right through you. I needed this. In some ways, I was used to it because my boss on the farm, Mr. Dean, could be the same way, and I never took it personally. And I never took it personally with Coach Cagle either, although he did piss me off at times, but I think he did that on purpose. Still, Coach loved all of us, and I know some, maybe even today, don't believe that, but I do. Not long after practice began, Coach took those on the team who could go to an indoor track meet at Pittsburg State. We saw a guy, I think it was Mike McCleod, run a 2-mile in under 9 minutes. Coach was like that. He cared for us and wanted us to be exposed to high-quality performances so we would know what they looked like.

It didn't take long for me to buy into Coach Cagle's philosophy, even though the enjoyment took longer. But what I did enjoy was being a part of his team. We had some pretty good runners, although, other than Burkes, it took some time to develop. But Coach Cagle was a good coach, and he was able to get a lot out of some runners over a period of time. Unfortunately, Cagle didn't remain long enough in coaching to get recognition, but I think he was one of the best high school track coaches in Kansas. I've been around the sport for 50 years, and few have been his equal. Plus, very few of his athletes got injured, and we never had serious injuries under his watch.

The first meet was approaching, and it was at home. In 1978, my sophomore year, I got a great gift from the Kansas High School Athletics Association – the 2-mile relay. In that year, Kansas added the 2-mile relay to the agenda of events, which I think many states did that year. I think it took the place of the medley relay in Kansas. One of the other races that was replaced was the 180-yard low hurdles with the 330-yard intermediate hurdles, which didn't affect me. This was terrific because I wasn't ready to move to the mile, so I could compete in two 880s per meet – the relay and open race. And as it turned out, I ran these two races in every meet as a sophomore.

The Parsons Invitational was the first of April, and I was not sure I was ready. But Coach made sure we had gradually worked up to harder workouts so we would be prepared. For example, we started out with three-mile runs during distant days and quickly advanced to four and five miles. Of course, Burkes was doing runs of 8 and 10 miles at times. Once we had our base down, which took a few weeks, we began some speed or pace work. These interval workouts could be done on the track or at a park and even at Oakwood Cemetery on the east side of town.

On the track, we started with 6x440 at maybe 70 to 75 seconds and, throughout the season, graduated to 10 or 12 440s in 68 to 72 seconds. When we were away from the track, the distances could vary and were never exact. I wish I had kept a training log, but during those years, I had never heard of one and had never thought about keeping a record of my workouts. In fact, I never thought about running on the weekends or twice a day. But today, I'm against most kids at the age of 16 running twice a day. I had also not heard of working out or training in the off-season. In fact, I don't believe I had heard the word "training" in the context of running. To me, you showed up to practice, did what the coach told you to do, didn't question the workout, and that was it. No other running was required.

When the Parsons Invitational arrived, I was indeed entered in the two-mile relay and the 880-yard run. It was a cool day, and as usual, I was nervous. Would I let down my teammates in the relay? After all, I was running the first leg, and I needed to be good enough for us to have a chance to place in the top six. Unlike junior high meets, we were given medals in high school, and only the top three received these precious awards. The two-mile relay was held early in the meet, so I didn't have to wait around long, in the cool weather, to run my race. The truth is, I don't actually remember what place I was in when I handed it off, but I do have memories of the race, but they are too fragmented to get the full picture. What I do know is we took 3rd running in the 8:50s, and I ran the leadoff leg in 2:14. Coach was extremely pleased with me because I had run a PR and was competitive. Burkes ran our anchor leg in 2:04 but couldn't catch the two teams ahead of us. And most importantly, I earned my first medal!

There was a fair amount of time between the relay and 880, so I had the opportunity to walk over to my house and talk with my dad about the race. He was also happy with the way I ran. My dad was terrific about these things because he enjoyed watching me compete in whatever sport I was doing but never placed any pressure on me. He just watched and gave me comments and never any criticism. Between races, I asked Burkes whether he thought I could run another 2:14 in the open 880, but his opinion was that it would be tough. I only ran a second faster than my previous best from 9th grade, but to me, it seemed like a lot more than that. Plus, the 2:14 was not nearly as hard as the races I ran the year before. In ninth grade, I could have never followed up a 2:15 or 2:16 with another 880 of equal time. I would have been hard-pressed to break 2:30 in a second race because I was usually spent after a race. But now, not only was I a year older, but I was actually in pretty good racing shape, at least as compared to my past. I was certain I could run a 2:20 in the second race, which was a hell of a lot better than 2:30.

I knew I couldn't get a medal in the 880 because high school track was a lot better than what I was used to. The year before, our high school team had a senior who ran 2:00 for the half, and he held our meet record in 2:04, so I expected that there would be a runner who would at least challenge the record. But I ended up being competitive in the race, and I finished fourth in 2:14. That's right,

2:14. I was surprised, and Coach Cagle was ecstatic. Now, 2:14 might not sound that fast, but it was blazing to me at that point. I think the winner, Jeff Norris from Labette County High School, our hated rival, ran 2:06. He was actually a great kid and was a year older than me. His dad was the principal at Labette County, and he spoke with me after the race and congratulated me on running well. He actually knew who I was because he attended church with my grandparents. I would have several good races against Norris over the next two years. I think I only beat him once.

In my opinion, and in the opinion of Coach Cagle and my father, I had a great day. And I admired that medal. It was in the shape of our school's Viking shield and was painted blue and yellow. Burkes, who was the kind of guy who seemed happier for someone else's accomplishments than his own, was happy with how I ran as well. I think that before track season, he had told coach I would be a good runner, so maybe his prediction was on the mark. Burkes had a good day as well, winning the 2-mile after competing in the relay.

It's interesting how much track and field means, or doesn't mean, to high school students. From a football game, it was highly probable that you would have several comments from students and teachers on Monday about the Friday night game. But in track, very few people even knew we had a meet. More were aware of a home meet, but when we traveled…. Still, a couple of people asked how I did. One was Mr. Wheat, who actually did work the meet but was running off a field event and wasn't sure how well I ran. Just because he didn't coach track anymore didn't mean he had lost interest in how we competed. When he asked me about my day, I told him I had run "two 2:14s." That's right, not a couple of 2:14s, but two 2:14s. I think it confused him at first, but he soon got it. I was proud, and that was revealed when I told him how I had done it.

Coach Cagle often ran distance runs with us, at least the shorter runs. As intense as Coach was, he also had a great sense of humor. We might run to a local park as a warmup before a speed workout, and Coach Cagle usually stretched with us, telling jokes or revealing funny stories. I can remember Coach getting overly excited telling us about a Steve Martin performance during his "Wild and Crazy Guy" days. Coach Cagle got so worked up telling us the story that I couldn't figure out if he had attended the show or not. If he had, I'm not sure where he would have traveled to see it because Parsons was not close to any place large. I guess he could have driven south to Tulsa or north to Kansas City.

As the season went on, I began to enjoy our workouts more and more, and my times improved little by little. We had a pretty good two-mile relay, and Burkes kept winning the two-mile and mile runs. Sometimes, he ran on the relay. Burkes could have handled three races a day, but Kansas rules didn't allow for this during those years. At mid-season, as the coach looked for a fourth guy to run the relay so Burkes could concentrate on his two races, he placed one of our quarter milers in the position. Buster Fuentes was a junior and one of those who could get the team points in multiple events, from the 440 to the long jump and high jump, and he even ran both hurdle races. Buster would have been a good decathlete if given the opportunity. In fact, as an adult, he has competed in triathlons and biathlons for years. Buster passed the 880 test on the relay in flying colors. This meant that the two-mile relay now consisted of me as the leadoff leg, senior Roger Smith and Buster as the middle two legs, and junior Ron Faulkenberry as the anchor. The first meet in which Buster ran the relay was in Fort Scott, and we ran 8:42.6 to take 3rd, with Burkes still as our fourth man.

Still, we were not a great relay team, but we always placed. We also had sophomore Eric Zink, who ran the relay at times. I remember that, for some reason, Eric didn't have track shoes. I think he couldn't find anything that was his size. I don't remember whether this occurred during our sophomore or junior years, but after I ran the lead-off, Eric was our third leg, and as soon as I finished, I turned to the infield, but not far off the track, and slipped my shoes off and

Eric put them on his feet. We had about 2 minutes to do this, and we pulled it off. Eric stepped on the track just in time to take the baton for his leg. I don't recall, but we might have even done this during our senior year at one meet. I had great teammates. And the middle-distance and distance guys were terrific. And my track shoes ran the mile before I did!

In reality, Burkes was the only guy on the team who ran a really good 880 times on the relay, but the rest of us did alright. One day, we ran our warmup a few blocks from the high school to Circle Park, which was not really a park but a round road with a few houses situated on the outside of the circle and grass on the inside. But it was a good place to do some pace work, so we occasionally ran there. I'm not sure where the conversation started and why, but Roger Smith started talking about some man he met or knew, and a couple of others knew him as well. I don't know the man's name, but Roger said the man told him he had run high school track a few years before in Missouri. He explained that the man asked him what he ran the 880 in, and Roger told him 2:13. With a smile on his face, Roger said the man laughed and said that it was slow. I looked at Roger and said, "That's not slow," and from my perspective, it wasn't, even though I knew it wasn't really that fast either. Roger asked the man if he had run the 880 in high school, and the man said "yes" in 1:53. That more or less put our times in perspective. At that point, my best score was 2:11, but I thought the man should have acknowledged that Roger wasn't a bad runner.

Toward the end of the season, I hadn't won a race. But then we participated in a triangular in Chanute against the home team and Coffeyville. After a good performance in the relay, in which we placed 2nd, I won the 880-yard run in my second 2:09 of the day. Coach Cagle was pleased even though I realize now it wasn't really a fast time. But in 1978, as a 16-year-old, it was fast to me. After the race, a couple of kids from Coffeyville who I had beaten asked me if I had lived in Parsons my whole life. I said I originally came from LA, and that seemed to impress them, and I even explained why I had won. Of course, coming from Los Angeles had nothing to do with my win, and even if the competition in California had helped me improve, I left the West coast at 6 years old. But I didn't let them know any of this. I could use this to my advantage when we raced again!

Our next meet was for sophomores in Iola, held at Allan County Community College. Besides our own, this was the only all-weather track we competed on during my first year of high school. I was entered in the 2-mile relay and the 880-yard run. I was surprised to learn after we arrived that my cousin Keith held the meet record in 2:03. Until my 10th grade track season, I didn't know which events Keith ran. But to learn he was a half-miler was interesting to me because that was my race as well. And I knew I wouldn't be able to break his meet record – but as long as I could win, I was OK with that. Sometime after our first meet, our vice principal and athletic director, Mr. Martin, who had once been the track and football coach, started telling me about this kid named Keith Cruse, whom he used to coach. "Do you know who I'm talking about?" he would say. And I'd answer, "Yes, Mr. Martin, he's, my cousin." Mr. Martin would tell me that, unlike Keith, he didn't think I had enough speed to break two minutes in the half. I told him that I thought I did.

When Mr. Martin told me about Keith as a track athlete, he revealed things I didn't know about him. My memories of Keith's track career only consisted of the celebration with his twin brother when he arrived home. He told me that Keith hated to practice, which sounded like me in junior high. Mr. Martin said that at the end of the school day, he would rush to one of the exit doors and try to catch Keith before he left school. On the days he guessed the door of which he was leaving, Keith went to practice. On the days he guessed incorrectly, well...you know the result. Mr. Martin thought the thing that made Keith so good was that he went to the skating rink several nights every week. True enough, I grew up at the rink as well, and

Keith had been there all the time when I was a kid. Mr. Martin said skating made Keith a strong runner. He might be right.

One night, when I was in elementary school, my sister and I were waiting for our dad to pick us up from the rink. It was after dark, and we were the only ones waiting outside. Suddenly, a car came sliding off the street into the gravel rink parking lot and stopped by a car. Everyone jumped out and broke a window or two, then jumped back in the car, raced around the end of the car, and slightly lost control before coming to a stop right by us. The person looking at us from the front passenger seat was Keith. He looked at us with wide-open eyes, and my wide-open eyes caught his. He knew what we had seen! Then the car sped off. I don't know who the others were in the car, but I could have guessed. The police arrived before our dad, and Karen and I never told them who we saw. And we didn't tell dad either. A couple of years before he died, I asked Keith about the incident. And he had a vague memory, but he did remember who was in the car with him!

Mr. Martin said they had a track meet in Iola at the stadium where we ran our junior high meets, and as the 880 neared, no one knew where Keith was. There was a carnival close by, and sitting in the stands, Mr. Martin could see Keith running across the field from the rides and making it to the starting line as instructions were given out. As the starter called "set," Mr. Martin saw Keith put something in his mouth, and then the gun sounded. Keith won the race while he chewed on peanuts he bought at the carnival. I'm not sure, but it might have been the sophomore meet. At the State Track meet, Mr. Martin told me that Keith was running a great race, but when he realized he wouldn't place in the top five, he slowed to a jog before crossing the finish line in 2:00.0. The school record was 1:59.2, from 1967, and Mr. Martin was sure Keith had it, but slowing down cost him. Oh well, he had two more years to break it. But it wasn't to be. His sophomore year was the only season he ran track. I don't believe Keith was in high school after 10th grade.

When I entered high school, the record was still 1:59.2, but I knew I had no chance as a sophomore. But at the Iola sophomore meet, my objective was to win, not attempt records. In the 2-mile relay, I ran the anchor. Eric Zink, Danny Ramirez, and Eddie Flashpolor were the legs before me. I received the baton in second place, a fair distance behind Pittsburg. I attempted to measure my run so that I didn't try and catch the leader on the first lap. I didn't want to die, so if I could catch the Pittsburg runner gradually, I would preserve my energy before taking him off the final curve. The plan worked great, except for one thing. As I came off the curve for the final stretch, I began to pass the leader but was never able to inch ahead and lost my nose. My leg was a 2:10, much faster than Pittsburg's anchor, but it didn't matter because they won. The Pittsburg kid did become a fine half-miler and qualified for the state meet in the 800 as a junior, beating me in the process.

When the 880-yard run rolled around, I was out of energy. I can't say it was the result of the relay because I had run both races in every meet that year and never had any issues with the second race. But I was spent this day. I think it might have been nerves because I knew I was expected to win the half, and I felt I had something to live up to after seeing that Keith held the meet record. When the race started, I didn't believe I would win. I ran the first 440 in a funk. That first lap was a disaster, at least for a young teenager trying to live up to certain expectations. But the thing is, and I only learned this later, most of the pressure was something I conjured up. It was all me. Sure, Coach Cagle wanted me to run well, and he expected me to give my all and do my best, but if I did those things and didn't win, he would be fine with that. With 330 yards to go, I was 35 yards behind the leader, but I suddenly had a burst of energy and started to kick. It was now or never, and I ran with complete purpose. My only thought was to catch the guy in first and pass him for the victory. It was the best kick I had my sophomore year, and I caught the leader down the stretch and flew by him for the victory. My winning time was only 2:12, but I had lived up to expectations, at least as I viewed them. The trip home in the school van that Coach drove was joyous for all of us because we had performed well as a team. Now, we needed to be ready for the high school league meet.

The Southeast Kansas League Meet was held on a Friday at Pittsburg State University. Their cinder track was the best of the non-all-weathers we competed on that year. As it was all season, I ran the 2-mile relay and the 880-yard run. We had some good athletes, but we didn't have the numbers to challenge for the win. Iola was the power of the League, and Coffeyville was good as well. And Independence had terrific athletes. But we did have the best distance runner in the League. Burkes' first race was the mile, and he ran well, but because Brad didn't have speed, he actually got out-kicked by a kid from Iola named Maxwell. Burkes ran 4:34 and broke the school record. Later in the meet, Burkes easily won the 2-mile in something just over 10 minutes. Brad had never run under 10 minutes on the track, but we knew he could do it because he ran 9:48 for the same distance at the state cross-country meet, where he took 9th.

In the 2-mile relay, I ran the first leg with Buster, Roger, and Ron, the other runners. I ran 2:09, but we were not in the lead. The other guys ran well, too, but we were just not good enough to win. We took a respectable 5[th,] though, and demonstrated improvement over the year. In the 880, I was relegated to the "slow" heat, but I thought I was faster than some of those in the second race. There were some in the "fast" heat who had never beaten me. But it was a lesson I would learn and be reminded of during my track career – coaches lie about the times and distances of their athletes. Fortunately, or maybe unfortunately, I always had honest coaches, and sometimes, that fact came back to bite me when I was placed in a slower heat when I should have been in the fastest one. This was especially true in college. I have learned throughout the years that there are plenty of dishonest and even horrific coaches, even at large universities, that don't know their asses from a hole in the ground. The level of bad and dishonest track coaches and other sports in this country is appalling. But I'll leave that discussion for a later chapter.

So, I was placed in the first heat of the 880 just after dark, under the lights. For some reason, races seemed more exciting when the lights were on, especially in a place like Pittsburg State, where the stadium was on both sides of the track and a stone wall hugged each curve. This provided the feeling of running inside the arena, more of a closed-in race. I usually ran well under those conditions. I don't remember who was in my heat except one of the Coffeyville kids I beat in Chanute. But when the gun went off, I didn't care who I was running against because I knew I was the best in the heat. This wasn't the unfounded confidence I had in the 8th-grade League Meet two years before. I had raced all of these guys and had not lost to any of them.

I took the lead from the beginning because I understood that waiting to out-kick the field would probably not get the team points, which was the top six finishers. I had earned the team points in every 880-yard run that year, which was every meet. But I also ran against the competition in every meet. This was not the case in the 1978 League Meet. If I was going to get points, I needed to earn them on my own, and I hoped the second heat didn't go extremely fast, with several runners being pulled too fast. Coach Cagle had me prepared and spoke to me about taking the lead from the start and trying to run away from the field. And I did just that. Except for the one kid from Coffeyville, who stayed relatively close, I blew the field away. But my time, which was equal to a personal best, was only 2:09. I was hoping for at least a 2:08 and possibly a 2:07. Those times might get me 6th place – that was my opinion going in.

I watched the fast heat with anticipation and wished I would have been in it. The favorite to win was Labette County's Jeff Norris, and he didn't disappoint. When he finished the race, there was only one guy relatively close to him, but I didn't know how fast Jeff ran. After a few minutes, Coach Cagle became overly excited as he began to jump and run around in his sweat suite in the cool evening air. I couldn't understand what the hell he was talking about as he jumped around the infield close to the finish line, but I knew it was about me. During those years, I can't remember any meets, other than those at the state level, in which coaches couldn't be inside the track. That's completely different today. Finally, he told me that I had taken third place, and he let the timers and judges know that I had run faster than the third-place finisher in the second heat. He didn't want them to forget my time and reminded them to combine the heat for the true places. I don't know if the officials actually needed help from Coach, but with his hyper-energy, no one was going to calm him down. Coach was as happy as I'd seen him. And then it was official – yes, I had finished third at the Southeast Kansas League Track and Field Meet, and I did it as a sophomore! My time wasn't great, but I still got a big, beautiful bronze League medal. Norris' winning time was 2:05. The "fast" heat was a slow tactical race, and I don't believe most even gave it a thought that if they didn't race fast, someone from the first heat would take a medal.

After League, the Class 3A Regional meet was eight days away. Roger Smith decided he didn't want to compete at Regionals, and I attempted to talk him out of this, but I couldn't change his mind. With Roger's decision, Coach replaced him on the relay with Burkes. Brad automatically took 10 seconds off the relay time, although I still wanted Roger to compete. We hadn't seen most of the teams we were to run against. Many of the teams in our League were 4A schools, with only Iola, Fort Scott, Columbus, and Labette County as the other 3As. Labette County competed in a different region, and I think Columbus did as well. Some of the schools in our region came from the Kansas City area, such as Bonner Springs, and they had a powerful program, especially for distance races.

Regionals were held at Allen County Community College in Iola on a very cool and extremely windy overcast Saturday. All that meant was that the times wouldn't be as fast, but the competition would be terrific. Coach Cagle didn't take a full team to Regionals, and we were already a small team. However, with the combination of those who selected not to go and those deemed not ready to compete at the level needed at Regionals, our numbers were small. I opened the 2-mile relay with a 2:13 leg, which was not nearly as fast as I had wanted, but I was still very competitive. I was either in 4th or 5th place when I handed off, and only the top three finishers qualified for the State Meet.

Buster, with a personal best of 2:09, and Ron also kept us close to 3rd, but as Burkes received the baton for the anchor, we were in 4th or 5th place, but it was fairly close for the last qualifying position. Burkes ran a courageous race, and his time of 2:06 was slower than his best, but he damn near caught the third-place kid. I don't think Burkes was overly tired, and he just lacked the basic speed to get around the third-place runner. The only advantage Burkes had was that they were kicking against the wind, and his strength might carry him through. But we took fourth by a couple of tenths. It was disappointing, and I blamed myself. If I had run 2:10, we would have given Burkes a better position and possibly finished third. We did break the school record with an 8:40.6, but of course, the event was new to Kansas in 1978. Bonner Springs won in 8:29.

Later in the day, I ran 2:10 in the 880 and took 7th in the same conditions we had run in the relay. So, I could have run 2:10 earlier in the day and helped us qualify for State. On the second curve, during the first lap, I was cut off by a kid who yelled at me because he thought I was the one running dirty. I just laughed at him. I can't tell you if I beat him or not. This was the first race in which I had not finished in the top six, but I came close. I wasn't the least bit disappointed with my 880 race because it was such a strong field, and I ran my best race of the year, especially considering the weather conditions. The winning time was well over two minutes, but as I would find a week later, there were at least two in the race who did break the two-minute barrier. Burkes ran the two-mile after my 880, and I do think the relay took a little out of him, but he took second anyway and qualified for State. He was the only one on the team to do so, but Coach decided to take some of us along not only to see Brad run but also to get a chance to witness the State Meet so we would understand when we qualified the next year.

The next Friday morning, a few of us piled into a school van, which Coach Cagle drove. Besides Burkes, the others going to the State Meet that day were Faulkenberry, Buster, Zink, and me. Usually, the State Meet was held at Wichita State University, but they were replacing their track. So, the different classes competed at different sites rather than the same one, and Class 3A was held at Augusta High School, close to Wichita. I had never seen an asphalt track, but that's what Augusta had. The meet was held over two days, but we only stayed on Friday. But it was exciting. For example, we watched a kid from Gardner High School jump 17 feet ½ inches in the pole vault. We thought Jeff Buckingham was the first high school kid to jump over 17 feet, but apparently, it had just been done by a kid from California and maybe even a few years before by someone else. The days before the internet!

The 2-mile relay came down to two teams. Early on, Wichita Kapaun Mt. Carmel led after their first leg, and a sophomore ran 1:58. But Bonner Springs, the team that won our regional, was close. The next two legs were exciting, but not as much as the anchor. Down the home stretch, the kid from Bonner Springs passed the Kapaun runner, leading his team to victory in 7:57. Kapaun was second in 7:58. I don't know how much energy Bonner Spring put into winning Regionals in 8:29, but it does demonstrate some degree how tough the conditions were the week before in Iola. I was as impressed as I could be. It never dawned on me that a high school team could have four kids average under two minutes in the half mile. And two teams did it in Augusta. I was still naïve about these things.

In the two-mile, Burkes ran the race of his life. Brad was one of several runners that compiled the second pack. The lead pack consisted of three runners who separated themselves from the rest early in the race. As the lead runners hit the 220 mark with half a lap to go, Rick Johnson of Kapaun unleashed the most devastating kick I think I've ever seen – even to this day. It looked to me like he was running a 220-yard dash. He crushed the field in that last, long sprint, winning in 9:19.0. Although I've since seen a number of faster high school two-mile races and a few significantly faster, I'm not sure I've witnessed a better one. At that time, I didn't know high school kids ran under 9:20. Burkes was good, and no one challenged him that year outside of the regional meet – not even close. I think Brad's best time was about 10:04. But 9:19 was stunning to me. By the way, Brad beat the second group to finish 4th in 9:42, so he ran more than 20 seconds under his previous best, and he finished ahead of the kid who beat him at regionals.

I yelled down at Brad his time, and I think he was surprised, but he also looked like he was in terrible distress. He then went over to the side and vomited. Then recovery began. After the meet, Coach took us to the local Pizza Hut for dinner. The coach was extremely happy about Brad's race but did tell him it would have been better had he not thrown up! We discussed some expectations for the next track season, and I know Coach Cagle wanted me to go out for cross-country, but I knew I had a great shot at earning a starting position in football. I just couldn't see giving up the game I loved so much.

A week after attending the State Meet, I ran the first of three early summer track meets. This was the AAU Junior Olympic area meet held at Fredonia. Although I just finished my sophomore year, I was required to compete in the senior division for 17–18-year-olds because my 17th birthday was before the end of the year. I was a bit worried because I thought there might be some good older runners entered, even though I had competed against high school juniors and seniors all season. In the end, there was nothing to worry about because I easily won the 880, and this qualified me for the State AAU Junior Olympic Meet. My next race was not in the original plan. A week or two after the area meet, I received a call one morning from Burkes asking me if I wanted to go over to Independence and run a little summer meet held there. I said sure, and we left a short time later. The problem is that I had been up all night with my cousins Mike and John Kerr, fishing at the KOP dam on the Neosho River. I hadn't got a wink of sleep. I don't remember whether we caught any fish, but I did catch a case of exhaustion.

When we arrived, it was clear this could be a fun meet. I decided to run the half mile, my bread and butter. I had thought about maybe trying the mile, but I wasn't really ready to live up to Mr. Hill's prophesy, especially with no sleep. As I warmed up for the race, I realized that the slight headache I had earlier blossomed into a full-fledge throbbing of intense pain. I could hardly think it was so bad. I didn't believe I could compete. I was standing by the backstretch in the grass when Burkes came jogging up and asked how I was doing. Maybe he could see I was in distress, or maybe it was just small talk, but when I explained my condition, he suddenly placed his hands on the top of my head, which was a reach because I was several inches taller than Brad and began to pray out loud for God to heal me or take away my headache so I could race. This just freaked me out because I wasn't sure I believed any of this stuff, or at least I had never thought about it. All I know is that when he was finished, my headache was completely gone. Nothing was there, no pain, no throbbing, just a clear mind, and now I felt like racing! Indeed, I went on to win, leading start to finish, in 2:09.0. This was the fastest time I'd ever run, and on no sleep on a slow cinder track. I was ready to run a PR at the State AAU meet.

Usually, if you are going to improve, you need to keep in shape, and I had hardly run a step, other than my two races, since the 3A Regional meets several weeks before. I'd gotten away with it in the previous two meets, but that was not the case this time. As in the previous year, the 1978 State AAU Junior Olympic Meet was held at Kansas State University in Manhattan. Several kids went, and we worked with Arvon Phillips, the Director of the Parsons Recreational Center, to find us a cheap place to stay and to help with gas. Arvon was able to work with his counterpart in Manhattan, and they placed us in an old gym to sleep. We brought our sleeping bags and camped out overnight on the basketball floor.

The next day, Burkes ran the 2-mile first thing in the morning while the rest of us had to wait for our events. My race was at the end of the day, but I didn't mind because I could take pictures with my little box camera. I even talked with the Kapaun sophomore, John Pyles, who led off their relay in 1:58 at the State Meet. Being June in Kansas, it was warm but not nearly as hot as it would get later in the summer. By the time the 880 rolled around, I was ready to roll, but because my time in Fredonia was not very fast, even though I won, I was placed in the slow heat. The officials didn't take into account that I had won, and the heat placements were based solely on time. But on this day, it didn't matter. I was not prepared to run a personal best, and I didn't win my heat, but I did run a respectable 2:11, or at least respectable for me. I don't know what place I finished in my heat, and I didn't know at the time. I just finished and was ready to move on. I wasn't upset, but track was now over, and I could focus on my summer and football in the fall. In the fast heat, Tim Gundy won in 1:57, which followed his 4:19 victory in the mile.

During the remainder of the summer, I worked in the hay fields for Don Dean, and this was terrific preparation for football. I also loved bailing hay and worked with a kid from another high school, and we became friends. Mike Giefer attended Erie High School, which is 18 miles north of Parsons. Although Mike wasn't tall, maybe 5 feet 5 inches, he was tough. We worked great together on the hay wagon and never got in the way of each other. Mike was a linebacker for Erie, and if he'd have been 6'2" and 220 pounds, I think big-time college football coaches would have salivated to sign him. Like me, Mike was going to be a junior. At his last high school game, when he was a senior in the fall of 1979, they played on a Thursday as opposed to our Friday game, so my cousin Phillip and I headed to Erie to watch him. Phillip and Mike became good friends years later when they worked together. Mike played a great game. I was amazed that, at his size, he could play as well as he did. He was physical. That was his game – small in stature with a huge, iron heart. And best of all, he didn't possess a Napoleon complex. Mike died a few years ago, and although he and I rarely saw each other over the years, I do miss him. Just the thought of Mike not being around makes me sad.

I think many of us on the team anticipated a good football season in the fall of 1978. We arrived for two-a-day drills in the dry August heat and soon found our positions on the field. When the coaches asked who wanted to be a defensive tackle, I was there first, and I started every game that season. But things didn't go well, even before the first game. We had several good players quit early because they got mad at coaches for childish reasons. For example, a couple of weeks before the first game, a senior clodhopper decided to quit in a tirade because an assistant coach made him hold a tackling dummy instead of a sophomore. This guy was dumb, and as he raged off the practice field, he barked f-bombs as loud as he could at whoever would listen while throwing off his equipment. Coach Barcus kept yelling for the kid to come back, but he just kept walking to the locker room, spitting and slobbering obscenities like the moron he was. He was actually a very good defensive lineman, and we really needed him, but I lost respect for him that day. I could see if the demand placed on him was serious, but this was nothing – just stupid pride from a brain-dead ass. As you can imagine, I despise people like him.

We had another incident during a mid-season game when one of our seniors, who was a defensive starter, became angry at one of the coaches in the second half and decided that he wouldn't try. He even announced this and said he was quitting after the game. It's my belief that he cost us the game against one of the best teams in the state. Our opponent figured out that he wasn't making tackles from his defensive end position and kept running to his side. He would come back to the huddle with a smile on his face. I told him to get out of the game, and I know a couple of others did the same. I did like him, but I should have called time out and told the coaches to get his sorry ass off the field. Our opponent scored in the final minute to beat us by two points.

In our first game, we held a 13-0 lead at the half. With less than a minute to go, we had the ball and a 13-12 lead and fumbled. Still, the other team had 60 yards to go for a touchdown and didn't have much of a passing game. But on their first play, they had a receiver get behind our safeties, and their bomb beat us 18-12. We had several really close games that season but never won any of them – 0-9. In the last two games, we were beaten by a total score of 107 to 6. These were two playoff teams, but one of the best teams we played all year only beat us 29-27. We had several players basically go through the motions those last two games. After we lost 6 to 0 in our seventh game, I think the heart was gone from several players the last two games. But we did have a few seniors who never gave up, and those are guys I respect today, even though I haven't seen most since high school. Despite the bad season, I played well, and I think the only game that I didn't play was our last one. I relied on quickness, and I was fairly strong. But their offensive tackle was not only a lot bigger than me, but he was also a lot stronger and even quicker.

Although the football season was long, made it that way by going winless, I made it through fairly healthy. But I loved football, so for me, the end of the season was bittersweet. Plus, as much as I loved the game, I hated school twice as much. I mean, I really hated Parsons High School. Not that I wanted to go anywhere else, and I'm not sure if my feelings for my high school were because of that particular school or school in general. But I knew I had less than two years left, and sports would carry me through. I certainly had absolutely no interest in the social life of the school. And that continued until I graduated.

After football season ended, I was convinced by one of the football assistant coaches to go out for wrestling. The coach was also a wrestling assistant and told me the sport would help me with my agility and quickness for football. And I think he was generally correct. But wrestling wasn't for me. I made it through the entire season but disliked the sport. There's no doubt it's a tough sport, but it's also difficult to come in with no experience and be good the first year, especially in a state with a rich high school wrestling tradition. In my second meet, I faced a kid from Oklahoma who had a losing record, maybe 1 and 3. I had one win and a loss, and my win was forfeited because the team didn't have a kid at my weight. Our head coach told me I had a good chance to win this opening match, but the kid was not only clearly better than me, but he was significantly better. I survived the first period but was easily pinned during the second. When I came off the mat, my coach told me that the kid was an Oklahoma state champ the previous year and had started this season with an injury. I asked him why he didn't tell me this, and he smiled and said he wanted to give me confidence. Of course, Oklahoma has a stronger high school wrestling tradition than Kansas. At any rate, at least I was in the loser's bracket the next round, which meant I had a real chance to win a match. But I lost that one, too. I wrestled better in that second match, but only because my opponent wasn't as good – but he was still better than me.

I liked my wrestling coaches and teammates, but all I really got out of the sport was a series of injuries, mostly to my ankles, which eventually took me off the varsity by mid-season. But this wasn't all bad as far as wrestling goes because I took second at the league junior varsity meet. The other big issue for me in wrestling was attempting to make weight. I wrestled in the 167 lbs. class, and at first, I had a hard time losing the weight. On the day of our first meet, which was held in our gym, I was about 8 pounds overweight. By the time of the weigh-in, I was 166 pounds. I was so weak that I had no chance in my first match. Plus, my opponent was experienced, and I doubt I would have won anyway. During the Christmas break, I took a trip to Guadalajara, Mexico, with four other students, our Spanish teacher, his wife, and two young sons, and decided not to worry about my weight. We had a great time, and when I returned, I was 163 pounds and wasn't concerned with my weight for the rest of the season.

However, when track practice began for my junior season at the end of February, I not only lacked energy, but my ankles were still hurting from wrestling. I wanted to run at the State Indoor Meet but was unsure if I could get myself in shape in time. I thought wrestling would get me in shape for track, but it's a different kind of condition; plus, sucking weight and the injuries took away any chance of being ready to run. Burkes and Faulkenberry would be running the State Indoor, but I needed to prove to Coach Cagle that I was ready. Beginning with my junior year, in the fall of 1978, Kansas moved from 5 classes to 6 classifications. Parsons moved from class 3A to 5A, which meant we would compete in the same classifications with the other schools from the Southeast Kansas League save two, Iola and Columbus, who moved to 4A.

At the 5A State cross-country meet, Burkes took 3rd place with a time of 9:39 on the two-mile course, well behind the leader, Steve Delano of Winfield, who won in 9:14. Faulkenberry took the final medal by placing 10th in 9:52. The team took 6th and ended the season on a strong note. These performances qualified Brad and Ron for the State Indoor Meet. If I were to run the 880 at the indoor meet, I needed to impress Coach, but in a time trial run with Faulkenberry, I would finish far behind my teammate. I can't say what I ran, and I'm not sure I knew the time then. I just knew I needed to get in shape before the first track meet, which wasn't going to be the State Indoor. I was actually upset with Coach because I believed I deserved to run at the State Indoor. But I was delusional. Coach Cagle was right – I had no business running at that meet. Burkes took 2nd in the State Indoor 2-mile, and Faulkenberry placed 4th. Brad also ran the mile but didn't place.

Leading up to the first meet, I asked Coach if I could run the extended speed work that Brad was doing because I believed it would help me get in shape quickly. But Coach decided that I needed to hold back some so as not to get injured. Of course, he was correct, but at the time, I wasn't so sure. As with the year before, our first meet was the Parsons Invitational, so we didn't have to travel. As usual, I competed in the 2-mile relay and 880-yard run. For the most part, I didn't have anything to gauge my fitness against. So, as I took the baton as the anchor leg in the 2-mile relay with a lead, I didn't know if I could hold it. Plus, we were in front of Labette County, and their anchor was Jeff Norris. I had a big task ahead of me if I wanted to remain in front of Jeff. I ran a little scared, but I was able to maintain the lead, and we won by a couple of seconds. Labette County actually took third. As I crossed the finish line, I slapped the baton across the tape, or string, in pure delight that we won. The next day, on the local sports page, there was a picture of me crossing the line, with a Columbus kid behind me and Norris behind him. My time was 2:11, and after I finished the race, Norris shook my hand and told me I was going to be tough this year. But I'm not sure we can say it played out that way. In the 880, I did place but failed to get a medal, and my time was not too great.

In our second meet, held at Independence, we had the best day as a team in my entire high school career. The old cinder track was loose, and it rained off and on during the meet. We ran well in the two-mile relay and won, and in the 880, I took second behind Faulkenberry with a time of 2:12 in heavy rain and even beat Norris. Ron, who won the 880 at our invitational, ran 2:10 at Independence. We took 2nd in the meet behind the host team, and we beat League power Coffeyville. It was my last good run for a few weeks. Even Ron, who ran so well during the first two meets, began to falter during the midpoint of the season. Burkes ran well, and Buster competed well, but many of us didn't.

One teammate who did run great was a new kid in our school, John Johnson. John arrived at our school as a junior at the beginning of the fall term. Then he was gone for a while, then returned before the Christmas break. During the winter, John started lifting weights with the football team, deciding he was going to play as a senior. I would have been lifting as well if not for wrestling. John and I were in the same Spanish class, and I saw him lifting while I was at wrestling practice. A couple of times, the wrestling and football coaches got together and had the two teams wrestle with each other. One day, I wrestled John. I didn't know John, but I found out that this shy kid was strong. I was a lot bigger than him, but John gave me all I could handle. I finally beat him, but only because I kind of knew what I was doing. The week before our first track practice, Coach Cagle held a boy's meeting after school in a classroom. As we were getting started, the door opened, and Coach Barcus stepped in with the pale, blond-haired John Johnson and said, "I have a new recruit for track." John looked out of place as if he would rather be somewhere else.

In our first workout, we ran three miles, and John, running with Coach and a few others, had to stop several times. However, as we progressed in those early season workouts, it was apparent that John had good speed. In the Parsons Invitational, Coach entered John in the 220, 440, and the mile-relay. In the prelims of the 220, it looked as if we made a mistake because John didn't run well and never came close to making the finals. In the 440, John looked a bit scared at the starting line, and it was apparent that he was not quite sure what to do. Unlike others, he didn't use blocks, and when the gun was fired, instead of going forward, John took a step back to gather himself and then took off. A quarter mile later, John won the race, but not before leaning at the wrong line. But he didn't slow enough before crossing the real finish line. His time might not have been great, but his 53 was pretty damn good for a kid who didn't have a clue what he was doing in his first meet.

John ran well in the meets that followed. One afternoon, while running a distance workout on the crossroads outside of town, Buster and I were running a nice pace, maybe 4 or 5 miles into a six-mile run. We heard a dog angrily bark behind us, and soon, John came scorching by. The dog chased him for a few feet, and John accelerated to get away, but when the dog gave up the chase, John didn't. It was the last time John finished a distance run behind us. In the final meet before League, Coach decided to try John in the half. I ran the 2-mile relay, and for the first time since 7th grade, I was not entered in the 880 and instead ran on a B-team mile relay. This was a home triangular against Coffeyville and Chanute. In the 2-mile relay, I finally ran a decent race with a 2:09 leg, my best so far that year, and we set a school record with an 8:36.3. In the 880, John ran with the small pack until 330 yards to go, and then took off, winning easily in 2:06. Coach decided then and there that John was on the 2-mile relay at League and Regionals. We needed a fourth person because we couldn't find anyone other than Burkes to fill the role. And even though Ron and I were not doing our best, we were far better than the others. And, of course, Buster was solid all season.

At League Meet, again held at Pittsburg State University, we hoped our relay team could come together and run a good race. The year before, although we had placed, we had not earned a medal in the relay. At League, Buster got us off to a great start and had the team in first as he handed off to Ron. He also ran well and extended our lead as he handed off to me. I ran the best race of my life up to that point, and I widened the gap even more. When John received the baton, there was little doubt we would be Southeast Kansas League champions. John closed with a strong 2:04, and we won in 8:23.5, shattering the school record and setting a meet record. But, of course, it was only the second year of the event. I ran a 2:06.0 880 leg that followed a 2:06.8 by Buster and 2:07 and change by Ron. Although we had won some relay races during the year, this was the first time we put it all together. And the gold first-place medal looked great.

After the relay victory, I looked forward to Burkes beating Iola's Maxwell in the mile. This would be Brad's chance to take the mile back from the Iola athlete. Burkes knew that Maxwell was a good runner and that if he didn't get away from him, Maxwell would win with a kick. Burkes pushed through three laps, but Maxwell held tight. Brad pushed harder into the backstretch, attempting to put some distance between the two, but the Iola miler didn't give an inch. Finally, with about 220 yards to go, Maxwell sprinted by Burkes and won in 4:27. Brad ran a fine race as well, and he broke his own school record with a 4:29.5. Today, over 40 years later, that is still the Parsons school record, although it is listed as 4:27.9 for a 1600m. And yes, 1600m is a ridiculous distance.

Brad came back in the 2-mile and won easily in 10:01. I ran the 880 and returned to my standard for 1979 and performed poorly with an unplaced 2:10. John didn't participate in the half but ran the mile relay instead. Nonetheless, I was upbeat about the relay and that I had finally broken out of my rut and run a good race. Maybe I was only good for one race a day at this point, but as long as the relay was first, I was good. Of course, I wanted to qualify for State in the half, but I knew my best chance was in the relay. At Regionals, held in Ottawa, we ran on a red-dog cinder track. I'd never seen a track with red cinders, only black. But this was the best cinder track on which I'd ever competed. As in the League Meet, we won the 2-mile relay with little trouble. John anchored in 2:01.1, Buster gave a 2:07 start, and Ron improved with a 2:03.9. But, although I thought I had run my third leg as well as I had at League, I actually barely broke 2:10 or was just above that time – Coach wasn't even sure. I was really devastated because I thought I had made huge strides, and now I was back to my old stuff. We won in 8:22.0 and lowered the school record, but Coach Cagle said he was considering replacing me with Brad.

We qualified for the State Meet with our victory, but I might not get a chance to compete. And maybe I didn't deserve to run. After all, I had not actually set the world on fire. And I didn't help my cause with a poor performance in the 880, but I didn't run that race with confidence. However, even though my time was not up to snuff in the relay, we were comfortably in the lead when I received the baton, and I never relinquished that lead. I would just have to see how Coach felt about the situation on Monday. Burkes easily won the mile run in 4:30 and did the same in the 2-mile, with Ron taking third, qualifying both for State. Brad had not run under 10 minutes all season, not even at the State Indoor. And except for the indoor meet, no one was ever close to him in the 8-lap race. At Regionals, Brad hit the mile in 5:01, and Coach Cagle yelled at him just past the mile mark, saying, "Burkes, if you don't break 10 minutes, I'm going to kick your ass." It was not really tactful, I guess, and not something a high school coach could do today, but Brad won at 9:58!

I worried about my opportunity to run at the State Meet all weekend, although I did have my work on the farm to take my mind off the subject at times. On Monday, Coach informed me that he was keeping me in the relay. I was relieved and attempted to concentrate on how I could improve my performance. The truth is that I didn't know what chance we had to get a medal or even place in the top six. My only reference was the 7:57 it took to win in 1978, and I knew we couldn't do that. But we might be able to run under 8:15, which was attainable. The 1979 Kansas State Track meet was the first one conducted in meters. All six classes, boys and girls, gathered on the same two days at Wichita State's Cessna Stadium. There were too many athletes and races, and I still think the meet should be split. Being held in meters, I had never heard of 1600 meters and 3200 meters. But Brad was running both those races, and we were running the 3200-meter relay. Our hurdler, Mike Burnett, was running the 110m High Hurdles, which is a legitimate race, I'd heard of it.

On Saturday morning, the second day of the meet, Brad ran the 3200. Ron was also scheduled to run, but when he found out that it was before the relay, he asked Coach to have him removed. I thought it was a mistake. How many times does one get to compete at the State Meet? I still think Ron should have run. Brad wanted to go out with the leader, who he knew would be Steve Delano, but Coach Cagle told him if he attempted to do that, he would probably get last place. Coach told Burkes that if he wanted a medal, he needed to start out at the back of the pack and move up during the race because that would be his best chance to finish in the top three. I think that was a mistake as well. I think Brad was good enough to hang with Delano. I doubt very seriously whether Brad would have won, but I think he would have had a good shot at second if he would have. One thing that would have helped Burkes is if he had run in the Kansas Relays in April. This would have given him the opportunity to run against the best competition around and prepare him for the State Meet. But Coach told Brad he wasn't good enough for the Relays.

Brad did run Coach's strategy to perfection, and coming down the home stretch, he was in third place but didn't have the speed to catch the second-place kid, a sophomore from Hayesville Campus High School, Kevin Wood, who won the State Indoor two-mile. Brad ran 9:37.7 for third. Delano won in 9:28, well off his best, but no one pushed him. One thing I do remember is that when Burkes crossed the finish line, the announcer said, "Faulkenberry." In the relay, Buster ran his leadoff 800m in 2:04.0. Ron followed with another 2:04.0, and then I took the baton; I didn't end up losing any places and held my own. I thought I had run well. We were in the middle of the pack when I handed it off to John. John was able to get us into 4th place on the second lap, but coming off the last curve, John began to tighten up. John had forgotten his track shoes and left them at home, so he had to borrow Mike's shoes, which were too small. As he tried to sprint down the home stretch, John said it felt like his feet were being squeezed.

We really believed John would run under 2 minutes for his relay leg, but it didn't happen. Over the final 30 yards or so, John got passed by a couple of runners, and we finished in 7th – out of the money. Only the top six earned team points. John ran a 2:04.0, the same time as the other two. When I got to the stands, Coach told me I ran either 2:09.9 or 2:10.0. I was surprised. I thought I had run much better than that. And this was 800m, about seven-tenths of a second faster than 880 yards. Later, in the 1600m, Brad ran in the 4:40s, his slowest time of the year, and didn't place. He said he was loose, but his legs felt like rubber. As we were about to leave, Coach asked us if we learned anything. I said I wanted to come back next year and compete better.

Chapter 5
Chasing a State Medal

If I was going to qualify for the 1980 State Track Meet my senior year, it would be done without Coach Cagle. Late in the season, he told us he was leaving for graduate school in Arizona. He also said he didn't think he would ever coach track again. There was a lot of uncertainty among those of us who were coming back. Who would be our coach, and would that coach be any good? I decided not to worry about it over the summer. I had summer track meets to run and hay to stack, and I had football in the fall. It would have to go better than my junior season – no more 0-9.

A week after the state meet, we traveled to Fredonia for the AAU Area Meet. I asked Coach Cagle during the school season if he would try me in the mile once, but he never did. So, I decided to give it a try in the Area Meet. I told Faulkenberry that I was going to run under 5:00 for my first time. He bet me I wouldn't. This was our second wager of the year. The first one, which I think was $5, was who would break 2:05 first, open or relay leg. Well, he won that. I don't recall the second wager stakes. What I do know is that I didn't want to lose to Ron twice. I'm surprised Ron actually bet because his father was a Baptist minister, but maybe the bets were low enough not to matter. I didn't expect to beat Ron in the race, but if I could stay close, I'd have a chance to win the bet. I ran as well as I could and finished 2nd behind Ron. I was tired, but with anticipation, I asked the timer what I had run. He said, as Ron looked on, "4:59.9." You can't make this stuff up; I had broken 5 minutes by a single tenth of a second! Ron couldn't believe it, but he was happy for me, nonetheless. I told Ron the mile was a tough race, and I wasn't sure I liked it.

Burkes won the 2-miles, opting not to race the mile, and Ron won the 880, with Buster second and I third. I'm sure Brad had a number of scholarship offers to run cross-country and track in college, but he decided to enlist in the Army, where he would spend time in Europe. But he wouldn't leave for boot camp until later in the summer, and we had a couple of summer meets left. We went back to the Independence meet, where I ran 2:09 the previous June. But this time, I decided to run my second mile. I ran a horrible race. I don't remember if I ran just under or just over 5:10, but either way, it was bad. In fact, it's a meet I really didn't think about over the years. Many times, when I have been asked about the mile races I ran before college, I completely forget about it, and I've even told people I'd never run a mile race over 5 minutes. I wasn't purposely giving false information; I had just totally forgotten. But the truth is, I did run one over 5 minutes unless there is another race or two; I conveniently forgot!

A week or two later, we headed to Manhattan to run the State AAU Junior Olympic Track Meet at Kansas State University. Burkes drove with me, and Terry Stover rode with him. Terry, whose nickname was "Tutum" and, as I remember, derived from "Too Tall" because he had once been big for his age, was a sophomore-to-be, was a good sprinter, and was involved in AAU track the previous couple of years. He had traveled with us before. Along the way, we picked up Eric Zink in Burlington because he was staying with his grandparents. Faulkenberry needed to go separately, and I'm not sure how Buster got there because he didn't travel with Brad, but he was at the meet. Buster and Eric decided not to compete even though they had qualified.

Brad arranged for us to stay at a Foursquare Church Camp on Tuttle Creek Lake in the Manhattan area. We were to sleep in one of the small cabins, and Buster and Ron weren't with us. This was a new world for me, and what happened was not expected. When we arrived, I realized that this would not be a comfortable stay for me, and I'm sure Terry and Eric felt the same. We were welcomed by a young man who knew Brad and then quickly whisked into a building where a man was giving a sermon to a bunch of kids and a few adults attending the camp. The "preacher" was ranting and raving about how a man in his 30s or older was only after one thing if he dated a young woman in her late teens or early 20s. He was probably right. All I know is I needed to get out of there but couldn't. I remember looking over at Zink, and we both gave each other a look of "what in the hell did we get ourselves into?" Finally, it was over, and we had a chance to get out of the bizarre situation. The young man who greeted us took us to our cabin, and we finally had peace.

But we didn't! The man wouldn't leave and began asking us questions about our spirituality and our relationship with God. Of course, Brad was completely comfortable, but the rest of us were squirming. He went around and asked each one of us if we were physically ready to race, mentally prepared, and spiritually ready to compete. To some degree, Eric got off easy because he wasn't racing, but he was still confronted with the question of spirituality. Today, this would be easy for me, but when I was 17, I was looking for the door. With Brad's father being a Foursquare minister, it was easy for him. He had been sick and missed quite a bit of training, so he said he was not physically prepared, but he was definitely spiritually ready. The rest of us could not answer that question. We each attempted to hew and haw around the question, but the man wouldn't let it go. Finally, after an excruciating amount of time, he left, and Eric took out a small bottle of whiskey from his bag.

The next morning, I couldn't get out of there fast enough. We left with an invitation to come back after the meet and take their challenge to run up a steep hill and see if we could break the record. But we were too tired by the late afternoon to return. When we arrived at the track, we met Ron and Buster. Brad ran the first race, and it was evident that the illness and lack of training took a toll on him. Still, he ran a fine race, finishing the 2-mile in 9:56, and took 6th place. Even in his best form, he wouldn't have won the race unless the winner would have dropped out. The winning time was 9:22 by Brent Steiner, who had won the 6A 3200 in 9:08. I think Brad had a 9:30 or slightly faster in him, and if he had been in his normal condition, he would have finished in the top four to qualify for the Missouri Valley Meet. Steiner, who was between his junior and senior years, went on that summer to run a 4:11.1 mile and 8:46.99 2-mile.

The big winner of the day was Ron Faulkenberry. He didn't win the mile, but he ran the best race of his life. I selected not to compete in the mile because I had been stung by a bee on the bottom of my foot, and it swelled to the size of a small football. By the day of the race, the swelling had subsided to some degree, but I still had to take the laces out of my track shoe and stick my foot in before re-lacing. Still, my foot barely fit into the shoe. I thought two laps would be easier to race with my foot issue, so I opted to just run the 880. Ron ended up taking 5th place in the mile, running 4:35. He wasn't close to the 4th place finisher, but Ron's mile race was still fantastic. The winner was Tim Gundy in 4:20, with Steiner second in 4:21, but much of my attention was focused on Ron. The two went on to run much faster in the subsequent meets that summer.

My bee-stung foot was the last of an accumulation of a track season that needed to end. My race was not only nothing special, but it was downright bad. I was placed in the first of two heats, which was for the slowest runners. And that's the heat I deserved. I didn't come close to finishing first in the also-ran heat, but at least I didn't finish last. If someone had paid attention to me in that race, and other than my teammates, there was no reason for anyone to notice, they would have thought it was nice to see a kid without much talent give racing at this level a try. But, of course, they would have believed that this kid with the farmer's tan had no future in the sport. I slogged through the two laps and was relieved that it was finally over in a pedestrian 2:14. Ron followed his good mile race with a steady 880, running 2:07 in the second heat. I was ready to do something else, anything else, for the remainder of the summer until football practice started. I would work in the hay fields to get ready for that.

The rest of my summer was pretty good. I worked on the farm bailing hay, got ready for football, and spent a week camping and trout fishing in Colorado with my dad and John Kerr. On our way to Cottonwood Creek, above Buena Vista, we stopped at a truck stop in Dodge City in the middle of the night. As we ate our warmed-up honey buns in the dining area, John and I watched some middle-aged drunk man cop a feel from an equally drunk woman who looked like she hadn't showered in a week, which I'm sure we looked like a week later. It's interesting what one remembers decades later. Somewhere around 3:00 or 4:00 in the morning on a dark highway in western Kansas or eastern Colorado, I can still clearly remember listening to Elton John's "Someone Saved My Life Tonight" on the radio! I can't recall if I was driving or if it was John, but my dad was asleep in the backseat. We had a great time fishing and caught plenty of trout, and John and I talked about how we thought our senior football season would go.

When two-a-day practices started in August, it was hot, as usual. We had two new assistant coaches as well, Gary Billions and Riley Cartwright. Unfortunately, we didn't have many seniors come out for the 1979 season. In fact, there were only six seniors on the team. John Johnson started out on the team but decided after a few days that cross-country was probably best for him. It was a good move on his part. He asked Coach Barcus if he could play football and run cross county at the same time, but Coach told him that it didn't work at a bigger school like Parsons. So, we six seniors were there to help lead the team to some victories.

I was supposed to play defensive end and running back my senior year. However, a couple of weeks before our first game, I pulled a quad muscle, and my lateral movement was limited. It wasn't a bad injury, but it kept me from playing running back, and although I was supposed to return to the position when I healed, it never happened. During our first game, I started at defensive end. Although I played tackle as a junior, I thought the new position would help my game. In the 5/2 defense, the ends stood up, much like outside linebackers, except we were on the line of scrimmage. This way, I could see the action and react, which was more difficult for me when playing in a down position at tackle. But against Fort Scott, I couldn't move side-to-side very well because of the quad injury and didn't play a good game. Fort Scott had a short, stocky, strong, fast running back, and I was unable to contain him. After this first game, of which we lost 34-0, I was moved back to defensive tackle.

Our biggest issue as a team is that we just lacked the basic talent of many teams, especially in the skilled positions. In other words, we were slow. Our quarterback was senior Mike Bolander, who was really a tight end. And, in fact, because of injuries, by the end of the season, Mike started at quarterback and nose guard on defense, which is not the normal combination. But Mike did an admirable job as our field general. Our attribute was that we were tough. I mean, we hit hard, and one of the reasons for this is because we hit in practice. There seems to be a movement today to avoid physical play in practice, and I get it. Teams need to avoid injuries. But if you are not physical in practice, how can you do the same in the games? I don't remember a single player in my junior and senior seasons who was badly hurt because of hard-hitting in practice. I went to see a high school game a few years ago, and I know the home team never had physical practices. In the first play of the game, their opponent hit them square in the mouth, and you could see the wide eyes of the home team from the stands. The game was over at that point.

During our second game at Iola, our opponent had a little running back who started to tackle me, a defensive player. It started early in the first quarter when I was rushing the quarterback, and the back was blocking me. As soon as the pass was thrown and I tuned to face downfield, this kid hit me in the back of my helmet with his forearm. I turned around, and he put his arms up in fists, ready to fight while laughing. I just ignored him. Like many teams we played, Iola ran option football, and as a tackle, my job was to take the dive back while someone else took the quarterback and another defender covered the pitchman. When this running back came through the line as the dive back, I tackled him as I was supposed to do, and the quarterback always pulled the ball out as I hit the back. The kid then got up and laughed at me, yelling and laughing that he didn't have the ball. Then he started to tackle me and complain to the referees. On one play, he went out of his way to hit me from behind, and I went down; as I attempted to get up, he hit me again, and the play went the other way. Then the referee said we were both kicked out of the game. I became livid and began to threaten the official. There was no reason for me to be booted from the game.

As I started to leave the field, I ripped my helmet off with all my hair flying about and started to throw it at Coach Barcus. Then, I had a moment of clarity. I remembered the previous year, also against Iola, when I threw my helmet at Coach after I was taken out of the game for a few plays. He didn't seem to see what I did as the helmet sailed over his head, but after the game, when no one else was around, he told me, in not-so-uncertain terms, that if I ever did that again, I would never play another down of football for him. So, in this game against Iola my senior year, I instead threw my helmet at Coach Billions, who caught it and tossed it back to me. I caught it and winged it back at him, at which point he threw it aside. I then proceeded to go over to the bench a break the damn thing. I was as mad as I've ever been. Everyone stayed away from me, and I looked over at Joe Woodworth and saw the shock on his face.

This was my senior year, and I knew I had only a few chances left to play football. I had already come to the conclusion that I would never play the game in college, and I wanted to play all I could. By halftime, I had settled down and attempted to apologies to Coach Barcus, but he wouldn't have any of it. I think I was almost kicked off the team, but I can't be sure. After the game, in which we lost 41-6 to a team we could have beaten, I walked over to the Iola bench and tried to talk to the player who got me kicked out, but he just laughed. I told him that he better not run the 880 in track because if he did, my half-inch spikes would be as sharp as a razor, and I would rip his tendon down the middle so he would never run again. Whether I would have done that or not is debatable, but I never saw him at a track meet in the spring.

On Sunday afternoon, I got off work from the farm early and went to watch the film of the game with the team. I dreaded the film session because I didn't want to face my coaches, and I wasn't sure I was still on the team. But when I saw the coaches in the parking lot, they were laughing. It seems that they had already watched the game film and saw what really happened. It was clear it was not my fault. Although throwing a fit was. But there was one thing I learned. On Monday, before the Friday Iola game, I had my four wisdom teeth removed. The pain medication caused me to doze off at practice a couple of times during the week. And, the theory goes, the medicine also made my temper escalate when I got angry, kind of like the Hulk, without the muscles. Anyway, this explanation works for me!

After Monday's practice, Mr. Martin gave me a ride home, the long way since I lived by the school, and told me he knew I was a good kid, but I needed to write the Iola principal and apologize, which I agreed to do. But then I began to hear things about how I was set-up by Iola because of how I dominated them when I was a junior.

And I decided that no letter would be written by me, and, in fact, I deserved a letter from them. I never wrote the letter, and Mr. Martin never followed up. As a side note, Coach Cagle visited the school that week and was all excited because he had heard about my incident. And on the farm that Saturday, Mike Geifer greeted me with "What the hell happened?" because he had already heard about it.

So, everyone moved on after Iola, but we didn't win our next two games. Finally, in game five, we played our archrival, Labette County. We traveled ten miles to the small town of Altamont to face LC with confidence that we could win. We had lost 13 games in a row, but we believed we could win this one. But our offense could not move the ball, and we trailed 6-0 at the half. The defense was playing well, and in the second half, our offense finally got on board. We scored to take the lead 7-6. But our offense didn't score again. With only a few seconds remaining in the game and LC more than 50 yards from our end zone, we knew they would attempt a long pass. Visions of Fort Scott from 1978 passed through my mind, but this time, when the pass was thrown, we intercepted it. It was dark outside, and the weather was cool and a little humid, with heavy dew on the field. When our safety ran down the sideline with the ball, I attempted to block an LC player but was hit on the other shoulder by another opponent, and both my ankles turned under me on the wet, slippery grass. As we scored a defensive touchdown when the horn sounded to end the game, I lay on the field, unable to get up. I couldn't celebrate our first varsity football victory because my ankles felt as if they were broken in two. They had to carry me off the field before we could kick the extra point, which gave us the 14-6 victory.

The next week against Pittsburg, our Homecoming, my ankles were in bad shape. I had finally fully recovered from the knee injury I suffered against Coffeyville in game three when I sacked Mike Lee, but now I had these fragile ankles. We played well against the powerful Pittsburg Purple Dragons and stayed close most of the game. They scored a late touchdown to beat us 21-6. After the game, while we were leaving the field, Coach Barcus apologized for not playing me more in my senior Homecoming game. But I told Coach that it was OK because I was a liability out there – he did the right thing by limiting my plays. But that's football. Injuries are a major part of the game, and sometimes, it's how you deal with the adversities that define you. I failed that test against Iola, but I wouldn't fail again.

Sometimes, things happen that most people don't expect, but if you believe, you can accomplish a lot. In our next two games, our defense played well, and I was healing up, although I would not be 100% the rest of the season. We lost to Chanute 15-0 and Columbus 14-0. Then we played our final game against non-league foe Perry-Lecompton. Like Shawnee St. Joseph from the year before, Perry-Lecompton was a 4A school who came into the game 8-0. But unlike St. Joseph, after we watched the film, we truly believed we could beat this undefeated team. Before Coach Barcus turned on the projector, he told the team that he thought we could beat Perry-Lecompton. We played in a much tougher league. I would challenge anyone to find three better leagues than the Southeast Kansas League in 1979 or any other year at that time.

On the first play from scrimmage, we intercepted a pass but were unable to capitalize. Perry-Lecompton did score first to take a 6-0 lead, but we came back to score and led 7-6 at half time. This was a rarity for us; we just didn't lead at the end of two quarters. We scored once again in the second half to win 14-6, to the surprise of the fans. Of course, we didn't make the playoffs, so beating an undefeated playoff team was our playoff game. It felt great to beat an undefeated team to end the careers of six seniors. I didn't play great, but I played solid enough.

When we returned to school on the other side of town from the stadium, my joy was somewhat soured. In the locker room, one of the school counselors, who was the PA announcer at the home games, congratulated the seniors for winning the game because they were "his" students, as he put it. But he walked right by me without one congratulatory remark, as if I didn't exist. I was not one of his fraternity of guys; I didn't count. I'm not bitter, but as one can see, I'm still pissed about it four decades later. But I decided not to allow his shallowness to ruin my senior year and the memory of that final game.

The next fall, when I was in college, I came home for the weekend, and my cousin called me up on Friday and asked me if I wanted to go watch a University of Kansas football game on Saturday. Of course I did! As we went up to a furniture store in downtown Parsons to get the tickets, my cousin told me to hang back because that school counselor had arranged for him to get the tickets and wouldn't approve of me using one. Part of me said I needed to refuse the ticket and stay home, but the other part of me decided to take the ticket. I hoped he would learn I went to the game so I could stick it to him, but I'm sure he never did. At any rate, we enjoyed the game, and KU won! I think there were others like him at the school, but I tried to avoid them, and I avoided him as well. I lost respect for him as a sophomore after I went to his office with some sort of issue, but he was too busy to see me, although it didn't look that way to me. Nonetheless, there were other teachers and school professionals that I did respect, and they far outnumbered the assholes. When I needed help from a councilor, I went to see Mrs. Whiteside. She was great! She went to college at what is now the University of Arkansas, Pine Bluff, and was our junior high councilor as well.

I decided during football season that my future in athletics was in track and field, so I devised a training schedule that I planned to start when the season ended. As soon as our last football game was over, I bought my first training shoes for running, a pair of Converse. I started out easy so I could build up, and I needed to lose weight as well. I was over 190 pounds when I started. I decided I needed to run twice a day during weekdays, and so on the Monday after the Perry-Lecompton game, I set my alarm early so I could run three miles. I never changed my alarm clock after day-light savings ended during those days, but I forgot about this, so I was out there running at 4:30 am instead of 5:30 as I had planned. I didn't know it was so early until I realized that it wasn't getting light. From then on, I adjusted the alarm to run at a decent time. On Christmas day, I ran 7 miles, which was my longest run of the winter up to that point.

I was progressing well, but I noticed a problem around the Holidays. Something wasn't right, and I wasn't sure what it was. But it began to affect my training. Through January, I continued to run, but not every day, and my work on the farm during the weekends and Wednesday evenings was affected. Finally, in early February, I came to the conclusion that I knew the problem. I told my parents that I needed to see our doctor. His diagnosis was what I expected, so he sent me to see a surgeon. A few days later, I had an operation to repair a hernia. I don't know how the procedure works today, but at that time, 1980, I spent three or four days in the hospital and couldn't run a step for six weeks.

I know that my surgery was on February 21, 1980, because the next evening, I watched the USA Olympic Hockey Team beat the Soviet Union at Lake Placid from my hospital bed. Like most people, I thought the game was live. It was only years later that I found out it was broadcast on tape delay. I don't watch hockey, and I've never followed the game, but like many Americans, I watched it with anticipation that night. My only issue is that it hurt to cheer!

My goal for my senior track season was not only to qualify for the State Meet in the 800m, which was not easy in the bigger classifications in Kansas but also to bring home a medal. Through 1979, Kansas gave out medals to the top three finishers. Burkes didn't get a medal for is 4th place 2-mile in 1978. However, beginning in the 1980 season, state medals were awarded to the top six finishers. I didn't think I'd have time to get in superb condition to qualify in the half. And it didn't seem as if we had the other runners to make up a good 2-mile relay. John Johnson was good enough, and maybe Eric Zink, but who else? And I might not be good enough to help make the relay competitive. And unfortunately, after I got back to training, Eric severely sprained his ankle wrestling me, and he was not the same the rest of the season. I felt guilty about this.

About two weeks after my surgery, John Johnson and I drove the 35 miles to Pittsburg to buy new track shoes. I wasn't sure how well I would do during the season, but I would at least look good. This was an era in which most track shoes were dull looking, but we bought the Nike Vancour, a colorful shoe in florescent green, yellow, and orange that was becoming popular. I believe the person who sold us the shoes was Rob McCleod, the former Pittsburg State All-American. John had already signed with Pitt State to run cross-country and track, but I wondered if I would have a chance to earn a track scholarship after surgery.

The cross-country team's new coach was Teach, and I think he did a fantastic job with them. The team qualified for the State Meet, which was not easy, and took 8th place. I don't believe the Parsons cross-country team has qualified for the State meet since. Teach didn't coach track, which was probably a good thing because he was also the new head basketball coach, being promoted from assistant, and he was still on the courts when track practice began. Our new head track and field coach was Gary Billions, with Riley Cartwright as the distance coach. Before 1980, Mr. Barcus coached the girl's track team, but I can't remember if he continued in that roll or coached weight events for both genders. But he was still one of the track coaches.

We got lucky as a team. The distance runners who returned from the 1979 team were worried about who would replace Coach Cagle. But we didn't miss a beat with Coach Cartwright. He was a great middle-distance and distance coach. We worked hard, and the workouts were terrific. We never had a lost day or workout, meaning everything we did was designed to help us improve, and we did. He never went through the motions, and he didn't allow us to go through the motions, either. Workouts were fun but difficult. Speed work was calculated, and each week was designed to build on the previous. By the end of the season, most of us were running our best.

What I learned from Coach Cagle was great, and Coach Cartwright continued the process. And Coach Billions was an outstanding head coach. As with the previous two seasons with Coach Cagle, we had some of the best coaching in the State of Kansas. Several years after I graduated Coach Cartwright said we spoiled him because he could never get the kids to work as hard as we did. He said that if he tried most would quit the team. He also said he "burned the midnight oil" with us, because he had never coached distance before and needed to keep a few days ahead of us. I never suspected it my senior year – he was that good. Anyone that says he wasn't a good coach (and I heard it a few years later from one of his track athletes) is dead wrong. You could never win that argument with me!

Before surgery I was playing recreational league basketball. John Johnson was my teammate. I still attended my team's games without playing, but by the last regular season game I couldn't remain on the bench any longer and decided to play anyway, defying the doctor's order. I actually didn't play badly, but there were times my incision hurt. One time I jumped to block a shot, and it felt like I ripped the incision apart – but I didn't. Finally, after several weeks, I was given the OK to run. I don't think it was six weeks though because the math doesn't calculate – it might have been five. The team had been practicing for several weeks so I was behind. I knew I wasn't in good condition, but I didn't realize how much I'd lost until my first practice. Coach Cartwright took the boys and girls out to a farm, and we ran on the grassy pasture. From the beginning it was clear that I was hurting. I had a tough time finishing the run and I felt horrible afterwards. The problem is that the first meet was only about a week to ten days away, and I wanted to run.

One athlete we wouldn't have in 1980 was senior Mike Burnett. Mike didn't make it out of the prelims the year before in the State Meet 110m hurdles. But I think he would have had a really good opportunity to get a medal at State in 1980 because our league had some of the best hurdlers in the state and Mike would have raced them week in and week out. And I think Mike would have been good in the intermediate hurdles as well. Burnett was a good athlete, and I think he could have dipped under 40 seconds in the longer hurdle race. As a junior he didn't get the chance to compete in a lot of meets because Coach Cagle didn't think he was ready early on. Maybe or maybe not, but as a senior Mike would have had the time to prepare for both hurdle races and I believe would have been a good leg on the mile relay. Unfortunately, Mike had a physical issue that prevented him from competing in athletics as a senior.

The coaches decided to allow me to compete in the first meet, the Parsons Invitational, so we could see what I could do. They placed me in the 2-mile relay and the 880-yard run. Our relay was a mystery because other than John Johnson the rest of us were unproven, even me with my lack of conditioning. Eric Zink was injured with his sprained ankle and couldn't run, junior Hando Martinez, who we looked at as a possible relay leg, was sick, and the others didn't seem ready. The coaches decided that our first leg would be sophomore Brad Strathe, the son of my 9th grade football coach, who only came out for track, as I remember, because he had a broken arm and couldn't play baseball. With Hando's illness, the coaches decided to run another sophomore, who had some success in cross-country. The problem is that this kid had a chip on his shoulder and threw a fit when he learned he was scheduled to run the relay. He told Coach Billions that he had trained for the mile and 2-mile, and he wouldn't run an 880 leg on the relay. Coach explained that this was only for one meet, and we needed him. He quit the team in an uproar.

I was fine with that. If he didn't want to run the relay and be part of the track team, then good riddance. I had no time or patience for a teammate like him, a prima donna. If that meant we wouldn't have a relay in the first meet, so be it. Goodbye, and don't come back! When we got out of school the next afternoon for the meet, we found out that the sophomore apologized and asked to be allowed back on the team. Coach Billions agreed, but he had to run the relay that day. I wasn't too happy, but I got over it quickly. Strathe gave us a strong first leg with a 2:12. He was someone that could work out for us because we knew he would improve. Then the quitter took the baton and dogged it. I know he did. He looked as if he was jogging the entire race. I think it was his way to protest, but selfishness cost the rest of us. And I think he did it so the coaches wouldn't place him back on the 2-mile relay the rest of the season. He barely broke 2:20, and he took second in the 2-mile run later in the day and ran a 4:39 1600m at the end of the season. I took the baton with a lot of trepidation. But the race didn't end up being that difficult. I passed a couple of teams and handed off to John in 3rd place. But we were quite a distance from second and John couldn't move us up. I ended up tying my best time with a 2:06, and John ran the same time as me.

I was surprised that I ran 2:06, especially off little training and coming back from hernia surgery. Although we only took third, it was possible that we might have a good 2-mile relay. Maybe Hando would work out, or Eric would heal quickly, and maybe junior Mike Butler could challenge, after all he had potential and was an important runner on the cross-country team. I now had some confidence as the 880 approached. Maybe my season wouldn't be a total bust after all. I knew I had a long way to go, and it's not uncommon for a runner to do well the first meet back from an injury, and then not compete well for a few weeks. But I didn't think that would happen to me. As it turned out, Hando did end up running the first meet. He was entered in the 880, but when he began to pull his sweats down, he discovered that he forgot to put on his racing shorts! A couple of coaches and some of our athletes encircled him so he could put on some shorts, because there wasn't enough time to go back to the locker room. I don't know where they found racing shorts so quickly, but he made it to the starting line fully dressed out in Parsons High School racing gear.

The meet record was still 2:04 from 1977, but John's goal was not only to win but break the record. My new goal was to finish in the top three and earn a medal. I knew that Labette County had a good half-miler in junior Danny Cleveland, but I didn't know how good the rest of the competition would be. John took the lead from the beginning, and I settled into third behind Cleveland. Danny was a member of our hated rival, but I personally liked him. I figured if I stayed with him, I could overcome my lack of training and run a good race, and maybe even out-kick him. Coming off the last curve, I was still close to Danny, but I could never pass. Still, I took third place and ran the fastest open 880 of my life with a 2:08.1, beating my 2:09.0 from my sophomore year. John bested the meet record at 2:03.8. It would be a good start to the season -- now if we could find a fourth person for the relay.

We next ran at Independence on their slow cinder track. Independence was an interesting place to run. The track was surrounded by a high wall except on the front stretch where the football stadium was located and at the beginning of the first curve where a small baseball-like stadium stood. On the other side of the fence was the Independence Zoo, and throughout the meet there were all kinds of odd animal sounds bouncing off the rock wall. You could even smell the monkeys or some other kind of creature on the back stretch when the wind was right. But it made for an interesting meet, and I never viewed it as a detriment. It gave character to a meet that already had tough competition.

In the 2-mile relay, Strathe, John and I ran solid legs, and we won in a meet record, although the time was still slow. Our new second leg was Hando, and he only ran about two seconds faster than the sophomore the previous week. Although he was not far under 2:20, Hando actually gave it a good effort, which was all we could ask at that point. Still, we needed a fourth guy to give us a good leg, and I wasn't sure Hando was the one. Plus, later in the 2-mile, Hando started to mess around during the race by coming up behind runners and placing his hand above their heads and giving the piece sign or doing a wave over their heads. His antics didn't play well with some of us as we shouted for him to stop being an ass. He just smiled or gave us a shit-eating grin and continued. I'm sure the opposing coaches weren't too happy, and neither were our coaches, who told him after the race that he would never do that again. A humbled Hando agreed, and he never again pulled that juvenile crap. If he had, I think he would have lost his opportunity to run on the relay.

In the 880, which was run under the lights, the pace was fairly slow the first lap, which was a disadvantage for John. For me, I don't think it mattered. I wasn't in good enough shape yet to handle a really fast pace, and my lack of fitness, combined with the fact the left side of my growing and the upper portion of my inner thigh were still really numb after surgery, meant that I didn't have much of a kick. Normally, John had the best kick in a race, but Steve Gaffney from Coffeyville was not only the defending League half mile champion, but he was also extremely fast. I think he had run around 9.9 for the 100-yard dash. I think there's a good chance he would have mostly run the short sprints if it wasn't for the fact that Coffeyville had two of the fastest three sprinters in the state. The fastest kid was from Independence, only ten miles away. Gaffney could also handle a fast pace, but when it was slow, he might have been unbeatable. Both runners ran 2:05, but John could not sprint by Steve and took second. I tried as hard as I could to get by Cleveland, but as with the race in Parsons, I couldn't pass him and took fourth.

We next traveled to Chanute for their invitational, and we wouldn't face Gaffney because Coffeyville didn't attend. Still, even if they would have been in Chanute, Steve didn't always run the open 880.

In the 2-mile relay, the three of us again ran well, but Hando's second leg was only 2:17, and we took third. In the 880-yard run, John and I controlled the race, and he controlled me, but we took the top two places running 2:04 and 2:06. Like many of the meets in which we competed during high school, there was a large school division and one for small schools. The winner of the small school 880 was Robert Skeen from Northeast Arma. It would have been nice to have him in our race because he won the State 3A 800m the next month in 1:58.0.

Two days later we competed in the Fredonia Invitational. Our 2-mile relay consisted of the same four runners. I was all for giving Hando a chance, but I hoped that Eric Zink would hurry up and heal. But something terrific happened on the way to our meet-record winning time – Hando ran a 2:10. Not a great time, but he improved 7 seconds in two days, and he looked as if he knew what he was doing. Maybe, just maybe we would have a good 2-mile relay team. We took 17 seconds off our previous best that season and ran 8:29. Although Coffeyville was at Fredonia, Gaffney didn't run the 880. John won easily, but I ran a poor race and took 7th. I think running two meets in three days finally caught up with me in the half mile and my lack of training reared its ugly head. But this was still good because racing in two meets in the same week helped me begin to race myself into shape and if we had a chance to have an outstanding relay, I needed to be at my best.

The team competed in the Labette County High School Invitational ten miles down the road in Altamont in our fifth meet of 1980. Their track was poor, but the competition was good as always. In the relay, all four of us ran good legs, but not fast, and we won easily in 8:33. Coach Billions was a little perturbed because our home-town newspaper had given Labette County glowing coverage the week before and had slighted us to a large degree. Coach told me, in no uncertain terms, to not let Cleveland beat me. This was a tall task because in the previous three races in which we competed against each other, I had lost to him each time. The pace was honest, and when I came off the last curve with about 55 yards to go, I was in second place. Then I felt pressure on my right shoulder as someone was getting ready to pass me. "Oh no," I thought as I knew Danny was about to pass. In my urge to not let Cleveland pass me I began to tighten up, and that cost me dearly. As I was being passed, I realized that it wasn't Cleveland – it was a kid from Columbus who I don't think had beaten me before, or we hadn't raced. At any rate, I was relieved it wasn't Danny who passed me as I crossed the finish line in third. But I should have been upset that I didn't get 2nd. Danny took 4th.

In our next two meets, the coaches changed things up a bit. John Johnson didn't run the 2-mile relay and was replaced by Eric Zink to see how he would perform. Unfortunately for Eric, he didn't have time to get in the needed condition, but he did give us a strong enough leg to do well. In the first meet, the Girard Invitational, contested at Pittsburg State's Brandenburg Stadium, we took second running in the 8:30s. John, who was recovering from a nasty leg injury, which he said happened when he ran into a tree, but I later found out was caused by a car accident when they hit a bridge on a rural road, won the 880 in 2:02. I took 10th in a slow 2:10. He followed that up with a nice 440 leg in the mile relay. At the second meet, a triangular in Fort Scott, I anchored the 2-mile relay for the second straight meet and brought us home to victory with a 2:04 leg. We ran 8:35, and Hando ran his second strong leg in as many meets. Eric improved a little but was unable to displace Hando or Strathe from the relay.

Instead of running the 880, I was entered in the mile, which I had wanted to try as a junior. This was my first try at the mile in a high school meet. But I had a problem. Because it was a small meet, I only had about 10 minutes between the relay and the mile. The coaches wanted to see how quickly I could recover. When the race began, I could still feel my 880 legs, and that meant no energy. I slogged through the first lap as a few runners widened their lead on me. This trend continued into the second lap. When I reached the halfway point, my 880 split was a pedestrian at 2:35 or a 5:10 pace. And I'm sure my second lap was slower than the first, so at that rate, I'd be lucky to break 5:20. But then the adrenalin and competitive juices began to flow, and I started to move up. I couldn't tell who was in the lead, but my goal was to pass those in front of me, and if I were in a position to make an attempt to win the last 220, then I'd give it a try. And that's just what happened. With about half a lap to go, I could see one of my teammates ahead of me. The sophomore who had run the poor leg in the 2-mile relay at our first meet. He had not run under 5:00 at that point, but he had run at 5:01 in junior high, and I thought I might be able to catch him, although I knew I had some distance to make up. I almost caught him, but he just held me off. He ran 4:50, and I ran 4:51. My last 880 run was at 2:16, and I began to wonder if maybe my future was in the mile. I even thought about asking the coaches if I could run the mile at Regionals because it might be my best shot at qualifying for State in an individual event. But I decided against it because I wasn't sure the recovery time between the relay and the mile was enough, and I knew it would take a mile in the 4:30s to qualify for State.

John Johnson warmed up for League with a 2:00.8 in the 880 at Fort Scott, and then came back to win the 2-mile in 10:16 off little rest. He made the 2-mile look easy. The coaches had us ready. Not only the distance runners, but some field events guys as well. Mike Bolander was throwing the javelin well and was a threat to win the League Meet. And the mile relay team was running its best of the season. Most of us peaked at the right time. One of our issues is that we didn't have any dominant sprinters, and in a league in which the best short sprinters in the state resided, we would have a difficult time scoring in the top three. There were nine schools in the Southeast Kansas League, and we were somewhere in the middle of the pack. But in those events in which we were good, we were really good.

League Meet was always held on a Friday and during my years it was contested at Pittsburg State. We arrived early in the afternoon, on a pleasant spring day. Most of the team was lying about under a tree in a field outside the stadium. Mike Bolander and I began to horse around little, when he suddenly hit me in my thigh and gave me a huge bruise. It hurt like hell, and I could hardly walk. I tried to work it out but to no avail. I knew this Charlie-horse was going to be a problem. I can't really blame Mike, but I asked him why he had to hit me so hard. We had the best 2-mile relay time in the League coming in and we weren't sure if anyone could beat us. What we didn't know is that Coffeyville had stacked its relay, and I don't think we were mentally prepared for that.

Brad Strathe and Hando ran strong legs to open a lead. In fact, Hando ran a personal best of 2:04. When I received the baton in the lead for the third leg, I knew I had to hold on. But my leg was killing me, and the bruise would turn into a nice shade of purple. Still, I was able to keep up a pretty good pace. I knew I had to gut it out. With about 220 yards to the handoff, I was passed by a Coffeyville runner named Pitts. He was a good runner, and I had no response with my aching leg. My kick was not back to full force anyway, and now I had no kick. I thought someone else was going to catch me, but we were well ahead of third. Regardless, I thought that I needed to keep it at least close so John could do his thing, and we would win. I was able to keep it real close down the stretch and didn't lose any ground after the initial surge past me by Coffeyville, and I ran a 2:05. Although I already knew that Gaffney was Coffeyville's anchor, I thought that John had improved enough to beat him here. John ran a 2:00, but so did Gaffney, and Coffeyville beat us 8:16.1 to 8:17.1. It was the first time all season in which I had been passed in the relay.

In the 880-yard run, I knew I was good enough to get third, but I also knew I might not even place. The race was after dark, and the lights lit up the track in a very eerie way. It's difficult to explain, but I was standing there, not able to determine whether the lights were bright or dim; my eyes couldn't adjust. I ran competitively, but with my leg hurting as it was and my lack of speed, I could not respond when I needed and was only able to muster a 6th place in 2:06.0. John ran the poorest race of his season and managed to hold on to second in 2:02.9 ahead of an Iola kid, who I think was Mike O'Meara. It's hard to say what happened to John, whether the pressure got to him, or he didn't feel well. But Gaffney ran away with the race and was League champion for the second year in a row, running 2:00.4. Gaffney didn't run the open half the rest of the season, but I'm sure that if he had, he would have medaled in the 800m at the State Meet. Steve's ability was off the charts. John was so distraught about not winning the 880 at League that he blamed it on the 2-mile relay. He said he wanted out of the relay, but I knew the coaches wouldn't let that happen. Maybe I was selfish, but I knew we had no chance at State without John as the anchor. By the next practice on Monday, John seemed excited about the relay again!

Regionals was eight days after League and was held in Ottawa, the same place as in 1979. I believed time was running out for me to earn a track scholarship. I'm sure no college coach paid attention to me and in an era before the internet, I don't know how they would have learned about me anyway. With John already agreeing to go to Pittsburg State, he was set, and I didn't want to go to Pitt State. I would have had to walk on there and I wasn't interested anyway. I'm not sure why I waited so long, but at some point, right before or right after regionals, I asked Coach Billions, Coach Cartwright, and Coach Barcus if they could help me find a college that would offer me a scholarship. Of course, they agreed. I believed that I needed to qualify for the State Meet in the 800m to have a good shot at a scholarship, but even without that incentive, I just wanted to run the half at State on its own right because it was my dream.

The Regional was held on a glorious Saturday in May. The Southeast Kansas League Schools in our Region were Fort Scott, Chanute, Pittsburg, and LC. In addition, there were a few teams from outside our league, such as the host school, Paola, and Blue Valley Stanley. Though we hadn't faced these schools during the season, we knew they had some good competitors. We were especially concerned with Blue Valley because they had a good half-miler named Pope and a pretty good relay as well. But we didn't end up having any issues in the 2-mile relay, and we all ran very relaxed, winning at 8:16.5, close to the same time Coffeyville had run the week before. My leg was healed, although I didn't feel my strongest, but I still ran 2:05. Brad and Hando also ran well, and John anchored in 1:59.4, his first time under 2 minutes, even though it was a relay leg. In the Javelin, Mike Bolander took third to qualify for the State Meet a week after he was League champion. The girls' 880 relay also qualified for State, and Char Owens qualified in the 400m dash.

By the time the 880 rolled around, I felt better and was ready to run. When the gun went off, I started strong, and at the break I settled into third place behind John, who led, and Pope. This ended up being a tactical mistake. I knew that only the top three finishers qualified for State and so I thought that's the position from where I should race. What I should have done is get on John's shoulder and stay there as long as I could. I'm almost sure I wouldn't have defeated Pope with this strategy, but I might have taken third. At the very least, I should have run on Pope's shoulder. When I came off the final curve with a little over 50 yards to go, I still held on to third place, and I thought I had it in the bag. But then a kid from Ottawa came up on me and with only a few yards to go I tightened up as I had never done before in an attempt to hold him off. It's possible had I relaxed I might have placed third, but as it was, I got beat out for the final State birth by a hair. And I mean a hair – it was that close. But I knew when we crossed, he had beaten me.

My time was 2:04.0, my fastest open 880 of my life, but it wasn't good enough. I do think that if I'd just kept up with John, I would have placed third, but hindsight gets you nothing, unless you use it to improve, and move on from the disappointment. I did move on, but not before I cussed loudly and made somewhat of an ass of myself until Coach Billions settled me down – I guess I did let my emotions get to me one more time! He knew my disappointment and empathized with me, but he also knew he needed to let me know how well I'd run. Yes, it was actually the best day in track I'd ever had. John won the race in 1:59.1 and broke the thirteen-year-old school record by a tenth of a second. For John, one week made a huge difference, and it would be different for him from then on. John's breakthrough meant that he would never go back to those days where 2:02 was fast – that would become nothing more than a jog. After the 880, Hando won his first 2-mile of the year in 10:19 and qualified for the State Meet.

Regardless of my 880 disappointment, I still had a chance at a State Meet medal in the relay. Coffeyville competed in a different Regional and I read in the paper that they took second in the relay behind Wichita Kapaun Mt. Carmel. John's adjusted 800m time was 1:58.4 and was about the same time of Kapaun's John Pyles from the regionals. The fastest regional time was McPherson's Jon Piles, the defending class 5A State champion, who ran 1:55.0. In the week of the State Meet, the coaches made sure we were ready. Our workouts were sharp early in the week and by the end of the week we were well rested. In fact, it was a real relaxed week, and the coaches didn't put any pressure on us as Friday approached.

Our girls 800m relay of Char Owens, Brenda Smith, Teresa Benson, and Jonnie Zetmeir ran a nice race on Friday, but they were unable to qualify for the finals. Char ran a real good 400m in 60 seconds but finished in 4th place, just outside qualifying for finals. Bolander threw the javelin fairly well but didn't make it to the final three throws. There were some outstanding performances at the State Meet. I saw Steve Stubblefield from Kansas City Wyandotte win the 6A pole vault in 17-0. He broke the national high school record with a 17-6 during the summer. And that 6A pole vault had some other great performances with Shawnee Mission North's Doug Lytle taking second in 16-5 (Lytle made the 1984 US Olympic team), and Mark Klee of Olathe finishing third with a 16-0 jump. I also saw 6A long jumper Veryl Switzer from Manhattan win with a 24-6 ½, and Clint Johnson of Shawnee Mission South win the shot with a national leading throw over 69 feet. I missed his 200-foot discus win. Johnson went on the set the high school national discus record with a 213-foot throw. I also witnessed a terrific 6A girls 1600 won by Shawnee Mission East's Lori Nelson in 4:55. And then there was Topeka-Highland Park senior Jocelyn Bentley, who dominated the three 6A sprints, with a 400m in 54 seconds. Unfortunately, I missed the 4A javelin won by Jim Russell with a throw of 234 feet.

The relay's turn came on Saturday. Unlike our other meets, State was hot – about 95 degrees by the afternoon. In the morning Hando competed in the 3200m, but he went out too fast and ran a poor race. We consoled him and said he needed to put that race behind him and get ready for the 3200m relay. Of the regional champions, we had the third fastest time behind Newton and Kapaun. My hope was that we would finish in the top 6 and earn medals. I was as nervous as I'd been all season, even more so than I had been the first meet of the year. As I watched Strathe run the first leg I could see that the race would be competitive and difficult. But Brad hung in there and remained close. As he sprinted down the home stretch to prepare for the handoff there was a traffic jam developing. Just as Brad handed off to Hando, several runners who had just passed their batons got their legs tangled and fell.

As Hando turned to run after taking the baton, he was shoved by an off-balance runner attempting to avoid the pile-up and pushed to lane six or seven. Since the Wichita State track was only seven lanes, Hando could go no further. Many teams took handoffs with the runner taking the baton facing the infield. But our runners faced the outer lanes of the track so when we took the baton, we could more easily see what was happening in front of us. I think our method saved Hando, because instead of tumbling with the other fallen athletes, he was able to keep on his feet, despite the shove, and recover. USAT&F teaches the other method, but I have always maintained that the handoff we used is superior, so I continue to teach it. But some meet officials don't understand that both handoffs are legal, so they make my athletes turn to the inside. That is wrong!

Strathe ran a personal best of 2:04.1 for his 800m leg, and Hando recovered quick enough to get back in the race, although I think the handoff incident cost him a second or two. But in a competitive race, the key was remaining close, and he did just that. In fact, Strathe had us in 7th place at the exchange, and when Hando got himself back in the first lane, we were still in 7th. Hando didn't move us up, but he ran a strong leg and kept us in position to earn a medal. And his leg was especially good after his performance in the 3200m. So, when I took the baton after Hando's 2:06 leg, we were still in 7th. Hando did his job well despite a slower leg than he expected.

My objective was to move us up as many places as possible. Any anxiety I may have had before the race was gone. I remember watching Hando run down the last straight toward me and I felt a moment of clarity and contentment. I was completely at ease. It's interesting that I can remember the legs of the other three better than my own, but I do have a couple of moments during my portion of the race that stand out. First is running the back stretch of the first lap in which I felt as loose and powerful as I ever had. I was running as uninhibited as one can feel. I passed a couple of runners to get us into 5th and I didn't have any worries that I would lose any places or that I might have gone out too fast. My first lap was a 57, which was as fast as I had ever run, although I didn't learn my split until after the race.

The second moment was in the last curve as we were headed for the home stretch. There were two teams right in front of me, and one was Newton who had the fastest regional time. I knew I needed to pass them, and just as I went wide to pass as we were coming to the straight, I heard someone yell from the side, "Go Parsons." I sprinted by the Newton runner and the other team, who I don't recall, and left both in the dust. The only team ahead of us at that moment was Kapaun, and I closed the gap. I handed off to John in second place with Newton in third. John ran a terrific leg, but was unable to catch Kapaun's anchor, John Pyles. John ran 1:57.9, and Pyles told him his time was the same. We had taken 2nd, which was much better than I expected.

I felt as if we had won the Olympics. Sure, I wanted a medal in the 800m, but hernia surgery had taken that away. But I had still earned that elusive State medal – a goal I had for three years. I truly thought I had broken 2 minutes, but my dad timed me in 2:01, and one coach had me in 2:01.2. I was also timed in 2:00.8. Regardless, we ran 8:08.83, about a second and a half behind Kapaun. Not only did we earn second place State Meet medals, but we also beat Coffeyville, who took 5th in 8:17. We smoked them, and they were surprised we ran so well. Coffeyville was a rival, and we were happy we beat them in the relay, but despite this, I was glad Coffeyville, a fellow Southeast Kansas League member, won the overall team title. Independence placed high as well. The League, as a whole, competed well. In the class 4A 3200m relay, Columbus finished 6th, which gave three teams from our league State medals in the relay.

In the evening, John ran the 800m. The first lap was not very good for him as he languished in 7th place, boxed in with no place to go. With 300 meters to go, he was about 35 yards behind the leader when he stuck his elbow out and told a Kapaun runner, who I think was Pyles' younger brother, to move because he was coming through. Then John ran a spectacular last three-quarters of a lap and passed everyone except the leader. John took second in 1:55.9, behind Jon Piles, who won 1:54.4. Kapaun's John Pyles took third in 1:56.4. John ended up as the third fastest 800m runner in the state in 1980. Steve Smith from Shawnee Mission South, who was a 4:07 miler, had the fastest in 1:54.3, with Piles right behind him. Our relay, of course, didn't make the top five times that year, but who cares!

Chapter 6
Running from Gunshots – or Maybe Not!

As we headed back to Parsons from the State Track Meet in the school van, traveling through the rolling Flint Hills on a long skinny highway in the darkness of night, I reflected about the achievement of that day, the past, and my future. All my track coaches, Coaches Kennedy, and Coons in junior high, Coach Cagle, Coach Cartwright, and Coaches Billions and Barcus in high school, had been such positive influences. These coaches were role models, and that's not always the case. I've seen plenty of coaches through the years that seem to be more concerned about their records, and the athletes come second, or even further down the line. I've seen high school coaches that have absolutely no regard for the kids and treat them like shit. I'm not saying our coaches never yelled at us because they did, but there was never distain in their voices. My coaches got it. They were in the profession for the right reasons, and education came first. Although I could have cared less about the education side at that point of my life, I knew my coaches did, and that was important.

Besides those I've already mentioned, I had wonderful teammates in high school. Tom O'Hara, who was a year behind me, was a tremendous teammate. I don't think Tom ran the mile under 5:20, at least during my time as his teammate, but you couldn't ask for a better person to run with and travel to meets. Tom was humble, and the friendliest person you'll ever find. Although he didn't become a good runner, he was an outstanding kicker in football. Unfortunately, we didn't score enough for Tom to attempt many extra points, but when we did score, he was true. I don't remember Tom ever shanking a kick whether it was an extra point, or a kickoff, in practices or in games. Kicking was Tom's athletic gift. Rob Mernan was a javelin thrower, and a terrific teammate. He was also younger than me, and he started 1980 trying to learn the technique of the javelin, but by the end of the season he was throwing quite well. And I know Mike Bolander helped a lot.

As for my future, it was much clearer that evening than it had been when I woke up that morning. Without my knowledge, the coaches spoke to the head football coach and athletic director at Coffeyville Community College. They told Coach Dick Foster to watch me in the 3200m relay because I was looking for a track scholarship. After the race, Coach Billions told me that he was taking me to meet Coach Foster because he was interested and was impressed with how I ran in the relay. I knew who Coach Foster was because he was already a legend in the area, and he had given the keynote at one of our sports banquets in high school. Coach Foster, who had a loud, deep voice that could penetrate a four-foot-thick brick wall, had a good visit with me, and he invited me to come to the college on Monday.

On Monday, the same day as our graduation, I drove the 35 miles to Coffeyville, a town about the size of Parsons on the Oklahoma border. John Johnson went with me. We met Coach Foster at his office in Memorial Hall, which was where the basketball teams played and was about two blocks from the small community college campus. Two months later, Memorial Hall burned at the hand of an arsonist. Coach Foster took John and me to lunch and spoke to us about the school and the team. They really hadn't competed in cross-country in a few years, but he wanted to bring it back. After lunch we went back to his office where Coach Foster spoke to us individually. He knew John was headed to Pittsburg State, and he didn't attempt to talk him into coming to Coffeyville, but if he ever changed his mind, they would be happy to have him.

In my meeting with Coach Foster, he spoke to me about my goals and what he would like to see happen with the track team. He then gave me a letter-of-intent from the Jayhawk Conference and asked me to think about it and sign and return if I wanted to attend Coffeyville. Coach was a great recruiter, and although he was a football coach of one of the true junior college powerhouses, he treated me like I was a superstar. I was impressed. I had not really considered going to a junior college to run, but this seemed like a good deal. I sat down with my parents and discussed the opportunity and decided to go to Coffeyville. I signed the letter and sent it back to Coach Foster the next day.

I was ready and happy to move on to college. The truth is, I didn't care for high school. I viewed cliques and clubs that were placed on pedestals as asinine and I had no interest in playing the popularity game, and I still don't. In college, because people come from various places, one didn't have to deal with local social politics, at least at the student level. I realize that this is probably not the case at all colleges, but I didn't experience these issues where I attended. Sure, there were groups and maybe even cliques, but no one group stood above the others. Oh, one or two thought they were, but there was no support or pressure for the rest of the groups or students to bow down to their "royal" egos and kiss their "royal" asses. Mostly they were ignored or mocked.

Although I would never be able to confirm this, I think Coach Barcus was pressured to start certain kids in football by some of the so-called city "fathers" or the "Monday Morning Elite." I doubt Coach ever succumbed to their efforts. I wouldn't be surprised that at some point he was told to start someone else rather than me. He was, I believe, relieved of his head coaching duties in football after four seasons because he didn't bow down to those jerks. He remained at the school as a teacher and track coach and would eventually come back to be an assistant football coach. Some might argue that he didn't win enough games and was fired for that reason, and there is merit for that. But that's not the whole story of his record. First, yes in 1978, we should have won four or five games, I get that. But overall, we didn't have the same talent as the other teams.

Second, I think those town "boys" who controlled such things, should have known that good talent was coming up through the system. But when the previous coach had two outstanding seasons before leaving, it made Coach Barcus' record appear worse. Plus, Coach was getting better at leading the team. I'm confident that he would have had tremendous success by 1983, just as the coach who took his place did. Those boys were just that much more talented than us, as were those before we began high School. A little bit of that talent was still there my sophomore year such as quarterback Vince Horton, but then it was gone. In a town like Parsons, the talent pool is cylindrical. I'm sure most of those city leaders who ran most aspects of the town's business are now dead. But at that time, I needed to leave that environment.

After the graduation ceremony, which took place at Marble Park Stadium, the same place we played our football games, John, Hando, and I took off for our graduation night. Of course, Hando was only a junior, but he wanted to party as well. For him it was more of a celebration of our 2-mile relay success at the State Meet. It's interesting to me that I can remember the graduation rehearsal but have little memory of the actual graduation. I don't remember walking across the stage, or whatever it would be called at the bottom walkway of the stadium, but I do remember that night. In fact, I remember little about my high school classes. I have the recollection of sitting in Spanish class and drafting and some coaching class that Mr. Wheat taught but not much else, other than gym class.

I remember shop class when I was a senior, sitting in the classroom with a friend, Randy Whitley, and not working on my project. The shop teacher, Mr. Weiderstein, would come in and ask if I was going to work in the shop that day, and I would only say "no." He would walk away in disgust shaking his head. One time, I told him that I didn't take the class to earn a grade and that he could fail me for all I cared. I just took the class to make a coffee table, I said to him. When he was gone, some of the burners would make small pot pipes out of walnut because they knew it would be difficult to get away with it if he was in the shop. I actually liked Mr. Weiderstein, and I should have acted as if I respected him more.

After John, Hando, and I left the drive-in theater, where we watched a movie or two and drank "liquor store" beer, we headed out to Parsons Lake in John's Oldsmobile. The lake was about 10 miles northwest of Parsons, and there was a graduation party there. But there always seemed to be a party at Parsons Lake, and this was just another excuse. On the way out, John drove, and he wasn't much of a driver in the first place, and after a few beers, I couldn't tell the difference. John kept saying he needed to drive carefully so we wouldn't wreck the car. The previous week or two, a local young man, who I knew, had been killed on his way to a party at the Lake. John indicated that he didn't want that to happen to us. Then, as we turned a corner where the road went from pavement to gravel, John hit the gas, spun the car, then panicked and hit the break as we flew into the ditch facing the opposite direction after we stopped. We all got out of the vehicle, and even on an extremely dark night, we could tell there wasn't any damage, and we were not the worst for wear and tear.

The three of us started laughing, but we couldn't get the damn car out of the ditch. Then, some guys we knew who graduated with us that night, including Mike Bolander, drove by and stopped to help us. With the extra help, we didn't have a problem getting that tank out of the shallow ditch. We then cautiously proceeded to the Lake, where we continued to party for a while. However, we found the whole scene to be a complete bore and decided to leave. Maybe the final straw for me was watching a kid who was paralyzed a couple of years before being fed a joint by a friend. But, then again, maybe that wasn't such a bad thing, but at the time, I didn't see anything redeeming about it. I hadn't been an angel during my teenage years, and I can't say I didn't do my share, but for some reason, it struck me as wrong at that moment. So, John, Hando, and I left the Lake and drove very carefully back to town. That was the last Parsons Lake party I ever attended, and I never missed it.

A week after the State Track and Field Meet, John, Hando, and I went to Fredonia for the area meet of the AAU Junior Olympics. I was three weeks too old to compete, although I wanted to do so. And I seriously thought about running. I didn't think it was right that just because my birthday was in December instead of January that I couldn't run, especially since I just graduated high school. Today, the rules are different, and if you don't turn 19 before the National Meet, you can still compete. At any rate, I decided not to run because I didn't want to break the rules, plus I had a very mild quad strain. John won the mile and 880-yard run, beating 3A 800m State champion Robert Skeen in the latter.

Two things changed in the AAU Junior Olympics in 1980. First, although the Fredonia meet was contested in yards, the running events in the remainder of the meets were in meters. Second, at least in Kansas, a sub-state meet was added. As before, the top three advanced out of the area meet but went to sub-state. From the sub-state meet, I believe the top three advanced to the State AAU meet. On the national level, something else was changing as well. National class track and field athletes revolted against the AAU as a result of the Amateur Sports Act of 1979 and because of a multitude of things that revolved around archaic and suppressive practices by the AAU. The Athletics Congress, or TAC, was formed to represent and serve the athletes, although eventually, I'm not sure it was any better for many of the national-level athletes, or anyone else for that matter.

Although the AAU lost its grip on adult-level track and field, it still controlled the youth.

The sub-State meet was held at Pittsburg State University. I wasn't running, but it was somewhat disappointing the meet was held on cinders, even if it was a good cinder track. However, it worked out well for me because I took the ACT that morning at PSU, so I was able to drive to another parking lot on campus, about two minutes away, and be at the track. I was originally supposed to take the ACT in February, but I was in the hospital and had to reschedule. During those years, a high school student took the ACT once. I don't remember anyone taking it more than once, but maybe some did.

I finished the ACT in time to watch John run the 1500m. In high school meets, John had never run the mile, so his first attempt was the week before in Fredonia, where he ran around 4:40. In the sub-State meet, he ran his first 1500m, winning easily in a time of 4:12, equal to about a 4:28 to 4:30 mile. In the 800m, John again beat Robert Skeen with a winning time of 2:01. This wasn't a fast time, but John won comfortably, even though Skeen was close behind. But John controlled the race. Skeen was a nice guy, and, like John, signed with Pitt State. We got to know Robert and his father a little during the few meets John competed against him. In the fall, Skeen and John were roommates at PSU, but Robert only lasted a semester.

Throughout the summer, John and I trained together several times a week and sometimes a couple of times a day. Sometimes, Hando joined us, but not too often. We occasionally ran in the morning, but we mostly trained in the afternoon or early evening, with some great short runs at Forest Park around 11:00 pm or midnight. Hando was usually with us during our late-night runs but chose to remain with the car. One particularly hot and still night, John and I ran about 4 miles around the park. Every time we ran by one spot on the east side of the park, we heard these guys yelling at us, using profanity, and calling us all sorts of names. We could tell they were drunk and just blowing steam out of their asses, but the comments were colorful! When we finished running, John and I decided to walk into the center of the park and see who these clowns were. It was so dark we could hardly tell where we were going, and we certainly couldn't see anyone in front of us. But we could hear them getting closer as they continued to act tough. They could see our silhouettes because of the streetlights behind us, so they had an advantage. But when we got up close enough for them to see who we were, their tone changed. They were just a few guys I'd known for several years, sitting in the core of the park getting drunk and high, and they never really had any intention of trying anything with us. It's a good thing because John and I would have torn them up. Hando had decided to stay with the car. But there was no need for a fight because I liked all the guys, and they had always liked me. We stayed and talked with them for a few minutes.

The summer of 1980 was blistering hot. I think Parsons had a point that it reached 100 degrees or higher 26 days in a row. Many of our training runs took place in the barrel of this heat. I'm not sure if it toughened us up or if we were just plain stupid. We had a choice. We could have run before or after the heat of the day, and we did. But we also were dumb enough to run in the late afternoon when the heat was at its worst. When I worked in the hay fields that summer, I didn't have a choice, so we bailed in the heat of the day. In one prairie hay field that had about 35 acres of grass, it only produced around 900 bales in 1980, compared to over 2,000 in 1979. But despite fewer bales, the work was just as difficult.

During the summer, we regularly went to the drive-in theater. Hando had stolen a bunch of cases of cheap beer from a Pittsburg disturber, and we drank that crappy malt beverage out of those old cans during our drive-in excursions. Much of the time, we just sat out on the benches next to the snack bar, and no one ever said a word about our beer drinking. Hando had an aversion to paying to watch movies, so he usually snuck in. There was a mobile home dealership next to the theater, and we sometimes dropped him off there. We would often see others get out of cars at this location and then hop the fence to the drive-in. The manager, who owned an old beat-up pick up, would chase the kids out of the theater area and out into a field with his truck. That's as far as he could go, and I never saw him actually catch anyone. Hando was too clever to be seen, and I don't think he was ever chased. The kids who snuck in over the fence were scared to death of the manager, who stood between 7'1" and 7'2" and probably weighed 400 pounds or more. I worked with him years later, and he once told me, "I'm not 7'2"; I'm 7'1." Hando didn't always sneak in over the fence. He sometimes got in the trunk. I always wanted to act like I couldn't get the hatch open and take a piss on the trunk to emulate the Cheek and Chong routine, but I never did. One thing I definitely remember is that I don't remember a single movie we saw at the drive-in.

It was after one of these drive-in visits that John and I experienced a very strange phenomenon. For some reason, Hando wasn't with us, and John's mom and siblings were out of town. After we returned from the movie, we found out that something wasn't right at his house. Before we left, John had placed his dog in the garage, but when we returned, the door to the garage was open, and the dog was in the house. It's possible that the dog had howled, and a neighbor took the dog and put him in the house. But the house was locked when we left. At any rate, it was strange. John didn't want to stay in the house, and he often talked about odd occurrences inside the home. I told him he could stay at my house that night, but he decided to sleep at his own house instead.

I have to admit that I had a strange feeling in that house, and we stood there deciding what to do, but it could have been my imagination. I was supposed to drop by John's house the next morning to pick him up. When I arrived, the front door was wide open, and no one was home. I walked in and called out to John but didn't get an answer. I searched inside all the rooms and then decided to go back home. When I arrived, John was sitting there with my mom – he had run the three miles to my house and wouldn't say what happened. From there, we ran out to the "special" pool where John's girlfriend worked as a lifeguard, which is where we encountered the light beer-drinking idiot with the mustache.

John and his girlfriend, Char Owens, our track teammate, broke up shortly thereafter. One of the things that I think contributed happened outside her house. Many times, Hando lacked tact and discretion. In fact, I don't think these things meant anything to him. Hando, who was extremely intelligent, liked to see how far he could go to insult people. We drove John over to Char's house in my car and waited for him outside. While we waited in the car, Hando spotted an elderly couple sitting in lawn chairs across the street from Char's house, and he began to insult them by yelling obscenities. He yelled such things as, "What the #%@$ are you looking at?" And there were plenty of other things said as well. I tried to get him to shut up, and it was clear the folks were extremely upset and emotionally shocked. Of course, Char and her family could hear every word, and as we found out later, the couple was very close to her family. Char was incensed, and I'm sure her parents were as well. After that incident, I guess John and Char felt it best to go their separate ways. It's sad, really, because I thought the two were a good couple. The interesting thing about Hando is that he could be extremely charming when he wanted.

My car, a 1968 Dodge Cornet, was the vehicle we used to do most of the things we did around town. After my wreck the year before, the passenger doors were caved in so much that they wouldn't open and close very well. Plus, the frame between the front and back doors was bent inward. I decided to go to a local junkyard and find two doors to replace the originals. I found two light brown doors to go on the greenish car. But the bent frame didn't allow the doors to close tight, so I used wire to keep the doors from flying open while I drove. This meant that the doors wouldn't open. I usually just kept the windows down on the passenger side, and John and Hando used to call it the Dukes of Hazard car because they had to crawl in. Although I'm sure my Dodge wasn't as fast as the Dukes' car, it still had a hell of a lot of power with its 318 motors. And it was fast as well, although, after 90 miles per hour, it shook like crazy.

Between the sub-State meet and the State AAU meet, my family traveled to the Black Hills. During a stay in Wall, South Dakota, I took a run down the highway south of town toward the Badlands. About a half mile into the run, I came across a rattlesnake that had been run over by a car. I turned around and headed back to the motel. A few days later, when we were about 25 miles from home, my mom said she was too tired to continue driving, so she pulled over at an intersection north of Thayer, Kansas – US 169, and State Highway 47, which we were on. I was sitting in the back seat on the driver's side, looking out the window. I could see a semi coming down the road headed south, then another semi pulled up next to us and stopped at the stop sign, obscuring my view of the southbound truck. Without thinking anything about it, I looked forward as my dad settled into the driver's seat. Then I saw a car crossing the intersection coming toward us when the southbound plowed into the car. It was the most gut-wrenching sound I've ever heard.

I don't know if the car didn't stop or if it stopped and proceeded without seeing the semi, but whatever it was, they would never do it again. The truck was a tanker transporting diesel fuel – thank God it wasn't gasoline. The car was thrown about ten feet off the ground, and the truck went right through it. The cab was a Mack flat-nosed, and the wheels seemed to be turned inward. It all seemed like slow motion as the truck slowly wobbled to the shallow but wide ditch, where it slowly rolled over onto the passenger side, but not before the car smashed into the back of the tanker. I swear it defied the laws of physics. Then, the truck cab caught on fire, and the driver of the truck next to us ran to help his fellow trucker. The driver of the wrecked truck smashed the passenger side window out with his cowboy boots and was able to crawl out with a bloody gash on his head.

My dad told me to stay behind, and he and a couple of others headed to the car. My dad said they were dead, and blood was everywhere. They could not get the doors open because of the damage created by the impact, which included the driver's side as well, and then the flames hit the tank, and it exploded, burning the hair off my dad's arms. They could not stay with the car any longer, and in a matter of minutes, after a series of explosions, the entire truck and the car were engulfed in flames. The truck driver was in shock, and the people in the car burned. As I read in the paper, the couple was in their 70s, which seemed old to me at the time. As I get older, I don't think that any longer. The diesel fuel fire was so hot that the ground remained black for years, and nothing would grow there. Several years later, when grass finally did start to grow, it was the greenest green I think I've ever seen.

A couple of weeks after the sub-state meet, we traveled to Wichita so John could run the State AAU Junior Olympic Meet. It was held at Wichita State University, on the same track as the State Track Meet the month before. We took John's Oldsmobile on the trip. Just before we got to Augusta, not too far from Wichita, the car began to overheat. We limped into town and stopped at the first convenience store we found. I asked John if he had checked the radiator lately, and he didn't know what I was talking about! Luckily, the store had a hose outside, so I filled the radiator and told John to get antifreeze in it before winter. Because of his lack of knowledge about the radiator, I asked John if he had checked the oil. I think he said, "It uses oil?" but I might be mistaken. But one thing is for sure: he had never checked the oil. The dipstick didn't register any oil, although the oil light never came on, and I don't recall how many quarts I put in the car; at least we were ready to go.

Hando's dad lived in Wichita and treated us to dinner. We stayed in a motel in the middle of town and got very little sleep. We probably slept two hours at the most, and I worried that John wouldn't perform well, being so tired. On our way to the stadium the next morning, we stopped for breakfast at a restaurant. We never eat at fast food joints because Hando would have to pay if we did. So, it was always sit-down places. On this particular morning, Hando did his usual routine after we finished by waiting for a group of people to go to the cashier to pay. Then, he would walk out with them as naturally as the grass growing in the sun. When he left the table, I picked up his check, and when he walked out with a group, he got caught, which was a rarity for him. The night before we ran at the State High School Meet, we were given a certain amount of money at the restaurant, and Hando walked out then as well, pocketing the profit.

But now he was caught, and I bailed him out. I told the lady at the cash register that I had his ticket, and I paid for both. Now, one thing is true – Hando usually only had about five dollars on our trips, so paying would be tough. Nonetheless, I felt he needed to ask one of us to pay. When we got back to the car, Hando decided to gripe because I paid his check, but I told him that the only reason I did what I did was to make sure we didn't get held up so John wouldn't miss his races. And this was the truth. I would have left him there to deal with the trouble himself otherwise.

As tired as he was and as inexperienced as he was in the 1500m, John ran a super race. On the back stretch of the final lap, he passed the leader and blistered the final 200m, winning in 4:04. As John crossed the finish line, I yelled, "About 10 seconds slower than you wanted," which was a joke because he didn't have a time goal, he just wanted to win. But I got a strange look from two guys standing close by who were wearing running shorts. I recognized them as Brent Steiner and Steve Smith from Shawnee Mission South. They weren't competing, and it appeared that they were just there to watch. I had never spoken to either one before, but they came over and talked with me about the race for a minute or so. The person who took second knew Steiner, and the three of us discussed John's kick for another minute or two.

John was happy about the 1500m result, but he turned his attention to the 800m, his favorite race. McPherson's Jon Piles was entered in the race, and John wanted to beat him this time. After John won the metric mile, Hand o I were looking at the heat sheet tacked up under the stadium to see who the 800m entrants were, when Piles and his girlfriend walked up to look as well. Of course, Piles didn't know who we were, and so he talked freely about the competition. He said to his girlfriend, "I think that's the guy who finished second behind me in the State Meet." I couldn't resist and turned and said it was him and he had run a horrible race that evening. And I was telling the truth. It was by far his best time, but John's race at State was strategically poor. But I told Piles this to psych him out!

I was not at the level as John with my times, but I was much more experienced, and so I told him how he should run the race to beat Piles. And there were other good runners in the race including Skeen. I told John that his strategy needed to be simple – stay within 10 yards of Piles the first lap, and then out-kick him. Piles liked to take the lead, so if he stayed close and out of trouble, everything would work out. John needed to give himself a chance. The strategy worked great. John was 10 yards behind Piles, who led, at the 400m mark. He moved up to Piles shoulder on the back stretch and coming off the final curve, he blew by the McPherson standout. John had a cheering section as well. My boss, Don Dean and his wife Nola and their family, were there to watch their granddaughter compete. They stood and cheered as John sprinted down the final straight to victory.

John's winning time was 1:55.6, and I think Piles ran 1:56.2, but I could be off a tenth or two. Piles indicated that when John went by him, he tried to gather himself and make one last drive to pass, but he just couldn't do it. Skeen was either third or fourth in 1:58, close to his 3A winning time at State. The top four qualified for the

Missouri Valley meet. I think it's been a few years since Kansas discontinued its AAU State meet, although it still might be contested. But I do know that the meet was run for at least 30 years after 1980, and through all that time, John still held the meet records in the 1500m and 800m runs. During the summer track meets we had the opportunity to get to know Piles, and he was an extremely nice guy and an outstanding runner!

As we left the track, we headed to a place to eat, and Hando decided to provide some unknowing young men with his wisdom. We were at a stoplight waiting for a green when these two men came up beside us on bikes and stopped. They were wearing dark dress pants and white dress shirts with ties. Hando hung his head out the window and said, "Don't step on that cockroach," which was a standard thing he would say. These two guys were not amused, and as the light turned green, they started to cuss us out. We had already decided to stop at a place to eat across the intersection, and when we turned into the parking lot, they headed our way with fire in their eyes. I think they must have thought we turned in to confront them, but it was only a coincidence. Hando got out of the big Olds first, and he was less than 5' 5". Then John, who was about 5' 9", got out, and the guys streaked towards us on their bikes. Then I got out, and I was about 6' 2". Standing next to Hando and John, I must have looked to be about 6' 6" because as soon as I stood next to my friends, they looked up and quickly made a 90-degree turn and sprinted away on their bikes as fast as they could. We were amazed and laughed as we entered the restaurant. Of course, Hando didn't pay.

As we had done in the past, I would go to the Rec Center and get money from Arvon Phillips to help pay for our trips and sometimes even find us places to stay. But for our trip to the Missouri Valley meet, which was held at Shawnee Mission South High School in Overland Park, Kansas, Hando knew a young family who lived near Olathe we could stay with. We did, however, get gas money from Arvon. I had relatives in Overland Park, but never considered contacting them. We took John's Olds, and I drove the 120 miles to the Kansas City area. When we reached Ottawa, we caught I35 and headed east to Olathe. Not long after we got on the interstate, we passed a car that was driving too slow. It must have pissed them off, because they passed right back and cut us off, almost hitting the car. There was construction on the interstate and the inside lane had been re-paved, but the outside had yet to be done, which meant that we had to drive off a small "curb" to get back over. We passed each other several times until about 125 to 130 miles per hour when our adversaries could no longer keep up. I then needed to maneuver off the inside lane, and like an idiot, I did it at well over 110 mph. Luckily, we didn't crash, but getting in a duel at more than 120 mph is about as stupid as one can get. We made it to the Olathe in one piece – and very quickly.

I don't remember the name of the family who hosted us, but they were very friendly. They were related to our teammate Tom O'Hara, and they might have had the same last name. They were a young couple with a couple of young children, and they fed us well. Although they had an Olathe address, their subdivision was in the middle of nowhere surrounded by cornfields. Hando decided to spend the day with the family, so John and I headed to the track by ourselves. The track was a fairly good one, but had a black surface, which radiated more heat than a red all-weather track. But the competition was good.

The first race for John was the 1500m. I stood by the starting line as the competitors mulled around nervously, waiting to get checked in (There were never heating tents. We had never heard of them). Suddenly this cocky loud kid ran up and said, "Who ran the 4:04?" John indicated it was him. The kid, who was from Missouri, complemented John but gave the impression that it wouldn't be good enough to beat him. His name was Jeff Pigg, and I could tell that John wasn't impressed as he looked over at me. The race was not quite as fast as the previous one, and I couldn't understand why

John just didn't run away from the pack. But John had a plan that was uncharacteristic for him. Fifty meters down the back straight on the final lap, John started to pass Pigg for the lead, but when he got next to him, he hesitated and ran stride for stride with Pigg for a few yards. I could see John's mouth move as he looked slightly over at Pigg, and then he took off and left his opponent in the dust. John won at 4:06. After the race, I asked John what he was doing on the backstretch and what he had said to Pigg. John said he just took the time to tell the kid "Bye." It was another easy win for John.

After the 1500, Piles showed up and we hung out with him awhile until they had to warmup. I know Piles wanted to beat John and I think he believed the best way to do so was by taking the lead. Piles best time was more than a second faster than John's, but he might have been losing fitness. I know John could have run faster than a mid-1:55 because he made it look so easy in Wichita. But I'm confident that Piles had the ability to run 1:53.0 then as well, and it's hard to say who was more talented. Piles told me he wished he had someone to train with like John did with me. That might have been the difference between the two that summer, not that I can take any credit for how well John ran. But Piles was correct that being pushed in workouts helped one remain in competitive shape. Piles certainly didn't take a backseat to John on the track, he proved that at the State Track Meet as a two-time champion. And it seemed to me that he liked competing against John and the two got along extremely well.

As in the State AAU Meet, Jon Piles took the lead early and maintained it through the first lap. John was about 10 yards behind at the 400 and followed a couple of other runners, including Skeen. But on the backstretch, John moved up to second and again placed himself on the leader's shoulder. As the two impressive young runners swung off the last curve, Piles in a purple shirt and gray shorts and John in a white top and blue shorts, they made a terrific run to the finish. This time, although John inched ahead, he never pulled away from Piles. But as they crossed the finish, John had beaten Piles for the second time in as many meets. The times were not as fast as in Wichita, but considering the heat, their 1:57s were pretty good. And their sprint down that final stretch was classic. Only the top three advanced to the Region 8 Meet, and unfortunately, Robert Skeen finished 4th in another 1:58. John doesn't hold the Missouri Valley meet records in either race anymore, but I was sure his winning time in the 800m was faster than the listed record the last time I checked.

After dinner with our hosts at their house, John and I decided to go to a drive-in movie we saw in Olathe along the interstate. Hando stayed behind. We knew we would be back late, so they decided to leave the backdoor unlocked for us. I do remember the two movies we saw – "Same Time Next Year," and "FM." The first movie was good, but "FM" sucked. However, the music was good. What an idea a drive-in was. The image on the screen was usually poor and the sound was crappy. Plus, you had to deal with bugs flying around including mosquitoes. Sometimes the food was good and sometimes not, and there was almost always someone blowing their horn. But I feel bad for today's youth, who have never had the opportunity to be a part of the great American cultural event of a drive-in movie. I loved it! But I have to say that I don't think I'd care much for it today. The drive-in was for young families and teenagers.

After we unwound from the day at the drive-in, we headed back to the house. But there were issues. First, where the hell was the sub-division? Second, after we located the oasis of buildings, we couldn't find the house. It must have been a new subdivision because there weren't any streetlights, and the houses looked so similar that we couldn't locate the home. Plus, the place wasn't set up on the grid, which, of course, is par for the course for subdivisions, it was just winding roads. We stopped at several homes thinking they were the right place, but decided they weren't. We looked for their car, but they must have parked it in the garage. Finally, we stopped at a place in the dark moonless night, decided to give that house a shot – and we hoped we didn't hear shots if this was the wrong home. We selected correctly and were relieved to get to bed.

To help John get publicity for his running exploits I decided I needed to get him on the radio. One day we had the radio on in my car listening to the local AM station KLKC. The DJ was a man who went by the moniker "Captain Kirk," who I knew. I'd been interviewed by him a couple of times for sports in high school and he called our football games on the radio. I'd also talked with him on other occasions. I guess I must have been a little brash, because when I heard the Captain on the radio that day, I decided to drive up to the station in downtown and ask him to interview John. We walked upstairs to the station, and no one stopped us. We watched Captain Kirk in the studio and when he played a record, we knocked, and he let us in. He had followed John's results in the newspaper and when I suggested he interview him he went for it! He interviewed John live. I think I took John up to the station three times and he was interviewed every time—the last time on tape. I had even convinced the *Parsons Sun* to take a picture of our 4x800m relay team and put it in the paper after the State High School Meet.

A couple of days before the 4th of July, we were driving by a convenient store in Parsons in my Dodge when Hando, sitting in the back seat spotted a beer truck parked in the alley behind the business with a couple of its doors up. The store was in a long building with a laundromat at the other end and another business or two in the middle. Hando wanted several cases of beer and maybe a keg. I was skeptical but parked on the east side of the laundromat a couple of spots from the alley. From where I was parked, I could see the alley and the corner of the building in front of me as John and Hando turned the corner and headed to the truck. At that point I couldn't see them anymore, but I waited as I watched the corner and the people doing laundry through the window. All at once I heard a man yell "Hey, what are you guys doing" or something like that and then I heard crashing cases of beer hitting the ground.

Then I heard several loud bangs as both of them came sprinting around the corner from the alley, flying by the car and around to the street where I lost visual of them. They were running from gunshots – or maybe not. The beer delivery man came around the corner looking for John and Hando, but they were long gone. The man didn't have a gun in his hand, so what were those loud noises? The man didn't even look at me and I held tight until he turned and walked back to his truck. He never suspected I was with them. When I caught up with John and Hando, I asked them what those bangs were because I thought they were being shot at. They said they were firecrackers from the house right across the alley from the convenient store! It certainly fooled me. Sometimes I think that moment was a microcosm of our summer.

On probably the hottest day of the year, we drove up to Topeka in my old Dodge to run a track meet. I hadn't had the opportunity to run a meet all summer, and I was looking forward to competing in this unattached meet at Highland Park High School, called the Sunflower Classic. I entered one race, the 800m, in order to give myself the best chance to run a PR and maybe even break two minutes. I had trained well, usually with John, and I felt ready for a good effort. Unfortunately, I wouldn't have the chance to compete against John because I was just old enough to be entered in the open division for 19–29-year-olds, even though I was still 18 at the time. John entered the 3000m run as well as the 800m, but they were in the high school division. Hando, who traveled with us selected not to race.

We drove the 150 miles early in the morning and it took quite a while to get there. During those years, the speed limit was 55, and even though I rarely drove that speed, the highway was teaming with law enforcement, so I had to take it easy on the pedal. This meant we were already a bit tired because my car didn't have air-conditioning and despite the early morning excursion, the weather was already hot. The first event was the 3000m around 8:00 or 9:00am, and the temperature was already in the mid-90s. John looked hot and pale during the race and wasn't pushed at all. Still, he didn't seem too exhausted after running around 9:20. I think he could have run under 9 minutes with competition, even with the heat and humidity. Then we both had to wait for hours until the late afternoon to compete again.

The trouble was that we remained at the track and mostly in the sun waiting for the 800m as the temperature rose above 110 degrees. At least the humidity burned away! During the 400m dash, a high school girl collapsed after crossing the finish line and had to be taken away in an ambulance. I think she might have been the young women who ran 54 seconds that year, but I'm not sure. Later that night, I watched the 10 o'clock news on a Topeka channel and they showed the girl's collapse. I was so hot that I didn't even realize that a TV crew was there, and I must have been standing right next to them while they recorded the end of the girl's 400 because the view on the screen was right where I was standing. The sports segment also showed a tennis tournament in Topeka that day and said it was over 130 degrees on the courts, which meant it was at least that hot on the black-surfaced track.

Finally, the 800m run arrived. John's high school division was first, and he out-kicked a competitor to win in 1:59. Next was the open division race. I don't remember how many were in the race, but the competition looked formidable. My strategy was to stay with the leader for the first lap and then see how much longer I could remain in that position. I thought this would carry me to a good time. I did just that but didn't hear the time of the first lap. I think I was told later it was about 55 seconds, which was much too fast for me, especially in that heat. I could feel the pace in my legs and in my breathing. My chest burned and the heat was draining me more with every step. I was passed on the back stretch by three runners, two of them identical blond-haired twins. It was all I could do to stay close to the twins, and all I could do to finish. When I crossed the line in 5th place, I thought I was going to collapse and even pass out. I couldn't recover and had to be helped off the track. My time was a slow 2:09. The winner ran 1:55, and we heard after the race that he was the Big 8 800m conference champion from Iowa State University. I don't know if I ever heard his name, so I can't verify if this is true. In 1980, Iowa States' best 800m runner was David Korir, but I don't know if it was him. Korir ran 1:46 for ISU that year, and 1:55 in that heat without competition seems reasonable, but who knows. I've never found the results on-line. Whoever it was, he was a lot better than me!

After the race I couldn't recover, no matter what I did. My head was pounding, and it felt as if my insides were burning up. We finally left the track after receiving our awards. We got into my car that had been closed up all day in that heat. It was like an oven, and it was probably close to the same temperature. We drove to a nearby grocery store to get something to drink, but to also find air conditioning. I bought a half gallon of orange juice, and we went to a sit-down soda fountain in the store where I drank that whole bottle in about a minute. I don't know how long it took to recover enough to leave, but I know it was at least a half hour. My chest was killing me as if I'd breathed in fire, and I was so lightheaded that I could hardly stand. In retrospect, changing temperatures so quickly from hot to overly cool was probably not the best idea because I was as cold as could be in that store, but I couldn't get myself to leave. When we finally left, we rolled down all the windows and headed back to Parsons. The hot breeze rushing through the windows didn't help much, but at least it wasn't still. At one point Hando and I began to talk to John, who was sitting in the front passenger seat, and he never heard a word we said. He was so hot that he completely spaced out. It's the worst conditions in which I ever raced.

The Region 8 AAU meet was held at Southeast Missouri State University in Cape Girardeau, Missouri, which was a hell of a long way from Parsons. To help pay for the trip I went to Arvon for gas money and to see if he might find us cheap lodging. As luck would have it, Arvon had once held a similar rec center position in Cape. He knew an old woman there who he said would be tickled to have us stay the night at her home. There were four of us going because our old teammate, Ron Faulkenberry decided to go as well. Ron had finished his freshman year at the University of Kansas and was home for the summer. With the Oldsmobile filled with oil, the radiator topped off, and with gas money and a place to stay, the four off were ready for our 400-mile trip to Cape Girardeau.

Ron loved to drive long distances, so he took the wheel of the large "boat" as we hit the highway. When we got to Joplin, Missouri, just across the border from Kansas we hit I44 and headed toward Springfield. We hadn't gone too far when we heard a horrible noise from the bottom of the car, and then the rubber of one of the tires came flying off. We pulled over and the tread was completely gone, but the tire was still inflated, so we proceeded on the shoulder with our flashers on until we came to the next exit with a service station. The man at the station said he had what we needed and that the whole thing would only cost us about $90. I said that was too much and asked if they had a used re-tread, which they did!

It ended up only costing us $10, and we didn't lose much time at all. We hit the interstate again and didn't get too far when we heard another horrible noise, but this time it was from under the hood. Now I've never been much of a mechanic, but I could tell that not all the cylinders were working. We pulled off I44 again at a small town and found a garage on their main road through the community. The mechanic looked under the hood and quickly noticed that we had blown a sparkplug, which he said he had never seen. As soon as the motor cooled enough, he put the plug back in place, charged us $10, and we headed toward Springfield again, wondering what could happen next. Luckily, the Olds held together for the rest of the trip! I'm thankful the tread didn't fly off west of Olathe when I was driving over 120 mph!

We reached Cape in the late afternoon and had a little trouble finding the home where we were to stay. We were grid people, and Cape roads were not the least bit straight. But we finally found the house, and the old lady treated us extremely well and fed us a great dinner. The next morning, she cooked a full breakfast for us, and you could tell she was in heaven hosting us and treating us to good meals. I wish I could remember her name, and I'm sure she is no longer living, but she was the sweetest, nicest women. Hando complained because he said the breakfast made him sick, but I think it was something else because the rest of us survived just fine. After breakfast we headed for the track, which we had found the night before so we wouldn't get lost the next morning.

The weather was already hot when we arrived at the track, which was brand new and looked very fast. Cape Girardeau is located on the Mississippi River, so in addition to the hot weather, it was also extremely humid. For some reason the 800m was contested before the 1500. In all my years in and around track and field, this is the only one-day meet in which I've seen the 800m before the 1500 or mile. I don't know who came up with the idea, but it was either a meet official who didn't know what he was doing (and yes, he, because women weren't meet officials in 1980), or he was drunk. I'm not sure it made a difference to John which race was first because either way, he was running two races. I thought John's best race was the 800, but I think he was beginning to think it was the 1500m. So, running the 1500 first would give him the best chance to qualify in that race. In retrospect, I think he was correct, but it didn't matter because the 800 was first.

Sometime before the start of the 800, Jon Piles arrived, and we hung out for a while. Just about the time that Piles and John were going to warm up together, this fairly tall kid came up to us where we were standing in the little bit of shade we could find and asked us if we were entered in the 800. John and Piles indicated they were. At that point John walked away, because he wasn't one for small talk with a competitor before a race unless he knew him. But Piles and I stayed and talked with him for a minute or so. He asked Piles what his best time was, and he proudly proclaimed "1:54," which I would have done as well if I had run that fast. Piles asked him what his best was, and he said 1:51, which he said he ran at the Atlanta Classic. I don't know why, but not only do I remember his time and where he ran it, but I remember his name as well – Cornelius Tate. He said he was from West Memphis, Arkansas. I could see that Piles was shocked and when Tate left, he looked at me and asked if I thought he had run that fast. At the State AAU, I had attempted to psyche out Piles, but I had no reason to do that here, so I told him that I didn't think Tate had actually run that fast, although in reality, I suspected that he was telling the truth.

Piles and John talked that morning about both making it to nationals in the 800, and to do so, they had to take first and second because only the top two qualified. But the Region 8 meet consisted of the states of Kansas, Missouri, Oklahoma, and Arkansas, and we didn't know how good those from the other states were. Like Tate, the other areas could have great half-milers entered as well. The Missouri Valley meet was Kansas and western Missouri, so John and Piles hadn't seen the kids from the St. Louis area, which was a gold mine of talent. And Oklahoma was known to have good runners as well. By the time the 800m was run in the early afternoon, it was already 108 degrees, and unlike Topeka, the humidity remained. I could tell that John was nervous, as, I think, was Piles. But Ron, Hando, and I were nervous as well because we knew this would be John's toughest race of the year. Ron had never seen John run under 2:00 and was looking forward to witnessing a good race from him.

When the race started, it was clear that Tate was not exaggerating his time. I took a photograph of the race just after the break, and

Tate is in the lead, wearing basketball socks up to his knees, with a huge stride, and the rest of the runners straining to keep up. John made a tactical decision not to attempt to stay with Tate, which was a very good move. Tate hit the 400m in 52 seconds, which was not only fast but even more so in the heat and humidity. Although John was in the middle of the pack, he still ran 54 seconds for his 400m split. This was the fastest he had ever gone out. In comparison, he ran his first lap in 57 seconds at the State High School meet. Even Tate couldn't keep that pace, but he burned off most of the competition without sacrificing his race. John moved up on the backstretch, and coming off the last curve, he moved into second place and ran away from third. He crossed the line in second in 1:56.3, behind Tate's 1:55.4. John's tactics were brilliant because if he had attempted to stay with the leader, I doubt he would have qualified for Nationals. Unfortunately, Piles fell back a few places and finished the race with a 1:59, which he said was the slowest he had run since he was a sophomore. Though he wasn't going to Nationals, Piles was headed to Kansas State University to run track.

Years later, after I moved to Arkansas, I looked up Tate on the internet and found that not only was he telling the truth about his 1:51, but he was still the fastest high school 800m runner to ever come out of the state, and that was not broken until 2023, when two runners ran faster, in a race I witnessed because I had an athlete entered. I'm not sure John was cognizant of what he had accomplished, because he was about to pass out. I had to help him off the track. There was a small tent set up on the infield for athletes who qualified for Nationals to declare. The woman at the tent asked John if he intended to compete at Nationals, but I'm not sure he heard her, so I answered yes for him. I then helped him to a shady area on the east side of the track where he passed out. We were naïve at that time and never considered getting John medical attention – that would never occur today. We would have medical staff there as quick as we could. When John finally came to, he asked how he did in the race. I told him what he had done, and he began to remember. Once he was able to get up and walk, we took him to a laundromat that had air-conditioning to help him recover and hopefully enough to be able to run a good 1500m.

Clearly, the extreme heat had taken its toll on John, and we were skeptical whether John could pull off another good race that day. Today, the AAU Junior Olympics is different than it was in 1980. For one, there are a lot more age divisions. But today, those competing in an age division, remain in that division all the way to the national meet. At that time the Intermediate Division (15/16-year-olds) was combined with the Senior Division (17/18), and I don't believe there was a national meet held for younger kids. In our area, the Senior and Intermediate Divisions were combined at the Missouri Valley Meet. That was significant at the Region 8 Meet in 1980, because some of the best in the 1500 were in the 15/16 age group. John had nothing left to give in the 1500m and the pace was fairly fast. Gradually, John fell off the pace and finished well back of the winner. I don't even remember how fast he ran, but it was no better than 4:12 and might have been a few seconds slower. The winner was Jim Jennings from Missouri, who was one of those Intermediate kids. He ran 4:01, and Jeff Pigg, who I also think was 15 or 16 years old, took second. I don't know what place Jennings got at Nationals, but I do know he set the Intermediate record in 3:59, and I'm sure it was against the senior level competition. That record wasn't bettered until 2018. I was at the stadium at Drake University when another Missouri kid broke it. As a senior, Jennings ran a 4:09 mile. In college I ran against Jennings and Pigg in a couple of small summer meets.

Throughout the summer, the three of us drove around town talking for most of the night on many occasions. We wouldn't even be drinking on these nights, so we weren't breaking any laws. There was a curfew law in town, but I was old enough that it didn't apply to me, and I don't think it affected John and Hando either. These were usually the nights John, and I ran at Forest Park. I wish I could remember some of the conversations because it's possible some

159

were pretty deep. If I worked in the hay fields the following day, I made it a practice not to stay out too late because I needed to get enough sleep to work well. Bailing hay could be a dangerous job and I wanted to be alert. But when John, Hando, and I had the chance to drive around half the night, we did.

I trained with John to help prepare him for Junior Olympic Nationals and to get me ready for Coffeyville. One of our favorite workouts was repeat work at Forest Park. We usually did our workouts at the park separately so we could time each other. We would run three to five repeats around the outside of the sixth tenths of a mile Park, which was the same route we did our late-night runs. John was always faster than me in this workout. I think he ran 2:45 for his fastest, and my best was just a little under three minutes. We did other workouts as well. One day I got the idea that the *Parsons Sun* should get a picture of John training for Nationals and do a little story, after all the paper did report his results for the summer meets, because I submitted them. To my surprise the *Sun* agreed to the request. I set it up to have the photographer take a picture of John training while he ran down Main Street. The photographer stationed himself in front of the Parsons Junior High School for our early morning run, and as we got a couple blocks away, I slowed down so I could drop back. I didn't want to be in the photo and had no reason to be in the picture. The photo ran in the paper within a couple of days. I also got John on the radio with the Captain one last time.

As I had done for the previous meets, I went to the Recreation Center and asked Arvon for money to send John to Junior Olympic Nationals. The meet was held in San Jose, California, and would not be cheap. The participants could stay in dorms, but the travel costs were high. Arvon didn't have the budget for this trip, so he went to the local banks and asked for them to donate, which they did. John came from a very low-income family, and there is no way they could have sent him to California on their own. I could get John to an airport, but that was it. And John would make this trip on his own.

Arvon helped John get a flight from Wichita to California, and I got him to Wichita.

A couple of days before we took John to Wichita, I was playing pool at the Rec Center with a high school friend named Calvin. It felt good to be inside because the severe heat. Calvin was a good guy. He had been on the track team when he was a sophomore, but his season ended late in the year when he broke his leg during a fight in gym class. In fact, I was there when it happened and when his leg snapped it sounded like a tree branch breaking. Calvin was in a hell of a lot of pain, and the kid he was fighting attempted to settle him down. His adversary, Tim, knew pain as well. In the fall during our ninth-grade year, he accidently shot himself playing with a pistol. Calvin was in the hospital most of the summer in traction and I went out to see him two or three times. And he came to see me in the hospital when I had my surgery during the winter of 1980. At the Rec Center, as we played pool, we talked about John running at nationals. When I left the rec, I saw Calvin walking at the northwest corner of Forest Park, where John and I always started our repeat workouts. We waved to each other – that was the last time I saw him. Late the following afternoon, we heard tons of sirens close by while sitting outside at John's house. It was just a few blocks away down by Labette Creek, and close to where Calvin lived, but we didn't think about that. Later that evening while getting gas at a convenient store, a kid I graduated with named Doug, drove up and told John, Hando, and me that Calvin had committed suicide by shooting himself – he was dead.

We headed to Wichita in my Dodge the day before John was to leave for Junior Olympics. Hando's dad took us out to eat, and we stayed in another cheap motel. The next morning, we took John to the airport, and when his flight left, Hando and I headed to the other side of town and stopped at Town East Mall. I needed to be back in Parsons by late in the afternoon, so I told Hando we couldn't stay long. Finally, while we were in J.C. Penny's, I told him it was time to leave. He said OK and as we left the store, he handed me a J.C. Penny's bag and said he would meet me at the car in a few minutes. In the car I threw the bag in the back seat and waited. But after a long while, I decided to go back inside to find him. I could only imagine what the hell he had got himself into. I was parked on the east side of the mall, so I entered on that side and walked the corridor to the main part of the mall. There I saw Hando in a jewelry store situated in a corner shop. He smiled and waved, so I headed back to the car thinking he was about to come out.

I waited for another long while and decided that I needed to drag his ass out so we could leave. I figured that he had moved on from the jewelry store, so I entered through other doors. When I reached the main mall area, I walked south. When I reached the jewelry store where I had seen Hando, I saw a lot of people rushing around in a panic. I knew immediately what that meant, so I high tailed it out to the parking lot where I saw the police chasing someone between the cars, and they had their guns drawn! I could see Hando's head popping up a couple of times looking to see where the police were, and I sensed that he couldn't find my car. The cops yelled for him to stop, or they might shoot. Then Hando got to the edge of a busy road that bordered the east side of the mall parking lot and sprinted across the traffic. It's a miracle he didn't get run over. I didn't know what to do, but I walked back to the car and decided to leave. But then I thought that there was no way they could catch him and if I drove through the neighborhood calling out his name, he could jump in my window, and we would get out of town as quick as possible.

I never found him and so I decided to leave. Then I made a stupid decision. I decided I couldn't leave Hando behind – he was a friend – so I went back to the mall to see if he had been caught. I parked the car and headed for the door Hando had run out and several people were discussing the incident. So, I asked what happened, and a couple of people said the police caught some Mexican kid and brought him back into the mall through this door. I was mad now, so

I headed to the jewelry store to find out what exactly happened. I told a cop that I knew Hando, but didn't know what he had done, although without telling the police, I had a strong suspicion. The cop was friendly and took down some information when Hando was led out of the store by an over-weight plain-clothed cop with a mustache. He asked me who I was, and I said I was his friend. As we got outside, the fat cop told the officers standing with me to watch me as he went back inside. The police officers and I were having a conversation, and Hando sat in the front of the police car smiling.

Suddenly, the plain-clothed cop came rushing out of the doors pointing at me saying "arrest that man!" Then the cops around me were not too nice anymore. As I was searched, I was so angry, that I began to insult the police. They handcuffed me and they asked me to take them to my car. We walked to my car and when we got there the cop car with Hando pulled up behind. Hando kept getting his handcuffed arms to his front and one of the officers said, "Hando quit doing that." As they searched my car, they found the J.C. Penny's bag, without a receipt. They looked at me and I said, "not mine." Then they looked at Hando through the rolled-up window and asked him, and he smiled and shook his head yes. I guess after hitting a jewelry store, what was a few bucks from Penny's? Then they threw me in the back seat of the same patrol car as Hando, and we headed downtown. Thank goodness I had checked the car a couple of years before, just after we bought the vehicle, because I found quite a bit of drug paraphilia. I don't know what would have happened to me if that stuff was still in that Dodge.

On the way to the main police station, Hando kept making jokes, and said he would have plenty of time to train for the Olympics now, and he referenced the TV movie "The Jericho Mile." The cop who was sitting with me in the back seat had the merchandise Hando had stolen, and he was making jokes that these items weren't worth what was listed on the price tags. He stole two items – a diamond ring with a price tag of $1500 and a gold-plated men's watch listed at $450. I can't say whether these items were worth the listed price, but I knew Hando had stolen $2000 of stuff, and that's a felony.

When we arrived at the downtown police headquarters, we were taken by elevator to a floor several stories up and when we arrived in the main area of the floor, a cop looked at us, wrung his hands, and said "we got two of them this time!" At that point they separated us and took us in different directions. They placed me in a small interrogation room with a metal table that was bolted to the floor and handcuffed me to the table. I sat in a small uncomfortable metal chair. The room was cold, and the metal table was cold as well. After a while I laid my head down and went to sleep.

I don't know how long I was in the room before they came to speak with me, because I had no reference point, but it was a long time. When he finally arrived, the detective told me if I wanted to talk without a lawyer, I had to sign a form. I said that I didn't need an attorney, and I told him what I knew, without revealing that I had actually looked for Hando at first. Then he came back and said I was free to go. They told me to stay out a Wichita for a while. Then they conveniently lost the key to the handcuffs. It was shift change at the station, and when they finally found the key, they took me down to the patrol car area, where I waited another half hour for a cop to show up to take me to my car. On the way to Town East Mall, the policeman pulled over a car on Kellogg and wrote the person a ticket, delaying my return even more. When I finally arrived in Parsons several hours later, my parents were not happy, and I had missed an appointment. My dad called his attorney with the Paine Ratner firm in Wichita, and they called back assuring him that I was not in any trouble.

Although I was advised to stay out of Wichita, I had to return three days later to pick up John. I waited at the gate for John to get off the plane, and when he did, the first thing he said to me was "Where's Hando." He could sense something wasn't right. I said, "I don't know, probably jail." Then I told him the story, and he just shook his head.

John hadn't performed well at Junior Olympic Nationals and didn't make finals. I asked him what won the finals, and he said 1:49. I told John that although he was talented, I didn't think he could have run that fast, and he agreed. The winner was John Marshall who made the 1984 Olympic team in the 800m. His meet record stood for close to 35 years. I saw the record get broken a few years ago by a kid from St. Louis, Charles Jones.

After we returned to Parsons, I dropped John off and headed home. It was a long week. Later in the evening I spent some time with John, and he said he saw Hando who told him the jewelry store didn't press charges, and his dad took him home. Amazingly, he didn't get in any trouble for the jewelry "Heist." Many years later, John's mother told me that John had wanted me to go to San Jose with him because I was the steady hand that could have had him in the right frame of mind to run well and keep him on schedule.

This was the last of our summer, and I didn't see Hando again until I came home from school a few weekends later. John and I went swimming at the public pool a couple more times before the start of the fall semester. We went swimming there several times that summer because Coach Billions managed the pool and let John and I swim for free. It was an odd summer, and I learned a lesson or two in the process. Hando told me later that if there was ever another incident in which he was arrested, to just leave him. I told him there would never be another incident like that, but there was – and I left him.

Chapter 7
Future Stars

I didn't know what I was getting myself into, but I was excited and nervous about college. I took my old Dodge and drove the 35 miles to Coffeyville, and when I got to town, I drove by the burned-out shell of the auditorium I had just visited three months before. It was still standing, and as I was to find out, there was still athletic equipment inside that wasn't damaged. Not long after I started school, me and a few of my new teammates went inside to gather some stuff to move to a temporary athletics complex on the northwest side of town that I think was at a park. Inside the burned hull was a severely warped basketball floor caused by the water the fire department used to put out the fire. A strange site was the rims that were bright orange, and what appeared to be new nets. Surely the fire would have damaged these things, but they looked brand new. Maybe it was a weird joke.

When I checked in at the dorm, I was told my new roommate was another runner, Eric Freeman, from Baldwin, Kansas. When I went in Eric had already put his stuff in the room and selected his bed, but he was nowhere to be found. A kid across the hall said he went out drinking with two roommates that lived in the suite. There were four rooms per suite with two people per room, and there was a bathroom and a lobby. The kid across the hall was a new track teammate, Carl Brown out of Wichita South High School. He was a sophomore and was a long sprinter and ran the 800m as well. Carl was a terrific guy and became an excellent teammate. Later in the night, Eric showed up drunk as could be. At that point I couldn't tell what kind of guy he was because he was too inebriated.

School began the next week, so after a couple of days in the dorms, I headed home for the weekend and returned for the start of school on Monday. Eric turned out to be a pretty good guy, although he and I were completely different people. Eric liked to put up the Playboy and Penthouse centerfolds on his wall and I always knew when his father, who was a minister, was coming because the photos were nowhere to be found. I'd say, "so your dad is coming by today?" and he'd say "yeah," with a real frown! Eric's brother also attended Coffeyville, or at least a trade school close by, and Eric attended the trade school as well through the Community College. I only ran with Eric once or twice that fall because he didn't seem to really like the sport, but I might be wrong. And he wasn't a bad runner. He took 3rd in the Class 4A 1600m and 5th in the 3200m run. After the fall semester Eric decided to transfer to Haskell Indian College in Lawrence, Kansas, and his brother left as well. I only saw Eric once after that when we ran a track meet at Haskell in the spring.

Although I went to Coffeyville to run cross-country as well as track, we never had formal practice in the fall – we just ran on our own. But I did get to know the core of my track teammates who weren't football players. In the spring, our team would grow as football players became part of the team. In junior college, spring football practice didn't exist, so some of the guys competed in track and field. During the fall, I didn't get the opportunity to know any of these guys, but I would become friends with some of them during track. The Coffeyville Community College Red Ravens football team was great – really great!

During the fall of 1980, the track teammates I got to know the best were Brown, and his Wichita South teammate, Verl McGaughy, as well as Jerome Phillips and Kenny Mitchell, both from Cooley High

School in Detroit. Early in the fall semester, I took Kenny to the local Walmart so he could buy a TV. He picked out the television he wanted, paid in the electronics area, and with TV and receipt in hand, walked to the front of the store to leave. As we got to the doors to exit, a worker stopped him because he thought he was stealing. This pissed off Kenny to no end because the receipt was visible in his hand. It was clear to me, and I'm sure to Kenny, that the reason he was stopped was because he was black. I hadn't thought about those issues too much in my life, but I was becoming more aware as I became an adult.

Kenny was a terrific guy and a pretty good sprinter. He was also a bit crazy. Half the time, when he got excited, I couldn't understand a word he said, but every other word was profanity. He'd come over to our dorm after dark on a regular basis to talk wearing nothing more than his pajamas. I also became a good friend with Dave Lusk, who was a shot putter from Mulvane, Kansas. Dave was a sophomore and after a couple of practices in the winter of 1981, decided not to compete anymore. Many evenings, while hanging out in Dave's dorm lobby, Kenny would stroll by in his PJs and stick around to chew the fat. Some of Dave's suitemates were from Iran, and they made a rice dish, if that's the best word to use, that was similar in taste to popcorn – it was great. One of the Iranian guys, who seemed older and might have lived somewhere else, was a self-proclaimed communist, and would talk shit all the time. He was very nice, and never confrontational, but his communist rhetoric didn't sway us in the least. He would invite us to walk 20 miles with him so he could talk to us about his political and economic philosophy. I don't think any of us ever took that walk.

I know the Iranian guys put up with a lot of crap. This was the time of the Iranian Hostage Crisis, and anyone who even remotely looked Iranian was viewed with suspicion. But I guess these guys got along OK. There were also two or three guys from Japan who lived in the dorms close by and hung out quite a bit as well. We'd spend time in the Student Center playing video games, and if one of these guys, I think his name was Toshe (I don't remember the spelling), got on the Asteroids game before you, then you had a long wait. I don't play video games anymore, and I couldn't tell you what game apps there are today, and don't care, but in the early 1980s, I spent far too much time on these addictive arcade games, and in 1980 and 81, Asteroids was my obsession. As time went on, I matriculated to other video games.

Early in the fall, I ran my first road race, which took place in Parsons. The race was hosted by the Recreation Center, and by a local Coors distributor, and was called the Coors Fun Run. A Rec Center employee told me that I had no chance to win because one of the guys competing was a wrestler from Labette Community College, and he was "good." There were two races, a 10K and a 3.2-mile race. You might think this is a typo, because the 5K is a 3.1-mile race, but because Kansas had 3.2 beer that was sold in regular stores, 3.2 miles was the distance of the race. I ran with Hando, and early on we took control. We decided to run across the line together hand-in-hand just like Tony Sandoval and Jeff Wells had the previous September in the Nike OTC Marathon. I don't remember our time, and it was not listed in the article about the race, but I do know we ran it in 18 minutes and something, a slower pace than Sandoval and Wells averaged per mile in their marathon! I think the Labette wrestler was 3rd, a fair distance back, but yes, he was a pretty good runner. I also won my first trophy, as Hando decided to let me receive it.

Because we didn't have scheduled practice, my training for Coffeyville cross-country was erratic. We had three meets on the schedule and had four runners who were officially on the team. Eric must have already decided to transfer because he wasn't included. Our first meet was hosted by Butler Community College in El Dorado, Kansas. Our coach, Dale Burkholder, was an assistant football coach, so he didn't come with us. In fact, we didn't have a coach with us, just an 18-year-old kid, who was a red-shirt football player, who drove us. Coach Burkholder was the new track coach, and he had called me over the summer to discuss my goals, but I hadn't met him until I got to campus. The Butler meet was the regular 5 miles. For me, this could as very well been a marathon. I was a half-miler, and five miles was an extremely long race. Sure, I ran more than five miles in training, but that's a lot different than racing.

Verl, Carl, and Jerome were the other Coffeyville runners, so we didn't have the required five to make a full team, meaning we wouldn't score as a team. I didn't start out too bad, but before long, the race began to feel long. I remember running in one direction and seeing the leader on the other side of some trees running the opposite way. He was from Haskell, and I think his name was Edison Eskeets, and he looked to be sprinting with a forward lean. He won the race in about 24:45. I ended up being our number one man in 30:15. I sure thought I would break 30 minutes; after all, that was only a 6-minute per-mile pace, and I think I had done that in practice for at least 5 or 6 miles. I don't know what place I got, but I did beat a few guys. I don't think my three teammates were too far behind me.

For some reason, the date on the schedule for our second meet was incorrect, so we missed that one. Before the third scheduled meet I placed myself on the disabled list. While standing on the step, in front of Dave's dorm, someone threw a Frisbee to me. As it got closer, I could tell it was going to fly way over my head, and maybe on the roof of the one-story dorm, so I jumped and caught the thing about 10 to 11 feet above the ground, and when I came down, only the inside of my left foot landed on the step, and I went down hard. I had severely sprained my ankle, but I didn't know how serious it was. What I did know was that I couldn't put any weight on that foot. For the next several days, I hobbled around the best I could, and then when the weekend came, I went to a Kansas football game with my cousin Phillip. On the way, we stopped in Iola to watch the Southeast

Kansas League High School cross-country meet before continuing to Lawrence.

On Sunday, when I woke up, my ankle was in terrible shape. The combination of hobble-running at the meet and walking up and down the steps at KU's Memorial Stadium played havoc on my ankle. By Monday, when I returned to Coffeyville, my left foot and ankle were as bad as they had been the previous week. I finely went to the athletic office to see what could be done, and after Coach Foster lectured me about not coming over the week before, he sent me to see the team doctor, who worked in a clinic close by. After X-rays, the doctor told me that my sprain was excessively bad and that I had torn some ligaments. He placed me in a cast that allowed my foot to move up and down but kept it stable enough not to let my ankle bend side to side. So, I missed the cross-country meet, which my teammates said was a peculiar race. Apparently, it was run like a relay, in which each runner ran a mile, and a teammate took over. Each runner ran several individual miles. But because I wasn't there, I'm not sure how it worked, and I don't remember where the race took place.

That was the last meet, so I hadn't had a real opportunity to experience a cross-country season. My ankle took what I thought was an extraordinarily long time to heal. In addition, during the summer, I hurt my back and went to see a chiropractor before I could work in the hay fields. My back no longer hurt, but it lacked flexibility, and I couldn't seem to get that worked out. Even after I got the cast off my foot and ankle, it wasn't easy to run. The doctor told me to keep my left leg elevated when I slept. In the morning, when I put my foot back on the floor, the blood rushing to my foot was excruciatingly painful. But gradually, even that got better. By the time Christmas break arrived, I was running normally again, although my ankle lacked flexibility and was still oddly shaped.

I'm not sure if my first college semester was uneventful, but it seemed that way. Most of the excitement I had was when I was in

Parsons for the weekends. But after a very eventful summer, a quieter fall was needed. Although we didn't have organized cross-country practice, track was a different matter, and we were told to be in shape come January. I looked forward to track season because I wanted to see if I had improved and whether the hernia surgery, I had the previous February slowed me as much as I thought. Although I was now 19 years old, I didn't see that there was that much difference in me physically from track my senior year in high school, although I had grown from 6' 1" to 6' 2". I felt it would be a good gauge as to how I might have done during the spring of 1980. Although this didn't really make a lot of difference, and certainly didn't change how I actually did, for me it was important. Nonetheless, I have felt for many years that the key to success in a race is using your strength to take advantage of the weaknesses of the other competitors. If one of my weaknesses during the 1980 track season was that I had surgery, then that was my issue, and the others needed to take advantage of my lack of training. Some did, but many others didn't. In the spring of 1981, I didn't have that excuse, so I needed to perform or shut up!

There are certain events that occur in life that we remember. On my 19th birthday, I was at Pittsburg State University in John's dorm room, and I had a great time along with Hando. John and I drank enough that we decided to run through the cemetery after dark, which was situated right next to his dorm. This was December 6, 1980. Two days later, as I watched Monday Night Football, along with a few million others, I heard Howard Cosell tell the country that John Lennon had been murdered. I've never been the type to place others on pedestals like gods, but Lennon was a true music legend and genius. He transcended the idea of a rock star and was even bigger than that without acting like it, at least as I saw him as a fan. It was devastating for so many, and I think I was one of those.

Not long after December 8, the semester was over, and I was back in Parsons for Christmas break. A family tradition was that we went over to my aunt and uncle's house, the Mercado's, and made holiday tamales. My cousin Mike, who worked for the MKT Railroad had to go to Denison, Texas for a meeting with a co-worker. At the last minute he asked me and his brother Phillip if we wanted to take the trip with him, and we said yes. It was already in the afternoon when we left, and by the time we were 50 miles or so in Oklahoma, it was dark. We caught a radio station in Oklahoma that we listened to all the way to Texas, which was playing a tribute to John Lennon. Mike was a huge Beatles fan, but Phillip kept saying he didn't like the group and didn't care for Lennon's solo stuff either. But every song they played he said he liked. After a while, me and Mike told Phillip that he had to like the Beatles, because he had listened to 10 or 15 songs and hadn't found one he didn't like. I'm not sure he ever admitted that he liked the Beatles, but Mike and I were in music heaven, even though the reason for the tribute was a somber one.

During the Christmas break, I spent time in Pittsburg with John. Hando, John, and I hung out, and we got into some training as well. During the fall, John's mom moved to Pittsburg, so we stayed at her house. One night, we all stayed at her home, sleeping on the floor in a small room. John's mom and youngest sister were the only ones not in that small bedroom. Those in the cramped room were John and his girlfriend, Hando, me, John's brothers Jerry and Joe, his sister, and three or four others I didn't know. At one point, as Aerosmith's *Toys in the Attic* played on a loop throughout the night, I turned over and saw the moonlight illuminate a bare female breast, and within 5 seconds, John's mom slammed open the door and yelled, "Not in my house." I don't know how she knew John had his girlfriend's top off, but she did. That stopped any shenanigans the rest of the night.

During the fall, I read in some running magazines that the training wave of the future was running 5 or 6 times a day, so I thought I'd give it a try during the break. The article laid out the plan, and for the most part, it was a series of shorter runs, usually 3 to 5 miles. On the first day of this experiment, Hando ran some of the runs with me. The second day, I ran on my own, and I realized that this was impractical, at least for me. And it would be especially unattainable when I returned to school because of my class schedule. I didn't attempt this training program on the third day and would never try anything like this again, although in the years to come, it was not uncommon for me to run three times a day.

In many ways, my time spent in Coffeyville is like it happened to another person. Looking back, it's as if it went by so quickly, and I wonder if it happened to me, even though I know it did. I'm not sure I actually got to know Eric Freeman, it's a flash-in-the-pan encounter. When I returned from Christmas break, I didn't have a roommate, but after a short time, I was assigned one. He didn't last too long before moving in with his girlfriend. I think he thought I didn't want him there, and he was correct, although it wasn't fair to him. I never gave him a chance, but he was a decent guy. Still, much of this is a blur. But he was a huge fan of AC/DC's *Back in Black,* and I allowed him to play my album when I wasn't around.

The one thing I do remember is the stink of Coffeyville. And I mean a literal horrible smell, or more of a rank odor, or odors. If the wind blew from the southwest, a bizarre, unexplainable, wretched stink came from the appropriately named Funks. I don't have a clue what Funks manufactured other than funky smell. If the wind drove down from the northwest, a bold rank of old body odor bellowed from the depth of the pit called Sherwin-Williams. And I don't mean the smell of someone who hasn't bathed in a few days, but I mean someone who reeks of not showering for months. Finally, on the rare occasion that the breeze whipped from the east, the pleasant odor came from a natural gas refinery. Believe me, it was quite beautiful!

I can't say I enjoyed my stay at Coffeyville Community College, but I can't say I didn't either. I made some good friends there. But to me, at least on the surface, Coffeyville was similar to Parsons – a town going nowhere. But underneath, I think Coffeyville might have been a little more progressive in business than my hometown. Coffeyville never seemed to be dying (despite the smell of death that permeated its borders) like Parsons. When we moved to Parsons in the late 1960s, it seemed so vibrant, which might have been the delusion of a kid, but urban renewal came in during the early 1970s and destroyed the town's character and soul. At least Coffeyville had a soul when I was there. Parsons was a community without a cultural and identity center. To me then, Coffeeville was a breath of fresh air, or wretchedness as it were. Regardless, it was great to be out of Parsons five days a week, if only by 35 miles.

Spring practice began in January with the start of the second semester. I don't remember running a lot of distance, but we did put together a number of spirited sprint and pace workouts. I had the opportunity to practice with several damn fast sprinters. Those doing middle distance did run some different workouts than the sprinters, but we did enough work with the sprinters to be beneficial. Besides Kenny Mitchell, we also had three football players who were the best athletes I've ever been teammates with. Melvin Gray, out of Virginia, was blazing fast. I believe he held the National High School record for 300m indoors at that time. Melvin was a running back and not that big, but he was tough. After two years at Coffeyville, he transferred to Purdue and then had a long career as a punt and kickoff specialist in the NFL. I think when he retired, Melvin was the all-time leader in kickoff and punt return yardage. I know that one year, he placed second in the fastest man in the NFL competition behind Darrell Green. It was not too bad finishing behind, in my opinion, the fastest man to ever play in the NFL. Maybe Bob Hayes might dispute this! Brian Smith was a second sprinter. He was a big, powerful running back who transferred to Ohio State after his first year, but I never saw him play there, and I never learned what happened to him.

On a trip to the University of Kansas for an indoor meet, I was asleep in the back of the van next to another one of the football sprinters.

During that time, I wore a gray cap or beanie, and I even ran with it sometimes. As I woke up, I placed my cap on, and the football player next to me asked me in a perturbed tone why I put his cap on my head. I was probably too dumb to be scared, and I shot back, "Man, this is my cap!" Then he realized that it was indeed my beanie that looked almost exactly like his, which was sitting on the seat next to him. I think he respected that not only had I stood up to him but that I also had the good taste to wear a cap like his. At any rate, Mike Rozier, from Camden, New Jersey, was a good sprinter, an even better javelin thrower, and a great football player. He was a junior college All-American and transferred to Nebraska after his first year, where he led the country in rushing his senior year with over 2,000 yards and won the Heisman Trophy. And that 1983 Nebraska team had what I think is the most powerful offense in the history of NCAA football. Rozier played professional football for several years, first in the USFL, and was an all-pro in the NFL. Melvin and Mike were future stars.

Many on the track team said that Rozier wasn't the fastest sprinter on our team until he put the pads on. He was a compact, strong man. He might have only been 19 years old, but he was physically a man, more than anyone on the team. I was probably three inches taller than Mike and physically mature and strong myself, but there was no comparison between the two of us. Mike was a human muscle. Years later, when I lived in Nebraska, I would hear things like Mike was not very smart and ridiculous things like that, but I never found that to be true. I'm amazed at how these rumors get started, but Mike was articulate enough. I know Mike was raised in a rough place, and he spoke like he came from the streets, but don't let that fool you. He was smart enough!

I remember Mike telling me a story about his last high school football game that never ended. With a few seconds to go in the game and Mike's team about to score to win, a shootout in the stands stopped the game. At that time, I thought he might be pulling my leg, but

176

three years later, when he won the Heisman, the network did a story about that game – Mike was telling the truth! I never played in that environment. The worst thing we had with our football team, besides a lack of talent, was when one teammate stabbed another teammate after practice during my senior season over stolen drug money.

I don't know what kind of track experience Coach Burkholder had when he came to Coffeyville, and I don't know if he thought the training through or not but making the middle-distance guys train with the sprinters was great. Up to that point, I didn't realize that I had good speed. But working with these guys forced me to find another gear I didn't know I had. When I moved on from Coffeyville, I became known as a 1500m guy with a hell of a kick. That didn't exist in me before Coffeyville. By the time I was 20 and 21 years old, I could run a 200 with a flying start in the 22s. Today, I'm sure some think I'm dreaming, but the truth is I had good speed, one level below the sprinters. And guys such as Kenny, Jerome, Karl, Mike, Melvin, Brian, and future Missouri defensive starter Reco Hawkins brought that out of me. Even Verl was fast – he could run a good 400 – and he was encouraging as well. And another 800m runner, Kelsey Loyd, who was from the small Kansas town of Sedan, had good speed. I was challenged every day at practice to break out my speed. I had to learn to adapt or get left behind – I learned to keep up. Coach Burkholder made sure I was competitive in those workouts.

One of my favorite teammates was Tim Wilson, a kid from Ottawa, Kansas. I knew who Tim was before I got to college, but I didn't know him. In my last two years in high school, the regional meet was held in Ottawa, and Tim was easy to remember because of his big afro. But he was also easy to remember because he was good – a good sprinter and an excellent long jumper. Tim placed second at the State Meet in the class 5A long jump in his junior year. For us, he jumped more than 23 feet. But Tim was just a great guy and fun to be around. And he was another of those who helped make me faster without realizing it.

Our first track meet was indoors at Pittsburg State University. I remember being there, warming up, and speaking with my old high school teammate and best friend, John Johnson. What I don't remember is actually racing. It's absurd to think that I can't remember my first college track race, but I can't. I'm not even sure what race I competed in, but I think it was the 880. I've racked my brain trying to remember the race, and I have even attempted to locate my training log, hoping the race is recorded, but to no avail. Our second meet was indoors at the University of Kansas. It's the only time I've ever been in the legendary Allan Fieldhouse. At that time, indoor track meets were held in the famous building. I was entered in the Mile.

Allan Fieldhouse was interesting because the curves went under the stadium area with beams right next to the track covered with pads. You didn't want to lean too much because if you did, you would separate a shoulder on a beam. I really didn't know what I was doing because I was not an experienced miler. I was placed in the first of two heats, which meant the slower race. On the last lap of the 220 track, I came flying out from under the stands on the backstretch, passing several runners, and I could hear my teammates yelling for me. I think I passed someone else in the last curve, where no one could see, and came screaming out in the open again to finish the race. I didn't win, but I placed fairly high in my heat. I ran at 4:41 or 4:42. Rozier was one of the first to get to me and just kept telling me he couldn't believe I could run that fast. He wasn't talking about my final time, but the last lap kick. So, my time was really, really slow for a college mile, but it was a good start for me.

Late in the winter, Hando and I went to Pittsburg to watch John run in his indoor district meeting. At this point, I was contemplating moving on to Pittsburg State at some point. John ran fairly well, and other Pitt State runners had good performances, such as in the 2-

mile in which two Pitt State runners finished in the top two places in a stirring race in just over 9:05. That evening, Hando and I went with John to a track party at the house of one of his teammates, Roddy Gaynor, an excellent 800m runner from Ireland. I didn't really get to know John's teammates, but I liked the ones I met. But I wonder how many cared for me after I drank too much, and I think I made a fool of myself. I tried to out-drink a distance runner on the team from Northern Ireland (who finished 2nd in the two-mile that evening), and after more than 30 beers, I couldn't stand up. John had to get me out of there before I did something drastic, and when we arrived back at his mom's house, I vomited on the front lawn until I thought I was going to die. It's the sickest I've ever been from drinking. Working out with the team back in Coffeyville two days later, I still felt like crap!

Our first outdoor meet in the spring of 1981 was held at Northeastern Oklahoma A&M College (NEO) in Miami, Oklahoma, which was not too far from Coffeyville. I was entered in the 800m but was placed in the slow heat, which upset me. The head track coach from Pittsburg State University was there recruiting, and I had determined by March that I would probably only stay at Coffeyville for my first year and was thinking about transferring to Pitt State, where I would again be teammates with John Johnson. The Pitt State coach didn't seem overly friendly, but he was nice to me that day, and we compared our hats, which were very similar. John told me that his coach was highly critical of me because I complained about my 800 heat and because I used bad language, which was probably true as an influence from some of my teammates.

Nonetheless, I also received reports from John about the Pitt State coach and how badly he treated John. Throughout the years of our college track careers, I never thought John's coach understood his difficult past and was insensitive to him at times. But of course, I got all of this from John and was not there to witness any of it. After the cross-country season his first year, John told me that his coach took away his scholarship and gave it to a foreign athlete who only remained at the school for one year. Because of this, John said he joined ROTC to pay for school and that this pissed off his coach. When a Pitt State representative visited Coffeyville Community College, I filled out a form to receive information about the track team and the history department. I soon received a packet of materials from the history department but was never contacted by the track coach.

I didn't run really well at NEO. I think I ran 2:04, and although it's been a lot of years and much of the meat is lost to time, I think I won my heat, but I don't believe I placed overall. After the meet, instead of going back to Coffeyville with the team, I drove to Pea Ridge, Arkansas, where there is a National Military Park. My Seminar in History class, taught by Frank Ortolani, was there to live as Civil War soldiers did in 1862. We slept in small tents, and it rained, and it was a cold March rain in northern Arkansas. We ate as the soldiers did, and we marched 20 miles one day. It was a cold, wet, miserable, and great time! It was one of the best classes I ever had. Mr. Ortolani's brother was the sports trainer at Pitt State.

Our next meet was the Arkansas Relays. The University of Arkansas had the first 9-lane track I'd ever seen, in fact, ever heard of. We ran in the junior college division, which was held on Friday. It was a beautiful day to compete. I was entered in the 1500m, which was run in the early afternoon. In the morning, one of the former Coffeyville Community College football players who was now playing for Arkansas came over to the track to talk to some of us. I wish I could remember his name, but for some reason, I got to know him a little during the fall when he was still in Coffeyville. I'm not sure, but it might have been Scott Chalene, but I can't know for sure. Arkansas was in the middle of spring practice, and he told me about how crazy Coach Lou Holtz was. I also watched Rozier win the javelin with a toss of 204 feet. It was interesting to watch Mike throw because he didn't utilize his speed. He just jogged up to the line and came to an almost complete stop, and then threw the thing with tremendous upper-body and arm strength – amazing! He was a powerful man.

This was my first 1500, and I really wasn't sure how I should run it. I was an experienced half-miler but not in the mile and metric mile. Although I had never seen a nine-lane track, I was stuck in the ninth lane on the waterfall start, probably because I came in without a time. When the gun went off, I strode to the inside and placed myself near the front. I remained there as long as I could. I don't remember who won the race or what the time was, but coming off the last curve, I mustered a pretty good kick, passed a couple of guys, and finished 5th in 4:11.0. Honestly, the time and my place surprised me. A coach from an Oklahoma junior college who had an outstanding 800m runner named Paul Williams congratulated me on a fine run. Williams, by the way, was the Big 8 800m champion for Oklahoma State in 1983. I was surprised by his compliment as well because I didn't know anyone besides my teammates and coaches paid attention. Coach Burkholder was extremely happy with me, and I was one of the few on the team to place. It's sad how badly some local newspaper writers know about track. In the Coffeyville newspaper, the reporter wrote that Carl Brown took 5th in the mile run in 3:27.3. Wow, a world record, and he didn't even win! Of course, our mile relay team, or more accurately, the 4x400m, ran 3:27, and Carl was one of the runners.

An interesting social side note is some of my black teammates from the north were a little concerned about being in the "South" because they had heard the stories about how badly African Americans were treated in the region. I guess Fayetteville is in the South, and I'm sure it had its share of racial tension. But nothing happened as far as I know to make them feel uncomfortable. That evening, Coach Burkholder went to see the movie *Raging Bull* and, at breakfast the next morning, expressed how disappointed he was that the movie was in black and white. I think very highly of Coach Burkholder; he's an outstanding man, but I must disagree with him on this one.

Raging Bull is one of the all-time cinematic greats, and the black-and-white filming only enhances the allure of the movie. On Saturday, we stayed to watch the university division, and it was a terrific meet, but it was cold and windy. Unfortunately, the Arkansas Relays only lasted a year or two after we competed in '81. But I still have my old and now raggedy Arkansas Relays t-shirt.

The most interesting trip and meet of the year was one hosted by Kansas City Kansas Community College. First off, it was cold and windy, but in addition, and in retrospect I'm probably wrong, but I swear the track was higher at one end than the other. In other words, the elevation was not level. It seemed like we ran uphill on the back stretch and downhill on the front stretch. Because it was a cold day, most athletes huddled in the fieldhouse to stay warm until their events. I was entered in the 800, which is usually contested toward the end of the meet, so I stayed in the building much of the day, only occasionally venturing out to see a teammate compete.

At one point, as it's prone to do, nature called, so I headed to the restrooms. I came to the first door, and it read "Women," so I headed to the next door and went inside. Without going into some details, as I was sitting there, I heard the door open to the room and then heard women's voices. I thought, "What the hell are women doing in the men's restroom?" Some others came in and I heard more female voices and laughing. I just remained in the stall until I didn't hear anyone speaking. I then gently opened the stall door, didn't see anyone, and hightailed it out of there without even washing my hands. When I went back through the door of which I entered, there was a male athlete from another team sitting on a table. He looked at me, and in a deadpan voice said, "I was wondering when you were going to come out of there." I looked at him and then looked at the door, which said "Women." The first door I looked at and this door went to the same restroom, they were just at opposite ends. I looked back at the guy at the table and just smiled and shrugged and headed for the Men's room to wash my hands.

The 800m was peculiar. Some idiot who didn't understand track or was stuck in 1976, decided that we would run in our lanes for the first 300 meters. We were placed at the 400m starting line for a two-turn stagger. I didn't think I'd seen this before, but in fact I had. The 1976 Olympics in Montreal ran the 800m with a two-turn stagger, but it was no longer used. I was placed in one of the outside lanes, and it might have been lane 8. This put me in a disadvantage because I couldn't see the competitors. For a 400m runner, this would probably not be a big deal because they run races in lanes and are used to running blind. When I cut in after that 300, I was at the back of the pack. I never recovered and although I didn't finish last, I was not competitive either. I don't know what place I got or my time, I just wanted to get in the van and get warm. It was one of the worst run meets of which I ever competed. Thank God I never had to run there again.

The van didn't provide much comfort, but it did have plenty of excitement. Not long after we left the meet in Kansas City, we were traveling down I35, when Melvin Gray and a teammate named Mike, who had run for Coffeyville's Field Kindley High School, got into a fight over a girl. Mike called his cousin a whore, and Melvin said she was his girlfriend. The argument quickly turned into a fight. Coach Burkholder drove over to the shoulder on the interstate and then told the two to get out and finish so we could continue in peace. What an amazing thing to do. I, for one, wanted them to get out and fight so I could see Melvin kick the hell out of Mike. Mike was a blowhard and talked and bitched too much, and he wanted no part of Melvin. It was OK to push some in the van, but a full-fledged fight outside in which Melvin had full range? Not a chance. Mike didn't move, and the fight ended. We still had three hours to go before we got to Coffeyville and Mike didn't mess with Melvin after that.

On one trip, Mike began to brag about Field Kindley winning the State Meet track title the year before. And it was something to be proud of, but Mike made it unbearable. Then he started to talk about my Parsons team and how we were nothing compared to them. And, he was right, they had an awesome team. But then it just went on too long, so I reminded Mike that although his team was better than mine, in the race in which he and I competed against each other, the 4X800m relay, Parsons beat Coffeyville. Yes Mike, my team beat your team! We finished 2nd and they finished 5th. That shut Mike up and our teammates laughed at him because I had put him in his place. Truthfully though, I did like Mike and his father as well, who I had talked with at track meets from Jr. high through high school. I had known Mike, to some degree, for a few years. We ran in many of the same track meets and we played football against each other for several years. Mike even ran a punt back for a touchdown against us our senior year. But Mike's mouth was too big, and it ultimately caused his demise on the Coffeyville Community College track team.

Late in the season we ran at the Fort Scott Community College Invitational. It was a low-key meet, but Fort Scott was our biggest rival, although they didn't have anyone that challenged me. We won the meet easily. But Mike was upset because he thought he was cheated in the long jump and complained about the official who he believed had done him wrong. The problem is that Mike wouldn't let it go. Our trip back to Coffeyville from Fort Scott was 100 miles in an old yellow school bus, which is extremely uncomfortable. But with Mike bitching about the long jump results and the "cheating" official the trip felt like 1,000 miles. The guy just wouldn't shut up. Coach Foster, the football coach and athletic director made the trip with us. When the bus finally parked back at our college, Mike just had to get in one more dig and wanted to know what Coach Burkholder was going to do about the unsavory long jump official. Well, Coach Foster had enough. I could have told Mike that if he continued Coach Foster was going to rip him a new one, and that's exactly what happened. Coach Foster started yelling at Mike and it was loud, thundering loud

– an explosion! Coach told him that all he heard on the way back was his bitching and he was tired of listening to him. Then he kicked Mike off the team, right there in the parking lot, screaming at him at the top of his lungs. Mike tried to get a word in edgewise, but he just couldn't do it. I never saw Mike again.

My second semester at Coffeyville, a kid moved into our suite that had a number of issues. I don't recall his name, but the guy that lived across the hall from me, Gregg I believe, nicknamed him Mud Flap because he said the kid looked like one when he walked with a stoop and floppy sandy blond hair. I remember standing in the doorway looking outside when Gregg said, "He look like a mud flap," in his usual lazy drawl. I don't think Mud Flap knew his nickname. The biggest issue he had, and probably because he was unable to stand up for himself, was that in his previous dorm, he was severely bullied by a couple of football players who were red shirting. The high majority of football players at Coffeyville were good guys, but these two were true redneck assholes. Like most groups, I find rednecks OK as well, but not these two. They never messed with me, but Mud Flap got the full treatment. They would piss in a cup and place it over his door so that when he walked out it fell on his head. And they defecated, placed it in a bag and put it under the door into his room. And these were the mild acts. Gregg didn't much care for Mud Flap, but when the two bullies showed up in our suite to give him hell, Gregg threatened them in no uncertain terms. Gregg was not a small man and didn't fear these two disgraces to the football team. Gregg had his issues as well. Karl Brown was his roommate, and Gregg was so messy that Karl left the suite after the first semester. Gregg smoked cigars and threw them on the floor when he was finished. The floor of his room was covered with cigar butts.

Mud Flap was a needy person who didn't drive, and I think craved friendship. I doubt he ever had a true friend, and I believe he was bullied most of his life. He also had a medical issue or two. I did become his friend, but he could be a bit much. He would wait in his room and listen for me to open the door to my room when I returned so he could catch me and have me go across the street to get him something from the store. He would tell me that he was scared to go out because he felt his medical condition coming on, and didn't want to have an incident, but I think the real reason was he feared being caught after dark by the bullies.

One night I got home from a track meet in the middle of the night. We had traveled 300 miles back from Dodge City, and I was tired and wanted to get in my car and drive home to Parsons. It was probably 2 or 3 in the morning, and I opened the suite door real quiet, walked through the lobby, and opened my room door as quietly as I could. I closed the door without making a sound and started gathering my things to make a getaway to my car. Then I heard a very soft knock on my door, and I knew it was Mud Flap. I thought about not opening the door, but I wanted to leave – I didn't want him to force me to be a prisoner in my own room! So, I opened the door, and Mud Flap said he had been waiting for me to get back so I could go to the store for him. I said that it was the middle of the night and that I needed to drive home, but he insisted that I go to an all-night convenient store. Then he said he wanted to go with me, but he had to get ready. It took him forever, and at one point he said, "I know I take longer than a woman, but I want to look presentable when I go out." At 3:00 in the morning? Finally, after he finished putting on the last chain around his neck, we took off. I don't remember what time I finally got to leave Coffeyville that night, or morning.

During spring break the team ran at the Emporia State Relays, but I didn't go. Instead, I headed to Vicksburg, Mississippi with Mr. Ortolani's History Seminar class. It was tough missing the Emporia meet, but I knew what I was getting into when I asked Mr. Ortolani permission to take his class. And as life experiences go, the week-long on-site class at the National Historic Site was one to remember. We spent every day at the Park studying the Siege of Vicksburg and how General Grant finally encircled the town on the Mississippi

River. During the evening, we all had a great time. On the way down, our vans stopped at a road-side store in the middle of no-where of southeast Arkansas. As we were paying, the women at the checkout said in a deep southern accent, "You all sure do talk funny," at which time one of our students shot back in a satirized southern accent, not too far removed from her own Oklahoma drawl, "We don't talk funny." Maybe you just had to be there, but at that moment it was hilarious, especially considering how deadpan Ms. Oklahoma delivered her putdown and how clueless that checkout attendant was combined with her puzzled stare. But I'm not so sure our Oklahoma student understood how profound her own accent was, but then again, she was pretty sharp!

We were so busy on our Vicksburg trip that I didn't get the opportunity to do much training. But one of the interesting things we did was run the park road in somewhat of a relay carrying a folded American flag. The run was to commemorate those who served at the siege. I don't recall the exact distance of the road that follows much of the siege line, but I think it was 15 to 20 miles. What I do remember is that I ran 7 miles. Three of us ran the relay as the rest of the class followed in the vans. The first leg was run by Greg Garrett from Parsons' rival Labette County High School. He was at Coffeyville Community College to play football. I was the second leg, and Mr. Ortolani was the last leg. Greg handed the flag to me, and I busted out as hard as I could. I needed a good, hard run to make up for lost workouts. As I finished my 7 miles, Mr. Ortolani seemed surprised. He told me later that he was not finished stretching because he thought I would take a lot longer to run my leg. No one timed me but I know I smoked those 7 miles – I felt great!

The most fun we had was two different nights we spent at this bar and restaurant. The first night we went there I had a little too much to drink and I asked the band if I could get up and sing with them, which, amazingly, they allowed. I must have sung a song or two but I'm not really sure, and it's possible my memory is completely wrong, and I didn't sing anything. I do know that I did actually get behind the mic and say something to the bar patrons. But who knows what that was? After we exited the bar, one of the students, who was a defensive lineman by the name of David Orvis, climbed the side of a brick building up to the second level and then jumped to the pavement below. The next day he thought he had sprained both ankles and he limped around the rest of the week. But after we returned to Kansas, he told me he learned that he actually broke his ankles. David was a big guy and a truly wonderful person who was fun to be around.

The second time we visited the bar; we eat all the boiled shrimp we could eat and gave toasts that were traditional for this class. Mr. Ortolani had been doing these for several years with each class on their historic visits. One evening many in the class, without Mr. Ortolani, drove over to the Louisiana side of the Mississippi River, and built a huge bon fire underneath the bridge that crossed over to Vicksburg. I walked up to the road level and even though it was after dark, I could see the smoke bellowing up from both sides of the bridge. It was an eerie sight.

After I returned to Coffeyville, we ran a meet at Butler Community College on an extremely windy day. I ran alright, but not great. However, we then traveled to Haskell in Lawrence, Kansas and the team competed great. I ran my second 1500m of the year and won by the thinnest of margins by outkicking another runner and leaning at the tape. I ran 4:10.0. I was tired after the race but could tell I was making progress. We won a multitude of races at that meet and finished second as a team, beating our big rival, Fort Scott. We were supposed to have a home meet, but rain halted those plans because the track at the high school was so bad that the deluge rendered it unusable. Someone had decided to fill holes in the track with sand from the long jump pit. Even when it was dry it was like running on the beach in some areas. So, our next meet was held at Fort Scott, on the same track we ran in high school. This cinder track was much better than the one in Coffeyville. I ran the 2-mile relay, which we won, and the 2-mile run. I placed 4th in the 2-mile in a very slow time of just above 11 minutes. But as a team, we competed well and won the meet, again beating Fort Scott!

Finally, we were ready for the Jayhawk Conference Meet hosted by Dodge City Community College. The track was a red dog cinder track, and it was in real good shape. But it was also a hot day in the 90s with a hot wind, which is typical in Dodge City. As a whole, we competed well. Rozier didn't make the trip, but most of the team did. I ran the 1500m and the 4x400, but we only ran a mere 3:35 in the relay. The 1500 was a good field. It's been so many years ago that I don't know who won or even who the other competitors were. But what I do vividly recall is how fast the start was. When the gun sounded, the field took off down the backstretch like a sprint. We slowed on the front stretch, but it was still fast. The first lap was run in 59 seconds, not too fast for a world-class miler, but plenty fast for a 19-year-old kid with a best 1500 of 4:10. The question for me was, could I hang on after a fast start in windy, hot weather? Plus, because of the wind, there was plenty of red dust in the air from the track that didn't help breathing. Despite all of this, I wasn't affected by anything. Two or three guys were able to separate from the field, but I remained competitive, and coming off the final curve, my sprint was really good, and I crossed the finish line in 5th place with a time of 4:09.9. The winner ran 3:59. I bettered my previous best by a mere tenth of a second, but I had run a better race, despite not winning. Considering the wind, heat, and cinder track, I think my Dodge City race was worth about 2 seconds better than my winning race in Lawrence.

Coach Burkholder was happy with my race, and I anticipated with excitement the Reginal Meet the next week, especially because it was run at Wichita State, my favorite track. Until I recently looked up the meet in Dodge City in the scrapbook my dad kept, I didn't even know I ran the 4x400 relay, so I don't know how I personally ran, it's completely lost to memory. But I clearly remember the 1500m I ran at Regionals. As much as I looked forward to running on the great Wichita State track, I ran equally as bad. There were two heats and for some reason I was placed in the first, or slow heat. This didn't make sense because I was one of the fastest 12 in the Region. But in retrospect, it didn't make a difference. I must have not warmed up well, because I was tight the entire race. In fact, I don't think I've ever run a race so tight. I felt horrible during the race, and I don't mean I was sick. I just couldn't get into a rhythm during the race and my kick was only average at best. I finished second in my heat in 4:14, and I doubt I would have run faster in the second heat that was won in 4:00. That was my last race for Coffeyville Community College.

Chapter 8
Going to Pittsburg? And Freshly Buttered Grasshopper

I decided during track season at Coffeyville that I wasn't going to return for my sophomore year. My plan was to transfer to Pittsburg State University and be teammates once again with John Johnson. John had a nice cross-country season at Pitt State but started off slow in indoor track and during the early part of outdoor season. But he finished strong late and placed at the conference meet in the 800m. Even though the Pitt State coach didn't seem to like me, and for what I could gather from John, wasn't impressed with my running, I still decided that is where I wanted to go. A year before I didn't want anything to do with Pittsburg – I had absolutely no interest in the school. When Coach Foster heard that I wasn't returning to Coffeyville, he called me into his office. I dreaded this because I'd heard the stories about such office visits. But our visit was very nice, and he just wanted to make sure I was making the right decision and if I changed my mind during the summer, a scholarship was waiting for me. Another issue about staying at Coffeyville, that had no bearing on my decision to leave, but made the decision easier, is that at the end of the season, Coach Burkholder indicated that he was not returning.

It could have been a difficult decision because I was leaving teammates I liked, but most were graduating or not returning. Some might have decided to return, but I don't know who those were. When I left Coffeyville, I never saw Karl, Verl, Jerome, and Kenny again. Verl gave me an address but when I wrote him a few months later, it came back as "return to sender." Because I was on an athletic scholarship, I had to return my books to the campus bookstore. The last morning at Coffeyville, I was returning my books when I ran into Tim and Rozier in the bookstore. We talked for a couple of minutes, and Tim and I agreed to meet up over the summer, but we never did. Mike suggested we keep in touch, but of course we didn't. I told Mike good luck at Nebraska, never thinking he would win a Heisman Trophy, and we said our goodbyes. I never saw them again, and don't know what happened to Tim Wilson. In fact, other than one teammate, I never saw any of them again. Of course, I watched Mike, Reco, and Melvin play football on TV. The only one I saw was Kelsey. I ran into him at a Wendy's in Branson, Missouri one summer. I knew I recognized him and when I went over to see if he was really Kelsey, he said he recognized me when I walked in. Kelsey was never one for a lot of words, so our conversation was short.

Ron Faulkenberry, my Parsons High School teammate, started college at the University of Kansas as a freshman in the fall of 1979. But after a year and a half at KU, decided to transfer to Baptist Bible College is Springfield, Missouri. After spending the spring semester at BBC, Ron decided to train over the summer because his new school had a cross-country team. Ron didn't compete for KU, and I don't think he ever meant to. I had tried to convince him to give it a try, but I don't think he was interested. Plus, he told me it was difficult to make the team as a walk-on. For a guy who took 10th in the class 5A State Cross-country Meet with a 9:52 two-mile, and who ran a 4:35 mile on the track, I don't think he thought he had a chance to make the team at KU. He said he was told that to make the cross-country team, he would have to break 15:00 for three miles. That certainly was tough, but I think Ron would have run between 15:45

and 16:00 at the High School State Meet if the course would have been 5,000 meters instead of two miles. And with some hard training over the summer of 1979, he would have had a chance at that 15:00.

But that didn't matter now, and we decided to train together that summer so he could get ready for the BBC cross-country season, and I could prepare for the Pittsburg State season. Ron was not in shape when we began to train, and he really struggled at first. I was surprised at just how out-of-shape he was. This was not the Ron that I knew as a competitive runner. But after a few weeks, his fitness and talent began to come around. During the mid-summer, Ron and I were on a run east of Parsons, clipping along at a nice pace and having a conversation. Ron was a great guy to run with, and a good friend, and our conversations could be lively. During the Kansas summers while we ran in the country, grasshoppers spattered in all directions about two to four feet ahead of us. Suddenly, a grasshopper about as large as a small bird flew into my mouth. I didn't even have time to gag or spit it out. Almost simultaneously it entered my mouth and slide down my throat as if it was slathered with butter. It was only at that point that I began to cough, but I realized it was too late, so I just kept running. At least that last half of my run was with renewed energy from the added protein. Ron didn't say much, only asking if I was OK – we just kept running.

About the time Ron started training with me, John Johnson and I went to Pittsburg State to watch Hando run at the Sub-State Jr. Olympic Meet. While there, John's coach at Pitt State had a conversation with me about running for him. He told me when practice began for cross-country, but he wouldn't give me a scholarship. I understood this. A kid who runs a 4:09.9 1500 as a freshman in college isn't good enough to earn a scholarship to an NAIA school. I actually don't know if I'm being sarcastic or not. But kids coming out of high school with similar comparative times in the mile got small college offers.

So, I was a year behind and had never had a cross-country season, save the one race at Coffeyville. You would have thought he would have recognized that I was under-trained and that my 1500m time indicated that I had potential. He never asked me about my training, and he probably never knew I had surgery for a hernia my senior year. If so, he would have realized that I would have had a good chance of running a 1:58 as a senior in high school, especially training daily with a 1:55 guy. And kids like that did get small-college scholarships. But I never got the impression the Pitt State coach wanted me to run for him. He wasn't unpleasant, but not cordial either. I was not a priority, and he just didn't seem nice to me. And although I was excited to continue running in college and again being teammates with John, to some degree I dreaded the idea of running for him.

A week or two after meeting with the Pittsburg State Coach at the AAU Meet, Ron and I went to Independence to compete in their small early-summer meet that we had run a couple of times before. Ron ran in the two mile and maybe the mile, and truth be told, he looked like a winded old man with gas attempting to waddle his way through the mud. I couldn't believe how a person could get that far out of shape in two years, Ron was young and was still thin and looked fit – until he ran! But Ron would come around. I competed in, and won, the mile and 880. I didn't run particularly fast, I think about a 4:50 mile, and I ran an easy 2:04 half. These weren't especially notable races, nor a meet that was memorable when it came to competition. But it did completely change the course of my life!

In both races I competed against a man who was several years older than me. I beat him in both races while he took second. His name was Elsie Miller who coached in Seneca, Missouri. He might have told me where he had attended college, but if he did, it didn't stick with me at the time. I do distinctly remember that he told me he competed in college cross-country and track. I told Elsie that I had just finished my freshman year at Coffeyville but that I was now going to run for Pittsburg State. I told him that I was not going to receive a scholarship, and I must have expressed my reservations for running there. We also discussed road races, and he said there were some in Joplin, Missouri, and that he could send me the schedule. So, I gave him my address and we parted ways.

Elsie, I believe, at the moment he asked for my address, had an alternative motive. A couple of days later I received a call from Elsie. He asked me if my heart was set on going to Pittsburg State. Enthusiastically, I said "no." Although I'm not sure I consciously knew it, I was looking for a way out of running for a coach who I was positive didn't like me and didn't want me on the team. I knew he was a good coach, but that didn't give me any comfort. He had terrific success and had coached several All-Americans, and one of them, Mike Nixon, who was a national cross-country champion, worked with my dad on the railroad. But if he didn't have an interest in me, I didn't think he would extend the energy to even try to develop my raw talent. Elsie said that he hoped he hadn't overstepped his bounds, but he had taken it upon himself to contact his old college coach about me. I was excited to hear this, and it came out of left field.

He said he had attended and graduated from the School of the Ozarks in the Branson, Missouri area. I didn't recall hearing of the school, but I knew Branson from the several trips I made with my family to trout fish on Lake Taneycomo and a visit to Silver Dollar City. Elsie told me his coach's name was Robert Osburn and that with my permission he would have the coach give me a call. Of course, I told him yes. Elsie explained that SofO, as many called it, was a unique school where students worked on campus to pay for their classes, room and board and meals. This was the first time I had ever heard of this kind of set up. Elsie also told me that if I was interested, I should start looking for those who could write letters of support. He said that my minister would be an excellent person to write one and asked if I had a pastor. I didn't. We didn't go to church and didn't even belong to a church. I couldn't have told you what my beliefs were. Brad Burkes had attempted to get me to attend his church, and he would continue to do so, but at this time he was in the Army, stationed in Germany. I never did attend the Four-Square Church where his father was the minister.

Ron's dad was a pastor at a local Baptist church, but I hadn't attended their either, so he wasn't an option for a letter. Ron said he knew that SofO was a Christian-centered liberal arts school about 40 miles south of where he attended college. But most interesting was that SofO was in the same conference as BBC. This meant that Ron and I would get the chance to race each other, although by the way he ran in Independence, it didn't appear it would be much of a contest. When Coach Osburn called me, we had a very good conversation. I could tell that he wanted me to come to SofO and he spoke to me with respect. Although he hadn't met me yet, he respected Elsie's evaluation, and he invited me down to visit the school with my parents.

Ron told me about a series of summer track meets held at Southwest Missouri State University in Springfield. I planned on running one of these Wednesday evening meets in mid-July, so we made plans to visit SofO that day. Coach had the application sent to me and I'm not sure who I ended up asking to write my letters of support – but I know not a single one was from a pastor. I do think Coach Riley Cartwright and Coach Gary Billions wrote letters. One of the questions on the application was to indicate religious affiliation, so my mom put down Christian, which wasn't un-true. We just didn't attend church. Maybe I should have counted the time I had to sit through the rantings of that sweating, spitting, raging preacher in that church camp at Tuttle Creek!

In the summer of 1981, I needed a job. John and I attempted to get jobs at the Wolf Creek Nuclear Plant in construction. They were building the plant at that time, and despite the controversy over building a new nuclear plant we knew they paid well. I had a relative who was an electrician at Wolf Creek, who encouraged me to apply. I made a trip to Burlington, where the plant was located, but no one at the construction trailer was there. John and I had made a trip there before school was out and never found anyone around. Finally, after failing to find work, my mom said I needed to apply to a place called Broderick's, which made sportswear. My mom, my aunt Judy, and my grandmother all worked there. Hando and I drove up to the company's main building and applied. Mr. Wall, who ran the company, asked me if Hando and I were a team to be hired together, but I said we weren't. So, I got the job and Hando didn't. I was placed in a building about a block away from the main building. This was the old Safeway store on Main St. just a half block from the Junior High School and across the street where we used to go watch fights after school between students. In fact, the best fight I ever saw took place on the west side of Safeway while I was in the 7th grade when two 8th grade girls attacked each other in a vicious display of fighting skill rarely seen. There wasn't a boy in that school who would have won against those girls. Unfortunately, at least as most of us watching at that time viewed it, a store manager came out and stopped it. I'm surprised he didn't get his butt kicked as he stepped in between those two fighting machines!

My job at Broderick's was to lay material. I would get an order that had a long white sheet of paper with it that had patterns drawn on it. The order indicated the type of cloth, the colors and how many of each. We had manual machines in which we rolled out the material. When we got to the front end, we pushed a button, and a knife cut the material off the role so we could begin the process again. When finished, we slid the stack down to the other end of the long table with the pattern on top, so the cutters could cut out the patterns. The manager in the building liked me because he had attended Coffeyville a couple of decades before. My aunt worked in the building as well and said the manager never liked anyone, so it was surprising that he took a liking to me. A couple of weeks after I started, Hando was hired, and we worked together as material layers the rest of the summer. After about two weeks on the job, my boss started me on the large $40,000 mechanized machine. It was the only one they had, and it was for the very largest jobs in which the stacks were extremely high. He told me I was the only one he trusted after the previous operator quit.

There were some interesting characters that worked there. My first hour on the job, this strange, and probably dirty old man, who lived across the street, gave me a sly look, and asked me to come over to his table to show me something. Out of his wallet, he pulled out an old color picture about 30 or 40 years old of a topless Hawaiian hula dancer and said, "Isn't she a beauty?" I was not impressed – with him! There was another fellow, a very young man, maybe 18 or 19 years old who had a brain worth about a penny-and-a-half. He was a nice kid with long blondish/reddish shaggy hair, who had a difficult time understanding the orders. On the next table was a man named Norman. Norman did his job with a smile on his face and sometimes even whistling. Several times an hour, we would hear, above the noise, the kid saying "Norman, Norman." I can't do his voice justice in words, but it was just weird and creepy. It seemed that Norman spent half his time helping the kid figure things out. Sometimes as a joke, Hando would raise his voice and say "Norman," in the kid's child-like voice, and he never caught on that he was being mocked.

The most interesting guy was a Hawaiian who had supposedly once driven his car off a cliff and landed in the Pacific Ocean. He had to get himself out of the car and swim to the surface. When I worked with him during the summer of 1981, he would drive at top speed into the parking lot each morning in an old beat-up car with no breaks. He would slam into the parking place, almost late, and get out of the car with a smile on his face. He was a great guy and could make you laugh just by looking at him. He was a cutter, and my memory is that he was the fastest of the bunch. He always had stories and told them so fast with his accent that I usually only got half the meaning. It didn't matter – they were always entertaining and hilarious. Besides my aunt, my favorite person in the building was Sam Strathe, who prepared the orders. He was the brother of my 9th grade football coach, and the uncle to Brad, my relay teammate. Sam was smart and funny!

Ron and I continued to train. Besides competing in cross-country in the fall, wherever that would be for me, we also planned to compete in a track meet in Lawrence, Kansas. Ron wasn't running in the Springfield meet and that would be contested before Lawrence. I went over to Pittsburg on some weekends and run with John, and I got in few runs with Hando in Parsons as well. Finally, the day came to visit SofO. I was nervous but I hoped it went well, because I didn't want to go to Pitt State. However, up to this point, I hadn't received word whether I was accepted by SofO or not. Here I was in mid-summer, and I didn't know for sure where I was attending college in the fall. I had not applied to Pitt State, and I didn't have a backup plan for another school.

But the visit went very well. However, not everything was revealed to me on the visit, and I'm not sure I would have selected to go to SofO if I'd known. But who knows, I still might have. After all, Pitt State didn't seem like a viable option anymore. My mom noticed that there were a lot of students on campus for the summer, but coach told us that some kids chose to attend during the summer months. I found out later that everyone was required to go to school in the summer. The name of the college concerned me as well, although I didn't bring this up with Coach Osburn. "School of the Ozarks" seemed like a name for a glorified high school, and not really fitting for an actual college. But when I visited, one could see that this was a college.

Coach did explain that students had to attend chapel until their senior years. He joked that the attitude was that if the College hadn't converted you by the time, you were a senior, you were considered a lost cause. I wasn't too keen about chapel; in fact, I had an aversion to organized religion. I felt, and still do really, that organized religion has caused enumerable major issues in the history of our world. I attend church now, and I'm even an elder, but I'm not enthusiastic about large churches, or the mega churches out there. I think they have too much political influence. We were also required to attend convocations, which didn't seem too bad once Coach explained how they worked.

At the end of the afternoon visit, Coach told me that he would see me at the Springfield meet in the evening. I didn't know he would be there! Now I got nervous. What if I didn't run well, would Coach Osburn still want me on the team? Coach said he was taking several kids to the meet to compete. I should have realized at that point that school in the summer was required at SofO. Before we went to the stadium in Springfield, we stopped by a running store in the University area. My intention was to buy a pair of Adidas training shoes that I liked. I had never worn them, but they looked good, and some famous distance runners wore them. But the salesperson told me that there was a better pair of shoes made by Nike called the Tailwind.

Eric Freeman wore a pair of Tailwinds and told me they were good, but I didn't pay much attention. I do remember that one could hardly tell the difference between the right and left shoe, and that they looked like gray boats to me. I reluctantly tried a pair on – I had never worn a shoe that felt so good! They had an air sole, that might have been Nike's first, and when I started to train in them, I couldn't believe how great they were. They were the best training shoes I would ever have, but Nike quit making them about that time, and I was always disappointed with my training shoes after that. Nothing was ever remotely close to the Tailwind, the greatest running shoe ever made.

At the Southwest Missouri State University track, we waited for Coach Osburn to arrive with some of the team. Finally, they arrived, and I spoke with him again. I decided to go check out the red dog cinder track. While jogging on the track, one of the SofO runners came over to speak with me. His name was Steve Davis, and he was three years older than me, but had run in high school for Iola, one of our Southeast Kansas League rivals. Because of our age difference, I never ran against him in high school, but he knew who Brad Burkes was as well as Ron Faulkenberry. Steve had attended Allen County Community College in his hometown for two years before transferring to SofO, so we had several things in common, and I think he knew who I was. We ran in the same high school league, and in the same Junior college conference. Over the years, Steve became a good friend, and after college he became one of Missouri's best high school distance coaches and is in the Missouri sports hall-of-fame. Among others, he coached a 9:00 two-miler and another kid at the same time who ran a 4:06 mile. With those two, his high school team finished in the top 10 at the Nike Cross-country National meet.

My only race at this SMS summer meet was the 880. I spoke with a freshman on the team who had just run a 1:59 800 meters in the spring during his final high school season. So, I was worried. I wanted to break 2:00 to impress Coach Osburn, but I also wanted to win for Coach. I wore a pair of yellow Sub 4 racing shorts, with a white mesh Sub 4 racing singlet, which were my favorite. This was Steve Scott's club, and I wanted to be as good as him. When the gun sounded, I took off on the firm and fast red cinders and took the lead. I ran with purpose if not a little tight because I knew Coach was watching. The first lap was about 58 seconds, and I felt pretty good but still a little tight. By the back stretch I expected the 1:59 kid to come up on my shoulder and try to pass, and there was a possibility that there were even better runners than him in the race. But no one came close and as I came off the last curve, I felt I had it won. The starting/finish line was in the middle of the straight, so I only had 55 yards left when I started for home. I felt strong, but not sharp, which was probably caused by the tightness that was a result of the anxiety.

I won easily at 2:01. I didn't reach my goal of breaking 2:00, but I impressed Coach, the 1:59 kid, and Steve Davis. Coach spoke to my parents and me after the race and was clearly enthusiastic about my coming to school at SofO. But I would have to sweat it out for a few more weeks before I found out whether I was admitted. Back in Parsons, Ron and I trained fairly hard, and he was really coming along. He was beginning to resemble the Ron I ran with and against in high school. We set our sights on the Lawrence meet and the possibility that we would race against each other in the fall. As far as the Lawrence meet was concerned, we wouldn't be entered in the same race. Ron decided that his best chance to run well was in the 3,000 meters, and he would also enter the 1500. My goal was to run a sub-two-minute 800m, so I would only run that race. If the 1500 would have been contested after the 800, I would have probably raced in the metric mile as well.

Although John didn't run in Lawrence, he did travel with Ron and me. The Lawrence Open was contested at Memorial Stadium on the campus of the University of Kansas. The stadium held about 50,000 people, but it was empty for this meet except for those competing and a few families and friends. I first heard of the meet in 1979, when Ron won the mile at 4:37. The meet had since been converted to meters. In the morning, vintage Ron showed up, and he took second in the 3,000 at 9:21, behind the winning time of 8:55. In the early afternoon, Ron again took second, with a time of 4:29 in the 1500m. Although Ron competed in the open division, the high school runners ran in the same race. Mike Reagan, the state class 5A champion in the 1600m and 3200m, won the high school division and finished ahead of Ron, but both were well behind the open winner's 4:02. But Ron looked good in both races, especially in the 3,000. I welcomed this. Not only because Ron was a friend but also because if I did attend SofO, I would have the opportunity to race against him when he was in good shape.

My race was last, and I eagerly anticipated the moment. The winner of the 1500 was also running the 800. He said he had run for Fort Hays State University but was now out of college. I knew I had my hands full, but this was great news because if he ran close to as well as he did in the 1500, he could pull me along to a good time. My plan was simple – hang on his shoulder until the final stretch and then attempt to out-kick him. And if the pace was too slow, I would take the lead and push. I don't think my red-haired competitor was in the same kind of shape that he was in college, but he was good enough for me.

When the race started, I settled in behind the former Fort Hays State runner and ran off his outside shoulder. On the backstretch, through the curve, and into the front stretch of the first lap, everything went as planned. The first lap could have been faster. I think we hit 58 seconds, and I would have preferred 57, but it was still fast enough for my goal, so there was no reason to panic. I've always been a competitor who tries to win, but sometimes, in some races, one needs to attempt to run a fast time, or hit a targeted time, because when you race against great fields in the future, you'll be ready to compete in a fast race. This was one of those races for me. Yes, I wanted to win, and I would try, but if my main goal had been to win the race, I might have taken the lead and attempted to control the pace by slowing down. But I needed to break two minutes, especially for my confidence.

On the second lap, I was easily able to stay with my competitor, and no one else seemed to be close, so I was sure I wouldn't finished worse than second. An advantage that day was that it wasn't too warm, and the wind was almost non-existent, both a rarity in hot wind-swept Kansas in July. Through the final curve I stayed with the leader. As we slung off the curve into the final straight, I tried to move up and fight him down the stretch. In retrospect, I think I could have matched his speed, but I didn't possess his strength at that point as a 19-year-old. But I was close. He never really pulled away with a quick burst, but he was able to put two or three yards between us that final 100 meters. He crossed the line about a second ahead of me.

Then came the excruciating wait. Had I run under two minutes? I heard one of the timers indicate that the winner ran 1:58.5. Now I was fairly sure I had also broken two minutes. But no one came up to me to tell me my time, although someone did ask me for my name. Finally, the result is that they forgot to time me!! Can you believe it? I was not timed. Did the person timing second place forget to start the watch (these were hand-timed races)? Or did he start the watch and forget to stop it when I crossed the line? Was the guy drinking a beer and just didn't care? Did the watch malfunction? I never did find out the cause, but the timers, along with the meet official, decided to give me credit for a 2:00.0. Man, I knew I broke two minutes; I just knew it! Luckily, Ron came to the rescue. Although I don't think my "official" time was ever changed, Ron timed me in 1:59.6. And that's what I went with. If I had not been confident that I really beat 2:00, I would not have accepted this as my first sub-two-minute 800m, but I knew that I had. This was my first race to break two minutes! It didn't matter that in an 880-yard race the time would have been just over 2:00 because most of my races from now on would be contested in meters. And I would get my chance to run well under two minutes in an 880.

I don't believe the Lawrence Open 800 was any better than the 2:01 880 I ran in Springfield. In the Springfield race, I was never pushed and, in fact, was on my own the entire race, and it was run on cinders. The KU race was run on a faster all-weather tartan track, and I had a good competitor to carry me through the race. Plus, the 880-time converted to a 2:00.3. The Springfield race just might have been superior. At that time, I didn't see it that way. Coach Osburn was impressed and happy I had finally broken through a mental barrier. Now my hope was that running under two minutes would be the norm, and hopefully training for and running cross-country would vastly improve my 1500m times.

After the Lawrence track meet, Coach Osburn said he was taking same kids to run in a 10k road race in Aurora, Missouri, a small town between Joplin and Springfield. I had never run a 10k before but decided to enter as well so I could have one more race in front of Coach. John and I decided to go to the race together, but I don't think he intended to race. I stayed with John that Friday night in Pittsburg so the drive the next morning to Aurora would be shorter. That night, John and I partied pretty heavily at an apartment where a friend of his lived. There were five or six of people there, including one of John's Pitt State teammates, Steve Ortiz. Steve graduated from Pittsburg High School in 1980, and I have a clear memory of him running the two-mile for them. I remember that as we partied, we listened to Frank Zappa, courtesy of Steve.

The next morning, I awoke with this terrible feeling. Something wasn't right, and it wasn't how crappy I felt after partying half the night, although I did feel like shit. As I looked at the clock, I realized that we over-slept. Did the alarm go off? I don't know, but we only had about an hour to make the race, which was at least 80 miles away. We would never make it in time, so we just didn't go. I felt horrible, but what could I do? I had made a big mistake, and I had to tell Coach that I missed the race by over-sleeping. This was not a good admission for a kid attempting to get into the college. I needed Coach's influence to get admitted at such a late stage in the process. If I'd applied during the winter, I don't think I would have had any issues, but my application was months after the deadline. I just hoped Coach understood. I got lucky, because instead of finding fault in missing the race, he just joked about the time a missed the road race. Of course, I didn't tell Coach Osburn the reason I over-slept! And he never asked.

Late in the summer, John, Hando, and I headed to Joplin one day to go to the mall. What this really meant for Hando is that he would have a field day stealing what he could. We went into a JC Pennies or Montgomery Ward and watched on one of the TVs, Sebastian Coe win a slow 800m race, I:46 I think (slow for him, blazing for most). After watching this race, I kind of did my own thing for a while. Then I found John and Hando again so we could leave and do something else in the mall. When I caught up with them, I noticed that two men in ill-fighting cheap suits were watching us and pointing at us as they spoke on radios. They were really pointing at John and Hando and didn't seem too interested in me.

I asked Hando what he took, but he wouldn't answer me. He just gave me this strange look. I indicated that we were being watched and followed. I said that whatever he had, just leave it because as soon as we left the store the stuff would be stolen items. But he didn't listen. I asked John what he had but didn't get an answer from him either. Finally, we left the store and walked to the other end of the mall to an arcade. As we left, the two men followed. Again, I told Hando that we were being followed. Hando told me I didn't know what I was talking about and that I was paranoid. He also said he was experienced in this kind of thing and that I wasn't. I told Hando in a very condescending way that might be true, but I sure as hell knew when we were being followed. When we got to the arcade, John stopped at one of the games in the front of the store while Hando and I walked to the back to buy game tokens from the machine, even though I was sure we would never get the chance to play.

When we got to the token machine, I turned around and told Hando that John was being arrested and that one of the men was walking back to us to arrest him. I wasn't sure if I would get arrested, but I wasn't worried – I hadn't stolen a thing! When the biggest man got to us, he forcefully nudged me aside and told Hando, "Young man, come with us." That was it. They didn't even look at me, and I watched the men take John and Hando away. And I remembered what I had told Hando the year before at the Wichita mall, so I left and drove back to Pittsburg.

As soon as I pulled up in front of John's house in Pittsburg, and before I could even get out of my beat-up Dodge Cornet, John's mom came flying out of the house screaming, "What the hell did Hando do this time?" She could tell that I was by myself, and in her mind, if John and Hando were not with me, then Hando would do something to get them in trouble. And, of course, she was right. I drove off with those two in the morning, and I returned without them in the afternoon. She was perceptive and knew Hando as well. I told her what happened, and we headed back to Joplin along with John's youngest brother, Joe.

When we arrived at the mall about 30 minutes later, we attempted to find out what happened to John and Hando but couldn't find anything. When we walked into the store where it all began, the terribly dressed store detective, with his belly rolled over his belt, recognized me. I told Joe that she was one of the men who arrested John and Hando. We left the store and stopped a short distance later at one of those stands in the middle of the mall that sells cheap jewelry or cheesy-looking black velvet paintings of fat Elvis. The detective stopped on the other side of the stand and just stared at us. Joe, never one to mince words, said in a loud, stern, and mean voice, "What the f... are you looking at?" at which point I laughed so hard while staring the man down that I thought I was going to wet myself. The dude looked horrified and quickly scuttled away. We never saw him again.

We left the mall and hurried our way to the downtown police station. John's mom went inside to see what she could find out. When she returned a short time later, she said that John and Hando had posted a bond and left. John had several hundred dollars of school grant money in his wallet. We hadn't missed them by much. She said they were charged with misdemeanor shoplifting. There were two main ways to leave Joplin for Pittsburg, and we basically dew straws and headed out of town. We didn't select correctly. Later, John told me they hitchhiked back to Pittsburg, and at an intersection of two highways, they saw my car fly by. In the end, John was fined around $150 for a $3 pair of Nike socks, and Hando was fined about $300. All for putting on clothes under the ones they walked into the store wearing. It's never worth it! John told me that one of the detectives asked them what the big guy took, referring to me since I was so much taller than John and Hando. They told him "nothing," which apparently satisfied him.

About a week later, my dad took me to Pittsburg so I could buy a bike for college. I didn't have my car anymore because I purposely didn't add oil when needed to see how long the motor would last. I already knew I was taking it to the junkyard before leaving for college, so I thought I would have a little fun with it. Well, during the week after the Joplin Affair, the engine gave out. I was able to limp the thing to the junkyard at about 5 miles an hour with my flashers on, the motor making a horrible noise that sounded like a dying whale, and black smoke rolling out the back. I got a whole $35 for the car. While in Pittsburg, I had dad take me by John's house. I hadn't heard from him since the thing in Joplin, and I wanted to see if he was OK. He was fine and was able to put the unfortunate incident behind and think forward to his sophomore year. John already knew I would not be his teammate, and I'm not sure if he was disappointed or not. But what I still didn't know, about a week out from the beginning of the fall semester, is if I was going to SofO. I hadn't received word from admissions.

I didn't see Hando again until the Christmas break. In fact, I didn't hear from him until I returned to Parsons after the fall semester ended. He really began to come into his own as a runner. He easily won the Regional two-mile in 10:02 on the home track in Parsons, and never looked stressed. The next weekend at the State Track meet he had a good chance to place in the top six and get a medal. I expected he would at least run a 9:45, especially since his two-mile time converted to a 9:58 3200m. But it wasn't to be. Around halfway through the race and running very well, Hando was hit in the head by the end of the pole vault crossbar. I saw the vaulter miss and hit the bar hard. Then the bar shot down to the first lane of the track like a torpedo, hitting Hando square in the temple and knocking him off balance. He wasn't the same the rest of the race, and he finished 8th or 9th at 10:08. It was a pretty good performance, considering. But he earned a track and cross-country scholarship to Neosho County Community College in Chanute, Kansas. Unfortunately, Hando squandered his opportunity. He quite the cross-country team about mid-way through the season and left school. During the winter, he was arrested for attempted armed robbery and spent a year in prison.

Most of the week after visiting John was a bit nerve-racking. If I did get accepted, I had already made plans with Ron to take me to campus because he had to be at BBC the same day. During the summer, Ron took a job working at a small truck stop about 10 or 12 miles north of Parsons on U.S. Highway 59. He worked late into the night, and I drove out to see him a couple of times and stayed until midnight. Finally, about three days before I was supposed to report to campus, and with the anxiety getting the best of me, I received the official word that I was accepted. I couldn't figure out why it took so long, other than the late application, and I was never told. Maybe it was my ACT scores. I never did see them, and I still don't know what I scored. Maybe I received a 12 or something lower, and Coach had to talk them into letting me in. Probably not; at least, I hope it isn't true!

The next spring, my cousin Phillip visited Southwestern College in Winfield, Kansas. He was there with some friends who were looking at the possibility of going to school there. I don't know why, but they met the track and cross-country coach. When he found out they were from Parsons, he asked them if they knew me and John Johnson, and of course, my cousin said he and I were related. The coach said he wished he would have had the opportunity to have me go to Southwestern from Coffeyville. Somehow, I guess, he knew I was at School of the Ozarks. He would have possibly known my name from some indoor track meets in which the schools competed, but I didn't know he knew me from Coffeyville Community College and Parsons High School and that John and I were high school teammates.

If I had known he was interested, I might have gone to Southwestern. Not only was it fairly close to Parsons, but they also had a couple of fantastic runners, including future NAIA national champion Steve Delano from Winfield High School and All-American Mike Lambing. Delano came from Class 5A like Parsons and beat Burkes at the State Cross-country Meet and State Track Meet when they were seniors. I guess we can all look back at many moments in our lives that would have completely changed the course. The coach at Southwestern may have never contacted me because he thought I would stay at Coffeyville for one more year.

Chapter 9
New Experience

On the Sunday before school began, Ron Faulkenberry drove me to the School of the Ozarks. When we arrived on campus, one of the first persons we saw was Coach Osburn. With Coach was a new freshman who was recruited to run, Kevin Bartholomeus from Springfield Kickapoo High School in Missouri, and Kevin's roommate, who was a freshman baseball player. We had a pleasant talk with Coach, and I could tell that he would have liked to have had Ron on the team. But Coach didn't ask Ron to transfer because he wouldn't have broken the rules.

That first week at SofO, as the College was called, I met an interesting person who had a strong personality. His name was Chris Marcak, and he was one of my new teammates. Chris was my age and started at SofO the year before. He was from West Plains, Missouri, which is a cross-country and distance running powerhouse in the State. Chris was one of the original West Plains Zizzers distance greats, if not the first. The school started cross-country in Chris' junior year, and by his second season, when he was a senior, the team won the 1979 class 4A state title (Missouri's largest class). As of 2024, West Plains has won many cross-country titles for boys and girls and most coached by the legendary Joe Bill Dixon, who started coaching Chris when he was in junior high.

DAM RUN

Chris was the best teammate I ever had. He could run, and he was the toughest runner and competitor I ever had the pleasure to call a teammate. Chris never looked like a distance runner. He was short and stocky, with huge calves, a broad smile, long sideburns, a thick mustache, and a flop of black hair. We used to call him the Miniature Shot Putter or Little Cave Man, and he thought those names were great. He was a brutal cross-country runner and could make a competitor crumble with exhaustion if he attempted to stay with him. I think Chris was made to be a cross-country runner, and I found him to be better on the grass and roads than he was on the track, not that he was a slouch on the oval.

The first time I met Chris, I was sitting on a wall outside Smith dorm, where my room was located. I was sitting with another teammate, Rod Land, who was a hell of a runner in high school in southern Illinois. I met Rod a day or so before when he came by Coach's office to tell him that he had just had an emergency appendectomy a week or so before and would miss the cross-country season. Rod and Chris knew each other from the previous year but were surprised to see him because Chris had left SofO at the beginning of the previous spring semester and transferred to Arkansas College, now called Lyon College. But Chris had returned to SofO. I was a little fascinated by Chris, especially with his profound Ozark accent and the fact that he had a wad of chewing tobacco or snuff in his mouth. A runner chewed tobacco? Seemed odd to me.

Chris was nice but very protective of his status as the best distance runner on the team. After a while, he said he was driving into Branson, or town, as he put it, and began to walk away. After walking about 10 or 15 yards, he turned around and said, "You'ns coming with me?" which sounded like Yuns to me. I didn't say anything and just looked at him. Then Chris said it again. I said, "Man, my name is Raymond," as I thought, "who has a name like You'ns?" I looked over to Rod for clarification, and he said, in his own southern Illinois accent, it means "You 'all." Well, I understood that, so I got up and went to town with Chris. Rod decided to stay behind. I don't think he was 100% after surgery.

SofO was truly a new world for me, a new beginning. First off, almost everyone was nice, but there was this religious thing, or more appropriately, a Christian thing, that hovered over just about everything that I wasn't used to – it was embedded in the School's DNA. No girls in the dorms other than the lobby and curfews were just a couple of things that were odd to me. And right off the bat, I noticed a double standard. The Girls' dorms were locked at midnight, but the doors to the Boy's dorms remained unlocked. Those first few weeks, I felt as if I'd made a big mistake. Not necessarily that I had not enrolled at Pitt State, but because I chose to attend School of the Ozarks. I didn't think I fit in; it was an alien world. When the front tire of my new bike was stolen in those first two weeks while it was locked in the bike stand by the dorm, I should have at least felt at home that this world was indeed not perfect. But instead, it just pissed me off. Right at the end of the first semester, the dorm supervisor, an ex-Marine, found the tire in one of the dorm rooms. I contemplated how I might kick the kid's ass, encouraged by the supervisor, but I never felt the urge to beat up the small kid.

The other big change was running. I had never trained like this. In fact, I had never trained for cross-country. The first run was on an extremely hot day, which was the one thing to which I could relate. Coach Oz, as we called him, said we would run 8 miles, which was not difficult for me. I wondered why we weren't running more. When we got to the end of the run at a place called Scenic View, Coach was waiting for us with a drink mix, sort of like Gator Ade. Scenic was indeed scenic. In fact, it was beautiful. It over-looked Lake Taneycomo, or the White River, Table Rock Dam, which I would come to love and hate at the same time, and a vast valley with small mountains beyond. Today, that view is ruined by Branson sprawl and a golf course.

I was exhausted by this 8-mile run. It was so hilly, and I mean steep hills, that I had a difficult time keeping up on the inclines. I had never run up hills like this. It was a beautiful route through the woods, in a valley next to the river-lake and up again through the woods that just kept going up! Then I was shocked – Scenic View was only halfway. We had only run 4 miles. I really thought we had run 8 miles. This was by far the most difficult 4 miles I had ever run, and I had to run the route, called Acacia Club Road, virtually every day. So, along with my teammates, I turned around and headed back to campus for the final 4 miles. The first half of the run back to school wasn't so bad, although not as easy as one might think, considering we were going down that two-mile mountain.

But the biggest challenge was when we began our ascent back to campus after the flat area by Taneycomo. I had not realized just how steep the hill was when we ran down, but now I was struggling to maintain any semblance of a running pace. I felt like I was almost walking. Just as we approached the hill, one of my teammates said something about coming up to Cardiac Hill. And he was right. By the time I reached the top of this hill that was at least a half mile away, my heart was beating so fast I thought it would stop at any moment. The deception of Cardiac was that the first half was extremely steep, but when you reached the end of the steep section and thought you had made the summit, you still had a quarter mile left of the hill; it just wasn't as steep. But it was still a grind after taking on the first half.

My campus workstation was in the cafeteria. This job didn't alter my training schedule or cause me any issues with practice. Some campus workstations caused all sorts of problems, not only with training but with classes and studying as well. For example, some team members had to work in the power plant during the overnight shift and had to find time to study, run, go to class, and sleep. In fact, the year before, Chris Marcak worked the all-night shift at the power plant shoveling high-Sulphur coal. Not only was it horrendous for the lungs of a runner (or anyone for that matter), but it got in the way of school and training. I think it might be a major reason he transferred. I think Steve Davis also worked in the power plant at one point before I arrived, but I don't know the shift he worked. What seemed exceedingly unfair was that the basketball players were usually given plush, easy jobs in the fieldhouse. Because we were on athletics scholarships, we worked 15 hours a week at our jobs, while other students worked 20 hours per week. We also had to work three 40-hour work weeks on breaks. I was told when I was recruited that I would get the break time off. However, only the basketball players didn't have to work those 40-hour weeks.

Practice started at 4:00 pm sharp, and we were expected to be there on time. But many times, we didn't actually begin running for a while. It was not untypical that after our stretching and abdominal work in the weight room, we went to one of the classrooms in the fieldhouse to have a meeting with Coach. These meetings could be short, but many times were too long, and the athletes cooled down too much. This wasn't a major issue the first month to six weeks of the cross-country season if we were on a distance run because the weather was usually hot. But if we did pace work or repeats, it did have a negative effect on us. In a distance run, we could use the few minutes to ease into the workout, maybe running 7:30 or so during the first mile. If it was an easy distance day, then 7:30 on the hills was the pace for the entire run, but on hard days, we would run 8 to 13 miles at closer to 6:30 per mile, and on really fast days, 6:00 or under for the distance, although it would be a while before I could run under 6:00 for long runs. But when we had speed work, we didn't get the opportunity to re-warm up, although sometimes we might get an easy 440.

One of my favorite workouts was kind of an odd one for cross-country. During the fall, Coach took us to a church camp called Kanakuk, which was situated on Lake Taneycomo and about 4 or 5 miles from campus. Because the lake, which was really a glorified river, flowed from the bottom of Table Rock Dam, the water was cold. In fact, Taneycomo is world-class trout water. When the breeze came off the lake, it created a fantastic cool sensation, even on hot days. Kanakuk had an old dirt track about 350 yards long that was rutted in places, and one end was slightly carved out of the side of the hill. I was not terribly impressed when we arrived for my first Kanakuk workout, but it didn't take long to change my mind.

It wasn't the track that forced me to reevaluate the workout, but it was the workout itself. Coach Oz had us run endless relays. He cut up a broken pole vault pole into baton-sized pieces and usually placed a member of the women's team with one of the men. Many times, I was paired with freshman Belinda Welcher from West Plains, who and like me, was a middle-distance specialist. I don't remember how many we actually did that first endless relay workout, but it was probably around 30. Coach Oz was notorious for losing count. He drew lines in the dirt for every rep, but it wasn't easy keeping track when the several two-person teams were spread over the entire length of the track after just a few runs. I found out when we did repeats on our all-weather track that Coach didn't keep good tabs on our reps there, either.

As the season progressed, our once-a-week endless relays increased to sometimes 50. In my junior year, we even ran over 70 on more than one occasion. I loved the Kanakuk endless relays, but 70 + was ridiculous. Of course, the rest period was minimal. It seemed as if I would just finish my leg when my partner was rounding the final curve to hand me the crude baton. To some degree, it was possible to cruise the run, but at some point, it would become obvious that you were slacking when other teams were lapping you. So, I just made sure I ran each one hard. Plus, taking it easy would not make me a better runner. When the workout was finished, most of us were vanquished, and then we had to climb the steep stairs to the top where the van was parked.

Like many teams, ours was made up of a hodgepodge of characters. I liked Kevin Bartholomeus, but he quit the team before the second semester began. On one day, Kevin could be a good friend, and I enjoyed spending time with him, but the next, he might not even acknowledge you existed, and it usually depended on who he was with. Nonetheless, Kevin was a good person. Paul Taylor was from Dalles, Oregon, and attended Oregon State University as a freshman but was not on their team. One of his older brothers had been student body president at SofO several years before, and another older brother was a small college All-American, I believe, at Lewis and Clark College, who had also raced in Europe. I remember Paul telling me that his brother finished second in the Oregon State Track Meet to one of Oregon's all-time great distance runners, Bill McChesney. Paul was a different kind of character and somewhat crazy with a unique view of the world, but all of this was good. Whenever I think of Paul, a smile comes to my face. He was just a great person to be around! He was also a unique racer.

Alan Hicks was a steady teammate from Lebanon, Missouri, who would push you in a race if you slacked off. I didn't lose to Alan much, but he did beat me here and there. Alan's older brother, Mark, was our pole vaulter and a pretty good one at that. He could have been a good middle-distance runner as well if he'd concentrated his efforts there, especially in the 800m and probably the 400. But he would have also been a strong, small college cross-country runner, in my opinion. Alan was a great person and teammate, but for some reason, he always seemed to be on Coach's bad side, while Mark was on his good side. This must have frustrated Alan, and to listen to Alan complain about the way Coach treated him, which wasn't really bad, was hilarious. Coach used to sometimes tease Alan a little, which I also found hilarious. Alan was a pretty strait-laced kid, and I was humored by how Paul's racing antics freaked out Alan.

Maybe my favorite teammate, and one of the nicest persons one could ever know, was Darren Wickliff. Darren was from Franklin,

Indiana, and was a pretty good runner. He ran 5 miles in the 27s and was consistent. For some reason, Coach Oz had issues with Darren at times, and I'm not 100% sure why. But Coach did like Darren, and, in fact, I've never met anyone who didn't like Darren. It might be a cliché, but Darren would give you the shirt off his back. He was also a great training partner. Over the years, I reconnected with Darren, and although we lose track of each other sometimes, we usually find a way to find each other again.

Ricky Sullins was another good teammate, but he only remained at school for the fall semester, although he did stay on the team throughout the cross-country season. I think Ricky was from the St. Louis area, but I'm not sure if he was from the Missouri or Illinois side of the river, and I don't recall if he was a freshman or sophomore. He told me that at a road race in St. Louis, while he was stretching during his warmup, he was accidentally kicked and turned to see that it was the great American distance runner and Olympian Craig Virgin who said "sorry" when he realized what he had done. That was Ricky's claim to fame! Ricky was also a steady runner. We were a very young team, and most of the members wouldn't be with the team long enough for us to build for the future. A couple of other teammates were only on the team for a short time, and I don't think they ran any meets. The 1:59 800m guy, I think his name was Larry, who I raced in Springfield, started out on the team but left sometime during the season and, I think, left school at the end of the semester. Arthur Tindle, who was a really nice guy, didn't remain with the team either. I might be wrong, but I think he had an injury during the fall. I think he also left school in December.

My mentality at that time was one of being competitive, and I looked at every workout in that vein. I learned this from John, who said that everyone on the Pittsburg State team was expected to work out like that. And I remember Coach Cagle indicating the same thing. Maybe or maybe not, but I was geared to think of college running like that. So, guys who left my first semester were viewed as collateral from the ultra-competitive nature of college athletics. I didn't give those who left a second thought, although I wish Ricky had stayed.

During the third week of practice, Coach Oz decided to run a trial to see where team members were in their racing fitness. But it wasn't really a time trial, although I'm sure it was timed. The "race" was a 4 mile on Acacia Club Road from Campus to Scenic View, an extremely grueling route, of course, so time meant nothing. We didn't have much in the way of experienced college cross-country runners competing for team spots, especially because of Rod's surgery and Chris' transfer ineligibility. Chris did run the trial as did Dan Mills, who had been Steve's teammate at Alan County, whose eligibility in cross-country was up, and maybe even another runner or two. But the core were the guys who ran on the team. I'm not even sure the girls ran the trial, but it seems that they must have. I don't think Paul Taylor ran with us that day, and I'm not even sure he had yet joined the team. I might be wrong, but Paul might not have been on campus yet.

I took off hard with exceedingly focused determination. My plan was to beat all the eligible runners. I could have cared less what my time was as long as I beat my teammates. I stayed with Chris and Dan down Cardiac and let the steep decline carry me, which was more difficult than one might think because of the pounding on the body. But when we reached the flat area by the lake, they were able to leave me behind quite easily. Still, I was ahead of the eligible runners, and I was able to put distance between me and them on the flats. I believed I needed this edge as I got to the difficult and long mile and a half or two-mile incline to the Scenic View finish, otherwise some of them might catch this Kansas flatlander.

As I began to climb that arduous hill in the woods toward Scenic View, my lungs began to burn as if the air was thin, but of course it wasn't. But the hot, humid air did cause me some breathing issues. Still, I ran strong, even though my legs began to feel like rubber the more I climbed hard. I finally reached the highway and turned right for the 100 to 150 yards to Scenic. I could see Coach's red car in the parking area, and as I turned to look to my side to see if anyone was close behind, all I saw was an empty road. I ran hard to the car and stopped in pain and satisfaction. No eligible runner came close. I don't know how fast I ran. It might be in an old training log, but I can't find it, and the years have erased it from my memory. I don't know who finished second, but it was probably Darren or Allan. What I did know was that after a drink or two of Coach's sports drink and a little time to recover, I ran an easy pace back to school. The four-mile run wasn't difficult until I reached Cardiac, but I ran as easy as I could up that monster and reached campus tired and hungry. Arthur Tindal and the 800m runner both said they believed I was going to be a good runner. It wasn't long after that both left the team.

For our first meet we traveled to Northwest Missouri State University. The five-mile race was run around a corn field. It's possible I raced an old high school teammate, Mike Butler, who was a freshman just up the road at Graceland College, right across the border in Iowa. We discussed this a few years later, but I never saw him at the race, and I was never sure he was there. Chris Marcak ran unattached, and I know the rest of us didn't run very well. I'm not even sure Chris ran well. With a best time of 30:15 from my one race the year before and knowing that I had a lot of hard training behind me over the last year, I expected this race to go a couple of minutes faster and a lot easier. It wasn't easier. In fact, it felt like 10 miles. I didn't think it was ever going to end, and all I kept thinking about was that I wanted to stop, and I hated cross-country.

I beat some teammates, but I don't know which ones. I know I beat our freshman 400m runner, Jerry Goodrich, a pretty good sprinter from the Boot Heel of Missouri. I think he ran 48 in high school. Jerry was recruited to run for the University of Missouri, and spent a few days there, if my memory is correct. But he came to SofO sometime in the first week of the semester. I asked him where he was from during the first week or two, but I couldn't understand what he said. He spoke too fast and with a southern drawl. I asked him several times, and he kept saying what sounded like "boody" or "booty." Where the hell is booty? And he would say, "no, booty." "That's what I just said" I told him. Finally, another teammate said, "he is from the Bootheel." "Ok, so what the hell is the Boot Hill, is it a town? I thought it was in Dodge City." It was explained to me that this was an area in extreme southeast Missouri that extends down into what should be Arkansas and looks like the heel of a boot, and it wasn't "hill."

At any rate, the race at Northwest didn't go so well for me but I did manage to run in the 29s, so at least I had a PR. Still, I didn't think I wanted anything to do with cross-country. I was an 800 and 1500 guy. I had no business running 5 miles. But on Monday I was back at practice with the drive to get in better distance shape and try and enjoy these marathon races. As we got passed the first meet and into the fall schedule, the races became easier and the training runs got longer, from 8 miles, to 10, and then to 13 miles. Our runs had names. The 8 miler was called the Scenic View or just plain Scenic. The 10-mile run was named Beard Mountain because that was where the turnaround was located. The 13 miler was the DX run because the place we turned around was next to an old DX service station across from the State Park on Table Rock Lake. The view when you ran past the Beard Mountain turnaround to the DX station was spectacular as it overlooked Table Rock. The highway was dangerous though because there wasn't a shoulder to get out of the way of cars, and RVs, and on the south side was a steep hill down to the lake.

These were tough, tough runs on hills. All these runs started on Acacia Club Road for the first 4 miles and ended on the same road for the last four. Then there was the 16 miler that went passed DX to Table Rock Dam. To make it a true 16 miler, you had to run across the concrete section of the dam before turning around to head back home. The highway crossed the dam. This was called the "Dam Run," and it was brutal for a guy from Kansas who had never run these kinds of hills and had never run 16 miles before SofO. The easiest part of the Dam Run was from about a quarter mile before the DX station to the far end of the Dam, and then back past DX where the long hill up Beard Mountain began – this area was flat. I ran the Dam Run many times during my years at SofO, and it seemed to be the workout that defined us. I think those on campus who knew we ran the 16-mile Dam Run thought we were crazy, but I got to a point that I liked it – most of the time! I also found out that there was a longer Dam Run later in that first semester.

Our second race was the All-Missouri Intercollegiate Meet at the University of Missouri in Columbia. This was a meet just for Missouri schools and most were there. The race was on a golf course and had some hills but was smooth running. When the gun sounded, I took off like there was no tomorrow. I was with the leaders for a good half mile, running with the big boys – that was the last time I saw those "big boys." By the time the race was over, most of my teammates had passed me. I might have beaten one, but I'm not sure I even did that. I barely broke 30 minutes on the 8k course, maybe running 29:45. I had not improved from the first race, and I had gone out much too hard for my fitness and experience. The winner was a soccer player from a rival NAIA school in our district. I'm not sure I ever raced him again. What I did know is that I hated this race more than the first one at Northwest Missouri.

As our third meet approached at Southwest Baptist University in Bolivar, Missouri, I looked forward to it with anticipation because I would get the opportunity to race Ron Faulkenberry. But I didn't get the chance. While working in the cafeteria, I was carrying a ten-gallon pot of boiling water with my teammate Arthur Tindle. We were carrying the water to clean something because the hot water wasn't working from the facet. As we slowly walked, some of the hot water splashed onto Arthur's hand, instantly burning him, and he dropped his side of the pot, leaving me holding the other handle. The ten gallons poured out onto the floor and much of the boiling water was dumped on my left foot, scolding it and as I attempted to move back, the now wet and greasy slick floor caused me to fall right in the middle of the water. I rolled out of the water, lucky to not get dangerously burned on my body, but my foot and ankle were not so lucky.

I was in severe pain, and I clocked out to head to my dorm room, although I'm not sure what I thought going there would do. I should have stopped at the campus hospital to see the doctor, but I just laid down in my room and tried to tough it out. Arthur felt horrible but it wasn't his fault. We should have never been allowed to carry that much scorching hot water that was filled to the rim of the large pot. As I laid in my room in pain, I finally went to sleep and missed practice. Coach was furious with me because I hadn't come to practice letting him know what had happened. My explanation of falling asleep didn't satisfy him. He got over it soon enough, and I think seeing the four-inch blister just below the outside of my left ankle as well as the other two or three smaller blisters caused him to see just what I was dealing with.

So, I couldn't race Ron on Saturday, and I missed a weeks' worth of training. Knowing that I couldn't race, my girlfriend asked me to spend the weekend with her at the family cabin on Lake of the Ozarks, but I declined. After pissing off Coach Oz earlier in the week, I didn't want to further exasperate the situation by telling him that I wasn't traveling to the meet with the team. Plus, I did want to see Ron. Ron was disappointed that we didn't get to race, and he didn't run particularly well. The course was several laps around a building and a field, maybe an athletics field, in an oval. Ron said the reason he liked cross-country is that it was different than track. But this course was like running on a grass track, in his opinion. Even though I didn't run the race, I had to agree with him. Nonetheless, I was disappointed as well because I wanted to run against Ron in that race.

Although the skin on my ankle was tender, I was back training by the middle of the next week. I placed some padding in the area below the outside of my ankle where the top of the shoe rubbed, and I wore an extra sock. It was not perfect, but I managed. In the middle of the season, we ran a pretty big invitational at the University of Missouri-Rolla. The first runner of each team received a watch, and I wanted the watch. I saw that Pittsburg State was going to be there, so I looked forward to racing and seeing John Johnson. But Pitt State never arrived. How disappointing. Later, John told me that his coach told the team he wasn't spending money to go to a meet just to give his first runner a watch. But I was still determined to win the watch on my team and ran the best race I'd ever run, finishing the five-mile course in 27:12 – I won the watch, and it would be the only one I would ever win. I would end up running on this course several times and just loved it. It was run on a campus golf course and had easy hills, and the grass provided great footing. I had taken more than two minutes off my previous best, and the race wasn't that difficult. I was becoming a cross-country runner. In a team meeting on Monday, Coach bragged to Chris about my improvement, but my new teammate couldn't bring himself to acknowledge that I had run a good race!

After I finished the race, I walked around to a place about 50 or 60 yards from the finish line to cheer for my teammates. As Alan came around the corner to the finishing stretch, Paul, competing unattached came screaming up next to Alan with legs flying in every direction and arms flailing, yelling at Alan and a couple of other runners, "Come on suckers, Come on suckers!" over and over with a freakish laugh. This caused Alan to look over at Paul in disbelief and it totally freaked him out. Alan's eyes were as wide as silver dollars, and he slowed to the point of fear. Paul beat Alan, and Alan couldn't for the life of him understand this bizarre behavior. I don't think

Alan was right for days. He just kept harping on the incident, totally dismayed. I thought Coach Oz would kill Paul, but instead he loved the antics. It was completely opposite of what I thought Coach would accept.

We went to St. Louis the next weekend to race in the Washington University Invitational contested in Forest Park. It was a great course with stiff competition and a lot of teams, even some from Indiana and some from the Chicago area. The problem was that it was raining heavily and had been all night. The course looked good, but there were several inches of standing water in many places and going uphill I sank in the mud to the top of my ankles. Of course, we all did. But I ran a horrible race and finished well behind most of my teammates. However, I wasn't too discouraged because I knew we had Conference and District coming up.

One thing I had never thought about was my spiritual belief. Sure, I believed in God, and the basic belief of my family was Christian. But I found that to many students at SofO being a Christian was not the belief in God and that Jesus died for our sins. To them, it was whether you had been saved, or in other words, did you get down on your knees with hands and head pointing to the heavens and ask God to forgive you of your sins. I had never heard of being "saved," and I was very uncomfortable with being confronted with the question.

One evening after studying with a group, one guy walked with me back to my dorm and asked me that question – "Are you a Christian?" I think I said yes, but I don't think this satisfied him. So, he asked me if I'd asked Jesus to come into my life. I didn't know what he was talking about, and he didn't get me to pray with him to ask God to forgive me of my sins. For the rest of my years at SofO, I had to deal with hearing these questions and the pursuit of Bible Beaters attempting to convert me. Years later, I did become a Christian, so I guess their pursuit paid off, but it just took a decade and a half.

DAM RUN

The Ozark Conference Meet was held in late October at a lake just north of Springfield. For some reason, the meet was held on the roads. So instead of grass we raced on the asphalt. I wasn't too happy with this, but in the bigger scope of things, it didn't matter, especially since I would finally get the opportunity to race Ron. We took 5 guys to the Meet because of injuries, although we only had six eligible runners left. The women didn't have a conference race, but Coach Oz brought along their best runner, Angie Pikschus. Coach might have had the thought of actually entering her in the race. She was, after all, an All-American and ran a 2:42 marathon after cross-country season. As it ended up, we needed her on the team. Although he traveled with us, Kevin was too sick to race. I found out later that he was just badly hung-over. I know there was a protest of some sort from the Park College coach, but she was allowed to race anyway. She was our fifth runner that day, being outkicked by Jerry, who wasn't about to let a girl beat him. Jerry took about two minutes off his best 5-mile time to beat Angie. Both ran in the 28:40s.

I had four goals for the Conference Meet: to help the team with a high finish, run a personal best time, make All-Conference, and beat Ron! Maybe I placed too much emphasis on Ron, and I'm sure he did the same with me, but it worked to our advantage. With both of us eyeing each other, we ran together for most of the race with a few others. I went out faster than I had before (excluding the All-Mizzu first half mile), and by this point of the season, I was finally comfortable being a cross-country runner. The races were easier, and I could run faster and be competitive. No matter how tired I got, I needed to stay with Ron, so I kept hammering away. In the last mile, I made the decision to leave the small pack I was in, which included Ron. I was still strong and felt this was the chance to make my move and finish ahead of my old high school teammate. I was running as our first runner, but I wasn't sure what place I was in. This was my defining move of the race, and I left the others in that pack behind. I finished in 6th place with a time of 26:43, not only a PR but an All-Conference performance as well. And I had finished ahead of Ron, who made All-Conference with an 8th-place performance in just over 27 minutes. Our team finished in 4th place.

Although it was on the roads, the course was hilly and a little difficult. Not any long hills, but a bunch of smaller ones that I would classify as rolling hills. After the race, I could tell that Ron was disappointed. He really wanted to beat me. But considering where he was in June when we ran at the Independence meet, he had come a long way. He told me after the race that I should have run cross-country in high school because it would have made us a stronger team, maybe even the top three in Class 5A. Maybe, I don't know. I'm not sure I was ready as a 16-year-old to be a good cross-country runner. But with Burkes 3rd at State and Ron 10th, if I could have been in the top 20, he might have been right. I do wish Ron would have transferred to SofO – he would have been a good runner there and a great teammate. He could have run in the 25s, I'm quite sure. I only saw Ron one more time, and that was for about 15 minutes several years later after I was married and living back in Parsons. Sometimes, and for whatever reason, you lose track of old friends. I do know that Ron died in 2020.

As well as I ran at Conference, I ran equally as bad at District. This meet was held north of Kansas City and was hosted by Park. It was also the National qualifying race. The top team qualified as well as the top 5 runners not on the winning team. I knew I had a legitimate chance after my Conference performance. But this course was unfairly difficult. A newspaper in Kansas City even did an article in which it questioned whether the course was unfair. I was still not used to the tough hills and was never competitive. I fell in the first mile when I stepped in a deep hole on a steep downhill. When I was sliding on the ground, a runner from Westminster, Barth Winkler, hurdled over me, and my momentum brought me right back up. I hardly missed a step and just kept running. The winner, an All-American from Park, who had run in the 24s for 5 miles, won in 28 something. I don't think it was the same runner who won the All

Missouri meet because I believe he left the team. Our first runner was Alan Hicks who missed qualifying for Nationals by one place and less than a second. Angie won the women's race and went on to make All-American again.

Despite my District meet race, overall, I was satisfied with my first cross-country season. I made big strides during the season and went from an also-ran to a fairly competitive runner, at least in some races. I now set my sights on finishing my first semester at SofO and the coming track season. Although my mileage during the cross-country season had increased, I had not reached 100 miles in a week. At most, I hit 85, which in retrospect was probably too much for a 6" 2" 170-to-175-pound kid. Nonetheless, I wanted to run a 100-mile week. Any member of the team who ran a 100-mile week received a maroon hat (team color) that read "100 Mile Club." So, a week or two after District I started out on my first 100-mile week. I ran much of this mileage with Darren and reached 105 miles in seven days. Even one of our 400-meter runners, Nate Lampkins, ran a 100-mile week. He wanted a hat.

I don't know if I did this during the 100-mile week or not, but I think I probably did. On a cool Saturday morning, Darren and I set out on the "second" Dam Run. When we got to the far side of Table Rock Dam, the 8-mile mark, instead of turning around we continued going straight. We sometimes called that running around the Dam. Once we crossed the Dam, we ran down the highway for a few miles until we reached Highway 76, or the Strip, in Branson. We ran down the Strip until we reached US 65 and headed south across the bridge over Taneycomo, up a long hill and then turned the last half mile or so to campus. In other words, we did a big circle, which was 21 miles. Darren and I ran a sensible pace and conversational, and in the end of the 21 miles, it really didn't seem so bad. But I had run a number of 16 milers on the Dam Run, so this was only 5 miles more. The next time I ran around the Dam, was a different story.

Chapter 10
Realizing I Was Fast

The last few weeks of the semester, Coach had all the men's track athletes run the Hollister Steps. These were very old concrete steps that started at road level across Tanycomo from Branson in the small town of Hollister. They reached the top of a cliff, and they were really steep and long. The steps were in several sections. After running one section, you would turn right or left, depending on the direction of the walk, and then begin to run up again after a few short feet of flat. In addition, the steps were falling apart and just plain dangerous. Like all the others on the team, I despised the Steps. For me it was not so much that they were difficult, but because I don't think they did me any good as a middle-distance runner. All they did for me were tighten my legs and take all the energy out of my body. I should have been running distance instead of climbing those stairs. Coach Oz had us run 100 stairs a week, for three weeks. By the end of the semester, my legs were crap. My knees hurt, my hips hurt, my tendons hurt, and I think my ass hurt, although that might be a mistake.

My saving grace was that the semester ended, and I could go back to Parsons, let my legs recover, and run some distance over the Christmas break. As I look back, I can't think but we might have had it wrong. In fact, I know we could have trained with better efficiency. But this was an era, I think, in which training tons of miles and intervals was the norm. But other coaches must have had a more progressive method and approach. I read during those years about Sebastian Coe and his method in which he followed his father's regimen of speed endurance training. I brought this up to Coach Oz, but he dismissed it. I spoke to him about Steve Scott's training, and he dismissed that as well. This didn't make sense to me at the time because they were the best in the world. But one thing is for sure, which I didn't fully understand then, is that there are many training programs that work, and some are better for some while other approaches don't work as well for some athletes. Coach was set in his ways, and I can see that now as I coach. I'm kind of set in my ways as well, and some of what I use is based on what I didn't agree with when I was in college, or in other words, what didn't seem to work well with me and my teammates. But I still try and stay informed about more recent approaches. One thing I'm certain of though, from near and far, yesterday and today, I would never recommend the Hollister Steps for a distance runner.

During the Christmas break, I spent some time in Pittsburg with John training and back home in Parsons running most days and doing a few runs with Hando. My goal was to be ready for the 880 during the indoor season. I still wasn't hooked on the mile, at least for indoor races. Eight or ten laps seemed too far for me and at any rate I still considered myself a half-miler, at least that's what I wanted to be. I still thought I had the basic speed, and today I still think I did. When I returned to SofO for the Spring semester, we traveled to Pittsburg State for our first indoor meet, which took place before classes began. This mid-January all-comers meet was not attended by many schools, and some of the races were not that competitive. That was the case in the 880. Including me, there were only four entered. I know Allen County Community College had one or two, and Pitt State had one. Although John was at the meet, he didn't run the 880.

I don't remember if John ran the 1000-yard run or something else or didn't race at all. It was difficult to talk with John at these meets because it pissed off his coach if his kids spoke with those from other teams, at least that's what John told me. I know the both of us got a hateful stare more than once when his coach caught us speaking with each other at these indoor races at Pitt State. I got off well in the 880 and took the lead from the beginning. The half mile on the Pitt State track was 5 laps and the surface was green rubber and there were no banked curves. But we could wear spikes, which was a tremendous help with grip on the curves. I liked the track, and one could run some pretty good times. For example, the best series of races on short indoor tracks that I witnessed came during that 1982 indoor season on that Pittsburg State track. Roddy Gaynor, the former Pitt State runner from Ireland ran a 1:51 880, a 2:10 1000y, I believe a 4:10 mile, and a really fast 600 yards during three or four meets we attended there. I didn't race him that winter because, by chance, I was entered in different races. I can't say I knew Gaynor, but it was at his house the previous year that I drank far too much and made an ass of myself.

During that first 880 at Pitt State, I was never pushed and just cruised the race. I was trying to run a fast time, but it was difficult to gage my pace when I was far ahead of the field. I tried to run as hard as I could the last lap, but I wasn't yet sharp. I was a little winded at the end but not tired. My time was 2:00.3. Not great, but about equal in time to my best outdoor 800m, but superior in effort. One of the runners from Allen County in the 880 who competed against me in high school when he ran for Iola, was shocked that I had run two-minutes in January and wondered if we had been running a lot of speed work. I told him no. I also saw one of my former high school teammates Mike Burnett, and he was impressed with how I ran. It reminded me of just how good he might have been in the hurdles if given the opportunity because he was very good athletic. My parents were there, and I really wanted them to see me break 2:00. Of course, the conversion was a little below 2:00 for an 800m, but they still didn't see me run under that barrier, as far as I was concerned. But I was ready for our next meet, which was right back at that same track.

During the winter I didn't train like a middle-distance runner, but more like an athlete that competed in distance races. I knew it would make me stronger for the outdoor season, but I wasn't sure how Coach would train us from mid-April on. Regardless, I felt ready for a good 880 at the second Pittsburg State Meet. Unlike the first race, this 880 had a strong field and John and I were entered. I knew John was the best half-miler in the field and I thought I might be second, but with other good runners in the race I was not 100% sure. I knew a couple in the race, besides John, were more accomplished than me, but their successes had come in longer races, even cross-country, so I thought I just might be better than them in the shorter distance.

When the race began, I placed myself in a competitive position and just followed. I don't think I heard my 440 split, but I was running comfortably and ready to pounce when needed. As we raced, as usual, the laps were called out to us, or rather, how many laps remained. Half a lap past the 440, as we crossed the start/finish line I heard "two laps to go." I felt great and thought about sprinting to the lead at that point. I wanted to take the lead so I could control the front and get a jump on John because I knew he liked to come from behind and sometimes he waited too long or let the others get too far ahead to make up all the distance. If this happed and I was in the lead, I could win the race, and maybe get a National Meet qualifying time in the process.

However, I hesitated and thought the better of taking the lead at that point, which in retrospect was a mistake. My new plan was to take the lead just after we cross the line with one lap to go. When we hit the line, and with me right on John's shoulder in about 4th place, the lap counter yelled "two laps to go." This caused me to hesitate for a moment. Had I miss-counted the laps? Were there really three laps to go when they yelled two laps the first time? I don't know, but as far as I could tell, the only two that hesitated were John and me. The others in front of us started to sprint. And they were all Pitt State runners, and one guy who had previously run for them. I thought they were going too early, and that John and I would smoke them. But something wasn't sitting well with me – something wasn't right. As we came off the final curve with just a few yards to go, I knew I'd made a mistake, and I realized this before John did as I easily passed him to take 5th or 6th place, I don't know, I was too pissed off to know or care. I wasn't the least bit tired.

I had beaten John for the first time, but it was hollow. I wanted to beat him or lose to him in a fair race. John was more upset than me. I ran a 2:01 and John was right behind me. The winning time was only 1:59, or 1:58 at the fastest. John believed this miss-counting of the laps was done on purpose, set up by one of his teammates to beat him, and it seemed suspicious to me as well. At that point I was no longer fairly sure I was the second best in the race, but I was positively sure. Those other guys in the race were not better than me or John. And the reaction of one of the Pitt State runners and the former Pitt State runner, both who finished ahead of us, one of which won the race, was peculiar. At that point I had little doubt that at least one of them had cheated and set this up. John pleaded with his coach to re-run the race, but the coach just blew him off. I asked Coach Oz to protest, but for an early-season indoor race, Coach didn't think it was necessary. I vowed to never let anything like that happen again.

I told John to tell his coach to have those two entered in the 880 in the next meet so we could show them who was boss. But when we arrived for our third meet of the season, again at Pittsburg State, those two were not in the 880. But John and I were. There were still good runners entered in the half mile, including two, I think, that finished ahead of us in the previous meet. I wasn't taking any chances here and I wasn't following anyone at the beginning, so I took the lead at the start. I wasn't running a fast pace, which was not necessarily the goal. I just wanted to control the race, and I made damn sure I counted the laps myself since the same idiots were calling out the laps. Somewhere in the middle of the race, just after crossing the start/finish line John surprised me by passing me in the curve. John had tremendous speed and before I could respond, he was by me.

I knew my speed was fairly good, but I hadn't realized yet that I had outstanding speed. My basic speed was superior to our other middle-distance and distance runners, but we had a 10.3 100m runner in Willie Williams, and a 10.5 guy is Trent Brinson, Willie's high school teammate, so I didn't have a good opportunity to see what my real speed was when running sprints against them, and other fast sprinters on our team. When John passed me on the curve, he cut me off, bumped me and caused me to break stride. I was far bigger than John so I wasn't off balance, but with my stride broken I didn't have the momentum to immediately attempt to pass him back, although I doubt I could have anyway. But despite that incident, and one in which John should have been disqualified, I never lost touch and remained right behind him. I knew my chance to win was small at that point, and I should have ridden up on John's shoulder and tried to pass him. At least it would have caused John to pick up the pace and we both would have run a couple of seconds faster. But I just followed and hoped John wasn't sharp that day.

On the final lap, I tried to pass him, but John had too much for me, although he wasn't able to create more space between us. John won in 1:58 and I ran 1:59. This was my first sub-two for an 880 and indoors and it didn't feel too bad losing to John. After we cross the finish line, and I wasn't tired, I looked down and saw blood pouring down my right shin from being spiked by John. I hadn't even known that I was spiked – it never hurt. John looked at my shin as well and instantly knew what he'd done. We shook hands and smiled at each other. I wasn't the least bit upset at John and I was happy he didn't get disqualified. In our way, we had demonstrated that we should have finished first and second the previous week, even if the others didn't. My biggest regret is that my parents weren't there to see me and John both break 2:00 in the same race. My parents were very fond of John. It would have been great to have our high school coaches there as well. I'm sure they would have been proud to see us run a competitive race. For me, I knew that although John was still better than me, I had significantly closed the gap since high school. This was the last time I would ever race John on the track. And that's odd because I raced on that track several more times, and John was always in different races. I wonder if his coach placed him in different races to avoid me.

I was happy to break two-flat and even happier that our next meet was not at Pittsburg State. We were headed to Central Missouri State to compete in the indoor Mule Relays, and they had a 220-yard track! The CMS meet was held on a Saturday only a couple days after the meet at Pitt State. Coach allowed us to have an easy training day on Friday so we would be ready the next day. Sometimes, we make stupid decisions, and that Friday was one of those for me. During the evening, I went out with Chris Marcak, my new teammate Mike Hueton, and former teammate Keven Bartholomeus. Mike graduated in 1980 from a high school in Des Moines, Iowa and ran in the 9:40s for the 2-mile. I first saw Mike toward the end of the fall semester when he came to talk to Coach Oz with his brother Eddie along for the ride. Mike spent the fall of 1980 at Northeast Missouri State running on their cross-country team.

Although Mike had to sit out the track season because of the transfer rules, he was scheduled to run the CMS 2-mile unattached. Chris was also in the 2-mile. As the four of us went out that evening, Chris decided to have a few beers and he and Kevin began to drink. I had no intention of drinking and Mike decided not to have any beers as well. At some point, early in the evening, I decided to have a single beer. Thirteen beers later, we made it back to campus. Mike kept his word and didn't drink, and Chris somehow consumed 15 beers. It was late and we had to be up early to take the trip to Warrensburg, Missouri for the meet.

When I woke up around 5:00am, I was still drunk. I hurriedly put on my track uniform and headed to Chris' room. I banged on his door to wake him up, and he came to the door, also still wasted, and said he wasn't going to the meet. I told Chris that if I was going, so was he, and I managed to convince him to get ready, and we headed to the fieldhouse. When we arrived, we realized that we were taking an old yellow school bus rather than the vans that we normally took. The men's and women's track teams were traveling together, which was rare, so the extra space was needed. But the bus ride would be horrible for two guys who were still drunk. Our goal was to avoid Coach, so Chris and I headed to the back and sat in the last seat.

About two hours into the ride, Chris and I were no longer drunk, we were just sick. The hills on US 65 between Branson and Springfield didn't help the situation. The trip to CMS was 180 miles and it was always slow-going. The bus stopped in Collins for a break and me and Chris were able to get some aspirin for our pounding headaches. I can still remember trying to avoid Coach Oz, but he somehow caught up with us and engaged us in a conversation. He could tell we didn't feel well, but, of course, we didn't reveal the reason. I can also remember after we left Collins and wondering as we approached Clinton, where the new Truman Reservoir was going to be as I stared out the window trying to decide whether I'd be able to compete. Finally, we made it to Warrensburg and the arduous trip was over.

The truth is, I felt like shit and was certain I either couldn't run, or I would embarrass myself on the track. I found a place to hideout and attempted to rest. The 880 was hours away, and I didn't feel well enough to watch my teammates compete. This was not the norm for me, because I enjoyed watching my teammates in competition. Throughout the day, I must have made more than a dozen trips to the restroom, and I just couldn't shake the pain and discomfort. I didn't have an ounce of energy and as my race got closer, I could tell my condition wouldn't improve. Finally, my race was fast approaching so I knew I needed to warm up, but I just gave up because I felt so bad. I don't even think I did much stretching. I thought about the lesson I'd learned and how this race was going to be the worst I would ever run. Four laps on an indoor track – how was I going to make it?

The 880 had three heats competing against time. That didn't matter to me because I wouldn't be competitive anyway. In addition, I was placed in the first heat, the heat for the slowest runners. Normally, that would upset me, and I was a little perturbed because I knew that I should at least be in heat number two, and maybe in the fast heat. So many coaches lied about the times of their athletes, and our coach was honest. In fact, dishonest coaches and other ridicules and unfair issues with the sport caused me to lose my religion, but not my enthusiasm, for track. Sometimes Coach Oz even forgot our best times and submitted times too slow. But, again, I was too sick to really care enough to complain. At the Central Missouri track, the bleachers for basketball were pushed back to expose the track straightaways. Right next to the starting line was a men's restroom. As they were about ready to start going through the list of runners for the first heat, I had to suddenly make a mad dash to the bathroom. I was going to miss the race, but at that moment, I had no option, and I bolted.

As I returned to the track, I fully expected the race to be at least on the second lap, but they were lining up the runners. I didn't hear the gun while in the restroom, so I guessed this was probably still the first heat. I asked which lane was mine, then a judge lined me up, and the gun sounded. I was probably only out of the commode 15 or 20 seconds when the race began, barely enough time to wash my hands, and at the break I pushed into the lead. For some reason, I forgot that I was sick as a dog and ran without pressure or even care. The race is a blur today, and it was then as well. I finished the four-lap race and was never challenged – no one was even close. My time was 1:57.8. I was, of course, stunned, but the race was easy. I should have run faster, I could have run faster, I knew I could have. I watched the second heat, and the winner was slower than me. Then I watched the fast heat, and only one guy, Bret Key from Southwest Missouri State beat my time. I think he ran 1:57.2 or so. I heard his coach tell Key that he ran "real slow." But I ran "real fast," at least to me. I couldn't believe it. I'd just earned a second-place medal, while hungover.

Coach was extremely pleased with me, and I don't think he ever suspected that I was out half the night drinking. My race might have inspired Chris because he was as sick as I was. In his two-mile race, although he didn't run great, he still managed a time of around 9:35. Chris was capable of something under 9:10 and I think he could have challenged the 9:00 mark. But not on this day. Still, I think Chris thought it would be a challenge to run 10:30. Mike, in his first race back from more than a year layoff, didn't manage to break 10 minutes – he had a long way to go.

My bad decision the night before caught up with me in the last event of the day. I wasn't scheduled to run the mile relay, but one of the guys was sick, and Coach asked me to run. I found out during the next few days that the person whose place I took, and I don't remember who it was, had went out and got high after competing in his individual events, and didn't feel well enough to race in the relay. So, I got the baton, the second leg I think, and tried to emulate my 880m race. But this second race felt like the first one should have. I had nothing in the tank and ran in slow motion with a 54 second 440 leg. Hell, my first quarter in the 880 was 56 and that was easy!

On the long trip back to SofO on that old school bus, as I had in the morning ride, I felt horrible. But at least I'd run a PR, and in a big way. Chris and I decided to never drink the night before a race again, and though I don't know if Chris followed through, I never again went out drinking before a meet. We also decided that we would wait a few weeks before we went out partying. As soon as we got back, I was going to bed to sleep this off. After we returned to campus, we heard about a party at a lodge a few miles south of the school that overlooked Table Rock Lake, so me and Chris piled in his car and headed south. So much for sleeping.

At the party, I saw Dan Mills, who asked me how I did. Dan was already feeling pretty good, and when I told him, he got excited and talked about how my 1:57 was an NAIA national class time. I don't think it was, but I went along. After spending some time at the party, Chris and I headed back to campus, fairly drunk again. Going down US 65, Chris drove cautiously because he was scared to drive too fast for fear of driving off one of the ledges. When we made it back to campus, we parked down the road so we could sneak back on campus. School of the Ozarks was in a rural setting, much more then than it is today. There is a dairy farm on campus, so we decided to take a trek through the woods and pasture on a very dark night. After getting scratched in a few briars, we finally made it back to our dorm and headed to or beds. It was only later that we found out that even though there was a midnight curfew, on weekends, we could park at the top of the hill, outside the gate, at Beacon Hill Theatre, and walk to our dorms after midnight, as long as we didn't cause a commotion.

The next morning the campus was abuzz about two students, a man and a woman, who had left a party and drove off into a deep hollow on US 65 and were severely injured. I had seen them at the party, and as Chris and I discussed the timeline, we realized that we probably went by the place they went over no more than 10 minutes before. At campus chapel later in the morning, I happen to be sitting next to Dan Mills, when the chaplain started talking about the evils of drinking and partying, which he brought up because of the wreak. Then the chaplain said something to the effect that he knew some of the students in chapel that morning was at that party, which caused Dan to bust out laughing. We were seated on the right side of the chaplain in the side pews, and all the old people who sat up front turned and stared angrily!

Students were not allowed to park on campus overnight except on Fridays and Saturdays. The student parking lot was at the top of the hill outside the gate, and the gate was locked at midnight. As with most students on campus, me and my friends walked down that hill almost on a daily basis. The road up the hill to the gate was split with the right lane headed up and the left lane headed down to campus. In the long island that split the road there was a sidewalk in the middle with grass to the sides. In the middle of the sidewalk were several light poles at intervals. The bottom light pole had an issue.

Tourism was big business on our campus. We had the Ralph Foster Museum, the Mill, and students made the school's famous fruit cake, jellies, and a few other things to sell. And this was the Branson area, so tourism was ready made. SofO had a tour train that left the gate area at the top of the hill in a visitor's center that included a cafeteria. The tourist train was on rubber tires with several cars that took guests to the Museum and other campus sites. It made students feel like they were animals from the zoo when people went by, and we called the thing the "Chicken Train." During my first couple of weeks at SofO, as the train was headed up the hill, the last car came loose with a load of deaf visitors, and rolled back toward the bottom, smashing into the last pole, and laying it flat. The pole was quickly fixed, but it was not the same.

Each pole had two short iron rods that extended at an upward angle form the post. These were probably intended to use for banners. I think the lights were 20 to 30 feet above the ground. The rods were about 10 feet off the ground, and I was the only one of my friends who could jump high enough to grab a rod. So, I would jump up, grab a rod, and shake the pole. This almost always made the light go out. But the next evening, it was always back on until I shook the light back out. One evening, after a couple of years of doing this, I jumped up, grabbed a rod, and shook – the whole damn light fixture glass came crashing down to the ground. No one got hurt, we didn't tell anyone what I did, and I never jumped to grab the light pole again.

We competed at one or two more meets at Pittsburg State. I ran a slow 1000y in 2:19 and an even slower mile in 4:34. I think I won the 1000 but I finished well back in the mile. I can't recall if these were run in a single meet or two, but I think they were in separate Pitt State meets. What I wanted was to compete in the NAIA Indoor National Meet, held in Kansas City at Municipal Auditorium. However, Coach Oz decided not to take me, although he did take Willie Williams in the 60y and Roy Dixon in the long jump, who's best leap made him an All-American. For some reason, the Distract 16 Indoor Meet, which encompassed the state of Missouri, was held after the National Meet. I don't know whether this was the norm for the NAIA across the nation, but I know District 10, which was Kansas, was also run after Nationals.

The District 16 Meet was held at William Jewell in Liberty, Missouri, which is in the Kansas City area. Their track was similar to the one at Pitt State only it had a slicker surface, and we couldn't wear spikes. Dan Mills had a pair of thin Nikes used for road racing that were a mild shade of cream and had a good grip. So, he let me borrow them. I was entered in the 880 and the two-mile relay. In the 880, I smoked the field, winning in an easy 1:59. My goal was to win, and not necessarily run fast, plus on the curves, without spikes, even with those good, borrowed racers, it was difficult to maintain great speed. The other thing about the building was that the air was extremely dry and made breathing difficult. The last event of the evening was the two-mile relay. We had a great meet going into this final event. But we needed to finish well to win the meet. We knew that Park College had the best relay in the field, and if they won the race and we finished third, it appeared that they would beat us for the team title. We were sure that Park would win the race, but could we get second?

Our first leg was distance runner Paul Taylor, who was strong, but not much of a half-miler. Still, he held his own. Our second runner was freshman Jerry Goodrich, who won the 440 earlier that evening and had just finished the mile relay. He did fine as well, but we were not in second place. Chris Marcak ran third and he ran a strong leg, but when he handed off to me, we were in about 4th place, with Park well in the lead. I ran my anchor leg as relaxed and with as much confidence as I have ever run. I didn't feel an ounce of pressure. I wasn't sure I could catch Park, so I decided to get by the third and second place teams and then cruise as to not die and get re-passed. I moved smoothly away from those I passed and was quickly catching Park, but they had too much of a lead to catch after a cautious first quarter. I did my job, and we won the team title by a mere three points over Park. So, we could have actually taken third and still won by a single point. I don't know what our time was, but probably no better than 8:10. And I don't know what my split was. Coach had an aversion to split times and rarely timed them. But I think I ran around 1:56 to 1:57. The SofO women's team won their team title as well – it was a great evening for the School of the Ozarks track teams.

After the District indoor meet, we had about a week until our first outdoor meet. During the days before that first outdoor meet, our training began to ramp up. We might do 25 440s or a high number of other interval distances. Our first meet was at home against Arkansas College. It was a low-key meet, and the weather was overcast and cool. But I was excited to race. I was entered in the 880. Our home track, which was yards, had a black all-weather surface, but I was never sure what it was made of. It was soft in hot weather, and harder when the temperature was low, but it still had some give. The most peculiar thing was the front stretch was not only 220 yards long, which I'd seen before, but also consisted of 16 lanes.

In the 880, I snuck in behind the leaders at the break because of the wind and just followed what seemed to be a pedestrian pace. And sure enough, when we reached the 440 mark, we had just barely run under 1:00 minute. My spilt was probably 59.7 or so, a walk in the park. The Arkansas College coach, Larry Rogers, who I believe had been a good 800m runner, yelled that we were running like a bunch of old ladies. True enough, and the comment made me laugh out-loud. With about 240 yards to go, I sprinted to the lead with speed and quickness that surprised me. I had never had that kind of quick acceleration before to top speed and I ran away from the field. My 660 split was only around 1:31, so we had slowed the third 220. I ran fast, but easy down the homestretch winning in 1:57.0. This was a 1:56.3 for 800 meters, and it was easy. In fact, it was as easy as I had ever run a race. I wasn't tired and I felt as if I could have run another 220 at the same speed. I had run my second lap much faster than my first and the final 220 in 26 seconds. I could see a 1:52 800m in a month or so. I realized, for the first time, that I was fast!

Chapter 11
Champion

In one of our early-season outdoor meets in 1982, I ran one of the best races I ever ran. The meet was held at Northwest Missouri State University in Maryville, which is about 35 miles north of St. Joseph. When the team got up on Saturday and headed out our motel rooms for this mid-March meet, there was a dusting of snow on the ground, and it was still snowing. The team had stayed in St. Joseph because Coach Oz's mother lived there. After the 45-minute drive, we arrived at the stadium and found the green all-weather track, which was as hard as a rock from the cold. The temperature never rose above 38 degrees, and the wind was strong from the northwest, with gusts of up to 40mph, which was indicated by the meeting's official results booklet. Our sprinters, most of whom hailed from Georgia, didn't adjust to the cold weather and ran poorly, although Willie Williams did manage a 10.55 hand-time in a severely wind-aided 100m. Still, for one of the best sprinters in the state, in warm weather with that wind, he would have run 10.0 to 10.1. For much of the day, most of us stayed in the fieldhouse, which had a 10-lap indoor track. This is where most of us warmed up, and where they contested the pole vault competition. I think all other events took place in and around the outdoor track.

Of course, the 800m was late in the day. My approach to adverse weather during races was different than most. I could have cared less. To me, a race was a race, and we all had to compete in the same conditions, so what difference did it make other than the times would be slower? There were supposed to be two heats in the 800m, slow and fast heats, and, of course, I was entered in the slow. But I think the meet officials wanted to get through the meet, so they combined the heats. Some athletes selected not to run, or their coaches didn't allow them to compete, but most of those who entered were at the starting line. This made the field much too large, but as far as I was concerned, that was just fine because I was about to compete against the best in the field. As I waited at the starting line for officials to get us lined up, I heard a lot of bitching from several competitors. As I stood there with my New Zealand Split shorts and my tank-top singlet, I smiled because I knew that much of the field, no matter how good they were, had already lost. I was ready to race!

Because of the size of the field, we were lined up on a waterfall start, and when the gun sounded, I quickly headed to the front and settled into second or third on the back stretch so I could get some protection from the hard north wind. As we headed north on the back straight into the strong wind, all of us were leaning forward as we struggled to maintain any sort of pace – but I was having fun! Through the first lap, which was covered in over 60 seconds, no one really wanted to lead and sacrifice their race, and I was perfectly content to remain in the top three or four as long as I didn't drop back. Although I knew the pace was slow, I also knew we had put in a pretty good effort the first 400m. Still, as cold and windy as it was, I was relaxed and not yet tired. As we reached the backstretch the second time, a huge gust of wind stood us all up, and the pace slowed again. I could feel the race being taken out of many of the guys. Then I got a burst of energy and the willingness to begin the race, and I bolted against the wind halfway down the backstretch and took the lead. This was my definitive move, one in which I attempted to steal the race. I ran strong and felt strong, and I know the move devastated most of the field. My best time of 1:56 was probably only the 10th or 12th best PR in the race, and I might have been further back than that. But that didn't matter, given that I had 250 meters to go in this arctic race.

Halfway through the final curve, I realized that my move didn't break everyone, as a runner from the University of Northern Iowa, who was wearing pantyhose because of the cold weather, got by me. But after his initial sprint to pass, he only gradually put three or four yards between us. Coming off the curve, I was in second place and attempted to make one final surge to pass the leader with the wind now at our backs. But Solomon Anderson, the UNI runner, was able to hold me off. About 10 meters from the finish, I felt the pressure on my right side from another runner. As I leaned at the finish, Paul White, the NWMS 800m school record holder, nipped me at the tape. I think Anderson's best time was 1:51 coming in, and I know White ran 1:52 in 1982. I beat a lot of good runners that day. Anderson won in 1:58, White ran just under two minutes in about 1:59.97, and I ran 2:00.02. White, who was bigger than me, said he thought the race was worth around 1:52, and I had to agree. Even with the cold and wind, the second lap was faster than the first. I received a bronze medal for my effort, and Coach Oz was as happy as I'd seen him. For years, even during track reunions long after I graduated, Coach bragged about that race, the day I went for the win against a strong field and horrible weather. It might be the best race I ever ran on the track.

As the season progressed, our training ramped up even more. Our mileage increased from 10-mile runs to 13, and our repeats increased as well. As a rule, we ran 4 miles in the morning, although Coach wanted us to run 6 miles. Steve Davis, whose eligibility was up, although he still trained with the team, commented that if 4-mile morning runs were good enough for Craig Virgin, then it was good enough for him! I don't know if Virgin ran 4 miles every morning or not or how Steve found out this information, but it sounded good to me. The number of 440s we ran was ridiculous. It was common for us to run between 35 and 40 440s in 63 to 66 seconds with a 90-second rest in between. And many times, Coach had us lined up at the minute mark. I know of one occasion during my time at SofO in which Coach Oz miscounted, and we ran 44 quarters, almost all under 65 seconds, at least for the best two or three of us on the team. Instead of decreasing the number at the end of the season, that's when we reached 40. What the middle-distance runners should have been doing by the last week of April was say a workout of 5 or 6 quarters at 55 seconds with three-minutes of rest between reps. Not all the guys could have averaged 55, but at least their speed would have been sharpened.

Coach also wanted a 16-mile Dam Run on Sundays, after a Saturday meet. It didn't matter if we were 800m runners or ran the 10,000m, Coach wanted a long Sunday run. One workout I particularly liked was a ladder session. With Coach, we usually went down the ladder rather than up then back down. So, the one that was especially beneficial was beginning with a 1320-yard run, or three laps on the track, then an 880, followed by a 440. We did three sets. Coach wanted us to run 65 seconds per lap on all the runs, meaning 3:15 for the 1320, 2:10 for the 880, and 65 for the 440. I thought this would be difficult, but as it turns out it was actually fairly easy, at least for Chris, Steve, and I. Mike was coming along, and he was close to running these times for the three sets. Paul Taylor was close as well. The best day I had running this workout is when me, Steve and Chris ran the first two sets in a little under 65 seconds per lap, and well under for the last set. I think we did 3:10 or so for the three-quarters run, 2:05 for the 880, and about 58 to 60 for the last 440 run. Mike, Paul, and Allen also ran well. It took me until I was a senior in high school to run a 2:05 half mile, and now I could run that pace in a workout for 3 three laps, and two laps multiple times, and it was easy.

In one distance run I ended up getting injured that seemed devastating at the time, but as I quickly learned, it was a blessing in disguise. Chris, Mike, and I went out for a typical 13-mile run. The pace was comfortable, a conversational pace. As we approached the DX station for the turn-around back to campus, we decided to run to the Dam, which would give us a 16 miler. To be honest, as I look back, a 16-mile run during the outdoor season, and on a weekday, seems asinine today, and it might have in 1982 as well. But we weren't finished adjusting the workout. When we reached Table Rock Dam, we made the decision to run through Branson and make it a 21 miler. Now that was just stupid for an 800m runner! At about the 12-to-13-mile mark, the outside of my left knee began to hurt. We ran on the left side of the road to face the oncoming traffic, and the outside of the lane, past the Dam, was severally curved down, which meant the right leg was a few inches above the left. I think this caused my knee issue. Mike and Chris left me because the pain caused me to slow down. I didn't stop running – where was I to go? I was miles from campus no matter which way I ran. I finally made it back to campus just as coach, with Chis and Mike along, picked me up right before the campus gate. I probably ran just under 21 miles.

I thought my season might be over because of that Dam Run. But I found out something beneficial. As long as I kept my runs less than 3 miles, I was OK! By this time, I had enough strength training, so speed work was what I needed. Because I couldn't run long distances, I spent most of my time on the track, and even stopped running in the mornings for a time. During the three weeks before my knee quit hurting, we ran a few meets. In one meet at Florissant Valley, near the St. Louis airport, I won the 800m in 1:57, on a cool but otherwise nice day. It was a solid run, but not especially remarkable. I took the lead from the start and was never challenged. On the way to St. Louis, the SofO track team, along with the SMS team, helped with the Hillcrest Relays in Springfield. I helped run the boys high jump along with our jumper Keith Rogers. On a cold and wet evening, with a grass run-up and small asphalt apron, the winner, a senior from Springfield Parkview, won in 7' ½". Bill Jasinski had the best jump in the country that year by a high school athlete at 7' 3" and later was an All-American at the University of Arkansas. Two days after the Flo Valley meet, on a beautiful Monday, we traveled to Jefferson City, Missouri to compete in an evening track meet.

The meet was held at Lincoln University. There were not many teams there, but the competition was terrific. Besides us and Lincoln, Northeast Missouri State (now Truman State) was there along with the University of Missouri-Rolla (Now Missouri S&T) and Southern Illinois-Edwardsville. There might have been another team or two, such as Westminster. This was an all men's meet, and I'm not sure why they didn't have women competing. Because of the small number of teams and the lack of women's events, the meet moved quickly. The track at Lincoln was at their football stadium and was where Missouri held the State High School Track Meet. Even in 1982, the all-weather track was old and worn. It was a reddish-pink tartan track that I assume was built in the early 1970s. It was originally a 440-yard track but was converted to meters at some point by changing the first curve or shortening it. The rubber surface on the adjusted curve was different than the old tartan. Instead of the slick surface of the rest of the track, this newer rubber was rough. The curve, because of the alteration, was oddly shaped. Finally, on the backstretch, there was a man-hole cover in one of the middle lanes, and it was covered with a red track rubber. The track looked like a mess, and I loved it! Despite its age and appearance, it was great and the best damn track I ever competed on.

The Lincoln meet was at mid-season, and Coach Oz decided it was a good time to see what I could do in a 1500m. I came into the meet with a best time of 4:09.9, which we could just say 4:10 to round it off, and that came from the previous spring. My single mile race indoors was a 4:34, which is somewhere around 4:17 for a 1500m, and this was accomplished in a race in which I was far behind the winner. So, what could I do? I knew I was in better shape than I was the year before, so I should run a PR. I thought maybe I could run three and possibly four seconds faster, so realistically, about 4:06 to 4:07. I thought that if everything went perfectly, I might slip into the 4:05s, but I thought that was probably out-of-reach at that point in the season. Maybe I could run a 4:05 by the end of the season.

The 1500 was run at sunset under the lights, and the weather was great. I don't think I ever ran a meet under better conditions. I didn't know anything about the field other than a Lincoln runner, Mike Lamb (I think that is his first name), who I was told was an NCAA Division II All-American at the event. Lamb didn't worry me because I knew I would be far behind him. I just wanted to compete well and run a PR. Even a 4:08 would be great. As we lined up, I tried to measure the field, but that was impossible. Then the gun sounded, and I tucked in toward the front of the pack. The pace was nice, but no one seemed to be in a hurry. I think I might have been ahead of Lamb at that point, but I knew he would take off and probably win when he felt the urge.

The first 400m was good, and I remained toward the front. By the 800m run in about 2:08, I felt comfortable and remained near the front into the third lap. When we hit the 1200m mark with 300m to go, I took the lead and tried to run for home. I felt strong as we hit about 3:12 or 3:13 at three laps. I led down the backstretch, knowing that Lamb and probably a couple of others would pass me, but maybe if I held on, I could place 4th or 5th. Midway through the final curve, I suddenly thought I just might win the thing. Maybe Lamb was not in good shape. But as suddenly as I had this thought, Lamb came blistering by me and smoothly moved away. As I ran down the home stretch, I could tell I would never catch Lamb, but I was still in 2nd, and no one ever challenged me for that position. I can't say I was particularly tired, but the pace did take something out of my legs; either that or Lamb just had blazing speed, especially after what was to him a slower race.

I crossed the line in second place, and I knew I had run a PR. Now, how fast did I run? I felt strongly that I had run at least 4:06, and I might have even surprised myself with a 4:05. As the timer came up to ask my name, I asked what my time was. She said 3:59.0. What? Surely that wasn't correct. That must have been the winner's time. I asked again – 3:59.0! To some out there, this might not seem like a fast time, but to a 2:01 high school half-miler, it was like running a sub-four mile. So, it was only my first sub-four 1500m, and I can tell you right now, without giving away the rest of the larger story of my running career, I never broke the 4-minute mile mark! So, this was my great milestone. Lamb won in 3:56, and I can't tell you what the person who placed 3rd ran, and I didn't know in 1982. Coach Oz was stunned, as was Chris Marcak. I think Chris saw himself as the alpha miler on the team, but now he had second thoughts.

For some reason, I got the impression Chris didn't think he could run a 3:59 1500, but of course, he could have – he ran a 4:18 mile in high school. Chris actually had a good evening as well. I think he took 2nd in the 5,000m at around 15:15. Willie Williams took second in the 100m in 10.3, which was a school record, but for some reason, it never got counted by Coach. One reason might be because Coach still had the record for the 100-yard dash posted and not the record for the 100m. The warmer weather brought out the best in Willie.

Although I continued to compete in the 800m, Coach Oz now saw me as a 1500m runner, and I had to admit that the race was my best distance. It took seven years, but I had finally grown into Coach Hill's prophecy from 1975 – I was now a miler, and I accepted it, cherished it, embraced it! After the Lincoln meet, my knee was healed, and I went back to training with the rest of the distance runners.

My next opportunity to race in a 1500m was at the Southwest Missouri State Relays in Springfield. Two days before the meet, Chris and I went to see the high school division of the meet. The day before, Chris asked me if I wanted to go with him to the meet. However, I had a major test in Latin American History, and Chris said he wouldn't wait. So, I devised a plan – I would study. Yes, I would actually study for the test so I would be prepared to finish early and be able to go to Springfield. My study habits at that time were atrocious, and it never dawned on me to study to achieve a good grade, although I did ace it. No, my motivation was to make a track meet. After attending the meet, since we didn't have the opportunity to work out that day, we decided to go out to the track that night and time each other in the 880s. Chris ran first, and because it was pitch dark outside, he didn't see a hurdle in lane one, which he almost ran over, and it caused him to slow down. Still, he ran 2:01. Then it was my turn after the hurdle was moved, and I ran a 1:59. I felt ready to run a good 1500 in two days.

The SMS meet was held on the same red-dog cinder track that I raced in an 880 the summer before. Because it was a traditional relay, there was not an 800m race, and there were multiple relay races. SofO didn't run a distance medley relay or a 4x800m, so I was only entered in the 1500. Although it was a cinder track, it was in great shape and fairly fast as non-all-weather tracks go. The field was a strong one. Besides me, my teammate Allan Hicks was entered. The best runner from SMS in the race was their 800m specialist, Bret Key, who won the 880 in the CMS indoor meet. Missouri-Rolla's best miler, Mark Stucky, was in the race as well, but I don't recall if he had run the metric mile at Lincoln University.

In the first couple of laps of the race, the pack was bunched together and not very fast, although not pedestrian either. I knew that Key was a good 800m runner, but I didn't know what his best time was for the season. I was also not aware that he was a 47 400m runner. But I still knew he had speed. My decision on whether I should go to the lead at the 800m mark to attempt to run the legs out of Key was never made. Stucky led the race at that point, so I just remained there. With one lap to go, the field finally began to string out. Key sprinted to the lead and attempted to run away from the field. I was able to stay with him, as was Stucky. On the backstretch, I became antsy, and I wanted to pass Key with 300 to go, but I didn't. I was still unsure of my strength and didn't want to move too soon. But with

250 meters to go, I hit a different gear and easily passed Key. Then, I just sprinted and moved away from the field.

As I crossed the line, I realized that I could have kept that same pace or sprinted for another 200 meters. I was not tired and was still full of run. I don't remember any of my spits, but I do know that the last 400 was in about 57 seconds and the last 200 in 26 or 27 seconds. My winning time was 4:01, and Key took second in 4:05. Key might have slowed the last few strides, but I'm not sure because I don't know how far ahead, he was of Stucky and the field. It was not as fast as the Lincoln race, but it was extremely easy. After this meet, Stucky ran a 3:53 1500 a week or two later and held the Missouri-Rolla record in the event for 20 years. Key ran a 1:49 800m that year and also took second at the NCAA Division II National Meet in the two-lapper a few weeks after our encounter. I remember watching that race on TV.

After my race, Chris Marcak ran the 5,000m. With one lap to go, Chris was one of three in the lead pack, and we yelled for him to sprint because he looked comfortable. But Chris just looked at us as Tom Becker of SMS and Scott Mantooth, Becker's teammate, slowly moved away. We couldn't figure out what was wrong with Chris; he just kept the same pace and never attempted to win, or at least that's what it looked like. Becker won the race, and Chris ended up third with a time of 15:30, which was a really slow time. After the race, when I asked him what had happened, he said he had taken third on purpose because he was mad at Coach Oz for not letting him run the steeplechase. Chris still might have taken third because Becker and Mantooth were terrific runners, but it would have been competitive. For some reason, Chris had driven himself the 40-plus miles to Springfield, so he didn't ride back to campus with the team. When I caught up with him at the dorm, Chris was smiling and no longer threatening to leave the team and transfer.

Chris always talked about transferring and maybe doing something to get kicked out of school. I don't think he was in total agreement with Coach Oz's training program, and he also didn't like the fact that SofO required summer school. He said he was needed back home in West Plains in the summer to help his dad with their farming, or haying, or something else that was needed – I don't remember all the issues. One night, the last week or so of the spring semester, Chris and I had been out drinking and feeling pretty good. We decided to leave our dorm, Kelce, and head across the alley to Smith Dorm to bother Kevin Bartholomeus. After leaving Kevin's room, we headed to the campus powerhouse to see a couple of student workers who had labored there all night, just as Chris had. On our way back to Kelce, which we had to do under-cover because it was past curfew, we cut through Smith and came out to the alley from the Smith basement. Then, Chris picked up a rock and flipped it toward Smith. He didn't throw or even toss the rock; it was just a flip of his wrist. But the rock flew and shattered a window in Smith Dorm.

When the glass broke with a loud crashing, echoing sound, Chris and I just looked at each other. And then, after two or three seconds, without saying a word, we ran in different directions. I ran to my room on the third floor of Kelce West and Chris to his room in Kelce East, which was on the first floor. I hit my room without stopping, and it's a wonder how I was able to unlock my door as quickly as I did. Meanwhile, Chris decided that he might get caught if he went into his room, so he flew down the hallway where his room was located, ripped through the lobby that connected Kelce East and West, and met me at my door just as I was closing it. How did he almost beat me to my room? He had to run twice as far. I asked him if anyone had seen him, and he said only Willie Williams, who was in the lounge. We knew he wouldn't say anything. I got into bed without even taking my clothes off, and Chris slid under my bed to hide. We heard people talking in the hallway, saying they had heard someone run to the third floor.

In the middle of the night, Chris slid out of my bed and went to sleep on the floor. My roommate, Dan Creed, threw him a pillow. The next day, we learned a little more about what happened after Chris and I got to my room. One thing was for sure: if caught, we would have been kicked out of school. Willie Williams saw Chris and asked him why he was running through the lobby at 2 am, but I don't think Chris gave him the answer. Willie didn't tell anyone that he saw Chris, but he was asked if he saw anything because the dorm authorities knew he had to have seen someone run through. He said he didn't recognize the person. Chris and I went out for a run that afternoon before a big dorm fish fry for the end of the semester. As we ran, we laughed about the incident, and Chris confessed that despite all his talk, he realized that he didn't want to get kicked out of school, especially as the semester was about to end. I don't think we were ever suspected!

Our last meet was District 16 at Westminster College in Fulton, Missouri on a bright excessively hot day. We wanted to emulate our performance from the indoor District Meet and the team came into the meet operating on all cylinders, except for Chris Marcak, who had sprained both his ankles in the week leading up to the meet and was relegated by Coach Oz to the 800m. This would be his only race at the District Meet. Chris would have been entered in the 1500 and 5,000m races. The track at Westminster was red-dog cinders and was not as good as the SMS track. But the meet was run smoothly by the Westminster head coach, Dick Ault, an extremely nice man who took 4th in the 1948 Olympic 400m hurdles in London.

Despite the heat it was a fun day. Willie Williams won the 100m and 200m sprints and anchored the winning 4x100m relay. Second in both sprints was Willie's high school teammate from Georgia, Trent Brinson. SofO had several guys place in the sprints including Roy Dixon who also won the long and triple jumps. We also had a part-time trackster, basketball player Herb Crocket from Arkansas who placed in both jumps. In the triple jump, with Roy, Wilbert Daniels, and me standing by the pit, Herb launched a massive jump that must have startled him because as he reached the third stage, he bailed. Roy was stunned that Herb didn't finish out the jump and pleaded with him that the jump would have been a 51- or 52-footer. Sure, Roy would have taken second, but he didn't care. Nonetheless, Herb still placed high in the event.

The first event of the day was also one of the most interesting, or at least until the second to last event late in the afternoon. The 10,000m run, just short of 25 laps on this old yards track, was started in the morning before the heat of the day. Paul Taylor and Alan Hicks were our competitors in this distance race. Throughout the season, Paul raced himself into good condition and was ready for a wicked run. Or at least "wicked" as I'm sure our rival Park College runners and coach viewed it. Paul was in peak shape to attack the field with his unique style of racing. As Coach Oz looked on in pure, unadulterated joy, Paul psychologically destroyed the majority of the field, and all but one of the Park runners.

David Mitchell, the best of the Park distance runners, and a damn good one at that, was good enough to pull away from the carnage and chaos behind him, but the other Park runners could not. As runners passed Paul, he would pass them right back in a short sprint, and when they attempted to pass him right before a curve, he sprinted to hold them off. Many times, the other runners would keep attempting to pass Paul on the curve, but he kept holding them off. Finally, Paul was unable to keep them from passing the second half of the curve. But as soon as they came off the curve, and with the competitors weary-legged from the hard curve drive, Paul just passed back. Paul did this for 23 or 24 laps, but on the final lap, Paul had mentally and physically broken the other guys. In the District Meet, Paul took second in the 10,000 meters, beating several runners who had run faster than him. Only Mitchell beat him. Alan also placed. Paul's tactics incensed the Park guys, and without our knowledge, they plotted their revenge, and I suspect their coach was behind it.

My first race was the 1500m in the early afternoon. By this time the temperature was already in the 90s. The field had some good competitors, including Park's Mitchell, and at least two or three of his teammates, and I think Westminster had a good runner as well. Alan Hicks was my only teammate in the race. My goal was to simply win, and I wasn't worried about my time. Earlier in the day, Mitchell asked Chris in the restroom how our half-miler was doing, and Chris told him I was now running the 1500 as well. I was actually in one of the stalls, so Chris called out asking me what my best time was, and I answered. I'm sure this didn't intimidate Mitchell, but I think the word got back to his coach and teammates that they might have some competition.

At the start, it was clear that the pace wasn't going to be quick. For two laps we just rolled along at a leisurely pace, and we hit the 800m mark in a slow 2:13. As we came off the curve in a tight pack with 500 meters to go, I saw Chris on the inside of the track and shouted out to him, saying "can you believe how slow this is? 2:13 at the half!" This was not so much to let Chris know the pace, but to psyche out the competition. But it really did feel slow, and I didn't feel as if I had yet run. However, Chris got on me for trying to have a conversation with him while I raced. With 250 meters to go, Mitchell, me and another Park runner had separated ourselves from the pack. I held back on the reins as to not take the lead because I thought the pace, or kick, was fast enough. Plus, although I was confident, I could win if I sprinted to the lead at that point, especially since Mitchell had already run the 10,000, I knew he was a terrific runner, so I just thought I'd wait a little longer, and because I had two more races. As we came off the final curve, I blew past the two Park runners and easily won going away in 4:01. Mitchell was second, I think in 4:03, in what was a good run after the 25 lapper.

I never felt stressed before or during the race. I expected to win and was never nervous or felt any added pressure. I ran relaxed and confident and knew I would win from the beginning. This wasn't the same kind of over-confidence I had in the 8th grade League 880. In this case I knew the competition and knew what I needed to do to win, and I certainly didn't take the race for granted. I don't know how fast I ran the last lap, but it had to be well under 60 seconds. The pace at two laps was about 4:10 for 1500 meters, and I ran nine seconds faster than that. During the couple of hours between the 1500 and my next race, I relaxed by watching my teammates compete, and at times attempted to find a cool place to rest.

SofO men had a great day at the District 16 Meet. Everyone we took scored. Our only weight guy, javelin thrower Dale Sanders took 6th. Besides Roy and Herb placing in the triple jump, Keith Rogers and Nate Lampkin also scored. In the long jump, after Roy's victory, Herb took third, Jerry Goodrich placed fifth, and Willie Williams jumped to a sixth-place finish. We dominated the horizontal jumps. Mark Hicks placed 2nd in the pole vault and Keith finished sixth in the high jump. We also dominated many of the running events. Besides Willie and Trent taking the top two spots in the 100m, Roy and Nate also placed. In the 200m, again after Willie and Trent, Roy placed 4th, Nate 5th, and Wilbert Daniels took sixth. Jerry won the 400m in 49.7, followed by Nate in second and Wilbert in third, which continued their rivalry from their high school days in Georgia. Keith placed 6th in the 110 hurdles, and Wilbert took third in the 400 hurdles. Finally, besides our victory in the 4x100m relay, our SofO guys took first in the 4x400 as well. We scored in every running event and won seven out of eleven events on the track. We also won the meet over Park College, 180 to 157 points.

The 800 came along late in the afternoon at the peak of the heat. As Chris and I mulled around the starting line as the officials began to organize their papers, one of the Park runners who ran in the 1500, looked straight at me and said to one of his teammates, "Oh no, he's in the race." I looked at Chris and said in a calm matter-of-fact voice, "I don't know if I'll beat anyone in this race, but I know I'll beat him." I said it loud enough for those at the line to hear while me and Chris laughed. And it was true. That Park runner was already defeated. But if I wanted to win, I still had to beat everyone else. At the break, I settled in right behind the leader and remained there for most of the race. It did feel hot, but I was still strong, and I didn't suffer any ill effects from the 1500m. Nonetheless, the first lap was slow, maybe 60 seconds or so and the pace didn't pick up until the back stretch of the second lap. Finally, the real race started and a runner from Park picked up the pace. Then on the final curve the sprint began, and the Park kid had really good speed. We pulled away from the pack but didn't put too much distance between the rest of the field. As we approached the finish line I inched ahead and won by a short yard in 1:58 – a slow time, but I was extremely satisfied. This was the race in which the small contingent of fans gave us a standing ovation as we crossed the line. Running on his two bad ankles, Chris managed to take fifth. Thinking back, that old track was 440 yards, so the race might have been an 880. I don't remember if the starting line and finish line were in different locations, but the race was counted as 800 meters.

Two races, two victories, but I had one more race to go, and it would turn out to be the most bizarre race I ever ran or witnessed. Unlike the time I had between the 1500 and 800m, I didn't get much rest before the start of the 5,000m. But that wasn't a concern because my job was to get points, and I was fairly sure I could do that with little rest. Plus, most of the competitors had already run at least one event that day, although I might have been the only one who ran the 800. When the race started on its twelve plus laps around the cinder track, I could tell this wasn't going to be a typical race. Three or four Park runners, excluding Mitchell, who immediately took the lead, began to attack Paul. Their goal was to prevent him from using his unusual tactics in this race.

One Park guy would get in front of Paul and slow down, one ran right next to him, and one up on his heels. I was right there with them, but they didn't try anything with me. They did joke with me, however. One thing I can say, because I thought it then, was if you try these tactics with me, I'll slug one of you right across the face. I tried to help Paul but there was nothing I could do unless I did something to get me disqualified. That was a thought, but I didn't know the team scores at that moment and thought we might need any points I could get. If I'd known we had the meet in the bag, I would have run those Park guys into the infield or shoved them down. I was far bigger than they were. I tried to pick up the pace so that they would follow me. My thinking was that they would not want me to get too far ahead of them, but their focus was only on Paul. What place they got was not relevant it seemed, so long as they made Paul's race miserable.

The problem for them is that they couldn't make him miserable. Paul had a great time playing their game and just laughed at them, which pissed off the Park guys even more. I actually thought the Park actions would get them disqualified. Once they had Paul boxed in the guy running next to him would run him into the infield. Sometimes one of the guys would shove Paul into the infield. Now, the Park runners only did this on the backstretch. I'm sure they didn't want to get caught shoving Paul on the front straight because of the judges, but I'm also sure everyone could see what they were doing on the backstretch. They also cussed Paul and used all sorts of profanity, and called him all sorts of vile names, but Paul just laughed. I don't think there has ever been a person who could have gotten into Paul's head, because he just didn't care.

Mitchell was fairly far ahead halfway through the race, and I wanted to keep up with him. But I can't blame the Park tactics on Paul with that because I wasn't able to stay at the lead. If I would have been fresh, I think I might have been able to race for a victory, but I also think Mitchell would have just run faster to avoid my kick. I was a better miler than Mitchell, but I can't truthfully say I was a better runner than him. I never beat him in cross-country, and I couldn't have finished ahead of him in the 10,000 on the track. The 5,000 would have been interesting if we were both fresh, but I think he would have gotten me in the end, unless the race was slow.

Mitchell won easily and I took 5th, and Paul, who finished behind me, I think in 6th, was disqualified. I could hear the Park coach crying about him to the officials and he was able to get Paul disqualified. Coach Oz attempted to get the call reversed, but to no avail. Paul's lost point didn't hurt us in the race for the team title, and Paul really won the psychological battle, because he didn't care. Those Park guys ran pissed off, it seemed to me, but I think Paul saw it as great fun! Down the road, in future races, Paul had the psychological advantage. And the Park guys never attempted anything on Paul for the next two or three years of his college career. It's possible I was told my time after the race, but I don't remember. And the school newspaper only indicated that I took 5th in the race. But I'm certain the time was not impressive, probably not far under 16:00 and maybe even over.

Whereas the Indoor District Meet came down to the last event, we easily won the Outdoor Meet. We were a small team, but we had good athletes. Several of our guys just had natural ability, such as Willie Williams. I think Willie was around 6'2" and was an extremely nice guy. But he was built, with large shoulders and huge thighs. And he didn't lift weights. But if you could get him to demonstrate his strength on the bench press, which he would rarely do, he could do several reps of 300 lbs. on dead weights. He was just naturally, massively strong. During that spring, a student who worked in landscaping with Willie, hid his timecard, which prevented Willie from clocking out to come to track practice. Apparently, Willie kept telling the kid to give him back his card and did so in a nice way. Student co-workers told the kid that it was a mistake to keep Willie's timecard hidden from him. Willie warned the kid that this wouldn't end well, and after what I was told was about 15 minutes, Willie hit the kid in the nose with a very short punch without a follow-through and broke the kid's nose and several bones in his face. I wasn't there to see it, so I guess the results could be exaggerated, but I doubt it, and Willie was too humble to say. At any rate, the next track season held promise, and we would probably have some new recruits as well.

This might be the meet in which I finally "got it." What I mean is that we didn't receive medals or any individual awards in the District Meet. And it didn't matter. I was over-joyed for just winning and the competition, not for an award. I had probably already evolved to this point, but I think this was the first meet I realized it. I was not the same competitor I had been in junior high, or even high school. Not just physically, but also why I raced. It was from the pure joy of it, and for the team. The fact is I loved to race, the competition, and yes, I loved to win. I knew I wasn't going to win many cross-country races, but on the track, especially is the 1500m and mile.... I knew that if I stayed relatively injury-free, and I remained focused, I would win the majority of my mile and 1500 races. Of course, I also needed to continue to enjoy racing and training. I could see myself running under 3:50 for the 1500m. I even had a couple of coaches tell me I had the ability to break 4 minutes in the mile. But the most important thing to me was that I was now a champion!

Chapter 12
"Come on, Raymond"

As soon as the spring semester ended, I headed home to Kansas for a couple of weeks before returning to campus for the summer semester. During my time in Parsons, I trained well, and didn't feel as if I'd lost anything when I returned to SofO. In fact, I felt the best I ever had. I was convinced that I could run under 3:50 for the 1500m right then. Regardless of the workout, I couldn't get myself tired. It might be a 10 miler in 55 minutes, it just felt easy. And the heat didn't make a difference. Many of my runs felt as if someone else was running – who was moving my legs and how come I couldn't feel the pace? This was the best shape I had been, or, as it turns out, ever would be. I later ran faster, but I never felt like that again except on an occasional run, and in the late spring and early summer of 1982, I remained like this for more than a month. Finally, in early July, I sustained a stone bruise on my foot, and when I altered my training to allow the bruise to heal, I lost that elusive edge.

During the summer we lost Willie Williams from the team. He was kicked out of school for having a girl in his room. I don't think it was actually his fault. The girl just walked in, and he tried to get her to leave. But it didn't matter – he was gone, and he went back to Georgia. This was a big blow to the team. Not just because he was a great athlete, he was, or because he worked harder than anyone, he didn't, but because he was a terrific teammate. He was fun to be around and extremely likable. I think every sprinter and jumper we had worked harder than Willie, but I don't know anyone who didn't want him on the team. I believe that if Willie would have worked hard at the 100m and the long jump, he would have run 10.1 FAT and jumped over 26 feet.

Another big loss for the team was our natural leader, Roy Dixon, but his was because he exhausted his eligibility. Roy worked extremely hard. A few years ago, I nominated Roy for the college's sports Hall-of-Fame, but he was never elected. This is ridiculous, because it is rare for a team to have the leadership ability that Roy possessed. Plus, he was an All-American. But I guess the powers that be didn't see Roy as fit to be a member of the Hall-of-Fame. In fact, there are few track and field athletes in the school's Hall-of-Fame. I've wondered over the years if it's political because of a rift between Coach Oz and others in the Athletics Department, although Coach is a member of the Hall.

I liked most of those in the Department, especially the men's basketball coach Al Waller, but the issues between Coach Oz and some of those in Athletics was apparent. I think I would have enjoyed playing basketball for Coach Waller, and I was as athletic as most of the players, but I would have never made the team, of course. He needed basketball players, not track guys! During the spring of 2016, the school dedicated its new track to Coach Oz, and I attended the special event. Maybe now, with a track named after Coach Osburn, and the college resurrecting the track and cross-country teams, the Hall will induct more track and cross-country guys.

Earlier in the season we lost hurdler Tony Peirce, who was kicked off the team. Tony was a good athlete, tall and strong and had very good potential as a hurdler. I was not in favor of Coach's dismissal of Tony, but one learned not to challenge Coach on these things. Coach was very principled. Tony had run a bad race at Flo Valley, and as he walked across the infield in disappointment, Coach began to call to

Tony several times, but Tony just kept walking away without turning around. I remember thinking "Tony, just turn around and acknowledge Coach, or this won't end well." So Tony was kicked off the team. I think Tony apologized, but it didn't matter. Tony should have been suspended for a couple of meets, at the most, but not kicked off the team.

Our best 400m runner, Jerry Goodrich didn't make it to the next track season either, other than the first one or two indoor meets. In an early season indoor meet in 1983, he took second in a very close 440, but he was soon after kicked out of school. He was ready for a stand-out sophomore year. I would have liked to have had Jerry reapply to get back in school. Jerry had three years left, and I think he would have run the 400 in 46 seconds before he graduated, but we'll never know. The best race I saw Jerry run was at the Lincoln meet. In the 400, as the field came off the final curve at the 300m mark, the runners blurred into one – in other words, it could not be determined who was leading, it was that close. Then, in a bullet-like burst, a tall runner, clad in purple, shot from the field like they were standing still. Future Olympian Ray Armstead from Northeast Missouri State just left the field and won in 46 seconds. But Jerry, instead of being devastated by Armstead's sprint, maintained his composure, and took second in 48. It looked like there were even better times ahead for Jerry. Sometimes Jerry got on my nerves, and often times tried too hard to act tough or cool. I liked Jerry despite the fact that he acted like himself sometimes. The last time I saw Jerry was when he was leaving campus to go home. He said to me, "Ray, you're the fastest white guy I've ever seen." Well, I've seen faster white guys than me, but it was a nice compliment. Jerry's departure from school was another huge blow to the team.

During the summer, Coach took us to the series of meets at SMS in Springfield. The series consisted of four meets, held every other Wednesday evening. If you finished in the top three in any event at any of the meets, you qualified for the championship meet that was held one week after the fourth meet. These meets were for fun and to give us some competition during the summer. The first of these meets was held during our first week back for the summer session. I won the open division mile in the 4:30s and the 880 in about 2:05. Slow times, but fun, and no one pushed me on either. One thing I noticed is that I held the 880 record for the series in the open division with a 2:01 from the previous summer.

When we got on the van to travel to this first SMS meet, I noticed a new kid already sitting. I didn't pay too much attention, but when we got to the meet, he entered the same races I did, although because he just graduated, he was in the high school division. His name was Mark Bollinger, but I couldn't remember his name for a while. We warmed up together and raced against each other because they combined the high school, open, and the masters' divisions into one heat. The next couple of days we worked out with him and on Friday, Mike Hueton and I asked him if he wanted to run a 21 miler with us on Saturday morning. Mike's brother Eddie was also a new freshman distance runner, but he didn't run the 21 miles. Chris Marcak went home for the summer, and we only hoped that he would be able to get back in school in the fall.

The next morning Mike, Mark and I headed out on the 21-mile Dam Run. After an easy first mile we picked up the pace. We zoomed by Scenic View, Beard Mountain, and the DX station on our way to Table Rock Dam. The only flat section of the run was the two miles or so from the DX area through the Dam and we ripped that part of the run. When we reached the Branson Strip, about the 15-mile mark, Mike, running next to me with Mark a couple of strides behind, looked over at me and said, "Do you want to see what the freshman has?" I said "yes," and we took off. This moment is significant for a couple of reasons. First, Mark couldn't keep up, and because he didn't know the way back to campus, he got lost. We hadn't considered this. When Mark got to McDonalds, he had passed US 65, which is where he needed to turn to head to campus.

266

He had to ask directions from the fast-food joint. He actually ran 22 miles.

The second importance to the moment is that we couldn't remember Mark's name, so we just called him "Freshman," which eventually got shortened to Fresh by mid-summer. It didn't take long before many on campus who knew Mark called him by his nickname. Even Coach Oz called him Fresh. After Mike and I finished the 21 miles in 2 hours and 10 minutes, the fastest I would ever run that course, which was around 6:10 to 6:12 per mile (and I think we could have continued for a marathon in about 2 hours 42 minutes), we had lunch and then went to the fieldhouse to play full court basketball. After a couple of games, Mike and I ran circles around the others, some of which were on the basketball team. Our long run didn't seem to have much effect on us, although it did take something out of my legs – I couldn't dunk that afternoon.

Mike and I saw Fresh that evening at dinner and asked him if he wanted to go to a party with us that night, which he agreed to do. So, the three of us, along with Eddie headed to a party before it was dark. We drank a lot that night, first beer and then whiskey. Late at night as we sat on the tailgate of Mike Montgomery's truck drinking with him, Fresh teased us a bit for being so drunk. Later as we were leaned against the front of Montgomery's truck, we decided to head back to campus. When Fresh stood up after leaning on the truck, he just kept going forward and fell flat on his face, passed out cold. He was fine when he was leaning on the truck, but something happened when he stood up.

I think the combination of not being used to drinking that much and the fact that his body was depleted after the 21-miler that day caused Fresh to lose control. He was like a wet noodle as we attempted to pick him up and get him to the car. Since we took Fresh's car, we had to fish the keys from his pocket. We were young and stupid and thought Fresh's condition was funny. His skin was pale and clammy and his lips a light shade of blue. This was an extremely dangerous situation, but we didn't know that then. As I look back, I think about how close we might have come to losing Mark that night. We got Fresh in the back seat, and I drove back to campus, which of course was also a stupid thing since I was drunk as well. I drove up Cardiac Hill and when we arrived at campus it was still before midnight, so we were able to park on campus. But we were still a long way from the dorms, and we didn't know where Fresh's room was, so we just left him in the back seat and went to our rooms.

As Mike and I headed to our rooms, I think the gravity of the situation began to become clear to us, so we decided to wake up early and go check on Fresh. The next morning hung over and feeling like crap, we headed to the other side of campus to check on our new teammate, and hopefully not our past teammate. As we walked, Mike wondered out loud what we would do if the freshman was dead. He thought we might take him to Table Rock dam and throw him off the lake side because Mike thought he would never be found. Was Mike kidding? He had to be. Anyway, when we arrived at Fresh's car, he wasn't there. This, we thought, was good news. We saw Fresh at lunch in the cafeteria and gave him back his car keys. He explained that he woke up when it became light, got his bearings, and headed to his room. His roommate must have been in because we had his room key as well. Interesting how things work out. Fresh, or Mark, became one of my best friends, he was later my roommate, and the best man at my wedding. My own son views Mark as an uncle. How things could have been different is scary. Mark knows the story about Mike's thoughts – we never kept that from him.

Mark recovered quickly. Despite stupidity, youth does have its advantages! During the next two SMS summer meets I ran the mile and 880 and won each time. The second meet I ran in the low 4:30s for the mile and about 2:05 in the 880. In the third meet my mile time was about 4:27 and probably 2:02 for the half mile. These, of course, were slow times, but easy wins. I just cruised these races and had fun. I can't recall that I was ever nervous before these races, and to me they were just these low-key meets in which I could spend time with teammates and get a meal after we were finished. During the couple of years that I ran these summer meets we had guys who came out for the team, or were recruited by Coach, but didn't last longer than the summer. They were fleeting teammates, and I don't remember the names of most.

In July, Mike, Fresh, Eddie, and I traveled to the University of Kansas to compete in the Lawrence Open. This is the same meet where I broke 2:00 in the 800m for the first time in the summer of 1981. Mike and Eddie's youngest brother, who was in elementary school, also made the trip and competed. I remember this little girl, I think her name was Jamie, who was just awesome. She ran the 3,000m in the morning and lapped boys who were three and four years older than her. But her father was rude and obnoxious. Because this was a summer meet, held in Memorial Stadium, which had a capacity of over 50,000, hardly anyone was there. So, in the bowl of this stadium, anyone who yelled could be easily heard. While this little girl ran, smashing the competition, her father yelled obscenities at her using every cuss word in the English language. Everyone in the stadium that I could see looked at him as if he was the biggest jerk they had ever seen. The scene was absurd.

I felt horrible for this girl. I found out she was a national record holder for her age group and there was absolutely no need for that kind of abuse. After the 3,000 her father ran lap after lap with her, just berating her with insults. I wish I'd had the guts to kick the guy right in the balls, but I would have never done that in front of his daughter. She won the 1500m later in the day and received the same treatment from her father as she had in the 3,000. My thought was that she was never going to enjoy running by the time she got to high school. I've witnessed similar treatment from parents over the years, but nothing compared to what I saw that day. It was so bad, I felt sick. In fact, I actually thought it was criminal, and I have not changed my mind more than 40 years later.

Despite the experience of listening to that horrible man, which came close to ruining the day for me (and I can't imagine what it did the little girl), I placed my focus on the 800m. I wanted a really fast time, and I hoped there would be great competition. But it was hot and windy and there wasn't competition in the '82 meet. Still, I thought I could run well on my own, and it's not that I ran badly, but I didn't come through with a great race. Oh, I won easily, but after a good first lap in 55 seconds, I was not able to maintain the pace. On the back stretch of the second lap, with the wind at my back I couldn't continue to run fast, even though I wasn't tired. It might be that I lost concentration or that the distance training I was doing to prepare for cross-country didn't allow me to be sharp. As I hit the final stretch, the south wind hit me square in the face and I struggled home. Just like the previous year, the timers didn't time me and they decided to give me credit for a 2:00, but two of my teammates had me in 1:59, and since the officials didn't time me and only guessed my time, I go with the 1:59. Plus, although it wasn't official, I saw 1:59 on the big score board when I crossed.

I liked running at KU, but after two straight years of officials failing to time me, I said I'd had enough of that crap and never went back to that meet. What I really wanted was the chance to run at the KU Relays. Coach took guys there in the 1970s, but he told us the competition was too tough and never took us. I don't know about too tough for the team, but it wasn't too tough for me and a few of my teammates. Our trip back to SofO from Lawrence, Kansas was a long one, and when we returned, we were exhausted. Somewhere on US 59 in Kansas, Mike was pulled over for speeding. His license was in his bag in the trunk, and he couldn't find it, but the Trooper let him off with a warning. Coach was not happy with me because I only ran the 800. He thought I should have competed in the 1500 as well and probably the 3,000m.

The next Wednesday, we ran the fourth of the SMS meets, and I didn't have a bit of energy. I only entered the mile run and SMS's Bret Key was in the race as well. I knew if I wanted to win against him, I needed to focus and stay close to him. The race was never fast, but I struggled to keep up with Key, who led the race from the start. On the back stretch of the fourth lap, Key got a couple of strides ahead of me and as we came off the final curve with 55 yards to go, I could never get on his outside shoulder to challenge. Key won in 4:25 and I was second in 4:26. He also took my series record in the open division mile. Speaking with Coach Clark, the SMS coach, I told him once Bret got that step on me, I wouldn't get by his 800 specialists, and he agreed. Bret said he was coming back the next week to run in the championship meet, so I knew I had my work cut out for me. Key's specialty was the 800 but he was a pretty good miler as well. I had to be sharp if I was going to match his speed. Later, Key won the 880, but I opted not to run the race that evening.

A week later, we were back in Springfield, and I felt terrific. Whatever had my energy down the previous week was gone, and I was ready to race and win! At the championship meet, they combined the open and high school races into one heat, and I think the master's might have been in the race as well. As they lined us up, the SMS coach, speaking on the PA system, announced the all-star field. He introduced Key as an 800m All-American. He also mentioned several other former SMS runners who had been All-Americans. Coach Clark introduced the 1982 Missouri Class 4A State 1600m champ, Branton White, from West Plains, who ran 4:15, and was headed to SMS.

As we readied on the waterfall start, I knew I could win the race, but I also knew that I had to run smart to beat Key. I wasn't worried about White, although our competitions were different. Still, I didn't want him to finish ahead of me. White became an outstanding 1500m runner in college, but he wasn't beating me on this day. The race began slowly with Key taking the lead. Although there were a

271

few former All-Americans, "former" was the key word. Some were still good runners, but they were not in their prime. Bret Key was the main competition for me. For three laps we ran, at best, a moderate pace, but because I was training for the cross-country season I wasn't as sharp as I could be, and I suspect Key wasn't either.

Our three-lap time was 3:21 and I was right on Key's shoulder. With 330 yards to go, Key picked up the pace and pushed hard. I wasn't tired but I found it difficult to keep up, and Key put a yard between us. On the back stretch Key pushed even harder, although it wasn't an all-out sprint yet. I went with him, but still found it hard to stay with the SMS half-miler. Nonetheless, I was able to keep up and even thought about passing him halfway down the back stretch, but I wasn't sure I could sprint that far out, even though that wasn't an issue during track season. In the final curve Key put it in another gear and I was able to go with him. As we came off the final curve I went wide to pass. Because the SMS summer meets started races in the middle of the straight, I only had 50 or 60 yards to pass, which I didn't think about on the back stretch when I decided not to pass. Although my acceleration wasn't quick, I still managed to get by Key fairly easily. I was surprised that I was able to sprint as well as I did considering how I felt on the back stretch. As I crossed the line, I still had plenty of energy, but I doubt I could have maintained that kick much longer.

I won in 4:20, and Key was right behind me in 4:21. My last lap was a solid 59 seconds. Although not sharp, 59 was a good final 440 off distance training. I also took back the series record. Coach Oz had this race videotaped and I watched it once. It amazed me just how slow it looked. That race was in 1982, and I don't have a clue what happed to the tape. My 880 race later in the evening upset Coach. Key didn't participate, so I decided to try a different race strategy for fun. I told Fresh, who was in the field as well, although in the high school division, that no matter how slow it was, I was going to run the first lap in last place and then see if I could win. Of course, this was risky because with kids as young as 15 in the race, I might be too far back to catch the leader in the final lap.

I don't know how fast the leader ran the first lap, but I ran 64 seconds, and he was well ahead of me. I was surprised with my first lap – I thought it would be slower, not that 64 isn't slow. After I crossed the line with one lap to go, I made a mad drive to pass everyone. I actually went into the lead with half a lap to go and ran the last 440 in 56 seconds for a 2:00. I should have run faster and finished in 1:59! It was just a hell of a lot of fun. These races didn't mean anything, although I guess the mile against Key was for pride. I hate to lose, but sometimes it's nice in a throw-away race to attempt something new. But Coach Oz didn't see it that way, and he kind of read me the riot act. My last race of the day was the mile relay with Fresh, Mike, and Eddie. We didn't run fast, but we won the open division, which is strange since Eddie and Fresh were in the high school division. I also won the trophy for scoring the most points in the Men's open division for the summer series.

I only raced Key one more time, and that was in a mile race the next year. However, he was redshirting as he recovered from an injury, so I don't consider that a race in which I beat him. I never raced head-to-head against Key in an 800. I wish I had because I'm sure I could have stayed with him. But beat him over two laps? That would have been tough, but if I could have pushed him, I'm sure he would have also pulled me along to a great time. By the time I was 21 years old, I believed I could have run under 1:50 for 800m, but I would have needed to be in a race in which others ran fast, and my training needed to consist of true middle-distance workouts.

We had two weeks between the end of the summer session and the beginning of the fall semester. One of those weeks I didn't train but spent that time camping and trout fishing in Colorado with my dad and a couple of his friends. If there was one thing, I enjoyed more than running, it was trout fishing in the mountains on streams and rivers. We fished the Taylor River, several miles above Gunnison. The four of us had a bet of who would catch the largest fish. It was low stakes – we all put in two dollars. On the last day, if fact, the last hour, I won the bet when I caught a 17 ¾ inch brown. And as I write this it dawns on me that it could have been 16 ¾. Fish get bigger as the years go by. It was the biggest trout I'd ever caught, and would be until the summer of 2016, when I caught a 21-inch rainbow from the Pecos River in New Mexico on the last day of a camping trip with my son. Someday that trout will be 31 inches!

When I returned from Colorado, I resumed my training, but I must have put in too many miles that week because I develop a hip injury. I didn't think a week away would hurt much, but I should have eased back into training with an easy week. When I got back to college, the hip injury got worse, so Coach sent me to the campus doctor, who diagnosed me with tendentious. Coach Oz put me on a reduced training schedule as the doctor treated the injury with medication. Because of the injury I missed the first meet, which was held at the University of Missouri-Rolla. Then, as my hip began to heal, I got sick, which was probably the flu, and I missed the second meet held at Northwest Missouri State. In fact, I didn't make the trip to Maryville. Finally, I was healthy and raced in our third meet.

We had a pretty good team in the fall of 1982, at least for a NAIA school, although it took until mid-season for us to come together. Our best runner was Chris Marcak, with Mike Heuten number two. By mid-season I was the team's solid third man, with Paul Taylor the fourth guy, and usually Allen Hicks number five, although Darren Wycliff sometimes was the fifth man. To round out the team we had three freshman, Jon Von Cannon, Fresh, and Eddie Heuten. We also had a kid who hadn't run before, Shawn Wiseman, plus Jerry Goodrich was still with the team, although he didn't run more than a couple of meets because we didn't need him to fill out the team as we had in '81. In one sense, our wildcard was Paul, because he was not in great form at the beginning of the season and, as usual, raced himself into racing shape as the season progressed. So, Paul might beat most of the guys, other than Chris and Mike, and then the next week be our sixth man. But by the middle of October, he was our strong fourth runner.

The older runners on the team realized that we had an opportunity to be good, so we made a pact. Chris, Mike, and I decided not to drink during the season and had Fresh and Eddie agree as well. We didn't have to worry about Allen, because he didn't drink, and Paul was always outside the group, plus we knew he wouldn't abuse alcohol anyway. We also knew that Jon wasn't a drinker, although he did prove us wrong once. In the fourth meet, Jon was sick as a dog and didn't race. He told Coach that he went out drinking the night before and got plastered. We couldn't believe he admitted this to Coach. He told Coach that he had never drank before, and no one doubted this was the truth. Coach told him it was OK as long as he learned his lesson, and that others on the team drank. Coach knew kids on the team drank? That surprised me, and I wondered how he knew and if he knew who drank. Someone out there must have been a snitch, but it didn't matter – Coach never brought it up to us.

My first meet was a quad back at Rolla, which was the third for the team. We ran alright, but we were beaten by Missouri-Rolla, and Southern Illinois-Edwardsville. We beat Lincoln University. Chris did win the meet in the mid-25s on the 5-mile course, but the rest of us only ran average. But for my first meet, around 27:20, was not too bad, and I felt good. We ran a dual meet at John Brown University in northwest Arkansas for the fourth meet. The women also had Oral Roberts to compete against, but they must not have had a men's team. Because I was healthy, the week between Rolla and John Brown involved intense training for me. I was so sore that I doubted I could run. My legs were stiff and running seemed impossible. But when the gun sounded, I took off with everyone else. It's surprising what one can do in competition when in physical distress, and I began to loosen up as the race progressed. But I still couldn't muster a good race and finished behind several of our guys. I think I was our sixth runner. The course was horrible with dangerous footing, and no one ran a good time. The surprise was that Chris got beat! He tied for second with Mike running 28 something. I suspect that Chris decided not to risk injury on that course. We did beat John Brown with ease, however.

Our second big meet, and first for me, was the Missouri Rolla Invitational. This was the team's third of four meets on the Rolla course. The Rolla race was contested on the school's golf course, and it was fast. I felt good but also knew I wasn't in great shape yet. Still, I managed to run a good race, and I think I ran just under 27 minutes, but it might have been just over. The team did OK, somewhere in the middle of the pack, and we were beginning to come around. Chris had an interesting race. I know that he wanted to run well and possibly win and so he took off with the leader, a runner from Maryville College in the St. Louis area. Although I was well behind, I could see Chris and the leader running by me on the other side of some trees. They looked like they were flying. When Chris hit the 2-mile mark and heard 9:15, he didn't think he could hold it and began to slow down. I think it was a mistake. The split psyched him out. Chris should have taken 2nd but fell back to fifth in a time of around 25:20. Chris should have run around 24:30, but the winner ran 23:23 – Chris wouldn't have won that day.

At the midpoint of the season, Chris and Mike had birthdays, and this ended our non-drinking pact. They rented a motel room in Branson, and we headed there to have a good time. I'm not sure why we decided to party while the season was going on, but I guess birthdays were a good excuse. There weren't too many there – Chris, Mike and their girlfriends, Eddie, Fresh and I think a couple of others, besides me. Fairly early in the evening I headed back to campus to wait on a good friend, a beautiful girl named Terri Cook. Mike, Fresh, and Eddie decided to go with me, and I drove Fresh's car. There was a school dance at the fieldhouse across from my dorm, but I needed to go to the dorm to wait for Terri, so the others walked over to the dance.

A while latter I received a call in my room on the intercom system from the lobby. There was some sort of issue, so I ran down and met Mike who told me Fresh was drunk and sick and could hardly stand. So, we headed to the parking lot behind the dorm and found Fresh leaning against his car. He was pale and pasty just as he had been at the beginning of the summer, but he was still conscious and standing. As students walked by on the sidewalk to the dance, most looked at Fresh with disgust because he had already vomited on the asphalt. It was dark, but the dim lights of the lot illuminated just enough for people to get a decent view.

Suddenly, while Mike and I stood next to him, Fresh threw up again as we jumped back so as to not be splattered with the spew. This meant we were too far away when he just fell over into his vomit on the ground. He was gone, passed out cold. He fell over like a toppled tree. We picked him up and threw him in the back seat of his car. Then Mike and Eddie decided to go back to the motel in Mike's car, which had been left behind earlier. I went back to the dorm and waited for Terri. When she arrived, we headed to the motel, but after a while, we decided to leave the party, and since I had Fresh's keys, we took his car. To be honest, Terri wasn't too thrilled to sit in a motel room watching several drunk guys make obnoxious fools of themselves, especially Chris! I actually wasn't drunk. So, Terri and I drove around Branson much of the night waiting for a café to open so we could get an early breakfast, all while Fresh was passed out in the back seat. Sometimes we checked on Fresh to see if he was breathing. Fresh didn't remember anything past mid-evening. Of course, he was passed out.

A week after the Rolla meet, the team competed at the Washington University Invitational held in Forest Park in St. Louis, which was the same place as the rain-soaked meet of 1981. But this year the weather was great, and the course was in fantastic shape. There were a lot of teams there, including some from Chicago and others from Indiana, Kentucky, and Tennessee. The team competed well, and I had my first real solid race of the season. Chris also ran well, taking third in a time of around 25:20, which was pretty good on a fairly tough course. The first and second place runners ran in the 24:30s, with the kid from Maryville who won in Rolla taking second. Mike ran 26:10 and was getting stronger every week and I ran 26:40. I don't know our places nor those of my teammates that finished behind me, but I think I was in the top 30. The team was emerging.

The final meet before conference was back in Rolla. It was supposed to be a duel, but I think Lincoln also ran. Coach Oz decided to give Chris and Mike a rest, so they didn't compete. Rolla's first runner also took the meet off. I had never won a cross-country meet but thought this was a good chance to do so. My racing condition was getting better, and I was our third man, plus I thought I could beat the rest of the Rolla runners. The pace was good from the beginning, and I ran with the confidence that I could win. By the halfway point, Paul and I led, and we began to pull away. Unlike his tactics against those from other schools, Paul ran "normal" against me that day. I kept thinking that I should push harder but I wasn't sure I could sustain it. But with a mile to go, I took off and put a little distance between Paul and myself. As I began to leave Paul, he yelled for me to go and win the damn thing. I ran strong the last mile and won comfortably in 26:11, and I felt that I had a lot more. Paul took a solid second in 26:23, which like me, was a big PR! Others on the team ran well also, although Rolla edged us for the team win. But we believed we had a good opportunity to beat Park at conference.

The Ozark Conference Meet was hosted by Park College, but it was held in a different location than the previous year's District Meet. The meet was held at Hidden Valley Park, close to Worlds of Fun Amusement Park in Kansas City. Although not unfairly difficult, the course for the Conference Meet was tough. There were steep hills and odd turns. Early in the race, running down a short, but very steep hill, with a 45 degree turn at the bottom right before a paved road, I slipped and fell. A runner jumped over me. My momentum allowed me to easily snap back up, and I was facing in the correct direction so I could keep running at the sharp turn. I looked over to see Westminster's Winkler running next to me. He was the one who just jumped over me and he looked over and said "Deja vu." He was the runner who jumped over me at the District meet in '81!

We competed well against Park, but they beat us by 5 points. Chris was Conference champion; Mike took fifth and I was seventh. Because of the difficult course, times were slow. Through four runners, we were even with Park, but their fifth man was better than our fifth runner. I tell the kids that I coach today that the fifth runner is just as important as the first guy, and sometimes even more so. And in 1982, this was the case with us. Chris was clearly the best in the conference, and there wasn't anyone even close to him. Winkler took second at Conference, and the first Park runner took third with their next runner in fourth. It didn't matter how far Chris won a race; it was worth one point. The first Park runner could have lost by a minute, but his place was worth three points. So, the fifth guys for both teams decided who won the team title. The race was much more bunched than that. Chris ran 27:20, and I ran around 27:50.

At the Conference Meet, after our top three, Paul was the fourth runner, Alan was our fifth guy, Darren Wycliff was close to Alan, and our seventh runner was freshman Jon Von Cannon. Fresh and Eddie didn't make the varsity, nor did Shawn Wiseman, so they didn't compete at Conference or at the District Meet the next week. Fresh decided to come watch the meet, and he drove up along with Chris' girlfriend as a passenger. This gave Fresh an opportunity to also visit one of his high school teammates, Chris Sylvan, who was a damn good half-miler and would go on to win the state title in the 800m as a senior. For some reason, there were some issues, and Fresh was late for the meet. It all stemmed from Chris' girlfriend who had Fresh's car and didn't return when she was supposed to. Coach Oz was really upset with Fresh, and I don't think he really understood that it wasn't Fresh's fault.

Chris' girlfriend tried to convince Fresh to drive them to the District Meet the next week, but he wouldn't have any of it. Despite our 5-point defeat at Conference, we still thought we had a good shot at winning District. If we won, the team would qualify for the NAIA National Meet. The meet was hosted by Westminster College in Fulton, Missouri. It was cold and windy that morning with a flurry or two. It was 20 degrees, overcast, and with that wind the chill was biting. The race began next to a gymnasium, which I think was at the high school or middle school and wound through a field of tall grass that was brown that time of the year. There was also a small creek, or more appropriately, a slew, winding through the field. At Conference, Paul took the lead early and attempted to hold off as many competitors as he could throughout the race. When he was in shape, Paul's best race results were achieved when he utilized this tactic. But at the District Meet, I think Coach Oz made a tactical mistake when he told Paul to hold back and try and move up in the pack during the race. Paul didn't race well using this tactic, and I thought about telling him to ignore Coach and just race as he always did. But I decided not to challenge Coach, even though I was only going to tell Paul.

As with the Conference Meet, this was a close and competitive race. A lot of times when it was cold, I would get warm as the race progressed, but not on this day. The cold didn't cause me to run a poor race, but I was never comfortable. I remember thinking somewhere between 3 and 4 miles that I wish this race would end. I could never get into a rhythm, but I remained competitive. In the last mile I kept thinking about qualifying for Nationals and that I needed to run as well as I could to help the team. I also passed two or three runners in the last mile, including Mike. As I approached the finish line there were two Park runners just ahead of me, but I couldn't catch them. I finished in fifth place, with Mike in seventh.

Chris won, and Winkler was second. The Park guys took 3rd, 4th, and 6th, which meant the teams were even after the first three runners.

Paul took 11th, and I know he should have finished in 8th or 9th, and maybe even ahead of Mike in 7th. I'm positive Paul's racing strategy cost him a few places. Coach should have realized we needed Paul to be Paul. Alan was again our fifth runner. Park beat us by 9 points. It was close again, but Park clearly had the better team that day. As with conference, times were slow. Chris ran 27:12, and I ran 27:35. I was happy with my race because I took fifth but upset that the team took second. But Chris' confidence took a hit because of his slow time. I tried to convince him that the cold had something to do about his time, and that it didn't matter since he won! Chris did admit that he thought about stopping in the race when he ran by the gym because he had to use the bathroom so bad, he wasn't sure he could finish. Thankfully he didn't stop. A year later, the Conference Meet was held at the same location, and I noticed that the course was somewhat different. The Westminster guys told me that when they re-measured, they found that the 1982 District course was about 600 yards too long. So, in reality, Chris ran his normal race. At 5 miles, wherever that was on the course, we all ran good times.

We did have a medical issue at District. During the break between the summer and fall semesters, Darren fell through a sliding glass door, and severely cut his foot. Glass was removed from the foot, and he was stitched up, and then healed. Darren didn't have any issues during the season, but in the District race, his foot, or ankle, began to hurt and as the race progressed the pain became severe. It's a miracle he finished the race, and, of course, he didn't have his normal performance. After the race he could hardly walk. We took a van and car to the meet. Chris drove the car back to SofO and Darren and I rode with him. After the long trip back to southern Missouri, Chris stopped at the campus hospital, and we helped Darren make into the building. Glass that the first doctor missed during the summer, began to push back through the muscle and skin to the surface. Again, it's a wonder Darren finished the race. This time, all the glass was removed.

Chris, Mike, and I qualified for Nationals, as did three women, Cheryl Smith who won at District, Linda Roberts in 5th, and the sixth-place finisher Terrie Camden. The entire women's team should have qualified. Our team tied for first with Park, but because their sixth runner beat our sixth runner, the Park coach convinced the powers that be that only Park qualified as a team. Later, Coach Oz said that he had made a mistake by not filing a formal protest, because he found out that was not the rule, and that both teams should have run Nationals as full teams, with Park still declared the District champion. But it was too late for our women because the National Meet had passed.

In the two weeks between the District Meet and Nationals, we had some good workouts. Some district meets were held the week before Nationals, and I can't say whether the National results prove my point, but I think we had an advantage because we had an extra week to recover and get in a few good workouts. On Tuesday after the District Meet Coach Oz had us do 5xmile repeats on the track with a three-minute rest between. This is probably the best workout I ever did. Steve Davis ran with Chris, Mike, and I, and we ran our first four in the low 4:50s. I think the slowest was the first in 4:53. On our last mile, we ran 4:39, although Steve was a few seconds back in the mid-4:40s. On Thursday, we repeated the workout and had similar results, although I got a stomach cramp on the second and ran 5:11. Otherwise they were all in the low 4:50s including the last. We were ready for Nationals, and I believed Chris had a good shot at All-American, which was the top 25.

We left on Friday morning and traveled most of the day to Kenosha, Wisconsin, where the NAIA National Meet was held, hosted by the University of Wisconsin-Parkside. On our way, we traveled through St. Louis. In the middle of the city, while we were on the freeway, Coach Oz came to a place where he needed to decide which way to go. Suddenly, he hit the break, and the van came to a complete stop as he contemplated to go left or right on the freeway. Mike, Chris, and I were sitting in the back two seats looking behind us as a semi, traveling too close, locked its breaks when Coach came to his abrupt halt. We thought we were dead. If you've ever seen a movie in which a person about to be in an accident has the face goes back and forth between a skeleton and face – that would describe the three of us. Instead of hitting us, the truck screeched to a stop and jack-knifed. Coach never saw it or heard it. He just continued on his way once he made the decision which way to go and left the carnage behind us. We never told Coach.

We made it through Chicago and arrived in Kenosha unscathed, but we had to change our shorts. The next day was cool but seemed to be a good day to compete. I'm not sure we slept well because we stayed in a shabby old motel north of town on Lake Michigan. You've heard of flea-bitten dogs; well, this was a flea-bitten motel. We had jogged and walked the course the afternoon before, so we knew the hills and turns. Although I trained on hills every day, I was not very good at them, and this course had some tough hills. The men watched our women compete, and they all ran well, but none came close to being All-American. Cheryl had an outside chance, but it didn't happen. Then, it was the men's turn.

The start line was a long one, and we were on the far-right end. The beginning of the race was flat with a tree in the middle, but it quickly turned into a long hill, which seemed like a half mile to me. As we waited for the countdown to start, we could hear a team to our left shout in unison, "We're only here for the beer," and repeat several times. The coach looked at us and said that the team wasn't focused enough and would perform poorly. I was later told that the team was Simon Fraser from British Columbia. They won the team title. I loved Coach, but much of the time, he was too uptight to have fun at meets. But sometimes, he surprises us, especially when he watches Paul race.

The start was interesting because as it was counted down over a loudspeaker, "10, 9, 8" and so on, when the count reached 3, a bunch of guys took off, and I was caught off guard but was able to recover. What surprised me was the speed of the start. In a five-mile race, or 8,000 meters, in this case, I'd never seen such a fast start. Then we started up that long hill that seemed to last forever. From the beginning, I had almost lost sight of Chris and Mike. I was sure they were ahead of me, but I hadn't witnessed it. When I reached the top of the hill, which was maybe a half mile into the race or felt like a half mile, I was exhausted. Later, I was told that from the starting line to the top of the hill was 1000 yards. Maybe, I don't know. It took me another quarter mile to recover, and I never did feel great. There were tons of guys ahead of me, and I couldn't see the leaders. And I realized that even if I suddenly became the best runner in the race and was full of energy, I could never win from where I was. Of course, I was not the best in the race, and I didn't have much energy.

At some point in the first mile, as I went around a corner, I looked to my side, and there was a sea of runners behind me. Somewhere in the second half of the race, we had to climb that first hill again, and it sapped my remaining energy. In the middle of the race, I passed a kid that I thought was wearing a Pitt State uniform. He had blond hair and ran like John. But when I got beside him, this kid had a tattoo on his upper arm, and I knew John didn't have one. Plus, although I hadn't seen John in about six months, I did see some of his results, and he ran a 5-mile race in 24:56 a few weeks before, so this couldn't be him. This guy was too far back to be John.

After the four-mile point, my goal was to finish as well as I could. Although I was far behind the leading runners, I still wanted to finish well for the sake of pride. Finally, as I was at the top of a small hill, I could see the finish line maybe 200 to 300 yards away. As I came off the hill, attempting to pick up my pace to finish strong, this guy came flying by me and yelled, "Come on, Raymond!" It was John, and I sprinted with him to the finish as we passed a fair number of runners who must have thought we were nuts. Yes, John and I were trying to beat each other, and we both had great kicks. When I realized that it was John who just passed me, he had a good stride on me, and we finished that way. We both sprinted just to get 274th and 275th places. When I looked at John in the shoot, I saw that he had a tattoo on his arm – it was John who I had passed somewhere around the three-mile mark. We ran in the 28s, which was damn slow. Chris and Mike didn't run well either. Chris finished ahead of Mike, and they both ran in the 27s.

Chapter 13
"Who's that guy mad at?"

Soon after the men's race ended, we left Kenosha and headed back to southern Missouri. We were disappointed with our performances, but we were also optimistic about the indoor season. On the drive back, Chris, Mike, and I discussed what races we would run and which events we would try to qualify for at Indoor Nationals. Chris thought he would have the best chance in the mile or two mile, while it was a given that Mike's best race was the three-mile. I would try in the 880, 1000 yards, or mile. Coach got in the conversation as well, and we also talked about a two-mile relay, or the distance medley, which was more realistic because we had some good quarter milers. But it was all for nothing.

A week or two after we returned from the National cross-country meet, Chris began to talk about transferring back to Arkansas College. Of course, I was against it, and I think once he brought it up, his girlfriend egged him on. I don't know if Chris was frustrated with the training program or if it was because we were in the middle of running the Hollister steps, but I did think his transfer talk would gradually fade away. Instead, he spoke of it more and more, and I was with him when he called the Arkansas College coach to tell him he wanted to transfer back. He was welcomed with open arms. Coach didn't lead on that he knew about Chris' contact with the AC coach, but I know he knew because he acted differently toward

Chris. And it wasn't anger that I noticed, but Coach Oz looked hurt, and I think part of this was because Chris didn't tell him. When the fall semester ended, Chris took off for home, never to return to SofO as a student, and his girlfriend went with him. In time, Coach Oz forgave Chris and blamed it on his girlfriend, who had been on the track team as well.

During the end of finals week, Mike got kicked out of school, and my two peers and friends were gone. It was a sad moment for me when I came to the realization that these two would no longer be my teammates. Although I had just turned 21 and the freshmen such as Fresh were only a couple of years younger than me, I didn't feel the same connection to them. That would change with Fresh because he became a great friend, and he still is. When Mike went to see the dean of students about his situation, I accompanied him for support. When he emerged from the dean's office, I asked him what happened, and Mike said he was kicked out. Without looking back, I made a not-so-flattering comment about the dean, and when I turned around, he was looking right at me. I hoped he hadn't heard, but I knew he had.

The next week, I was still on campus to work one of my three 40-hour work weeks that was required at SofO when grades came out. I received two very low grades that I didn't deserve, and I thought one was going to be an A. I knew what this meant. As a professor, I always told my students to stand up for themselves and go see their instructors if they didn't agree with a grade. However, I never did this for myself, even though I fully intended to do so when the spring semester began. In fact, that incident is the reason I tell students to meet with their professors. I was so upset with the situation that I called my dad and said I was transferring. After all, it would be easier to leave now that my two best friends on campus were gone.

I thought about following Chris to Arkansas College, and Chris encouraged me to do so. I thought about Southwest Missouri State and Coach Clark, but I was sure I'd never run at Nationals again at a

Division I school. I even thought about Southwestern College in Kansas. I couldn't think of another place I wanted to consider, and I certainly didn't want anything to do with Pittsburg State's coach, although teaming up with John again would have been nice. My dad had a level head and told me I should stick it out one more semester, and if I still felt the same way, we could talk about transferring at that time.

In the spring semester, my new roommate was Fresh, and we failed room checks during the first three weeks. One more and the two of us would be suspended from school. After failing on week three, I confronted our RA and asked why he failed us and didn't receive an answer. So, we got the dorm supervisor to take a look, and he said, "This room flunks," even though it was spotless. I had once liked the supervisor who lived in the building with his family, but I had changed my mind well before this moment. Then Fresh and I asked Alan Hicks, who served as a RA on a different floor, to view the room, and he said it looked great. He was puzzled as to why our room failed, but I wasn't. What did concern me was why they were taking out their revenge on Fresh when I was the one who screwed up. But Fresh was friends with Mike. Mike's brother, Eddie, was still in school, and thank goodness he was spared the crap. I knew I could go to Coach, but although he might have had clout on campus at one time, he no longer did, so I didn't approach him about the issue.

As week four approached, I began to prepare to leave school and thought about what to pack first. I still went to practice and did a good job in my workouts, but I knew I'd be gone in a few days. For some reason, I didn't pack, and when I checked the list after the fourth week of inspection, I was surprised to see that Fresh and I easily passed. What a surprise! We passed week five as well, and I never had another unfair issue during my remaining time at SofO. It just stopped. I think it was a message – don't mess with us! The school almost made my pending transfer easy. I came that close to leaving – or forced to leave. When the spring semester ended, I decided to remain at SofO, and although I'm sure I could have ended up being a lot better at SMS or somewhere else, I'm glad I stayed.

During the Christmas break, I was able to get some training, but not nearly as much as I wanted. After running three weeks of Hollister steps, I had some issues with my legs and hips and needed the first half of the five-week break to rest them and heal, although I did get in some light running. In the last couple of weeks, I got in some good runs in Parsons, but I wasn't in the kind of shape needed to race well early. I had decided to attempt to qualify in the mile, but after a slow but winning 2:00 880 at our first meet at Pitt State, the realization hit me that the mile was out of the question, so I turned my attention to the half. Although that first 880 was slow and I was spent after the race, I knew I could get in fairly good half-mile shape quickly, while the mile would take more strength work, and I wouldn't be ready for the longer race until the outdoor season.

I managed to get under 2:00 minutes in my next race, and my condition steadily improved. Late in the indoor season, the team competed at Central Missouri State on their 220-yard track and Coach had me entered in the mile. We had one more meet after CMS before Nationals, and I was to run the 880 in that one, so the mile was a good chance to run a longer race before attempting to qualify in the half mile. I competed alright and remained competitive most of the race but ended up close to 10 seconds behind the winner. My time was a decent, at best, 4:25. As I came to the finish, I attempted to pass SMS runner Scott Mantooth, a fellow Kansan, and a really good long-distance runner, but he finished just ahead of me. Scott coached with Mark Bollinger at Westminster College a few years ago.

One week later, we were at the University of Missouri for the All-Missouri Intercollegiate Indoor Meet. There were three heats in the 880, and as usual, I was entered in the first or slow heat. I knew if I was to qualify for the NAIA Nationals, I needed to do it on my own. I had hoped to race against the best half-milers in the state, including

Missouri's Scotty Davis, even though I knew I would probably not beat him. But I was really coming around quickly, and I believed, as I still do today, that I could finish second or third in the race.

I went out hard from the start to establish my pace, and for the first time all season, my legs felt fresh. I quickly moved away from the field and hit the 440 in 55 seconds. I knew I was on pace for a good time and to qualify for Nationals. On my own, I tried to finish the last two laps strong, but it was hard to gauge my pace. I knew I slowed some, but I ran the last 220 well. I was a little tired at the finish, and my legs were a little heavy, but I was sure I'd run 60 seconds for the last 440. Because it was an automatically timed race, I didn't get the result at the finish, but two or three of my teammates had me in 1:55, which is what I expected, and even Coach Oz, who was notorious for stopping the watch late, had me in about 1:56 flat.

I watched the second heat with keen interest and timed it myself, but they didn't come close to my time. Then I timed the "fast" heat and watched Scotty Davis easily win in 1:52. I knew I wouldn't have run that fast if I'd raced in that heat, but I was sure I would have placed high. When the results were finally posted, I took 6th place overall, which was a good performance considering that I had run in the slow heat. But what did surprise me was my time – 1:57.32. That didn't make any sense whatsoever. Sure, hand times are faster than FATs, but I surely had run faster than that. Although 1:57 was my official posted time, Coach believed that I was given credit for the 6th place time in the last heat, and I think that's viable. My place was correct, but I had probably run between 1:55.5 and 1:56.0. At any rate, when I'm asked what my best 800m is, I say 1:55. For the metric distance, it's possible it's a high 1:54, but I don't think it's faster than 1:55.0. This wasn't the last time my correct time was an issue, and it happened one more time in my track career.

Some people might question whether the timing could be wrong, but I've seen it in many AAU meets since I've been a coach. For example, a few years ago at the Arkansas Association AAU meet, I watched a kid with a best 800m time of 1:53 run 1:59 winning the 800m, but when the "official" results were posted, he was credited with last place in a time over 3:00. And this was FAT timing! This good runner was not on our club, but when the results were posted online a few days later, I protested, to no avail. And there were several other timing issues that day. It's so bad I've considered leaving youth track, but I love coaching the kids too much to leave right now. I've thought about leaving the AAU for USAT&F, but that organization is weak in the youth track in Arkansas. With my situation at the All-Missouri Meet, I think it was just a simple oversite with no intention.

The next week, I was in Kansas City to compete at the NAIA Indoor National Meet held at Municipal Auditorium in downtown, along with four teammates, Keith Rogers, Nate Lampkin, Wilbert Daniels, and Reggie Burton. Trenton Brinson might have competed as well. The team stayed at a hotel in the arena area, so everything was confined, including the track. I had never raced on a board track, and this one was a twelve-lapper, meaning twelve laps for a mile. Even then, I thought it was ridiculous to contest a national meet on such a short track. One lap was just under 147 yards. For a taller athlete such as me, I was 6' 2", this was too short. The curves were banked, which helped, but I had never run on a banked track, and I found out it does take some practice. There were some fine 220-yard tracks in the country in metropolitan areas if that was the requirement, but the NAIA had to put the indoor meet in a closet. And it didn't appear to me that a major city was needed since cross-country and outdoor track Nationals were held in smaller cities and towns.

Despite the track issue, it was a competitive meet, a great meet, really. The 880 heats were in the evening. I don't recall how many heats there were, but I was in a really tough race. When the race began, I didn't sprint at full speed, which I should have done to get a position at the front. As I came off the second curve, I tried to use the curve to propel me by some runners, and I sprinted down the straight, which I think was no more than 35 yards long. I was able to actually pass a couple of guys, but I couldn't cut into the first lane because they were too close, and by this time, I was running up a hill at the start of the next curve, so I lost my position. This happened for most of the six laps. I just couldn't get by anyone long enough to keep it. And the pace was slow, and I could feel that it was slow, but I couldn't push to the lead. It was slow for most, if not all the guys, but that's how prelims can go. One or two runners at the front controlled the pace.

As I came off the last curve, I sprinted and passed one runner and almost caught another, who was taller than me. He was as frustrated as I was. I'm not sure who he was, but I think he won the outdoor 800m at Nationals a few months later. But neither one of us qualified for the finals. It was frustrating because I thought I could have qualified, but that's the way it goes. As an athlete, you need to make adjustments and do what it takes to come through and I didn't – it was my fault. The thing that struck me was that it seemed to me that all of us could have continued at that same pace for a couple more laps. I can't speak for those behind me, but the guys I saw didn't appear tired or in distress at all, including me. The race felt so easy that I was sure I'd run about 2:04. I never heard the 440 spits, so I didn't have a clue what the pace was other than slow.

When the results were posted a little while later, I was surprised with my time, just as I had been the week before. But this time it wasn't because the time was too slow, but because I'd run much faster than I ever would have imagined. My time was 1:58.31 (I might be a couple of hundredths off). How did I run 1:58 FAT when I essentially jogged the race? Now, 1:58 is not fast, and I know it, and the winner only ran in the 1:56s, but I never thought I had come close to running under two minutes, let alone 1:58. I don't know what place I got anymore, and at the time I didn't know when the race finished because it was too bunched. For all the 880 heats combined, I think was 13th or 14th. Despite my disappointment and squandering my opportunity to be an NAIA All-American, I was encouraged because I knew I was now in good form and ready to tackle the 1500m during the outdoor season. I knew I could have run a 1:54 on that rinky-dink track, so that gave me confidence.

The next morning, I watched John Johnson easily qualify for the 1000y finals by winning his heat. His final was in the evening, but our team left for home before the race, so I didn't see him take 5th and make All-American. John told me that he made a tactical mistake and didn't respond when the pace quickened and found himself boxed and unable to get by guys when he did get out. It was similar to my situation in the 880 heats. Like me, John had a hell of a kick, but he was quicker than me, meaning he could reach top speed faster than I could. And even with his explosive acceleration, John couldn't pass anyone on the short straights. Still, he ran 2:14, which is much faster than I ever ran the race. John told me he was so upset about his poor race that the next week at indoor districts he hit 1:53 at the 880 on his way to a 1000 in 2:12.

Our District 16 Meet was also the next week at William Jewell. I was entered in the mile, 880, and 1000y. We had a strong team in 1983, but we didn't have the same firepower we had in '82. Our goal was to defend the team title, but we placed 2nd behind Park. I won the mile in an easy 4:31 or 4:32. In the 880, I was pretty much attacked by a couple of Park runners. One tripped me from behind and the other pushed me, then they tried to box me in coming off the final curve and I was elbowed and cut off, costing me the victory. Of course, with my size, I was able to stand my ground, but it was too late to sprint to the lead. Then, I was disqualified, but the Park guys were not. Coach Oz said that the Park coach was able to get in the official's ear and convince him that I needed to be disqualified. Coach did protest, but he was outvoted. Coach knew, as did my team, that there was a conspiracy against SofO at that meet, and we lost points, although I'm not sure what place I took.

I didn't have time to think about it much because I had to run the 1000 in 15 minutes. Coach had my legs iced down. He had recently read that this would help in the recovery by slowing down the buildup of lactic acid in the muscles. Maybe it's true, I don't know, but I wasn't competitive in the 1000 yards. When I lined up for the race, one of the Park runners were shocked that I was in the 1000 so close to the 880. I was not close enough to the front to have them try anything with me, but I knew that when I raced those guys again and they tried that same shit, I'd knock them silly. I liked the Park guys that I knew, but their reputation was that they would use dirty tactics, and I witnessed it more than once. Some of their guys wouldn't engage in such shenanigans, but others did. However, no one from that college ever tried anything with me again. I believed their actions had to come from the demand of their coach.

The school newspaper indicated that I ran on the two-mile relay as well in which we took 4th, although I have no recollection of the race. In the days that followed, many athletes on campus heard of the incident and asked me about it, but other than answering them, I put it behind me because I had the outdoor season as my new focus! Our first outdoor meet was nine days after the district meet, so I decided to run a 100-mile week beginning on Monday to gain some strength. I ended the 100-mile week on a Sunday, and our first outdoor meet was the next day, a late afternoon meet on our home track against Southwest Missouri State, Missouri Rolla, and the University of Tulsa.

Coach had me in the mile for the first meet. It was a cool, overcast day, with a slight breeze, although the sun came out for a short time during the mile. It was not a bad day to run. The team had a good day. Freshman Reggie Burton broke the school record in his 440-victory running 48.8, and Mark Hicks, who was a senior set a school record in the pole vault jumping 15' 9". Although I had just finished with a 100-mile week, I still thought I could run a decent race. I wasn't concerned with how fast I could run yet, after all, I had run those miles to help me later in the season, especially as I did more track work. I felt that if I could run around 4:25 that would be a good indication that I could go significantly faster on fresh legs. But in reality, I didn't give a time much thought. I just wanted to compete and win if I could.

After the race started, I settled in the second position and followed on the heels of the leader, Tom Becker of SMS. Key was in the race but was running unattached because he was redshirting. I wasn't concerned about him because I knew he wasn't fit. SMS freshman Branton White was also in the race, and I believed I did need to watch him – he was talented. But White wasn't a factor that day. It would have been great to race White later in the season when he ran a fast 1500. I think Mantooth was in the race as well, but I'm not 100% sure. But it was just Becker and me racing for the win. I followed Becker through the first lap, and it didn't seem fast although I wasn't sharp either. By the 880, split in 2:09, I was comfortable staying right behind Becker and he didn't seem in a hurry to try and leave me, and I didn't feel compelled to go by him and press.

If this had been mid-season I might have tried to go, but 2:09 at the half was good enough after a hard distance week so I was content. Nothing changed as we crossed the line at three laps, and I'm sure it mirrored the end of the first lap and the end of the second. On the backstretch, Becker picked it up a bit, but not anything close to a kick, and I had no problems staying with him. Into the final curve I decided that I would try to pass coming on that final straight. I knew that I would not be explosive, but I felt good and strong so a steady drive to the finish line was in order. In the curve, Becker started his kick, but I could tell that's all he had, and although I didn't have my full kick yet, I didn't see any issues in being able to pass him.

As we started to come off the curve, I went wide to pass. Then I saw Becker look to his side at me and then he stepped out into the second lane and cut me off. I broke stride so I wouldn't fall. If I'd had my usual explosiveness, I would have sprinted right by him before he could respond, but not on this day. I gathered myself and went wide to pass and he did the same thing to me again. I was sure he would be disqualified, if not for the first incident, then the second. Now I was pissed and didn't even think about whether I was tired or not, which I wasn't. With a little more than half the straight left I decided on a new approach. I waited a second or so while running right behind him and then he looked to his outside again and at that moment I put everything I had in my kick and passed him on the inside while he was still looking for me on his outside. When he realized I was in lane one, it was too late for him to respond, and I easily beat him to the finish line.

My winning time was 4:18.3, which was a school record, and Becker also ran under 4:19. To be honest, a 4:18 is not a great school record, but to be fair to my school, the record in the 1500m was 3:50. Oh, and Becker wasn't disqualified. It was our home meet, but Coach didn't get involved in officiating the meet and let the lead official run that show, which is the way it should be. But after the race, I was glad Becker wasn't disqualified. Coach was really happy with how the team competed in the first meet and indicated it was the first time in school history that three records fell in the same meet. In another week, Becker would get his opportunity to try and return the favor against me.

Our next meet was at Rolla, against SMS as well. This meet was held on the Rolla High School track and contested in meters. It was cooler than our first meet and somewhat windy as well as cloudy. Although Tulsa was not at this meet, the field in the 1500m had many of the same guys entered as were in the mile at our place. The pace was not as fast as the previous meet, but it developed almost the same. I tucked in behind Becker and followed through three laps. But before we reached the 1200m mark, I had made the decision to pass Becker with 300m to go to surprise him. This way he wouldn't be ready to step out in front of me when I tried to pass. I also decided

296

to mess with him. My usual way of messing with competitors was to talk during the race, but I had other things in mind here.

With 300 meters to go, I sprinted by Becker. I was much sharper than I had been in the mile at SofO, so I didn't have a problem getting by him. Then, instead of attempting to sprint away from Becker, I slowed to a point that he tried to pass me back. This is what I wanted. As soon as he got next to me, I sprinted again and put a few yards between us, and then I slowed again and repeated the process. I did these three or four times until finally maintaining me sprint with 50 meters to go. The reason I did this to Becker was to get back at him for trying to trip me, twice, the previous week. I wanted to punish him, and it worked perfectly. He fell for it. I won in 4:03.6, which wasn't fast, but it wasn't supposed to be. Becker finished 2nd and Mantooth was 4th.

After the race, Becker headed to the short chain-link fence past the finish line that bordered the outside of the track. He was leaning on the three-foot high fence when I approached him to shake his hand. I held out my hand and said, "Good race," but he wouldn't shake. He then began to cuss all sorts of file language as he repeatedly kicked the fence with his right foot! I couldn't resist, so I started laughing and walked away. I wasn't the least bit offended – after all, I was the one who pissed him off. I was never sure he was angry for losing or because I messed with him. In reality, I was not a better runner than Becker, just maybe a better miler. Becker was really a very good runner, who I whole-heartily respected. About a year and a half before our two races, he was hit by a car while standing in front of a building I think, not even on the street. I don't remember the details, but I think he was standing with some friends during the SMS football homecoming weekend, and someone drove up on the sidewalk and hit him. I do know it tore up his knee and he went through a long rehab. I remember reading about his rehab in a pool in a newspaper article. I don't think I ever raced Becker again.

Our third meet of the outdoor season was at Northwest Missouri State University, and as it was in 1982, it was cold in '83. It was in the high 30s and when we arrived in the morning, there was a thin layer of ice in the track. It also became very windy. Early in the meet, the 4x100m relay was contested. I was standing against the fence on the outside of the track in the first curve. Our SofO team was in one of the inside lanes. When the gun sounded the athletes took off fast, and only a few strides into the race, one of the runners in a middle lane, wearing a purple uniform, slipped when his spikes didn't penetrate the ice covering portions of the track. He was a very tall runner, and when he fell, his momentum caused him to spin on the ice as his body quickly headed straight toward where I was standing. In the process, he took out a team or two who were in lanes to his outside, and right before he hit the fence, I jumped back as a reflex. Our team went on the win the race. The runner who slipped was, I believe, Northeast Missouri State's Ray Armstead, the future gold medalist.

In the 1500m, I believed I was one of the best in the race and had a chance to win, even though the field was strong. I knew the time would not be good considering the conditions, so I just focused on the competition. Although I knew I had a chance in the race, I also knew the best runner was Northwest Missouri's Jim Ryan, not to be confused with the great miler Jim Ryun. Coach Oz was related to Ryan, but I'm not sure how. Ryan was an outstanding runner, which included the steeplechase. As the race started and the field headed down the first straight directly into the wind, it was a battle not to take the lead, so the pace dwindled quickly, or never materialized at all. We just bunched up in a tight group and waddled around the track. I don't know who was in the lead, but I was in the middle of the cluster.

The second lap was the same, and the third as well, but when the race hit the 1200m mark with 300 to go, I got caught napping and didn't respond quick enough to get up with the leaders and found myself back in about 10th or 11th place. I could see Ryan sprint away, but I was too far behind when I did start my kick. I should have moved up to third place with 500m to go so I would have been ready for the move when it occurred. When I went, I had a good kick and passed several guys to finish in 5th place in 4:15 (although it might have been 4:17). Ryan won in 4:10. These were slow times, but the race was tough. I'm not sure what my last 300m was, but probably 44 or 45 seconds – I never heard my 1200m split, I was too busy falling asleep. Ryan went on to run 3:46 or 3:45 that year and I think he took second at the NCAA Division II Nationals in the metric mile. I don't know if this was his fastest time, but he was a good one. In fact, he was tough enough for me to beat if I'd went right with him, but impossible when I didn't give myself a chance.

I was upset with myself. I should have taken 2nd in that race at worst. Ryan was better than me, but I wanted to have a chance to see if I could race with him, and I failed to do so. I still had the 800m to run so I headed to the indoor track area to get warm and think about my next race. I might have been tired after the 1500m, but I was too mad at myself to notice. When we lined up for the 800, it was as cold and windy as it had been. And there were a lot of guys bitching about the cold. I told myself right then that I was going to try and win this thing, redeem myself from my poor 1500, and beat these wimps who cried a little, or a lot, because of the weather. Like the 1500, the 800 was slow and the race took on the same feel, a bunch of guys bunched together running the first lap in about 63 or 64 seconds. But I kept myself toward the front this time and instead of waiting for someone else to make the first move, I decided to be the one. On the back stretch, I took the lead and tried to sprint for home. I kept the lead as I fought the wind going into the final curve, but as I came off the curve I got passed. At least I could still get second. Just as I was about to cross the finish line, a big runner out leaned me and I had to settle for third, and the bronze medal. When I crossed the line, I saw it was Paul White, who got by me the year before at the tape. He tuned to shake my hand, smiled, and said "Deja vu." He remembered it was me. It was the second time in six months someone said that to me! My time was a very slow 2:02, but my second lap was good, and I wasn't upset because I knew I had not made any mental mistakes in the two-lapper. I also vowed that I would not get caught sleeping again.

Our next meet was again at home against Iowa's Loras College and Tulsa. But a few days before the meet, I got sick, and I mean really sick. I vomited and was just sick as a dog for about three days. I'm sure I had the flu. When race day arrived, I was lucky we didn't have to travel – I just had to walk 200 yards from my dorm to the track. It was another cool and overcast day, but with only a slight breeze. But I felt horrible. I was depleted of energy, and I was entered in the mile, and I might have been in the three-mile as well. I didn't want to race that day. I wasn't in the throws if the worst of the flu, but I was still achy. But there I was at the start of the mile waiting for the gun to sound.

The field wasn't big, and I didn't know what kind a milers Loras had. Tulsa didn't have a miler who could compete with me on a day I felt well, but maybe today would be different. A Loras runner took the lead, with an unattached athlete right behind him, a young man who I think was a Loras assistant. I tried to stay close, but it was a struggle. I don't remember the middle of the race anymore, but I do remember, clearly, the last lap. With 330 yards to go, I was about 35 yards behind the leader from Loras and his coach. I had not fallen asleep as I had at Northwest, but I was well off the lead. However, I decided to give it a go and see if I could get close, so I started to sprint, and I was amazed that I had as much speed as I did. It only took about 230 yards to catch the leader, who had left his coach behind. As I came close to the Loras runner, his coach yelled at him that I was about to catch him. But there was nothing he could do, and once I passed him and was sure I had the win, I slowed because I thought I might throw up if I didn't. I won in 4:18.7, and the kid behind me ran 4:19. Steve Davis was my official timer, and he came out to give me my time and pat me on the back. But I just hoped I wouldn't vomit on him. Of course, my time was a shock, as well as my last 440 in 57 seconds. This was one of the few races that was videotaped in which I competed, and when I watched the tape, I couldn't believe I slowed so much. I was almost at a walk when I crossed the line. Today, I don't know if I ran the three-mile race that day, or even the 880, but if I did, it was slow, and I was badly beaten.

This race gave me tons of confidence. I was sick and ran 4:18 and almost came to a stop at the finish – I was fit! I was sure I could run a mile in 4:05 to 4:07 and a 1500m in something under 3:50. But would I get the chance? I wasn't sure if I could run those kinds of times on my own. I really thought I needed to be in a race with others running those times, or close to it. I even thought if everything went right, I might be able to sneak below 4 minutes in the mile in a year or two. There were good meets coming up and I believed I could at least run a 3:55 1500m on my own, even if the weather was not cooperative. I really wanted to compete at the Mule Relays at Central Missouri State, where I knew the competition would be good. I also wanted to run at the Kansas Relays and the Drake Relays, but Coach felt these meets were too tough for some of the guys. But we had men on the team who could compete at that level, and I at least believed we should go to CMS, but we didn't.

Training went well throughout the season and except for sore knees and hips in the morning, I didn't have any concerns, and I didn't worry about soreness in the morning either. We still ran lots of miles, which was Coach Oz's philosophy, and we did tons of repeats on the track. As with the previous track season, we typically ran 30 to 40 440 repeats with 60 to 90 seconds for rest. Jon Von Cannon would run the first few, maybe 8 to 10, faster than the rest of us and Coach praised him and questioned our effort. But we ran 63 to 66 seconds just as Coach wanted, and Jon ran 61 to 62 seconds, just enough to finish ahead of the other runners. Several times, around the twelfth one, I would tell the other guys not to worry about me because I was going to burn a few to make Jon drop out, so we could resume our workout in peace. So, I would run the next three or four in 55 seconds or so, and, of course, Jon attempted to stay with me. It was rare for Jon to reach 18 quarters after that, while the rest of the guys continued well past 30.

Without Chris Marcak around the season was certainly different, both on the track and socially. Although Mike was no longer in school, he was still around most days because his brother Eddie was still enrolled. Mike trained with the team and with Steve Davis. A new freshman who started school in January was Mike Saunders, and he was a distance runner. Mike was a good kid, and I can't think of anyone who disliked him. And Fresh and I became closer friends not only because we were teammates, but because we were roommates as well. Through the course of the semester, Fresh and I came up with Tuesday wine night. We would buy three of four bottles of cheap wine and go out to the Tower of Power; a name we gave the observation tower about a mile off US 65 south of campus. If we bought three bottles, we split the third. We should have called it "Ripple Tuesday." It's a miracle some of us competed as well as we did.

As a freshman, Fresh struggled to find his race and confidence. But this is common for freshman. And I think Coach Oz tried to find the best race for him as well. Was he an 800m runner, a 1500m guy, or a distance runner whose best race was the 5,000? Was he a middle-distance runner, an 8 and 15 guy, or 15 and 5 athlete? I don't think we ever knew that first year. Fresh wanted to be an 800m runner first with his second distance as the 1500. He was a 2:01 runner at Jefferson City High School, but I think he was tugged back and forth between different races and never fell into a good rhythm. If he could have focused on the 800m, let's say, I believe he would have raced much better. I think Coach should have avoided the 5,000 with Fresh, except for a couple of early season races.

I tried a few things with Fresh to help him. Sometimes I built him up to give him confidence, sometimes tore him down to piss him off with the hope that it would make him try and prove me wrong, and other times I didn't pay attention. But nothing worked. I also think a lot of it was that Fresh was over-worked or over-trained. He has told me over the years that it wasn't so much the miles that we ran, but the hard pace. I have a feeling as a college coach, Mark used a lot of what he learned his freshmen year and what to avoid. Mark should have been a 1:55 guy in college and a sub-4:00 1500m runner. I can't say he was a real gifted runner, but he wasn't bad either.

We ran a meet at Flo Valley in St. Louis on a Saturday, and I won the 1500 and 800 is slow races. On the way to St. Louis on Friday, the team helped with a high school meet in Springfield, along with some SMS track athletes, just as we had the year before. I helped run off the shot put in a muddy landing area. I noticed when it was my turn to retrieve shots, when I threw them back, I was sometimes hitting around 45 feet. Although I was a middle-distance runner, I could bench press 260 pounds on dead weights, and occasionally 265. And I could press 225 more than 15 reaps. So, I was strong, at least for a miler! The meet I was waiting for was only two days later on Monday at Lincoln University. That same old worn-out track with the manhole cover on the back stretch was still there and I was ready to race.

The meet in St. Louis was chilly, but the weather on Monday was perfect. It was sunny and the temperature was about 70 degrees. I felt great when I warmed up. The year before the 1500m was run under the lights, but it was earlier in '83, so it was still sunny. I was determined to run well, and if needed take the lead early. But when the race started, I decided that the pace was good enough and there was no need to attack in the early stages. On the second curve as the field approached the 400m mark, I large bug flew into my mouth. I coughed or gagged two or three times and was never able to conclude if I swallowed it or spit the bug out. At any rate, I never lost stride, and it didn't have any impact on my race. I was comfortable in second place and was running smoothly through the second lap. My 800 split was 2:06, which wasn't too bad, although I wished it had been faster. But that was my fault for not pushing after the first lap – maybe I was too comfortable.

On the third lap I don't think I ever thought about taking the lead, although in retrospect, I should have. I think this was the best I'd ever felt in a race. I hit 3:11 at the 1200, and I blasted to the lead in a furious kick. I was full of run at that point, and it felt like a fast 300 in a workout. I couldn't believe how well I felt and how fast I was. I just completely left the field. With 200 meters to go, I shifted into my final gear and smoked the curve, and I was able to maintain it all the way down the stretch to the finish line. Except for being a little winded from the sprint, I was not at all tired. This was the easiest 1500m or mile I had ever run, or any race for that matter. The timer came up and asked my name as I turned to shake hands with the other competitors, and I thought she said I ran 3:57. I didn't give that time too much thought, although I wanted to run faster. But after the race, as I went into the infield to put on my sweats, the time didn't make much sense, especially after a teammate said I ran my last 400m well under 60 seconds, and maybe as fast as 57.

If I'd run 3:57, then my last 300m was a 46. No, that certainly wasn't correct. But I didn't have much time to think about it because I only had 25 minutes or so before the 800. As with the previous year, the Lincoln Meet didn't have women competing and not many teams – but the teams there were good. So, the meet was run quickly. But before the 800, the results of the 1500 were announced over the PA and my winning time was 3:52.0. Maybe I didn't hear the timer correctly or she thought the 2 was a 7. I don't know, but I wasn't sure I'd run 3:52. Later, when I was back at school and thought about it, 3:52 made a lot more sense. That would mean my last 300m was 41 seconds and if I ran 57 or 58 seconds my last lap, and I didn't begin to kick until 300 meters to go, then 3:52 was correct. I actually never saw the official results I just heard them.

When I lined up for the 800m, Coach pointed to an unattached runner and said stay with him the first lap. I didn't know who the guy was, but I told Coach "OK." And that's just what I did. I was in third place at 400 in 54 seconds, and I was right with the leader, the one Coach told me to stay with, and the second-place runner. But when I heard my split, I made a tactical mistake by thinking too much. The pace wasn't bothering me, but I thought I hadn't had enough time to recover from a fast 1500 to run my first lap that fast. So, I slowed, and several people passed me on the back stretch. With 80 meters to go, I realized I wasn't tired, and I began to kick, passing two runners to take 4th in a very disappointing 1:57. The winner, who Coach told me after the race was a former Northeast Mo runner who ran 1:46 in college and won the Division II Nationals, won the race in 1:52. Why hadn't I stayed with him throughout the race? I should have run 1:53, but that's how it goes when you think too much. I don't remember the winner's name, and maybe I didn't know then.

I thought my day was over, but one of our best 400m runners, Wilbert Daniels, tweaked his hammy running a 21.6 200m, so Coach recruited me to take his place in the 4x400m. Wilbert had moved down in this meet to work on speed and had a great day, running a PR in the 100m as well in 10.6. He didn't think the tweak was bad enough to keep him out of the relay and was hoping for a 47 leg. But Coach wanted to be cautious, which was the right move. So only 20 minutes after the 800, I took Wilbert's place. Our first two runners ran well, then I took the baton as the third leg, and that's when I felt the first two races. It's not that I was extremely tired, but my legs were heavy, and I didn't have my normal speed. Coming off the final curve, I was about to pass a guy when one of his teammates standing in an outside lane yelled, "He's their miler!" I guess it was embarrassing for a college 400m runner to get passed by a miler. So, he dug in and held me off. I handed the baton to Reggie Burton, and we finish the race in 3rd or 4th in 3:21.0. Going against his norm, Coach had a teammate time my leg and it was 52.0. Not bad, but much slower than Wilbert would have done. No doubt fresh, I would have run 48 or 49. But not that day.

Our next scheduled meet was the SMS Relays in Springfield, and I really looked forward to racing Branton White, because his recent results were outstanding. Unfortunately, I didn't get the opportunity to race him because the meet was cancelled. It had rained a lot, and the cinder track was in no condition for a meet. Fresh was disappointed as well because he was entered in the freshman 1500, and this was a good opportunity to place well against his peers. Although White was a freshman, I doubt he was entered in that freshman race. So, we ended up with a long break from racing. Today, college teams don't compete often, but we raced once or twice a week back then. I think for middle distance runners, racing every week is beneficial. And even distance runners can race often if they only run the 5,000 and 10,000 a few times. They can run shorter races to work on speed. I don't know if today's trend is to keep athletes fresh or because of athletic budget restrictions.

We ended up with more of a break than expected when our meet at Arkansas Tech was postponed because of bad weather. But finally, that meet was rescheduled, and we headed to Russellville, Arkansas on a cold and cloudy day, and it was windy as well. On the way to Tech, traveling on the very scenic, and somewhat dangerous, Hwy. 7 in Arkansas, Coach almost drove the van off a cliff or something close to it. Luckily, I was traveling in a car behind the van with three other teammates when the near disaster happened. Mark Hicks was driving the car, and I thought we were all going to have heart attacks, but I can't imagine what those on the van felt. I swear the back passenger tire was over the side. But Coach just kept on driving as if nothing happened, because I don't think he knew it happened. All I know is the guys on the back of the van looked back with pure fear in the faces.

Of course, we made it to the meet safely – we always did. I was determined to take the lead in this race and push like hell from the start, regardless of the crappy weather. After all, this was nothing like the day at Northeast Missouri! I took off like a shot when the gun sounded in the 1500m and pushed hard and quickly left the field. The track was rubber asphalt like my high school track, accept this one had held together much better. But the cold weather made it hard as a rock and my spikes didn't seem to penetrate the surface. It was like running on the road with spikes. When I came down the home stretch for the first time, the PA announcer enthusiastically said, "Who's that guy mad at?" It almost made me laugh. My 400m split was 60 seconds, one of the fastest first laps I'd run in the 1500 or mile. I wanted 2:02 at the 800m, but I hit 2:04 instead. This was my best 800m split, but I could tell this would not be a PR Day. The hard track was unforgiving, and my legs were beginning to suffer from the pounding. I kept plugging away and I tried not to slow on the third lap, but I knew I was.

With 300 to go, I didn't have the explosiveness I had at Lincoln and I was spent, as I hit 3:10. That was one second faster than the previous race, but I was slowing at an alarming rate. I'm told with 300 to go I was 30 to 35 meters in the lead. But coming off the last curve with a little over 100m to go, I was caught and being passed. Then something happened. I got mad, not at myself and not at the kid from Arkansas Tech trying to pass me. But I was just mad. I guess I sort of answered the PA announcer. My anger stemmed from the fact that I led the whole race, and now I was about to get beat. I remember thinking to myself, "You led the whole race and I'll be damned if I'll let you lose it!" And so, I dug. The Tech kid, named Dietz, inched ahead but I wouldn't let him have the race and I dug some more. I was completely exhausted, and my legs felt like 200-pound weights, but I just kept moving my arms and digging some more. When I finished the race, I could hardly stand, but I'd won the race, 3:57.57 to Dietz's 3:57.95. My last 300 meters was run in 47 seconds, which was just good enough. Dietz gave me all I could handle and made it a great race the last 150 meters.

I had just missed the meet record by a couple of tenths, but I didn't care. A few days later I received a letter in the mail from someone who graduated from SofO the year before. Judy Jones saw the article about the track meet in the Russellville newspaper, where she was living, and sent the results and a picture of me and Dietz battling off the final curve. And I looked like I was dying! She wrote in her letter that when she saw the picture she said, "I know that guy!" The newspaper results had my time as 3:57.95, but that was Dietz's time. In an Arkansas newspaper that the SofO library received, it listed the top college performers in the state throughout the season and listed his time as 3:58.0, which is rounded up from the hand-time result from the meet.

I still had to run the damn 800m and unlike the Lincoln meet, there was plenty of time between races. But I was not even competitive. The winner ran 1:53, but I struggled home in 2:06, two seconds slower than my split in the 15. Thank God Wilbert's hamstring was good, because I don't think I could have replaced him in the relay. Although I was not happy with the 800, I was more than satisfied with the 1500m. While the Lincoln 1500 was the easiest one I ever ran, the one at Tech was the hardest. In fact, I was extremely happy with the 1500m, and I could live with a poor 800 after running such a strenuous race. It's amazing how an athlete can perform in a competition and the next time it's completely different. If the weather would have been nice at Tech, I'm not so sure I'd have run a PR. Each day is different.

Despite the meet at Tech on Saturday, I traveled to Springfield on Sunday morning with a couple of teammates, including Fresh, to run the Pepsi Challenge 10k road race. This was just for fun. If I was going to go for a distance run that day, why not make it a race? I wasn't worried about my time or place, but I did want to give it a good effort. The day was beautiful. The race started at a park and was two laps through a neighborhood. When I reached the 5k point, which was where we started, I heard someone yell my name and saw Steve Davis to the side. I joked with him, and he told me that if I was that fresh, I needed to run faster. On the second lap I was passed by a runner in his 30s who was from the area and ran some good marathons and 10ks. After the race, in which I ran around 33:10, and finished 11th, Steve got on me for letting the guy beat me. I told Steve that I had raced hard the day before, so I wasn't up to par. Steve said that this guy had raced in a marathon the day before in the 2:20s. So that put it in perspective. Today, I wouldn't recommend a college runner competing in a 10k road race in the middle of track season, but we did these things because we loved to race.

Our last meet of the season was district held at William Jewell on an old cinder track, that I swear was on a slight hill, but it probably wasn't. The meet was contested in yards, and it was another cool and windy day. The evening before the meet, I was with three or four teammates, including Paul Taylor, playing miniature golf, when Coach came by upset. He told us that there was no way we could be concentrating on the meet playing this game the night before. I tried to argue with Coach, as did Paul, but our mini golf game was over. Of course, relaxing with a non-strenuous game, the evening before didn't hurt our performances the next day, but Coach was convinced it would.

My races at the District 16 Meet were the mile, 880 and 3 mile. With three races and the cool, windy weather, I wasn't worried about times. I did think about trying to run a 4:15 mile so I wouldn't be bothered with kicking to win, but that didn't make sense if I wanted to place in the 3 mile later in the meet. The mile was easy. I just stepped in behind a Park runner and waited and waited. I don't remember my spits and I might not have paid attention anyway. About midway down the back stretch on the last lap, I decided it was time. I was antsy and needed to run. So, I took off around the Park guy and sprinted home. With a lap to go, some Park runners pleaded with their teammate to go now because they knew I would smoke him on a short sprint. But I would have smoked him on a long sprint as well.

My winning time was 4:24, and the Park runner was second in 4:29. I then rested for the 880, but then something happened. My back began to tighten up, and I had never had this happen before. I worked it out, but it was still not good by the time of the 880. I didn't run well, and my kick disappeared. And it was a real slow race, but I took 2nd in 1:59, losing to Ron Chisolm of Park who ran 1:58. I'd beaten Chisolm already that year, so I was disappointed, but he was a real good half-miler. But I had beaten their other good 800m runner, a guy named Eddie Hicks, who I believe ran 1:52 during his college career. And then my back got worse. I tried to find a place to lay down and when it finally came time to warm up for the 3 mile, I was not in good shape. I went to Coach and told him my lower back really hurt and I wasn't sure I could run the last race. But Coach told me to run it anyway because it might loosen up in the race. Well, it hadn't loosened up in the half!

So, I lined up for the 3 mile with Paul and Fresh. I told Fresh I would try to pace him so he could have a good race, but I wasn't sure how long I could do so before dropping out. I'd never dropped out of a race before, but I didn't see any other option. I stayed with pack to help Fresh, but I felt horrible as Westminster's Winkler took the lead. He had won the 6 mile in the morning, and I don't remember if he ran the mile. But as I ran three or four laps, something else happened – my back began to loosen up and the pain went away. Now I was in a race. I didn't attempt to move up because I was already with the pack, except for Winkler who had a decent lead. And I continued like this lap after lap, not running fast, but staying competitive, hoping Fresh would stay with me. With one lap to go, I knew I wouldn't catch Winkler, but I knew I was getting second. As in the mile, some Park guys yelled at their teammate I was running behind to take off and they told him my kick was too good for him to beat me with half a lap to go. But he didn't try to leave me, and I easily kicked by him with 220 yards to go. My kick was only temporarily gone. My second-place time was only 15:23.9, but I was happy with it. Winkler won in 15:09.9. Unfortunately, Fresh wasn't able to remain with the pack the second half of the race. As a team we took second behind Park College.

Chapter 14
Injured

I hoped that Coach Oz would take me to Outdoor Nationals, but he didn't. I also thought Reggie and Wilbert deserved to go as well as Trenton Brinson, and the 4x400, which those three were on. And Nate would have been on the relay. Mark Hicks deserved to compete at Nationals in the pole vault. I was sure I could make All-American in the 1500. I didn't think then, and still believe this today, that there were six 1500m runners in the NAIA who could beat me. But I never got the opportunity to find out. I'm not trying to indicate that I was great, but in the small college world of the NAIA, I was pretty damn good. Yes, there were some world class guys in the NAIA such as Kenya's Joel Ngetich who was world ranked in the 800m in 1981, but there was usually only one in an event, and most didn't have that. I don't think the 1500 had a world class runner in 1983. I believe the National meet was held in Virginia that year and Coach said it was too far away. But we went to Wisconsin for Cross-country Nationals. Nonetheless, it was a good outdoor track season. I ran in eight 1500 and mile races and won seven of them. I was not the same runner I had been in high school – I was in a different league now.

When the semester ended, I headed back to Parsons for two weeks and continued to train. I spent some time with John Johnson and did a few runs with him. I had spent two or three days with John over spring break but only had the opportunity to get a single training run with him because he had practice with his team. During my short early summer break, I began to feel a slight discomfort on the outside of my lower left leg, but only after I was finished with my run, so I didn't give it much thought. My opinion was that if it didn't bother me while I ran, then why worry, especially since it went away quickly. If I put pressure on it, it seemed to help, and it didn't bother me after every run.

My training resumed with my teammates when I returned to SofO. We had a full racing schedule for the summer, and I wanted to do as well as I could in some of the races, especially an 8k in Wichita during July. I decided to run the 2-mile a couple of times at the SMS summer meets to help prepare for cross-country. To get an idea of where I was with my fitness, I ran a 2-mile time trial on our home track. I wasn't trying to hit a homerun, I just wanted to run a steady pace. Fresh and Eddie timed me. I hit the first mile in 5:01 and ran the last lap well to finish in 9:52. So, not too bad on a hot afternoon. I timed Mark Bollinger later in the day and he ran 10:02. I was sure Fresh was coming around and would have a good summer and cross-country season.

One of the interesting things about the SMS summer meets are the guys who were members of the team for the first time and didn't stay on the team after that. As I look at the fragmented results that I kept from those meets and the articles in the school newspaper, I'm surprised at how many there were. And the list usually only includes those who placed. As I look at the names, some I remember such as high jumper Len Jones, who began his career at Arkansas College. But other names are lost to my memory. I just can't see their faces. It's quite possible if I did see a photo, I might recall them, but it's difficult to say. I wonder why these athletes didn't stick with us. I don't think too many were scholarship guys, but I know that one, when I see the results, was a decent shot putter. Most didn't run distance but were sprinters or field event competitors.

In the first SMS summer meet I ran the 2-mile. My goal was to win and run a nice pace, but I wasn't looking for anything fast. I didn't think there would be much competition but when I lined up, there were two very good runners in the race. Both were University of Missouri guys, Jeff Pigg, the same kid John ran against in AAU, and Jim Jennings, who ran a 4:09 mile in high school. But as it turned out, neither was race fit, and I won easily in 9:46. It would have been nice to have them running their best, even if I wasn't expecting competition. I never did race these guys when they were in great shape. I think Pigg ran a 3:43 1500m a couple of years later, and he made All-American in the NCAA Division I indoor 1000m. I think he transferred to Florida later in his college career. I don't know how well Jennings did in his career. I do know he was the guy who won the 1500 at the Region 8 AAU meet in 1980, the race in which John faded after qualifying in the 800. And I know that Jennings ran the 15-16 age division record at the AAU National Meet that year. His record was finally lowered in 2018, and I was in the stadium at Drake for that race.

In the next couple of meets in Springfield I won the mile in average times. I was training for distance races and wasn't concerned with how fast I ran four laps. Unlike the year before, I wasn't trying to win the overall outstanding athlete award at the SMS meets. As the summer continued, however, the issues with my lower left leg progressively got worse. For the first half of the summer, it still didn't bother me when I ran, but when I finished it did hurt and it took longer to alleviate. Before the 8k race in Wichita, I ran a 6-mile road race in Aurora, Missouri, which I won in about 33 minutes. I also ran in the Heer's 5 miler in Springfield but had lost some fitness because of some hip issues. I think I only ran around 27:10 or 27:15 in that one. We had 15 days before the Wichita race, and I needed to get fit. Luckily, the hip issue had already gone away before the Springfield race, so I could put in some good training. I was still in good shape, and although I had to back off the training for a couple of weeks, I knew I was really close to getting back my edge.

At the Heer's race, Mike ran 25:07, which was big PR for him, and he was looking for a great race in Wichita. My lower leg issues didn't keep me from training well leading up to the 8k, and although the one-mile race I won at SMS during those two weeks was only 4:29, it did give me a shorter, faster race before Wichita. On July 9, 1983, Mike, Fresh, Eddie and I traveled the long trip from the Branson area to Wichita for the Rainbow Couples Classic 8k road race. The next day, as we lined up for the race, which began in a park near the Arkansas River, I realized that this was the best field I had ever raced or was about to race. I noticed some familiar faces from my high school days, such as multiple state champion Mike Regan, now a runner at Georgetown, and Tim Gundy from the University of Kansas, as well as Rick Johnson, who had delivered that devastating kick in the 2-mile in the 1978 State Meet and ran just over 30 minutes for 10,000 on the track while competing for Wichita State. The best runner in the race that day was Fred Torneden, a name I knew, but I didn't know what he looked like.

If I wanted to run a personal best, I knew I needed to get out well, but not blistering. At the start, it was a mad dash, and I ran harder than I would have liked just to keep from getting mired in the middle of the pack. But I had anticipated doing this, so I was prepared. The best few runners just took off and I never saw them again, except when they passed me after the turn-around. My first mile was good, a 4:54, but I could feel the pace, and my stomach didn't feel well. I really felt like I had to use the bathroom. But, for some reason, despite the discomfort, I was able to continue running well. My 2-mile split was around 10:02, and I didn't feel any worse than I had at the mile, but I didn't feel better either. I can't say I was in a rhythm. Sometimes when you run, whether it's a race or workout, the pace feels automatic, and the rhythm is great. But other times it's a struggle and one needs to concentrate. When I felt like this, it didn't mean I was not going to race well. At the District 16 Cross-country Meet the previous fall, I felt like that, and raced very well.

315

My split at 3 miles was in the 15:15 range, so I had basically maintained my pace for two miles. But I was hurting at this point. My stomach didn't feel better, and I had to work to not slow significantly. But I kept running. I don't remember my 4-mile spit, but I do remember thinking when I heard it that I had a good chance to get a PR and get under 26 minutes. At 4 miles I must have been around 20:35, which meant a fourth mile in about 5:20, my slowest. I started to dig that last mile, not as a sprint, of course, but just grinding. And I felt sicker the more I ran. A couple of times I thought I was going to vomit. But I can truly say that the way I felt never affected my race, I just felt like shit. An 8k race is just short of 5 miles, 4.97 to be exact, or about 8 or 9 seconds faster than a full 5 miles. So, I knew that if I was to break 26 minutes, I wanted to run under 25:50 so I could be sure it was a sub-26 for the full 5 miles. As I approached the finish I could see the big clock – 25:25. 26, 27, and so on. It appeared that I was closer to the finish than I was, but when I finally crossed the line, I saw 25:42.

My official time was 25:44, so I had run a PR by about 20 seconds. The first thing I did after seeing Mike at the finish was head to the porta pots. Mike ran the best race of his life finishing in 16th place in 24:39. I finished in 29th place out of several hundred, maybe even over a thousand, and I beat some really good runners, including Rick Johnson. Fresh ran a PR as well, I think in the 27s, although I'm not sure his name was in the results. I know he wanted a time in the 26s, but this was a good sign. I don't remember Eddie's time, but he might have run 27 something as well. I believe that even today, the 1983 Rainbows Couple's Classic is the fastest 8k/5-mile road race ever held in Kansas. Torneden won in 23:28, and second was a 23:30. It was the second fastest time for a race of this distance in which I'd ever run, but this was a much deeper field. I knew I was ready for cross-country.

The 8k race gave me confidence, and I believed if my training went well, I could possibly run under 25 minutes by the end of October.

One issue about running fast times is that many of our cross-country races were contested on tough hilly courses, but there were a few where a good time was possible. But a tough course was not my biggest concern. After Wichita my leg quickly got worse. Now it bothered me in workouts, but I still didn't back off on my training and continued to race. Throughout the summer, Steve, Fresh and I did a few terrific workouts at the State Park on Table Rock Lake, which was close to the Dam. We ran half mile and mile repeats on the roads of the park in the heat of the day, and we ran them fast. These were the types of workouts, along with distance runs that I needed to be at my best for cross-country.

After the Couple's Classic, I competed in the last of the SMS meets before the championship meet. Mike and I decided to race in the 2-mile and try and run fast times, maybe under 9:20 and possibly as fast as 9:10. The plan was for me to take the lead early and push the pace, hopefully around 2:15 at the 880. This Wednesday evening meet was only three days after our Wichita race, but I didn't think it would be an issue. I couldn't have been more wrong. The first of the eight laps was good and fast as I led the field that also included Jeff Pigg. Mike was supposed to let me lead through the mile, but he passed me before the end of the second lap. He hit 2:14 and I came across at 2:15. Although I was running a 9:00 pace, I knew a 9:10 was out of the question, at least for me. I couldn't speak for Mike, but he looked strong.

But as I began to slow, so did Mike ahead of me, and he didn't leave me behind. I still thought a 9:25 was possible but when I crossed the mile in 4:40, I wondered if I could even do that. I was tired and my legs were heavy! My second 880 was a 2:25, and I was slowing. With a lap to go, Mike was actually in striking distance for me and with my speed, and the fact that Mike didn't have a kick, I thought it might be possible to catch him. But when I summoned the magic of my kick, it didn't answer. I had nothing. It didn't matter that I could run a 400m at least eight seconds faster than Mike, I wasn't going to catch him. I still stood in second, but in the last 220 yards I was passed by a guy who I'd raced for a couple of years in these meets, and then by Pigg. I'd never lost to the first guy, and I wish I could remember his name. He was a good runner and a really nice person. Mike won in 9:39 and I was about a second behind Pigg in 9:46 and took 4th, the same time I ran in the first meet. My second mile was a slow 5:06 and I felt horrible when I finished. Mike Saunders ran a good race and almost broke 10:00. I apologized to Coach for running such a poor time, but he told me there was no reason for that because I gave it a good effort.

A week later I decided to run the mile at the Championship Meet, and I won in a slow, but steady 4:29. But my leg was as bad as ever. Instead of taking a week or two off to see if it would heal, I went to Anderson, Missouri to compete in a late summer track meet. My problem is that I loved to race, just loved it! In high school I liked to race, but I hated the hour or so before. I got so nervous at times that I wanted to sneak into the stands and hide. But in college, although I still got those same butterflies, I learned to embrace the nerves. I believe there were many times in Jr. high and high school that the nerves took away energy, and it was detrimental to my races. But not now. I could harness the nerves and use them to my advantage. So, I loved to race, and I tried to race as much as I could.

I traveled to the Anderson meet with one of our jumpers, Kenny Holstein, a West Plains native, who was also training to be a decathlete. We almost didn't make it to the far southwest corner of Missouri when, as we went around a sharp curve, a vehicle was over in our lane. It should have been a head-on, and as we somehow passed by without an accident, I didn't see any way we could have missed each other. But we made it to Noel, Missouri in one piece. Mike Saunders lived in Noel, about 10 miles south of Anderson, and we stayed with him, sleeping in a trailer tent. Noel used to be a resort town, but even in 1983, it was quickly losing its luster. When I was a kid, we used to take trips with the Parsons Rec Center to various places such as Worlds of Fun, and one of those trips was to Noel, which included a cave visit.

One of the events I learned during the summer while Coach Oz was not around, was the javelin. Coach would not have been happy to see me try the event. But I liked to try new things, and plus, I came from Kansas, a huge high school javelin state. I say I learned to throw it, but not very well. Kenny and I competed in the javelin and there were only a few guys throwing. During those years, the javelin was not contested in Missouri high schools, so you didn't see a lot of guys in the event, outside of college. I don't remember my exact distance, but I believe it was between 115 and 120 feet. I probably didn't have much of a future in the event! I selected to run the 800 and nothing else because, one, it was 108 degrees, and two, my leg was not in good condition. The heat didn't seem to get to me very much and I won the race easily in 2:04. That was the end of my summer racing schedule. Unfortunately for the team and for those of us who were friends with them, Saunders and Eddie left school at the end of the summer.

During the two weeks between the summer and fall semesters, Fresh and I spent a few days in West Plains with Chris Marcak, running hard distance on the rugged hills outside of town, where Chris lived. One day we ran a hard 18 miler in the severe heat. Boy, I could really feel the pain in my lower left leg during these runs and it didn't seem to improve much afterwards. It was especially bad after the 18-mile run. The three of us also spent an evening at the drive-in theater watching a Cheech and Chong movie and drinking too much. Sometimes I'm amazed what I remember. Why can I recall that it was a Cheech and Chong movie? After a few days I headed back to Parsons, and I invited Chris to come stay with me a few days.

I drove my car, and Chris followed me on his motorcycle. The trip between West Plains, Missouri and Parsons, Kansas was 250 miles, and Chris was exhausted by the time we reached my hometown. Fresh was unable to visit that time, and he left West Plains for his home in Jefferson City, earning a speeding ticket along the way when a local small-town cop pulled him over at a place where bushes and a tree hid the speed limit sign. So, he didn't know the limit had changed. I went through that town later, and sure enough, the sign was covered, and a cop was waiting on the other side! But I already knew the situation, so I wasn't speeding.

Chris and I had a plan to get in some killer runs on the lonely gravel roads outside of Parsons. In one of our runs, Coach Barcus saw us and stopped to say hello. Every run was hot, over 100 degrees. But the heat wasn't the issue for me. My leg was killing me, and I struggled to finish a couple of the runs. One day we did a 17 or 18 miler. On the day before Chris left, I could only finish part of our run. The next morning, Chris ran a 10 miler on his own and then headed home, while I wondered what the hell was wrong with my leg. I had a few days before I needed to be back at SofO, and I didn't run the remainder of the time.

When I returned to SofO in mid-August, I tried a couple of runs, but I wasn't any better. After a couple of weeks, Coach Oz sent me to a specialist who ordered a bone scan, which revealed a stress fracture in my fibula. The doctor said this was better than having a stress fracture in the tibia. He said if I could take the pain, I could still run, but it would eventually completely break, so he didn't recommend continuing! Coach said the risk was too much and he redshirted me. As a rule, Coach didn't always understand injuries and that one needed to rest at times. But in this case, he didn't want to take the risk. So, I went swimming to help me keep in condition, but I didn't swim nearly enough – I hate swimming laps! Eventually I also rode a stationary bike, but my leg took forever to heal.

In December, Fresh, Mike, and I went to Jefferson City for a 10k road race. I didn't run because of my leg, but Mike and Fresh did. The race was coordinated by one of Fresh's high school coaches, who knew American 10,000m record holder and Olympian Craig Virgin and convinced him to race. He won in a little over 30 minutes on a bitterly cold morning, and Mike took third in just over 31 minutes. Afterward, Virgin signed autographs and answered questions in the warmth of a bank lobby. I asked him about my stress fracture, and indicated that it was not healing after four months of not running. He said that seemed much too long to him and advised me not to do anything on it for a month or so and to see what happens. When I went home for Christmas break, I didn't do anything even to give the impression I was training, and when I returned to school in a few weeks, my leg was better, just like that. Craig Virgin's advice worked! Of course, he didn't know it, and he didn't know me from the man on the moon, but he helped me resume my running career.

Just because I couldn't run during the fall didn't mean I didn't have fun. On Halloween, Fresh, Steve Davis and I egged the hell out of the school after curfew. We even got into the gym and egged the heck out of that as well. The next day, I avoided going to my campus job in the gym and when I arrived for practice (even though I couldn't run) the place smelled like rotten eggs. And I'm glad I didn't go to work because I would have had to help clean it up. Some of the basketball players had to clean up the mess, and when I asked them who they thought did it, they said it was probably some local high school kids who had been on campus the previous evening causing trouble. I agreed that it was likely them!

After my first year and a half at SofO, I was transferred to the gym for my campus workstation, and in a few weeks, I worked for Coach Oz. Some days, many days, about mid-morning, Coach would tell me to go check out the pump house road on campus to see if it was muddy or good enough for the afternoon practice. This was code for "go run five miles to the pump house and back." The pump house was on Lake Taneycomo, and the old dirt road was 2 ½ miles. Sometimes, Coach Smith, the baseball coach and the one who I thank was in charge of workers in the fieldhouse, would clock me out when he didn't see me in the building while I was running. I suspect there were times that an athlete who worked in the athletics

321

office told Coach Smith because he was jealous of my position. But I always went to Coach Oz to get an override. In the fall of 1983, I couldn't run, but I did plenty of jobs for Coach, and in the spring of 1984, I painted hurdles with Theresa Brown from the women's team. I loved working for Coach Oz. He treated me extremely well, and I know I helped him with the many things that needed to be done.

The cross-country team did alright in the spring of '83, but by mid-fall, the makeup of the team changed. Mike, who was back in school, ran the first three meets and won two of them. His only loss was at Harding University in Arkansas against our old teammate, Chris Marcak. For some reason, the course judges, or maybe just some working the meet, sent Chris and Mike in the wrong direction somewhere in the middle of the race while they were running together. They were far ahead of the field, so when the mistake was realized, they just had everyone race the incorrect route. No one gained an advantage, but Mike was upset. After the third meet, Mike was again kicked out of school. This is a real shame because I think Mike had a better-than-average chance to make All-American. But sometimes, you only have yourself to blame. Chris ran a 24:36 five-mile time in cross-country that year competing for Arkansas College, but he hurt his back during the season and didn't make All-American either.

Fresh had a decent season but didn't round into form as we thought he would. The only guy to qualify for Cross-country Nationals was Paul Taylor. Paul came up with the idea that running too many races, especially early in the season, was detrimental to having a good season. To implement his plan, he decided to upset Coach Oz enough that he would leave Paul home for a few meets. It worked perfectly. Paul ran very few meets, but at the end of the season, he was back on Coach's good side, just as he had planned. Paul didn't run great at Nationals, but not bad either. At the end of the semester, another team member, a freshman, was kicked out of school for stealing, and he never returned.

One new member of the track team, who started in the fall, was actually an old team member. Mark Adkerson, who was from Eureka, Missouri, outside St. Louis, arrived as a freshman in the fall of 1980. He left after one semester and transferred to Northeast Missouri State, but I don't believe he ran for them. Mark ran cross-country, but he was really a hurdler. In time, Mark and I became good friends and roommates. He was also crazy. Rod Land attempted to make a comeback in the fall of 1983, and he did compete, but his tendon would never let him be the same runner who ran a 3-mile cross-country race in high school in the mid-14s. Sometimes, it dawns on me just how good we could have been if all the stars had lined up. And I'm not talking about kids who might have signed with us out of high school. We did lose some good ones who originally said they would attend. But I mean runners who were on the team and performed well at some point in their careers – we could have been an NAIA power. But a lot of teams in any sport can make the same claim.

During the Christmas break, my dad became extremely sick with pneumonia. On Christmas morning, Dad got up to open presents, and he didn't look well. He hardly remembered that morning. A little while later, he came out and said he needed to go to the hospital. There was snow on the ground, the temperature hovered around 0, and the roads were icy, but I drove him to the Katy Hospital. This was not the main hospital in town, but because dad worked for the Katy Railroad, the Katy is where I took him. The sidewalk leading up to the building was icy, so I had to hold on to him as we walked. I didn't know how sick he was until he got out of the hospital a week later and found out he almost died that first night. The doctor told him a few days later, when he was out of danger that he was surprised to see him alive the next morning.

When I first arrived at School of the Ozarks, there was a guy hanging around who ran for the College in the mid-1970s. Coach Oz was really fond of him. Mark McGarity was mysterious, at least to me, during that fall of 1981, and I didn't get to know him at that time. What I did know is that he ran really fast in his workouts. And it didn't matter whether he was running 10 miles or 16; he blazed on those rugged Ozarks hills. He often ran with Steve Davis and Dan Mills, and the hills didn't seem to challenge them as much as they did me. What I didn't know at the time is that he had trained for the 1980 Olympic Marathon trials in Colorado with some of America's top road racers who were also training for the marathon trials, so the combination of altitude, mountains, and great training partners made the Ozarks seem like anthills. Plus, he had run these same hills I struggled on while he was in college. And, of course, he was a talented distance runner.

At some point, and I think it was during the fall 1981 semester, Mark was gone. I'm not even sure I realized he had left for Naples, Florida, but I came to realize that I hadn't seen the guy in a while. Of course, since I really didn't know Mark, there was no reason for him to tell me he was leaving. I'm sure to him, I was just another face on the cross-country team he passed coming and going on Acacia Club Road during our training runs. I remember one summer; he showed up on campus in a van with some people from Florida on a trip to Colorado. I don't remember the year, but I think it was the summer of 1982. I said to myself, "Hey, that's the guy who ran those fast workouts my first semester here and would say 'hi' as he passed us on the roads." Then he was gone again, and he only stopped by for an hour or so to see Coach Oz.

Then, in the late fall of 1983 or winter of 1984, Mark was back. He enrolled again at SofO to get his teaching credentials so he could return to southwest Florida to teach science and coach. McGarity was from New Orleans but had matriculated to Naples sometime after graduating from SofO. I think that was in the late 1970s. Mark was not only going back to school, but he also became our assistant coach. Mark knew running and was a great asset to the team. Mark was also one of the craziest guys I've ever met. He trained with us quite a bit, and he ran like a beast! In reality, he was the yin to Coach Oz's yang. Mark was not much older than we were, in his late 20s, and had much in common with the team's middle-distance and distance runners.

The hardest part of Mark being an assistant coach for me was not his knowledge or how he coached us – that was great. But it was those damn morning runs. I am not a morning person, so our four-mile morning runs were torture for me. I could never get loose, and I was barely awake. Of course, it would've helped if I didn't go to bed at 2:00 am and get up and run at 6:30 in the morning! But Mark ran these morning workouts like he did the ones in the afternoon. I could barely work my stride up to a foot and a half, and he was ramming these runs like he was competing in a 10k road race. Really, none of us on the team could keep up with him on these morning excursions. I don't remember ever finishing a morning run with McGarity in view.

I don't know Mark McGarity's best times, but like several of us, I know he never reached his potential. I think Mark ran in the low 2:20s in the marathon and maybe faster, but I know he could have run under 2:15, and in the late 1970s and early 80s, that was really good – and it's still not bad. I believe we all benefited from Mark's presence, and even though I was recovering from the stress fracture, I learned a tremendous amount as I attempted to get back in shape. In the summer of 1984, several of us were driving to a 5-mile road race in Springfield. John Johnson was with me, and his Camaro was parked by McGarity's van. We were late for the race and had over 40 miles to reach the starting line in a short amount of time. I drove because I knew the way, and when I started the car, which didn't have a muffler, Mark came flying out of the van startled. He had overslept and was also late for the race. So, he jumped in, and we headed north to Springfield on the hilly US 65, sometimes reaching 90 mph. We arrived about three minutes before the race, and as we piled out of the Camaro, Mark headed to the registration to get race numbers (during those years, you could show up and pay the registration on-site). Without a warmup and lack of sleep, Mark ran 25:03 and took third. I think he would have run under 24:20 and won if he'd had time to prepare that morning.

As the spring semester began in January, I started to train again, but Coach redshirted me for track because I wasn't in shape. I had ballooned to over 190 lbs. and knew I needed to lose weight, but my extra pounds made the runs difficult. However, gradually, I became somewhat fit, and I shed the pounds rather quickly. In late January, or possibly early February, Coach Oz took a few of us to a road race in Rolla. I didn't go to the 5-miler to compete but to get in a good run. I ran with Rod Land, who was also attempting to get in shape again. We stayed together from start to finish and ran 35 minutes, a steady 7-minute mile pace. I'd like to say it was easy, and it wasn't exactly killer, but at the same time, it was a bit difficult. I was surprised that I had to work at running five miles at a slow pace. Three weeks later, several of us went to a race north of Springfield to run in another 5miler.

By the Springfield race, I was down to my normal competition weight of 170. This race was part of a triathlon in which the competitors swam in a pool in the morning, biked a little while later, and ran the road race in the afternoon. You were allowed to run in the road race even if you didn't compete in the entire triathlon. McGarity was probably going to win, and I knew I wasn't in good shape, so I told Fresh that I would pace him as long as I could so he could run in the 26s. I told him that I wasn't sure I could hold a 5:20 mile pace to the halfway point, the turnaround, but maybe I could pace him for two miles. Today, I don't recall any of my splits, but before we reached 2 ½ miles, I left Fresh and the field, except for McGarity. I tried to get Fresh to run with me, but he was unable to do so. I felt good at the turn-around, but I still believed several runners, including Fresh, and another teammate, freshman Kenny Nobles, would catch me. It never happened. I felt good the entire race and finished second behind McGarity in 26:20. Mark won in around 25:40, and Fresh ran in the 27s. I was perplexed how I had worked hard to run 35 minutes three weeks before and now ran a comfortable 26:20. I couldn't answer the question, but I was happy about it.

During the indoor season, I went with the team to a couple of meets. One meet I didn't attend was at Central Missouri State, but I wish I had. Brad Burkes, running for Butler Community College, was there and asked about me. He was told I was still on the team but injured. So, I missed an opportunity to see him. The night before the first indoor meet, held at Pitt State, Mark Adkerson, Fresh, and I went to a town south of Springfield to pick up girls. We met some women, and they invited us to their apartment in Springfield. After spending a late night there, we headed back to campus and had to get up early for the meet. We were all exhausted. The morning after the meet, I woke up extremely sick and thought it was probably from lack of sleep. But as the day progressed, I got as sick as I'd ever been at that point in my life. I had the flu, and it remained with me for several days, which might be the reason the 35-minute 5-mile race was difficult a week or so later.

During that first evening, several people came and went from our room. Rod Land spent some time there, mostly visiting with Fresh because I was in bed trying to survive. Adkerson came by, and so did Kenny Nobles, but I was too sick to visit. We had one more visitor that evening, and I won't mention his name, but we all knew him well. He stood behind my bed for a minute or so, which is where my built-in desk was located, and then he abruptly left without a clue why he dropped by. The next morning, although still sick, I realized my room key was missing. I kept the key on my desk, just where our "friend" had stood. Even if he hadn't stood there, Fresh and I knew who did it. The others who visited our room would have never taken anything from us, or anyone for that matter.

Although I was sick, I still got out of the room the next day. I broke my fever by taking an extremely hot shower, although I doubt that was a smart thing to do. That evening Fresh discovered that his wallet was missing. He looked everywhere but couldn't locate it. We knew what happened. The next day, a Monday, his wallet was found in the student parking lot area and turned in. When Fresh retrieved it, all his money was missing. We never suspected that the person who found the wallet took the money. Again, we knew who did it. A couple of days later, when I was feeling a bit better, I broke into this guy's car (it was unlocked) parked on campus and tried to find my room key. I didn't find my key, but I did find more than a dozen dorm room keys he had stolen. So, I took all the keys and threw them on top of the fieldhouse, one at a time. At least he wouldn't be able to break into those rooms, although it's possible he already had. This might sound odd, but I did like this person, and I guess to a certain degree I did forgive him, although he never knew that we knew what he did.

While I was growing up, I rarely got sick, but at SofO it seemed that I was constantly ill. There are several reasons to consider. One, I was running a lot of miles, and not getting enough sleep, plus, to top it off, I didn't eat right. But I have another theory. The campus powerhouse burned coal, and I think it was coal with a high Sulphur count. It was not uncommon to be walking on campus and get covered with a fine grit from the power plant as it drifted in the breeze. I just can't imagine that this was healthy for students. And it smelled bad! My issues might be a combination of my running, sleep habits and the power plant. Who knows, but since college, I have not been one to regularly get sick.

In the fall of '83, a Rolla freshman, Randy Gray, came to SofO. Randy was a hurdler, and I didn't care for him much. In fact, I didn't like him at all, and the feeling was mutual. But that changed over time, especially in the second semester, and we eventually became good friends. I don't even remember why I didn't initially like him, although he could have remembered why he didn't care for me. It might be because he got the sense from me that I didn't like him, or maybe I got the impression he disliked me. But that didn't make any difference by the spring of 1984. Another new freshman was Jim Rector from Anderson and was a high school teammate with Mike Saunders. In fact, the first time I met Jim was at the summer meet in Anderson, and he said he would be beginning at SofO in January. He was an 800m runner and a great person to be around. Like many others, however, he left school in a short time. For him, it was at the end of the spring semester.

I continued to train and get in better shape, and McGarity's presence helped. Before the outdoor season began, Coach Oz decided to have us run time-trials on the track. So, on a beautiful Saturday morning, members of the team gathered at the track to run some races against each other. Although I was redshirting, I ran the mile and 880. The first trial for me was the mile, and although I was not in great form, I beat my teammates with a slow 4:40. A short time later I won the 880 in 2:04. I thought I would have issues beating Kenny Nobles, who broke 2:00 in high school in Georgia. It felt good to race on the track, even though it wasn't official, and although I wasn't pushed much in my trials, and could have run faster, I could still tell that I was a long way from being back. If I would have competed with the team that spring, I don't think I could have run better than 1:57 in the 800 and would have struggled to hit 4:05 in the 15. So, remaining a redshirt was the best option for me.

I did run an 800m in an early season meet at SMS. Because I was redshirting, I competed unattached. I thought I would be able to break two-minutes in the race, but I didn't have it in me. I competed well for 600 meters, but the last half-lap was a struggle, and I only ran 2:01, and didn't come close to winning. Of course, I didn't expect to win, but as with the trials I ran a couple of weeks before, this race demonstrated to me that I had a long way to go. The 26:20 five-mile time I ran was fool's gold. It gave me the impression that I was much further along than I really was. That 5-mile race was probably just an anomaly. But by April 1, I was able to really train well, and I could tell my fitness was turning around. I think I ran one more track meet during the spring, at Flo Valley, but I just can't remember, and I'm unable to locate my running logs to give me the information. But I know I went – and if I did race, did I run the 1500 or 800m?

The one race I do remember is the 10,000. Paul had trained and raced himself into form. There were three runners from Principia College, Indiana in the race, and at least two came in with better times than Paul. During the 25 laps, Paul used his usual tactics on the competition, which by the mid-way point only consisted of two of the Principia guys and him. It's the best race I ever saw Paul run, and it was classic! Lap after lap, Paul fought these two, passing and being passed, and as usual, Coach was ecstatic. But with two laps to go, one of the Principia runners began to pull away from Paul as he continued to run with the other. Paul was unable to hold off the leader and pass him back. Maybe Paul would take second.

Early in the last lap, it appeared that Paul would get 3rd, when the second Principia runner created a little cap. But the first Principia runner looked as if he was struggling, and with 300 meters to go, Paul launched a vicious kick, quickly taking over the guy in second. Then, I think, Paul could see the leader fighting to maintain, and by the middle of the last curve, he flew by the first Principia runner and won going away. Unlike the Park runners, these two guys were not only impressed, but congratulated Paul for such terrific race tactics. Paul's winning time was 32:12, by far the best he had ever run, and even his 8,000-meter split of 25:40, or so, was a PR. The two Principia guys had run faster than Paul's winning time, and the second-place guy said that Paul's tactics completely exhausted him, physically and mentally.

Redshirting is a bummer when you're injured, but for me it was exacerbated because SofO hosted the 1984 District 16 Outdoor Championship Meet. Instead of getting the opportunity to compete for one or more District victories and helping the team, I was relegated to helping create the heats in the days leading up and then working the meet that day. It was a nice day and a competitive meet. I thought Fresh would place in the 880, but he fell just short. Paul didn't run well either. For some reason Paul decided that he could get better by running high steps for several miles, but he did this, for the first time, the week of the meet. In the 6-mile run, he didn't place and it's a race he should have taken second. His older brother, an outstanding runner in his own right, attended the District Meet and told Paul he was crazy for running that workout.

No one on the men's team qualified for Nationals, so the end of the District Meet meant the end of the track season. After the semester came to a close, I headed home to Parsons for the summer to train and watch the Olympics. Although students were required to attend summer school, we were allowed to take one summer off, which I did in 1984. I was optimistic that I could get myself back in cross-country form by the end of the summer, but I also had a busy schedule for those three months. I wasn't really worried about the 1500 or 800 during the spring of '85 because I knew I could get in really good condition to race the middle distances, but cross-country was different. I had wanted to run under 25:00 for five miles the fall before but the injury put an end to that goal. And I wasn't sure I could get strong enough to run 24 something by the first of November. However, I did think I could run around 25:20 and I knew that should be good enough to qualify for Nationals.

Chapter 15
Olympics

When I said I planned to watch the Olympics, what I really meant is that I was attending the Olympics. The year before, my mom entered me in a lottery for Olympic Track and Field tickets, and I was awarded them for five sessions. I was excited to attend the Olympics, but before I traveled to Los Angeles in July, there were a lot of things to do. And, I didn't want to have anything interfere with my training, although that would be tough to maintain. Before the spring semester ended, I began to show signs that my fitness was getting better, especially for longer races. By the first of April, I was training hard, but I must have increased too fast because I sustained a mild quad strain, and I had to back off on the training and even take a few days off.

In April I went to Fayetteville, Arkansas to compete in the Hogeye Marathon Relay. This race started in Fayetteville and went to the small town of Hogeye, and then headed back, ending at the football stadium at the University of Arkansas. There were several options to race: one could run the entire marathon or enter as a relay. There were two person relays in which each ran a half marathon, or four person relays in which each leg was 6.55 miles. There were also mixed relay divisions. I ran in one of the all-male four person relays.

This was a fun event, and I had attended the year before to watch some of my friends run. My team had Eddie Hueton and Fresh and other man that I don't remember. Our other team had Mike Hueton, Steve Davis, Mark McGarity, and a man who I believe owned a local running store. Mike and I ran the second leg for our teams. It was a terrific morning to run, but I was unsure how I would do in a race over six miles. When I took off on my leg, we were in third or fourth place and far ahead of Mike's team. I took off strong with the goal of catching the team in front of us and then catching the next team. I knew that Mike was in much better condition than I was, and although I knew we had a significant lead on his team, I wasn't sure how far ahead I was because their first runner was not in sight when I began my leg.

When I crossed the seven-mile mark, which was just short of a half mile into my leg, I looked at my watch. At nine miles I looked at my watch again and saw that I'd run those two miles in 9:54, so I was moving quite well. I didn't think Mike would make up much difference in the 2 ½ mile stretch, but he ran that same two-mile distance under 9:30. Still, I was well ahead and at that point I didn't know Mike was flying. Of course, I slowed significantly after that, but I was still strong. Eventually, I took the lead and moved away from the second-place team. When I passed the runners that were ahead of me, I held my breath and acted as if I wasn't in any distress. I could sense that this demoralized those runners, even though in reality I was not as comfortable as I seemed.

Still, I wasn't tying up and when I touched hands with our third leg, Eddie, we were in the lead, and I knew I put in a good effort. But Mike had made up a lot of distance on me and he was close when I finished. I timed myself in 34:53, and the official time by the race timers was just a shade over 35 minutes. Mike ran around 32:50, as I recall. I knew we wouldn't win because the last two legs of the first team were much better than our final legs. Steve quickly over-took Eddie, who still ran well, and McGarity widened the lead over Fresh who also ran a terrific race. We ended up in 3rd, which was a good position for us. Of all those who ran the 6.55 legs, I had the second fastest time, with only Mike faster. I think I probably hit the 10k mark in the high 32s, and Mike was more than likely just under 31 minutes.

Within a minute of touching Eddie's hand, my quad, which I thought was healed, began to hurt and it continued to get worse throughout the day. My injury wasn't healed, and it set me back another couple of weeks. Coach Oz was upset with me because I ran the race and aggravated my quad, but he hadn't shown this concern before I went. But the strain didn't end up being a big deal and I was training well again by early May. Of course, if I would have run a race or went out on a hard training run, the strain would have come to the surface again.

During the late spring there was an event that I think changed several of us. One afternoon, before track practice, Mark Adkerson, McGarity, Fresh, Rod Land and I were hanging out on the outdoor patio by the indoor pool, when Randy Gray dropped by. Randy was injured so he wasn't practicing right then. Randy had become a good friend and just a couple of days before, he and I, plus Eddie and Natalie Newberry from the women's team went to Springfield to watch a high school track meet. Randy's campus job was with construction and while at the pool, he talked about the trench, 18 feet deep, that they had dug for foundation footing as part of a new wing of the Ralph Foster Museum, which was located on campus. After a few minutes, Randy threw on his shirt and said, in a joking tone, "Well, time to go down in the hole," while the rest of us headed off to practice. Little did we know that Randy's life was about be altered.

Not long after practice started, we heard the fire horn on campus and then heard the fire truck head to our end of campus. Honestly, this was a common occurrence, and no one at practice seemed alarmed. SofO was unique in that it had its' own fire station with student firemen who lived at the station, and it was also their campus workstation. When practice ended, we headed to the cafeteria and heard that there was a major accident at the museum construction site that involved Randy. At this point it was all rumor, but we headed to the museum where we found the fire department with many students watching. Then we were told that it was Randy, and that he was dead. Then word came back quickly that he was alive but crushed, with multiple broken bones.

When I think about this today, I can get very emotional. While down in the deep hole, the walls began to collapse, and Randy was the only one who didn't make it to the ladder. The walls of the trench had not been reinforced and so the earth just came down. Randy was at the bottom, possibly crushed, maybe dead, and most assuredly severely injured. His friends waited for what seemed forever, and it might have been a couple of hours, I don't think I knew how long it took – time stood still. I don't even know if we made it to dinner. When I think about our student firemen and the adult supervisor, risking their own lives to save Randy, I still find it amazing. They couldn't rush into the hole and start digging because it was unstable, and more of the side could collapse. When they finally brought him out of the hole, I heard one of the student firemen say, "How do you spell relief?" And Randy was smiling. Those student firemen were true heroes.

Several of us headed to the Branson hospital and beat the ambulance and when they wheeled Randy into the emergence room, he looked up at me with a big smile on his face and said "Ray!" But Randy was hurt and hurt bad. This was serious, and he was really broken up and even had nerve damage. Of course, we didn't know that then. Randy had tickets to attend the Olympic Track and Field Trials at the LA Coliseum, and we had been discussing his trip and my Olympic trip at the same location. But now, Randy was in a fight to regain his health. Before school was out, Fresh, Adkerson, and I went to see Randy at the hospital at Fort Leonard Wood, where he had been transferred, because his dad was military. He was in good spirits, but he was also unable to get out of bed. Later in the summer, I made a trip back to SofO from Parsons to visit, and Randy was visiting as well. He looked gaunt and he walked slowly with a cane. But as usual he had a smile on his face – and he was alive! Unfortunately, Randy died in 2021 of COVID. It's a huge loss.

After visiting Randy, we headed to Fresh's house in Jefferson City. Fresh and I were attending the State Track meet the next day, and Mark was going to see his brother graduate from Mizzo with a master's degree. At the State Meet, which had several tremendous performances, one athlete caught my eye. I already knew who he was, and I'd seen him race earlier in the season on a cool day on a cinder track. But this didn't prepare me for what I saw that day. After watching Joe Falcon win the 1600m in 4:08, followed by victories in the 800 and 3200, I believed I was witnessing America's next great miler. So, a 4:08 is about a 4:09 to 4:10 mile, and although fast, it is not necessarily a time that would give one the impression that a world great is in this kid's future.

Every year, high school milers run 4:08 and even faster, but virtually none become one of the best in the world. And if I would have just seen the results without watching the kid compete that day, I would have been impressed, but nothing more. But I did see Falcon race, and he was the most impressive high school runner I had ever seen. He went to the University of Arkansas and won multiple NCAA titles, and his range was incredible. He was a great 10,000 runner and a great 1500 guy. Maybe I'm wrong, but I can't think of a better all-around college distance and middle-distance runner, other than Prefontaine. Suleiman Nyambui, from my era, certainly could be part of that conversation, and much more recently, Edward Cheserek qualifies, but it's hard to argue against Falcon. Falcon ran a 3:49 mile in 1990 in winning the prestigious Dream Mile at the old Bislett Stadium in Oslo, Norway.

Another kid I was interested in watching that day was Jason Pyrah, who was only a freshman. He didn't come close to winning, but I had watched him in two or three track meets that spring and I could tell he was special. At his conference meet in Branson, one in which the SofO track team helped work, with Steve Davis as meet clerk, I watched Pyrah get beat in a 1600 by a good sophomore. For some reason, after my job was finished, I found myself next to Pyrah and struck up a conversation. I asked him what else he was doing that day, and he said the 3200m. I told him that he could beat the kid who finished ahead of him in the 1600 by pushing in the middle of the race because I didn't think he could handle a hard pace for eight laps. I don't know if he followed my advice, but Pyrah won the race. After that race I told him that I believed he could run a 4:10 mile as a senior. But I was wrong. He ran a 4:03 mile as senior. The year before that, Fresh called me up and asked me if I remembered Jason Pyrah. "Of course," I said. Fresh said "you won't believe what he did today at the State Meet." And then told me that Pyrah went out in 1:56 for his first 800m of the 1600 and won in 4:05. Now that impressed me! Pyrah eventually became a two-time Olympian in the 1500m.

As soon as the semester ended, and before I headed home to Parsons, Adkerson, Rod, Fresh and I took a trip to Florida with McGarity. On our way down we took a kid in the military to a post in the Memphis area. We left in the evening and drove south into Arkansas. We also had lots of beer. McGarity, who was driving, didn't have any, and Rod didn't drink alcohol, but the rest of us got smashed sitting in the back of the van. We just had sleeping bags laid out because there were no seats in the back. I remember driving through the Little Rock area on I40, and the next thing I remember was stopping at a roadside rest in eastern Arkansas. We all headed to the restroom and as I stood there doing my business, an old man was watching me with a strange look on his face. As I looked down, I realized I was taking a piss in the sink. Youth and drinking....

When we piled back in the van, I was out like a light and when I awoke again, we were stopped letting our passenger out at his base.

His name is lost to time, but he is in one of the photos. Then I was passed out again and I woke up with sunlight glaring in the front window and I didn't have a clue where we were. There were pine trees everywhere and McGarity said we were in northern Alabama. After stopping for breakfast, we continued south on I65 headed toward Panama City Beach, Florida. Along the way, McGarity pointed out a strange square running track at a school in Birmingham that we could see from the interstate. It's the one and only time I've seen a track like that. We reached Panama City in the late afternoon and set up camp in a beach campground.

Our intention on the trip was to have a great time and get in some runs. After getting established in our campsite, we headed out for a run along the beach. Then we went for dinner, and after that, the nightlife of Panama City Beach. I found it hilarious that men had to wear collared shirts in some of these dumps, but I obliged. At one bar along the beach, which was a little classier, I enjoyed watching overweight guys in shorts, and collars of course, with their bellies hanging out, trying to pick up women as they danced while holding on to a sand pail full of Long Island Iced Tea. Maybe the women got drunk enough – but I doubt it. This was classic '80s. After witnessing the scene of beach yuppies for a while, Adkerson and I headed to the van to have a couple of beers, when someone knocked on the van. When we opened the side door a security man scolded us, saying we couldn't drink in the parking lot, even if we were in our vehicle. If we were to stay, we had to go inside and pay for extremely high-priced, water-downed drinks. No collarless shirts and no drinking in the parking lot! But we had fun anyway.

The next morning, after another run along the beach, we went out to the beach for the day, and in the evening, we loaded up the van and headed to Naples. This was a long, long drive of 550 miles and 9 or 10 hours through Tallahassee, Gainesville, Tampa, and Fort Myers, before we reached southwest Florida. When we arrived in Naples, the sun had just come up, so the first thing we did was head straight for the beach. We parked at the end of a street at the edge of the beach and stumbled out of the van. There was only one guy there, so we had almost free range. Suddenly, McGarity got excited and said that the young man on the beach was Rob May, who he had coached and would be our new teammate in the fall. We knew we were getting a new kid on the team from Naples, but we didn't think we would meet him while we were there.

In Naples, McGarity arranged for us to stay with some very good friends of his that he had known since his New Orleans days, and they were a running family. Bill and Mary Briant had a teenage daughter and one or two older sons, if my memory is correct. One thing is for certain, the bars in Naples were far superior to those in Panama City Beach. We spent our time in Naples doing three things – spending time on the white-sand beach, running, and partying. We actually did one other thing. McGarity knew a man who had a speed boat. He dropped by the beach where we were spending some time, so we swam out to him, got loaded on the boat, and headed out into the gulf to waterski. We went way out, maybe three or four miles. I'd never been waterskiing before and I didn't exactly do a great job then, in fact, I'm not sure what I did can be described as waterskiing. I mostly did a front fall into the water. I think I could have caught on to the technique if I hadn't swallowed so much salt water. Of those of us who had never attempted this before, only Adkerson was able to finally remain up on the skis for a while. But we had a hell of a time!

We spent our days on the beach and ran in the late afternoon, while bar hopping in the evenings. Some of the bars were quiet pubs, which were my favorites, and a few others were like the yuppie bars in Panama City Beach. But most were cool places with a mix of music and loud conversation. One evening I put on a nice shirt that I brought along, but it didn't have a collar. It was a nicer, more expensive shirt than 90% of those worn in the club, but they made me leave. McGarity had a collared shirt in the van, so I put it on, but it was about two sizes too small. Good thing I was in shape, so my belly didn't hang out. I didn't want to emulate those rhythm-less, overweight yuppies we encountered in Panama City Beach. At one place I had to talk my way in because my Kansas driver's license didn't include my photo.

We had some great runs in Naples, although some were still rough because of our constant nightly alcohol consumption. It seemed we were attempting to run off the previous night's indiscretions. Some of our runs included the Briants. Bill was an ex-career Marine, and an ultra-marathoner. Mary competed in all sorts of distances including marathons I believe, but I don't think she ran ultra-marathons. Bill jokingly told us that he didn't even get warmed up in a 10k race, although I think there was a lot of truth to that, especially for a man who competed in 100-mile races. Bill and Mary were outstanding runners and were great to train with. It was on one of these runs that Adkerson told me that no matter how fast I ran in our cross-country races he was keeping up.

Before we left Naples, Adkerson became preoccupied with a young lady he met on the beach. She was from the Miami area, and they wrote several times after we returned but the long distance didn't allow for the pending relationship to develop. I had a girlfriend at the time, so I didn't attempt to pick up women.

On our trip back to southern Missouri, we dropped off Rod in Orlando. Rod, who majored in criminal justice, had relatives there and he wanted to get a job with the Orlando Police Department. After leaving Rod, we headed toward the Florida Panhandle. We were exhausted and Fresh was especially irritable and slept almost the entire trip home. He would wake up and move to the front seat to let one of us go to the back to sleep and then before you knew it was bitching that we slept too much, and he wanted to return to his perpetual nap. What we didn't know is that Fresh was in the early stages of mono, which he blamed on a woman he picked up during one of our excursions to the Springfield area that spring.

While traveling along I10 between Tallahassee and Pensacola, McGarity was pulled over by a trooper for speeding. Mark got out of the van and met the officer at the back end of the vehicle and tried desperately to talk his way out of the ticket. While McGarity pleaded with the trooper, the other two Marks and I laughed our asses off. We couldn't see McGarity because of the lack of windows in the back of the van, but I swear he got down on his knees and begged. But to no avail. He received a ticket, and it must have been a big one because the speed limit was 55 then and McGarity got back in the van so pissed he didn't say a word. Fresh, Adkerson and I didn't say a word either. Of course, this was easy for Fresh because he was asleep in a matter of seconds after we resumed.

While McGarity drove, the rest of us slept most of the time. I remember waking up in Mobile, Alabama and going through a tunnel, and again on the moon-lite night somewhere in the hinterland of Mississippi. I was sitting in the front seat when I awoke and looked out the window to an eerie scene of flat nothingness illuminated by the moon. McGarity said we were somewhere in Mississippi when I asked, and I quickly fell back asleep. The three of us woke up again as the sun was coming up behind us, just before we made Vicksburg. As we crossed the bridge over the Mississippi River into Louisiana, the first time I'd seen that bridge since the spring of 1981, my mind drifted back to the night we built the fire under the structure and when I went up to the top to look at the smoke. During our trip we had talked about going to the Keys and maybe to New Orleans, but we came to realize that we would probably run out of money.

We didn't have credit cards and not long after crossing the border from Louisiana into Arkansas we determined that we might not have enough money to make it back to the Branson area. The four of us pulled our money and come up with just enough to pay for our gas. We rolled into the SofO campus on fumes, but we made it! Since I was taking the summer off, I no longer had a dorm room, so I stayed with Adkerson that night, which is where I also stored my things during our Florida trip. Fresh had his car at campus so he headed back to Jeff City that evening. Too tired to run, Adkerson and I scrounged up some change from his room and went out and bought some beer, but we found we were too bushed to drink much. The next day, my dad picked me up and we headed back to Parsons.

I had a full summer ahead, which included a couple of trips back to school, a camping excursion to the Colorado Rockies, and of course the Olympics in Los Angeles. But I also had a lot of down time. Because I had a tight schedule, I decided it wouldn't be worth getting a job and I also knew that this was probably the last summer of "freedom" of my life. My girlfriend back at college thought this was strange and I think it might be one of the reasons we broke up that summer, although I think there were other issues as well. Because I didn't work, I stayed up late, which until the last few years, was natural for me anyway. But it also meant that I slept late, and for the first time in my life, I woke up with horrible-splitting headaches.

My normal routine was to wake up around 11am to noon, eat something and then go out to the back yard, lay down on the wooden swing, and go to sleep. When I woke up, my headache was worse than ever, and the only thing that got rid of the pain was a run. So, sometime in the afternoon, during the heat of the day, I strapped on my running shoes and headed out for a long run. I put in some good training, but I needed to get out of that rut, so I headed back to SofO for a few days to see friends and train. I went with John Johnson in his Camaro, and he had visited a few times, so he already knew some of my friends. It just so happened that Fresh was visiting at the same time while he tried to recover from mono. We ran with Adkerson, McGarity, Kenny Nobles, and a few others. We also ran in the Heer's 5-mile race in Springfield, but I didn't run well. One reason might be because I didn't get a warmup, but I still should have been able to run a decent race. Fresh went with us but didn't run because of his condition.

In addition, Randy visited SofO that week as well. He had just been dismissed from the hospital and was very weak, but it was great to see him. Of course, he couldn't run yet, and his recovery was long, but at least he was on the right road. It took a year, but eventually Randy got back in school and rejoined the track team, although my eligibility was up by then. I made one more trip to SofO that summer and this time it was by myself. But this trip was marred by all sorts of problems, most, if not all, with my girlfriend. She started getting on me for not having a job and was dumbfounded that I didn't know how many days I was visiting. Needless to say, our relationship didn't last the duration of my vacation. I left for Parsons and never saw her again as she left school at the end of the summer. But I still had a lot left to do before fall, so my mind was preoccupied for the next month and a half.

At mid-summer my dad and I headed to Colorado to go camping and trout fishing. John Johnson came along, and it was his first trip to the Rocky Mountains. We camped along the Taylor River on the west side of the Continental Divide above Gunnison. We didn't get in much running, but I did teach John how to trout fish. I've always thought it would be great to train for a long period of time at 9,000 ft. altitude, which was approximately where our campground was at. But we were only there for a week and mostly fished, which didn't give us much time to run. Plus, without the luxury of showers, running everyday didn't appeal to either one of us. We caught lots of trout and as John learned the intricacies of trout fishing in fast running water, he also caught plenty of rocks at the bottom of the Taylor.

The last couple of days of the trip we drove to the east side of the divide and stayed in a cabin in Buena Vista. We headed up the canyon to fish Cottonwood Creek, one that I had been fishing for several years. It's one of my favorite creeks to fish, and Buena Vista has one of the most beautiful views in the country with the Collegiate Peaks to the west. We also fished Chalk Creek in the

Collegiate Peaks. Because we now had showers, John and I went out for a 4 or 5 mile run in the evening. Although Buena Vista is around 8,000 ft., we didn't feel the altitude because we ran on a mostly flat highway along the Arkansas River in the upper valley. Today, I live close to the Arkansas River and cross it every day from Little Rock to North Little Rock to get to my museum job at Camp Robinson. The River in Arkansas looks nothing like it does in the mountains of Colorado. I'd like to see them try and take a barge up the Arkansas in the shallow rapids near the headwaters.

After returning from Colorado, I only had a couple of days before driving to Los Angeles. My mom took this as an opportunity to visit relatives and friends in California and one of her friends from Parsons came with us. We left early in the morning, and it took two full days to make it to Lancaster, where my aunt and uncle and cousins lived. During the trip we stayed the night about halfway in Grants, New Mexico. Once arriving in Lancaster, I still had a few days before we needed to go into LA, so I stayed with my cousin Bob Smith and my mom stayed with Peggy and Wayne Smith, my aunt and uncle. Peggy was my dad's sister and was four or five years older than him. Their youngest son, Lee, was in high school and still living at home.

Because Wayne's health was poor, he mostly sat at the kitchen bar and eat popsicles. I also had a chance to see my older cousin Kathy Smith. We went to eat with her at a Chinese place and it was the first time I'd seen or even heard of Mongolian barbeque. But it was great! Kathy was heavy with tattoos on her arms, which was not common on women in the mid-80s. And she was blunt. I thought she was going to get us killed by some of the things she said in that restaurant. Wayne didn't get along with his oldest daughter and tried to dissuade me from going out to eat with her. Now I could see why! But I got along well with her, even though she could be mean. But she wasn't mean to me, although she was puzzled why someone would run (unless running from the law) and why anyone would waste their time attending the Olympics. But years later, after moving to Parsons, she was exceedingly nice to my son Ryan when we visited Kansas. Kathy died at the age of 62 in early 2017 in a nursing home in Parsons. Her hard life took its toll. Aunt Peggy died in the winter of 2019 in the same nursing home.

After a few days we headed to the Valley and I stayed with friends Neil and Chris Patrizio, and their sister Bubby. When I was born, my mom and dad lived across the alley from the Patrizios. They lived on a side street, and we lived on the busy Victory Boulevard. I don't remember living next to them because I was still a baby when we moved a few blocks down on Victory, but mom and dad had made life-long friends. By 1984, Neil and Chris lived in the family home, and their parents, Vince and Deedee had moved to Ridgecrest, California. During my week or so in Burbank, this was my home base during the Olympics, while mom went with Vince and Deedee to Ridgecrest for a few days.

We had obtained the bus schedule and routes before we arrived in LA, so my mom, her friend, and I took the bus to downtown the morning of the first day of track competition. Once in downtown LA, the city bus system had buses that fingered throughout the city to the Olympic venues. Of course, I was headed to the Coliseum for track and field. I think the shuttles left from Pershing Square. I bought my shuttle passes for my five days of track and waited for my bus to leave for the Coliseum, as my mom and friend went to Olvera Street to eat lunch and wait for her friend's family who lived in LA. Taking the bus and shuttle buses from Burbank to the Coliseum was much cheaper than driving myself. In fact, it only cost me $5.00 a day – 50 cents to go to downtown, 50 cents to go back to Burbank, and $2.00 for the shuttle each way. There was absolutely no parking at the LA Coliseum, so I would have paid a fortune to park in someone's yard, and the gas would have been considerably more. Plus, the aggravation of the traffic would have been enough to drive me crazy. But LA was ready for the Olympics, and everything ran like a well-oiled machine. I had no issues getting to and from the Coliseum, which was about 20 miles each way.

Each day I walked several blocks to "beautiful downtown Burbank" to catch my bus, and I got off the bus at the end of the day at Burbank airport where Neil picked me up. My only issue each morning was getting across the extremely busy corner where Victory and Burbank Boulevards intersect. But once I crossed that mess, it was free sailing to my bus stop. On days I didn't go to the Coliseum, I usually headed to a sandwich shop on Burbank Boulevard for lunch to get the best damn pastrami I've ever had. This pastrami was so fatty and stringy that I can still taste it, and it was so good, the sandwich didn't need a single condiment. I've never found that kind of pastrami in the Midwest or South. When Neil picked me up at the airport, and other days as well, we usually headed to this little fast-food joint where you eat outside, for triple chili cheeseburgers. I think the place was called Tommy's, and these were the best damn burgers in the world, and their fries were great.

The first day of the Olympic track and field competition had a number of exciting events, although most were preliminaries. My seat was located at the far curve of the track opposite the columns and scoreboard. They were great seats about halfway up and I sat next to the coach of the Wesleyan University track team and his wife. They were both very pleasant and it was great to sit next to someone who was knowledgeable of the sport. As is often the case reflecting back so many years, I can't remember his name. I watched numerous events, but the most exciting for me was the first round of the men's 800m. I watched the eventual Olympic champion Joaquim Cruz run his opening race in 1:45, and Sebastian Coe, who took the silver for the second consecutive Olympics, also ran a 1:45 in his heat. Both ran so easy that it looked as if I could have run right with them. Their performances looked effortless. But, of course, I could have never run with those guys. I witnessed other greats such as Americans Earl Jones, who took the bronze three days later, and

Johnny Gray, who made the finals, but didn't perform well, although he did earn an 800m medal in the '92 Games. And I saw the defending Olympic champion Steve Ovett move on to the quarter finals.

One unique thing about the '84 Olympic 800 is that they ran four rounds – heats on day one, quarterfinals on the second day, semis on day three, and the finals on the fourth. To medal in the 1984 800m, one had to be a man! Cruz took the gold with a 1:43.00, an amazing time racing for a fourth consecutive day, especially after running a high 1:43 in the semifinals. Unfortunately, Ovett, who made the final on a last gasp fall over the finish line in the semis, had a severe health issue and ran poorly. The other anticipated event for me was the men's 10,000 heats, which went late into the evening. The world recoded holder, Portugal's Fernando Mamede, made the finals, where he would drop out, and American Pat Porter, who came out of an NAIA school like me, made the finals. Craig Virgin didn't make the final, but I was rooting for him the entire 25 laps. But I also watched Italy's Alberto Cova compete. He won the gold two days later.

The day ended late, and as I headed out of the stadium to get to a shuttle, I realized I didn't feel well. It wasn't too bad, but I had a headache that worsened on the short ride from the Coliseum to downtown. When I got on the bus to head back to Burbank, the bus was so full of Olympic attendees that I couldn't find a seat, so I stood with many others. But my headache got so bad that I almost passed out and I was sweating profusely. It felt like someone had taken an axe and split my head open from the top and down across my left eye. I remember a lady who had attended track that day trying to comfort me. It got to the point that I thought I was going to vomit. But I couldn't get off the bus to throw up or try and recover because I was on the last bus of the day to Burbank on this route. When I finally arrived at the Burbank airport, I called Neil on a pay phone and waited outside on a bench.

When he arrived, Neil asked me if I wanted to get a triple chili cheeseburger, but I felt so bad that I just asked him to get me home. I had a difficult time getting to sleep and when I woke up the next morning the pain was gone, but I could still feel where the pain had been. To this day I don't know what happened and why, but I was grateful in the morning that the headache had dissipated. It took two years before that kind of headache returned and they occurred every day for about two weeks. After that, I went through years of severe migraines from four to seven days a week. They abruptly stopped in 1993, when I moved to Iowa for a new job. I've only had a handful in the decades since.

During my days at the Coliseum, I witnessed some great competition and all-time greats. For example, I was at the track for the last seven or eight events of the decathlon. The second day of the men's multis was great, as the defending Olympic Champion, Britain's Daley Thompson outdueled the German Jürgen Hingsen. Thompson was maybe 6 feet tall, compact, and powerful, while Hingsen, the world record holder, was tall, about 6 foot 7, but also built like Atlas. Thompson tied Hingsen's decathlon world record by beating the West German. Although I didn't get to watch the women's 100m final at the stadium, I did see the Olympic Champion, American Evelyn Ashford run in the heats. Like many, I knew this was probably her last chance to win the Gold, and after being boycotted out of the '80 Games, when she was at her peak (although I think she was injured), it was great to see her win the 100 in '84, even though I watched on television in Burbank! Even today, along with Calvin Smith and Gail Devers, she is one of my favorite sprinters.

Unfortunately, Calvin Smith didn't make the Olympic team in the 100 and 200m dashes. He won the 200m at the inaugural World Championships the year before but finished out of the money at the Olympic Trials in 1984. But I still got the chance to see Smith race at the Los Angeles Olympics because he made the Team in the 4x100m relay. They won, with Carl Lewis running anchor in a world record of

37.83. I wasn't there for the final, but I saw the team run in the semis. One of my big joys was sitting on row 13 on the far curve during the men's 200m final and the men's 400m final. Carl Lewis was not a fan favorite over the years, and I guess I thought he could be a bit aloof, but I also didn't have a problem with him, and I was rooting for him to win four Golds. So, I was there looking at him from my seat on the 13th row with binoculars. When the gun sounded, the field ran toward me on the curve, and then away to the straight. It was great to witness Lewis win in 19.80, an Olympic record, but also to be there as the Americans swept the medals, with Kirk Baptiste taking 2nd and Thomas Jefferson winning the Bronze.

The other joy that day was watching American Alonzo Babers win the 400m in dominating style. American Antonio McKay was one of the favorites, but drew the unfortunate lane one, I think the most difficult lane, maybe along with the outside lane, to win a 400m. McKay finished in 3rd to win the bronze, and I remember hearing criticism about him because he didn't win the Gold—all ridicules. I wonder how many who have never raced at a high level, or even a small college level like me, really know what it's like to race against great competition? We know the answer. McKay ran great – a bronze medal from lane one – no shame in that. Plus, McKay won a Gold by anchoring the American 4x400m relay, along with Ray Armstead, the Northeast Missouri State sprinter.

During the early afternoon one day, and it might have been the first day of track competition, while I waited outside the Coliseum for it to open, I very tall and strikingly beautiful women, dressed to the tees, sat down next to me, and struck up a conversation. I was not sure why she selected to sit next to me because there were plenty of other places to sit, and some didn't have a single person sitting on them. But she seemed to want to talk, and she was interesting. I don't remember her name, and she told me her husband played in the NBA, but I don't recall his name either. We had a conversation for quite a while, until the stadium opened, and I never saw her again.

One of the nights that finished late, I sat on the bus from downtown to Burbank when there were only four or five riding. There was an old person on the bus who appeared to be homeless, and I couldn't tell if the person was a man or a woman. But the person was reciting a poem that lasted the entire 15-mile bus ride, and I don't know when it began, and it was still being recited when I got off at the airport. But it was horribly racist. Although I couldn't determine the gender, the person was clearly white, and other than the bus driver and the old person the other couple were African American. I thought at any moment one was going to confront the poem person, but no one ever did. In fact, the person was completely ignored. I determined that the few people on the bus rode it nightly, and this was nothing new to them. When Neil picked me up, we went to an all-night lighted golf course, I think in Van Nuys, and hit golf balls on the driving range, which put me at ease after the drama of the bus ride.

In 1984, I thought it was great to see the resurgence of American high jumper Dwight Stones. I watched him jump at the Olympics and rooted for him, but he finished 4th with the same clearance as the Bronze Medalist. One of the best performances at the Olympics was Valerie Brisco-Hooks winning the difficult 200m/400m double. In addition, watching Al Joyner win the triple jump was great. In the heptathlon, his sister, Jackie Joyner, as I recall, was leading the event going into the last event, the 800m, but she was unable to hold on to first and ended up with the silver. Of course, we didn't know she would go on to win several Olympic Gold Medals in the heptathlon and long jump. People can argue with me all they want, but they will never convince me that she is not the greatest female athlete of all time, and maybe she's the greatest athlete ever. It's a tough call between her and Bo Jackson.

Possibly the best thing I witnessed was Joan Benoit winning the Women's Marathon. And it wasn't just because American Benoit won the race, and I was pulling for her, but because the race was historic. It is the first time that the women's marathon was contested in the Olympics. For some reason, the opinion forever was that women couldn't compete in the longer races. Even in the '84 Olympics, women ran the 3,000 meters, but not the 5,000 or the 10,000. Now, women run the 3,000m steeplechase at the Olympics, like the men, instead of the flat race, as it should be. Women also compete in the 5,000 and 10,000. At that time, women also didn't pole vault as they do now. So, the sport has improved for women's participation. But I think we have at least one more step to go. The heptathlon needs to be scraped and replaced be the decathlon. Why can't women compete in 10 events? Men do!

There is just too much that I saw at the Olympics to mention. But a highlight was watching the men's 20k Walk. Every time the race was shown on the big screen, Mexico's Ernesto Canto was leading, and a fan from Mexico, sitting close by waived the Mexican flag and shouted "Canto, Canto" several times. This fan's enthusiasm was refreshing, especially compared to the steeplechase prelims when a middle-aged clown, passing himself off as a fan, stood up and yelled "get wet" every time the runners reached the water jump in front of us. Actually, I'm insulting clowns when I shouldn't. This man had the head of a donkey. When Canto entered the Coliseum in the lead, the Mexican fan shouted Canto's name while swinging the Mexican flag back and forth as the walker circled the track to the finish, winning the Gold. I never thought I would get so excited watching race walking, but the fan turned the race into a wonderful event for those of us in his section.

On the last day of track and field, I had a ticket for the morning session but not one for the afternoon and evening. I wanted to watch the finals in the 1500 and 5,000 as well as the 4x400m. After the morning session ended, the crowed left the stadium, and I walked around trying to buy a ticket for the later session, but the prices were much too high from the scalpers. Of course, I never found a ticket at face value or even twice the price, and I would have taken a ticket for the worst seat in the house. On one of the days, I attended a morning session. I was located in the last row on the far curve, and I could still see everything clearly. I could even look over at USC and see the swimming and diving arena, which was outside. But on the final day of competition, outside the men's Marathon, I couldn't even get a seat in the clouds for an affordable price. So, I headed back to Burbank and watched the finals of those races on TV, which wasn't a bad seat, as it turned out!

On the morning, I was placed in the upper reaches of the Coliseum, I sat next to a husband and wife from Great Britain and there was no one else seated close to us. He was part of the media, and the English couple had attended the Olympics since 1948, as well as numerous other world events. And they had driven across America several times since the 1950s. I'm not sure exactly what his job was during the 1984 Olympics, but I think he said he was head of international commentators for boxing. Anyway, I know he was involved in the boxing competition held next to the Coliseum at the Memorial Sports Arena. Strangely, he and his wife had never visited Los Angeles during their American visits. He told me that LA was "like a bloody foreign country," with distain. He said that he had a bag that was given to him as a gift from a famous athlete, which might have been Daley Thompson, and the "damn thing was lifted" the first day of boxing while it sat next to him. He said the bag contained an expensive camera, which he said was easily replaceable, but the bag was special.

Nonetheless, they were extremely nice, and he told me several stories about past Olympics and other competitions. I guess he could have been pulling my leg, but he did show me his press credentials. He had the morning off from boxing and they decided to get a couple tickets for track. The morning sessions were never sold-out, so they were easy to get.

When the Olympics ended, we stayed in Lancaster for a couple of days, and then drove back to Kansas with Aunt Peggy along so she could visit. It's the last time I saw Wayne, as he died the next year. Later, Bob told me that he and Lee were fishing at Lake Isabella, northeast of Bakersfield, when he got a strange feeling, something wasn't right at home. So, they left their fishing trip early and found that their dad had died when they arrived. I've only been back to Los Angeles once since the '84 Olympics and that was in 2008 for a conference, and it was nowhere near the area of which I was familiar. But Bob along with Lee's family came down to see me in West LA where I was staying, and we went to Santa Monica to eat and walk out on the Santa Monica Pier.

Chapter 16
The Highs and the Lows

My final year as a college athlete was not on par with my previous seasons but there were flashes of the past. But, of course, I didn't know that as I headed toward the 1984 cross-country season. After I returned from Los Angeles, I only had a short time before I had to return to college. But that was enough time to run a couple of 5k road races and determine where I was with my fitness. My training during my time in California was erratic because of my schedule, so I wasn't sure how I would test out in these races. I can emphatically say that I failed miserably. I could have probably beaten the fields in these races if they would have been 800s! But not in 5k races.

The first race was in Coffeyville and there were some good runners from Oklahoma entered, and I heard a couple indicate that they ran for the University of Tulsa, but they must have been recent additions to that team because I didn't recognize them. It was a hot morning and not long after the race started on the simple, flat, out-and-back course I could tell I was not fit. Somehow, I reasoned that I would catch the leaders after the half-way point. I don't know what gave me the impression I'd catch a second wind when I never had a first. When I reached the turn-around I attempted to make an effort to pick up the pace and catch the front runners, but instead I continued to slow. At the end of the race, in which I finished 11th in 17:20, I was completely exhausted. It was disheartening to think that I might have wasted my summer by not training enough, especially since I knew I could run two and a half minutes faster when I was in peak form. But I also thought I might not be too far away.

The next weekend, I ran a local race in Parsons. I trained well during the week and didn't have any issues. I planned to win this one no matter how I felt, but as in Coffeyville, I was not ready to run a strong race. I competed better, but the competition was not as good, and I finished 3rd in a time only a few seconds faster than the previous Saturday. Although I felt better in this second race, I couldn't determine if I'd improved or not. Regardless, I knew that I needed to get in shape quickly if I wanted to compete well in cross-country, which was just around the corner. Luckily, Coach Oz wouldn't allow me the pleasure of being lazy once I returned to school the next week.

As it turned out, I really wasn't far from being back in form. I think I was just tired from my late summer in LA and needed three or four weeks of training to get myself back in racing shape. Four weeks after the Coffeyville race, I'm sure I was in 15:30 5k shape or better. When I returned, I quickly got back in my training routine. However, I wasn't going to be able to go on those course checking runs for Coach because I no longer worked for him. The work coordinator for SofO didn't place me back in the fieldhouse, and I never did officially work for Coach Oz because that was not a real workstation. Coach was able to work it out with Coach Smith that I would work for him, but I officially filled the slot as one of the fieldhouse workers. So, in the fall of '84 there weren't any places open in the fieldhouse. I couldn't argue that I had worked for Coach Oz when I don't believe I was really supposed to work for him. The work coordinator, who I'm sure never knew I worked for Coach, placed me in one of the worst workstations on campus – the laundry. The laundry was usually reserved for freshman, but I was a senior. I asked if I could instead go to work in my original station, the cafeteria, and he reluctantly agreed, as long as I promised to keep my nose clean.

When I worked there before there were some issues because some of the cooks, as far as I could tell, were scared to death of me. But I didn't have any issues with my return.

The SofO cross-country team was quite different than it had been. Obviously, teams are fluid from year to year, but we really had almost a completely different team, and we were young. Paul Taylor and I were the senior veterans, and Fresh was experienced but he ended up injured and redshirted instead. I don't think he fully recovered from mono when the season began. But we did have talent. One of our new runners was Keith Schepker from Helias High School in Jefferson City. Keith graduated a couple of years before but didn't immediately go to college to run. His sister Sandy was a member of the women's team. Keith ran a 9:30 or a little under in the 3200m as a high school senior and took 2nd in that race at the Class 3A State Meet, and as a junior finished in 4th place. Adkerson, who was a hurdler, although I think he could have been an outstanding 800m runner, was also on the team. Adkerson had good speed and was faster than I was. And I think he believed he could run a good half, and he hoped that cross county would give him the strength required. In addition, cross-country training would make him a much better 400mIH runner. But he got injured during cross-country, and although he was fine during track season, he missed the opportunity to get a good distance base for the longer track races.

Two other new members were Rob May, who we encountered on the Florida beach, and a kid from Missouri, Jim Dautenhahn. Sophomore Tony Pate, from Tahlequah, Oklahoma, had potential as well. And we had Kenny Nobles, a returning sophomore from Swainsboro, Georgia who was an outstanding all-around athlete, who hailed from the same place as Wilbert Daniels. Ironically, I had an aunt who taught school in Swainsboro but was retired by then. Although I knew my aunt, at least a little, I didn't know at that time that she had taught school in that Georgia town. In addition, Coach

356

recruited a man who was a little older than us and came with his family. Because he transferred in, he wasn't eligible in the fall of 1984.

I believe his last name was Teggs or something similar, and he was supposed to be a great runner, and he seemed as if he was when I trained with him. He might have run under 30 minutes for a 10k, but he would never say. As it turned out, he only stayed in school in the fall, so he never competed for SofO. I'm sure he would have been a tremendous teammate in the spring. In 2011, I was helping run the high jump at the AAU regional meet in Lawrence, Kansas, and the man running off the event looked familiar. It suddenly came to me that he was my old, one-semester teammate. He said he recognized me but didn't say anything about this until I asked him. Other than looking a little older, as of course I did, he looked the same.

Our first meet was hosted by Arkansas Tech University in Russellville. Before we left for the meet, Keith checked the small cooler he took along to hold his insulin. As a Type 1 diabetic, he needed to make sure he ate right and took his insulin twice a day if he wanted to run tons of miles – and he did. About halfway down to Russellville on the 120-mile trip, Keith needed to take his shot, but when he checked the cooler, the insulin was gone. Someone removed it! It was stolen. He told Paul first and then let me know. We both told Keith we needed to let Coach know so we could return and get more insulin, but he said it was OK. Still, we tried to convince Keith that we needed to go back, but he indicated that we would miss the meet. "To hell with the meet," we told him, "Your health is more important!" But Keith said he would be fine, and all he needed to do was double up that evening. After some discussion at the back of the van, we determined that one of our teammates took the insulin to beat him in the race. We had our suspicion, but we could never prove it. Keith said the ploy wouldn't work because it wouldn't bother him until the evening.

Keith was right, he raced well and beat all his teammates save for me. But the course was anything but good. It was a pasture where cattle had trampled when it was muddy and left deep holes where they sank. Footing was not only horrendous in places, but downright dangerous. There were areas in which we ran into a different field where the cattle hadn't been for a while, or at least when it was muddy, and one could maintain a decent pace. I decided, that although I wanted to run well, it wasn't worth the risk of an injury. My old teammate Chris Marcak, now running for Arkansas College, tied for first with two of his teammates in 26:02. I actually ran fairly well, and although I don't think I was ready to compete with the winners yet, I still managed an 8th place finish in 27:05. What was encouraging was that I knew I had a lot left in the tank and would have run 30 or 40 seconds faster if I hadn't tiptoed through the potholes. That's not to say that I would have necessarily finished higher than 8th because I know others decided to be cautious as well. I don't know if Chris was careful or not, but he was a terrific runner. The previous year he ran 5 miles in 24:36 before he hurt his back. I always regretted not trying harder to convince Chris to stay at SofO. In the fall of 2017, I took my high school team to run a meet at Tech. The Tech coach, Tom Aspel, was the same one they had in 1984. I asked him where that '84 meet was held, and he pointed across the road and said it was over there in the cow pastures. Funny, because I had thought it was a few miles north of town, not part of their campus.

The next weekend, we were back in Arkansas, and this time, we were at Harding University. I looked forward to this meet for two reasons. First, my performance at Tech helped build confidence, and second, I wanted to see if I could compete with Chris. Two things went wrong. First, I ran like crap, and second, Chris' back issue flared up and he didn't run. From the beginning of the race, I could tell it wouldn't go well. I didn't have energy and could not pick up the pace. Somewhere in the middle of the race, Chris shouted at me to pick it up. Once a teammate and friend, always a teammate and friend. I told him this was all I had, and it was. I know that Paul and Keith beat me, and I'm not sure if any other teammates finished ahead of me, but Kenny might have. I don't even know my time, but I'm sure I didn't break 28 minutes, and I bet I didn't finish under 29.

Although the Harding race was awash, my training was going well, and I could tell that I was getting in good shape. Sometimes, one can't explain why a performance is poor, and sometimes, it's best not to be concerned about it. One has to move on and not look back, and that's just what I did. On several occasions, Coach Oz took the team to a state park campground for RVs and campers in Forsyth, a few miles from campus, to run mile repeats. These were competitive and spirited workouts, especially with Teggs running with us. Although we never knew how fast he had raced, it was clear he was really good. I know his presence was a tremendous help in not only getting me in a race condition but also making me a much faster 5 miler than I'd ever been, although it would be a few weeks before that became clear.

By mid-season, I was working and racing my way into form when we traveled to Fayette, Missouri, for the Central Methodist Invitational. There were a number of schools there, but none were top teams in the area. I figured I'd have the chance to win this race if I stayed focused. Coach Oz told me before the race that I could win and even suggested that I should win. Although the team ran in the meet the previous year because I redshirted, this was my first race on the course. In fact, I didn't travel with the team in '83, so this was my first look at the course. But Mike Hueton ran the race a year earlier and told me it was a tough course because of the odd footing in some places. Mike's winning time was in the 26s, which was around two minutes slower than his best that year.

Mike was right. There were places in which we ran on a hill from side to side with one leg significantly higher than the other. It seems to me the course was run in a park, and the start and finish straight were the only places where the course was smooth. That portion was possibly on a golf course. Despite the issues of rough ground and odd running angles, it was much, much better than the Arkansas Tech course.

I decided not to be concerned with how fast I ran but instead just concentrate on competing. My goal was to win. I didn't care what my splits were because my strategy was to run with the lead pack, and if anyone attempted to pull away, I'd go with him. The race started with a moderate pace, and I didn't have any issues staying at the front. By two miles or so, there were only two runners in the lead, and I was one of them. We steadily pulled away from the field, and by three miles, I knew I would win unless I fell. Throughout the last two miles, I was itching to take the lead and run away from my competitor, but because of the bad footing, I decided to wait until we reached the final smooth section. I think the last straight was about 300 yards. It went downhill for a short distance and then turned into a steady but easy climb to the finish. Going from the rough grass to the smooth grass was abrupt, and from there, I took off and went away. It was truly an easy run, and I don't think the guy I passed was especially tired. He just didn't possess my speed. My time was 27:12 on what Coach Oz described to the school paper as "a very slow course." Although not fast, I knew I was ready to run in the mid to low 25s, and I believed that chance was the next week on the fast golf course at the University of Missouri Rolla.

As with so many things in our lives, a good race at Rolla was just not to be. By Thursday before the Saturday race, I was sick in bed with the flu or something akin. I was vomiting and couldn't keep anything down. Strangely, I still thought I could recover and race well in two days. On Friday, I was no longer vomiting, but I was so achy that I couldn't run, and any movement was painful. In the evening, I felt a little better, although not well, and it appeared that my fever had broken. So, I decided to go to the track and run a couple of laps to see if I could do it. This was not an intelligent move, and after a lap or two, I painfully walked back to my dorm room, still determined to race the next day.

On Saturday morning, I felt terrible, as I should have expected, but I guess I was still seeking a miracle. I traveled with the team and ran those pitiful five miles and stunk it up. In a picture of me running in the Rolla race, I'm beat red. I had no business racing that day, and I should have stayed in bed. Somehow, I did manage to run 29 minutes and beat a teammate, who I criticized for allowing me to finish ahead of him while I had the flu. I was disappointed, but what can you do when you're sick? I didn't let it bother me for long. The only positive was that Randy Gray attended, so I got to see him.

On Monday, I was still weak but recovering. The bug hit me hard, and I took time to get back to normal. However, my strength steadily improved throughout the week. One thing I didn't do during the week was run in the mornings as I usually did, so I just put in one workout a day, which was during practice. On Friday, we left for St. Louis to compete in the Washington University Invitational in Forest Park. I liked the course, and although it was more challenging than Rolla, a good time was attainable. I felt fine by the end of the week and didn't seem to have lasting effects from the flu. I rarely sketched out a race plan in cross-country based on spits, but I decided to do so for the Washington meet. I wanted to hit four miles in 20:40, a 5:10 mile pace, and try and run the last mile in 5:10 or faster.

The warmup went well, and when the gun sounded, I sprinted to the lead pack and attempted to settle in. I was running well but felt weak. I could tell this was going to be a struggle. In the first mile, I was running next to a Maryville runner, Pat Zinn, a former West Plains runner, who was very good. I thought that if I could stay with him, I might be able to work out my early race issues. There was a long flexible pole with a small flag on the top to help mark the course. A competitor ran over it several feet ahead of Zinn and bent the pole to the ground, and when it released, it snapped up like a wipe and hit Zinn between the legs. It didn't sound very good. Zinn took off, appearing to be angry, and I never saw him again in the race.

Meanwhile, I steadily slowed and finished well back. Although I think I ran for 28 minutes, I wasn't concerned about my time at that juncture, and I never learned how fast I ran. In retrospect, I was still weakened by the flu, and I wondered if my final cross-country season would end in a whimper.

After the Washington race, we only had two meets left, conference and district, with the possibility of a third if we qualified for Nationals, which didn't seem likely for me. The conference was a couple of weeks after Washington, which was the time I needed to gather myself and get back on the right track. Training went well, and I began to believe that my health issues were behind me. I needed to regain my confidence and strength. On Thursday, the day before we were to leave for the meet, Coach asked members of the team if they had been running in the morning. I had resumed two workouts a day by then and, in fact, began after the Washington meet. I told Coach Oz this, but he wanted to know what I did before that. I told Coach that I didn't run in the mornings for a week and a half when I got sick before the Rolla race. Coach was not satisfied and was angry with me. He said I should have run in the mornings anyway, at least the week leading up to the meet in St. Louis. Coach asked me if I wanted to run in the conference meet, which, of course, I did. He said that the only way he would take me was if I ran 5 miles the following morning. I told Coach that I had to be at work at 5 am in the cafeteria, and we were leaving for the meet at mid-morning. But he stuck to his guns.

During the fall 1984 semester, I went to work early several days a week to make breakfast biscuits, and although I wouldn't say I like early mornings, this was a good gig. There were few cooks around and only a few students preparing for breakfast. But I had 5 miles to run! I could have lied and told Coach Oz that I ran my miles, but I never considered that. So, I was out running a little before 4 am so I could get to work by 5:00. Because SofO had a curfew, I wasn't sure if I was even allowed to be out on campus at 3:50 am. I had never had a reason to challenge the rule, at least after getting up. Of course, I rolled onto campus after curfew, but that was different. If you worked on campus, you could walk to your job during the curfew hours if required. But I ran my 5 miles and was never approached, and security did see me!

When we left for St. Louis later that morning for conference, Coach Oz didn't ask if I'd run the five miles. That was disappointing. But I had run those damn five miles, and I at least knew it! I'd experienced the highs and lows of competing that fall, and now I wanted to get back to the top. After the course we ran the District 16 meet on in 1981, this course, run at Missouri Baptist, was the second hardest of which I had ever raced. I had already decided that I was going out conservatively and then try to move up in the field. The reason was that I was still unsure about my strength, and I didn't want to burn myself out early. And now that I saw how tough the course was with its steep hills, I decided that this was the best strategy. My race plan worked, and I passed a number of runners in the last couple of miles. Times were extremely slow, but that didn't matter on that course. Unfortunately, I finished 11th, my worst Ozark Conference finish, and one place out of all-conference honors. But I was encouraged because it was a good race, and I knew I left a lot out on the course. My strength was back, and even though I knew I'd have to run better at district, I believed I could qualify for nationals.

We had a week between the conference and district. I wasn't going to gain anything in my training, so the key, as it was for everyone on the team, was to remain healthy. Our team was already depleted because of injuries. Besides Adkerson, Keith was also injured with a stress fracture in his upper leg. Other than Paul and me, at the end of the season, those healthy enough to compete were Kenny, Tony, Rob, and Jim. I believed I was ready for a good race, and I knew that Paul was in form. He made All-Conference the previous weekend and seemed to be in a good state of mind. The other four were not necessarily running poorly, but they hadn't distinguished themselves either. But they were sophomores and freshmen, so that was understandable. Plus, we had two good teams in the district in 1984, Park College and Missouri Baptist. Normally, only the top team from district qualified for nationals, but in 1983, Park finished in the top ten at the National Meet, so in '84, two teams qualified.

On the morning of the District 16 Meet, which was held in Springfield, the team gathered at the fieldhouse and prepared to board the school bus. I'm not sure why we didn't take the usual vans, but for a short 45-mile trip, the bus didn't seem too bad. The driver was a student who had driven for us before. After we were boarded, someone asked where Coach Oz was, and someone else in the back, a male, shouted that Coach told him that he was driving up in his car, so the bus should leave for the meet. I was sitting toward the front and didn't pay attention to who indicated we should leave. As a senior on the team, I should have followed up by going inside the fieldhouse to make sure we could leave, but I didn't. I took the direction at face value, as did the rest of us on the bus. The ride didn't take long, and when we arrived, members of the team strolled off the bus and hung out, waiting for Coach to arrive.

And Coach did arrive, with Coach McGarity and Teggs. Coach Oz looked angry and ordered everyone back on the bus, including the driver. Then he asked in the angriest tone I've ever heard from him, why did we leave him? At this point the question was directed at the driver who said he was told to leave. The driver's only response was it was someone in the back and he explained to Coach what was said. Coach didn't buy it, but it was the truth. The incident on the bus was tense. Then Coach began asking team members who told us to leave. He asked me but all I could tell him is that a male member of the team sitting in the back said we should leave, and I said the same thing the driver told him. This was the same thing others told Coach as well. The person who said that Coach told us to leave would not speak up. He must have been scared or a coward. I spoke up and said that the person who directed us to leave needed to come forward, but he didn't.

After what seemed an eternity of high tension, Mark Adkerson spoke up and said he told us to leave. Although he was injured, Adkerson made the trip. Now I know Mark didn't tell the driver to leave Coach behind. For one, he was only a seat or two behind me, and second, I knew his voice. Coach Oz looked straight at Adkerson and said, "no you didn't." Coach knew that Mark didn't tell us to leave. Of course, Mark attempted to take the blame when it became apparent that anyone who qualified for the National Meet might not get to go. And Coach knew that Mark would have spoken up at the beginning if he was the guilty party. In fact, Coach looked right at me and said "Ray, do you want to go nationals if you qualify?" Which, of course, I said "yes." Coach answered back, "We'll see." So, Mark tried to take the fall, but Coach wouldn't have it. No one ever came forward to take the blame, but some of us believed we knew who it was, but we couldn't prove it, so we never told Coach because we were not completely sure. I wasn't about to place the blame on someone when I was still unsure.

Coach left the bus still pissed, and probably even more so than when he entered the vehicle because he knew he had a coward on the team. Now one thing is unclear. Did Coach actually tell the kid to let the bus leave? It's possible because Coach did sometimes forget things. But forgetting in such a short period of time seems unlikely unless he was preoccupied with getting things together for the meet. Plus, Teggs and McGarity were with Coach, and they didn't hear Coach say that the bus should leave, although they might not have been with Coach every second. Since no one came forward we couldn't ask if the other two were with Coach. And finally, if Coach wanted the bus to leave without him, why didn't the person who Coach allegedly told, let the bus driver know to leave when he boarded the bus? Coach never got mad at Adkerson for attempting to take the blame. In some way, I think Coach admired what Mark tried to do, however misguided Coach thought it was.

When Coach Oz left the bus, I was pissed. In fact, I was incensed, and I laid into the team. I directed my anger to the couple of teammates that I thought might be responsible, although I'm sure most on the bus didn't see it that way because all appeared to be in my cross hairs. Paul and Mark knew they weren't part of my rage, and neither did Fresh, who rode with us. I said that the one who was responsible was taking away the chance for those who had a legitimate chance to qualify from running at Nationals. I said this person was selfish because he knew he didn't have a shot in the dark of qualifying. I said if I ever found out who the person was that I'd kick the shit out of him. With my yelling, cussing, and threatening, I know I scared the wits out of some of the younger women on the team, which I truly regretted after I cooled down. But I didn't regret my reaction on that bus. I wonder now if Coach could hear me, but I think he left in his car. How can a team leave a coach behind?

When I exited the bus, I was so mad that I hit the side of the bus with my left fist, possibly breaking it. But that was not my biggest issue. I exuded so much anger with my bus tirade that it sapped me of all my energy. During the women's race I was numb and my goal of qualifying for Nationals was dashed. My desire to race was gone. I was so excited about this race after getting sick in mid-season and knowing I was back in form. But now I was just spent and didn't possess an ounce of enthusiasm for the race. I thought about all that training going to waste.

I watched the women's race hoping it would take my mind off my race and I cheered them on, and I truly wanted them to run well. But when we lined up for the men's race, I didn't know if I could muster more than a jog. My warmup was poor, and I didn't think I was stretched enough. But I didn't feel tight, in fact, my body felt like a wet noodle, and I felt as if all the blood had drained from my head and extremities. The weather was good for racing. It was a cool day, but nowhere near cold, and the sun was bright. But as I stood there while the meet director gave us directions, the breeze felt cold to me. I just wanted to turn around and walk away. I felt hopeless while I stood there realizing that I wouldn't qualify for Nationals my senior year. This was now going to be my last college cross-country race, and I wanted nothing to do with it. Then the gun sounded, and I ran the greatest race of my life!

The early pace was blistering and after the first mile, a fair number of runners fell back. My mile split was 4:37. Of course, the race didn't continue at that pace and those of us who remained competitive settled in. Two runners were well out in front by two miles, and they were even ahead at the mile. But there were three of us behind them running together, and it was a steady pace. Two miles was crossed in 9:39, so we slowed to 5:02 for the second mile, but that was a good pace for me. The same three of us were together at miles three and four, hit in 14:42, and 19:47. The pace after mile one remained steady, and we covered that three mile stretch in 15:10. The course was rolling hills, and mostly run on asphalt, which was highly unusual for a cross-country meet. I think the hard service made the race slower, but who can tell. The two runners with me were from Park College, and I believed at that point I would beat both and finish 3rd.

Just after the four-mile mark, maybe 10 seconds past, I caught a severe stomach cramp that slowed me and the two Park guys moved away. I tried to take deep breaths and work it out. I went around a curve and looked to my side to see how close the next competitor was behind me, and I saw that it was Paul Bringman of Missouri Baptist, who won the 3200m in the large school division at the 1982 Missouri State Meet in 9:19. So I needed to relieve the stomach cramp. I was in 5th place, and we weren't sure how many individuals qualified for Nationals. In past district meets it was the top five individuals not on the winning team. But with two teams moving on to the National Meet in 1984, some said it was only the top five places in the race. So, it was possible no runners not on the top two teams would qualify. So, I needed to run that last mile well. And I did. My cramp soon went away, and I began to catch the two Park runners. By the time I could see the finish line I had already moved into 4th and was fast approaching 3rd. But his coach shouted that I was catching him, and he had enough of a spurt to finish ahead of me.

My 4th place time was 24:54, and I qualified for Nationals. After the race, I could tell it was the fastest I'd ever raced over five miles, because my legs severely cramped. But I didn't even care, although that is extremely painful. Park won the team title, Missouri Baptist was second, and we were a distant third. Danny Bryant a great runner from Missouri Baptist won in 23:57. He took 7th at the National meet that year to make All-American. Paul Taylor ran a PR in 25:38 and was "officially" told that he qualified for the NAIA National Meet because the top five individuals not on the two top teams got to go. I was extremely happy but couldn't figure out why I could run so well when I felt like I did at the starting line. I still don't know today. Maybe taking all the pressure off when I didn't think I had a chance, relaxed me and I ran uninhibited. Whatever it was I was grateful! I also think it's the most fun I ever had in a race. Coach Ault of Westminster said it was about time I ran that fast!

That evening a few of us caught up with McGarity at the liquor store where he worked. We asked him if Paul and I were going to Nationals since he rode with Coach back to campus. He said he didn't know what Coach Oz was going to do. On Monday afternoon Paul and I showed up for practice without knowing Coach's plan. Paul looked at Coach without mentioning the bus incident and asked him what he wanted us to do. Coach said, "you want to go to Nationals, don't you?" And with that we knew his decision and he sent the two of us out on a distance run.

Unfortunately, at mid-week, Coach got word from the NAIA that Paul had not qualified for the National Meet. I thought this was cheap. Don't "officially" tell a guy that he qualified for Nationals at the District meet, and then come back a few days later and take that away. Just make sure in the years that follow the rules are clear before the race begins. I know this hurt Paul. He ran at the NAIA National Meet the year before and he wanted to go back, just as I did. I don't think Paul was the same after that. I rarely hung out with him, but he was a great guy. He stopped coming to practice and he left school at the semester break.

Between the District meet and Nationals, SofO had its basketball homecoming during the first game of the year. Teggs, who rented a home from Coach Oz, decided to throw a party the night of homecoming. He bought a huge stereo system and several albums from Walmart because he knew he could return them when the party was over and get his money back, which is what he did. That evening, I attended the homecoming dance with some of my teammates and even danced with Teggs' wife. She said he was setting up for the party.

The home that Teggs and his family lived in was to be torn down so Coach could build a new home on that location. Coach and his family lived on campus across from Kelce dorm for years, but most of the faculty housing was being removed. Teggs had to be out of the rented home at a certain date, so he held this party as a last hurrah in the house. When Fresh, Adkerson, and I arrived it was so dark along the road leading to the house that one could barely see. There were tons of cars already there and when we walked up to the home, although dark there too, we could see several pieces of heavy equipment in the yard, including a bulldozer. When we went inside, the house was completely void of furniture. But it was wall-to-wall people in every room, many that I knew. The music was loud, but our objective was to find the keg, which we located in a closet in one of the back bedrooms.

I found out quickly that when I needed a refill, it was difficult getting back to the keg, so once I made it to the keg closet the second time,

I just stayed, acting as the one who pumped the keg for everyone and filling up my own cup when needed. After a while, I heard someone yell from another room that the police were here. I couldn't leave and try to get away because I was trapped. So, I just stayed there until the cops came into the room and told us to head to the front room. Well, what became apparent is that Teggs already vacated the house, as he was required, and already lived somewhere else, but hadn't returned the keys to Coach Oz. I kind of suspected this when I saw the equipment outside and no furniture inside. The police didn't want to arrest anyone and told us all to leave. One cop said, "I can appreciate that you cats want to party," but said it couldn't be there. "Cats?" Who used the word "cats" in the 1980s other than Keith Richards? Even today, when Keith Richards uses "cats" it's cool, but not anyone else. So, we left – no harm done!

The District 16 Meet was held on a Friday, so I think homecoming was the next day, because the next Saturday, Fresh and I went to Springfield to watch the NCAA cross-country regional hosted by SMS. Their race was held on a golf course just off I80. Unlike our meet in the same city the week before, the weather was bitterly cold. But the races were great. In the Men's race I believe the winner was Yobes Ondieka of Iowa State, who took 3rd at the NCAA National Meet, and Brent Steiner, the great distance runner from a Kansas high school, now running for the University of Kansas, took second. Steiner placed 7th at nationals. For me, although I didn't need the lesson, it did put things in perspective about my cross-country running. There were multiple competitors who had five-mile splits faster than my district time and they had over a mile to go. And we had good conditions, while they had extremely cold temperatures.

On a Thursday afternoon, Coach and I left for Kenosha, Wisconsin for the NAIA National Cross-Country Championship. We didn't have any women qualify in '84, so it was just Coach and me. It would have been great to have Paul competing as well. We only discussed the bus incident once and only for a few seconds, which probably doesn't count as a discussion. I only told him that I didn't know who told us to leave, and he dropped it. McGarity told me that Coach was actually laughing about it when they returned to campus after the district meet. After dark, somewhere in Illinois on I55, Coach and I noticed something odd ahead of us. It appeared that cars were running off the road and some were headed left to the center area. Then as we got closer, we realized that a car was barreling toward us in the wrong direction. Coach quickly turned to the shoulder as the car screamed past us. I think the car was going 80 miles an hour or more. Thank God, it didn't hit us. I don't know if the vehicle ever hit anyone that night – we never heard. Ironically, it wasn't Coach who caused the highway havoc this time. The incident reminds me of the scene, which takes place on the same stretch of interstate, in *Trains, Planes, and Automobiles*, with Steve Martin and John Candy, although that movie came out a few years later.

In the week leading up to Nationals, Teresa Mather asked to borrow some money because she wanted to travel to the meet. Belinda Welcher also wanted to go and asked me for some money, but she decided not to attend. When I arrived on the course the morning of the meet, I didn't see Teresa. She wasn't there for the women's race, and when I was on the starting line for my race, I didn't see her then either. I just figured she decided not to make the trip. But I wasn't concerned because I had my race to run. I was lined up next to Adam State University, the best NAIA cross-country program in the country. I saw this as an advantage. If I could stay with them up the long first hill, I would be in good position. Adam State was the team favored to win. Coach Oz must have known the Adam State coach, Joe Vigil, because they struck up a conversation as if they were friends. Most NAIA distance runners knew who Coach Vigil was, or they should have. He was already a legend.

When the race started, I attempted to stay with Adam State runners. But at the start, I slipped in the mud and went down. It didn't really slow me down much, but when I regained my form, the Adam State guys were several strides ahead of me. I told myself before the race not to let anyone in my area get a jump on me. I had learned my lesson two years before when, as the count went down to the start, tons of guys took off two seconds before the official start, and I got left behind. And there were just too many in the race to pass enough to make all-American. In 1984, they did the same thing, and I responded, but the slip cost me a little. I still had time to sprint 40 yards to get up with Adam State, but I never did. I knew I had an outside chance to make All-America, but I also knew I would have to run the best race of my life – better even than district. Realistically, a top 75 finish was certainly possible.

When I made it to the top of that long opening hill, I was pretty far back and I knew I wouldn't finish in the top 25, which is what it took to be an all-American, but I knew I could still run a good race. However, I never got comfortable, although I kept fighting. I wasn't running badly, but I was not running really well either. I don't know what place I got, but it was over 200. My time was in the 27s over the 8k course. Although it might be difficult to determine from the results, I believed at the time that it was my second-best race of the year, even better than my win. I was disappointed in my performance, but when I looked at how well I ran at the District 16 Meet, the NAIA Nationals was just gravy. If I'd been a legitimate contender for a top 25 spot, then that would have been a different story. But because a great performance on my part would have been 50th, then it didn't make a difference that I was in the 200s. My district race was my pinnacle for the season and that was just fine. And, I was a middle-distance runner, an 800 and 1500 guy, and indoor season was around the corner. I planned to qualify for Nationals in the mile and make all-American. I knew a 4:10 to 4:12 mile indoors was realistic and that could get me to my goal.

After the race was over, I saw Teresa with an old track teammate who ran for the women's team in 1982, before leaving. She had arrived in time to see the race but couldn't find Coach and me. I thought I had heard a women's voice cheering for me at two or three places on the course, so that must have been her. After speaking to Teresa for a little while, Coach and I left. I didn't see Teresa for about three weeks. Back on campus, some of her friends asked me if I'd seen her at the meet and did, I know where she was now? I didn't know. Although we were teammates and I lent her money to travel to Nationals, I didn't hang out with Teresa. She was at parties I attended, and she had some close friends who were good friends of mine, and we did know each other fairly well, but we were never close. Three weeks after the National Meet, at a school dance in the lobby of the fieldhouse, Teresa came sprinting through. I tried to ask her what happened, but she acted as if she didn't know me. I doubt we said 10 words to each other my remaining time at SofO. It wasn't out of spite, at least from my point of view, I just rarely saw her. She came back to campus with some guy she met, I think in Chicago, and that's all I knew. It didn't make a difference to me. I'm not sure I ever got my money back.

Chapter 17
I'm Done

I find it interesting how I'm not remembered by those who were around me every day, after being one of the best athletes on the track team in the early to mid-80s. For example, a few years ago I went back to the College for a homecoming. At our class gathering I said hello to one of my former teammates who I knew well, although we didn't hang out. He didn't have a clue who I was and didn't remember me. We were only teammates for three years! His wife, who went to SofO with us but was not on the track team, knew who I was, and he knew other teammates who were there, but didn't recollect me. At the dedication for the new track in 2016, one of the members of the women's team didn't remember me as well. She recalled names of those who didn't have my career, but we did have different track coaches so it's more understandable. The moral is, do as well as you can, make good friends, and don't worry who remembers you when you leave because you can't control that aspect of your life. I also teach that history doesn't happen in a bubble. What happened in the past affects the future. But when you are on a team, you are in a bubble of that time, and when all the teammates you had are finished with their athletics careers, no one on the team after them can remember you, because they were never your teammates.

And so, this is the reality when you're done. I didn't know that after the spring 1985 season I'd be done. Sure, my college career would end, but I fully planned to continue competing. As soon as cross-country Nationals was over, our training switched to the Hollister Steps. For three weeks we did virtually nothing else, and it tore up my legs. Coach wanted at least one week in which we did 100 of the steps, which for him was similar to a 100-mile week. But it didn't work that way for most of us, at least for those who ran middle-distance and distance. Instead of doing a short distance buildup for indoor track, the steps not only played hell on our legs, but hurt our running fitness as well. I was never as happy as the day the semester ended, and I could go home to Parsons to get in some easy runs and let my legs recover.

Unfortunately, it didn't turn out that way. Only a few days after I got home, my left Achilles tendon began to hurt. At first it was soreness after I ran, but within a week it hurt when I ran and even when I didn't. The pain was high in the tendon, and I finally made the decision that I needed to take a few days off. What choice did I have? I needed to be in shape for indoor season so I could qualify for Nationals in the mile and make All-American. But if I continued to run, I would be too injured to run during the indoor season. After a few days off, I ran again, but the tendon was no better, so I took a week off. But even after a week the damn thing was just as painful. The best decision I could have made was to take two or three weeks off and prepare for outdoor Nationals and try to make All-American in the late spring. But I knew one thing for sure – Coach was not likely to take me to outdoor Nationals no matter how fast I ran, so if I was going to be an All-American, the odds were that I'd have to do it indoors.

I made the choice to continue to train and try to work around the tendon injury. It was apparent early on that I wasn't going to be able to qualify in the mile. Because of the injury and the Hollister steps, I was not in good enough shape to run a fast mile. I thought I might be able to approach 4:20 but that was much too slow to even think about being an All-American. But the tendon issue also took away my natural speed, and so it would handcuff me in the 880. My compromise distance, and it was not much of a compromise, was the 1000 yards. But that distance is only 120 longer than a half mile, so it took good speed as well. In my first indoor meet I ran the 880 and didn't even break the lowly 2-minute barrier. The next meet I failed again to break 2:00. I also ran poorly at an indoor meet at Harding University in Arkansas, and I think it was in the 1000y. Finally, at the Mule Indoor Relays at Central Missouri State, I won my heat in the 880 and took third overall in 1:58 FAT. Not too bad, and in fact, it was the first time my parents had ever witnessed me breaking two minutes in a race although my dad had timed me in a 1:59 a couple of years before in a practice run.

Our final meet before Nationals was at Pittsburg State. Coach entered me in the 1000 yards, which was my final opportunity to run a good time and go to Nationals. I didn't feel particularly confident, and I knew my strength was diminishing quickly. I was only training once a day because if I ran in the morning the afternoon workout was arduous with my tendon that was increasingly getting worse. In addition, I didn't run on Sundays so I could at least rest the injury one day a week. The Pitt State race went surprisingly well, although, by all means, not great. I was leading at the 880 in 1:57.9, but I was shadowed by a good runner from Southwestern College, and I could tell that my speed had went the way of the dodo bird. Before the final curve, the kid from Southwestern sprinted by me with excessive ease, and I did all I could just to hang on. I crossed the finish line in 2nd with a time of 2:17.1, one second behind the winner.

Despite taking second and running a snail's pace last 120 yards, I was happy. It wasn't a great performance but considering the injury and my lack of conditioning, it was adequate. But in reality, even though Coach Oz said he would take me to Nationals, I knew that 2:17 is slow. My encouragement was that 1985 was not a particularly strong year in the NAIA for the 1000 yards. If I would have been in any kind of shape, I would have run at least a 2:14, and I think a 2:11 or 2:12 was possible. But at the same time, if I would have been in 2:12 shape, I would have been running the mile at Nationals!

In the short time between the Pitt State meet and Nationals, I attempted to maintain my fitness without worsening my tendon. I'm not sure I succeeded. Coach took several to the NAIA National Indoor meet in Kansas City, held at Municipal Auditorium. This was the same location the meet was held when I competed two years before on that dismal short track. As I looked at the competition, I thought I had a chance to be one of the seven to make the finals. And, despite my injury, I did have a chance. I'm not sure why but my 1000-yard prelim heat only had three competitors. The other two were All-Americans from the previous years so that was an advantage because only the heat winners were automatic qualifiers. But if the heat was fast and I finished close I would make the finals by time.

When I came out onto the track for my heat, Coach was sitting at trackside working the meet. I don't know what capacity he was involved, but he couldn't really say much to me as an official. I had a small patch of hair under my bottom lip, sometimes called a soul patch, that I had all winter. But because of my light hair, this mini beard was blond, and apparently not noticed by Coach until that moment. He told me later that if he would not have been working the meet, he would have pulled me off the track and not allowed me to race. Luckily for me he didn't do that.

My strategy, no matter how many were in the race, was to take the lead from the start so I wouldn't get caught in the pack and boxed in. I learned my lesson from the 1983 880 heat. When the gun sounded, I quickly headed for the front and the other two didn't challenge. I thought that one, or both would go by me early and try to push the pace, which I welcomed, but they just rode my shadow. I tried to push, and my 440 split was 58 seconds, which wasn't too bad, but not fast either. If I could hit 1:58, I knew I'd have a legitimate chance to make the finals because 2:16 was in reach. I didn't think I slowed much, but my 880 split was 2:00 and knew I needed to really kick hard. I was still in the lead at the half mile, but the other two quickly sprinted by me. I stayed fairly close to them, but not enough to run 2:16. I had nothing left. My kick was non-existent, although I wasn't tired either. I just didn't have enough. My best chance to make the finals was if one of the other two would have taken the lead early and run 2:15, then I think I could have run 2:16. Instead my time was an extremely slow 2:18.9. If I'd have run a 2:17.1, as I had the week before I would have easily made finals, but you know what they say about "ifs" and "buts." My philosophy in racing is to use your strengths to take advantage of the weaknesses of others. My weakness was my injury. No one needed to feel sorry for me or to take it easy on me. My injury was my problem. I'm sure in my career, I took advantage of the injuries of some of my competitors.

I was disappointed. I wasn't immediately sure if I made the finals until the results were posted, but I was almost sure that I didn't. Other than the comment about my odd beard, Coach didn't say anything about the race. I watched the finals later and the winner, who won my heat, only ran 2:15. But that's how it goes. I wasn't sure what the rest of the season held for me, but the next weekend was the District 16 Indoor Championships, and for the first time in my college running career I didn't want to compete. I felt tired and uninspired, which was new for me. The one thing that was certain is that I traveled back to SofO from the National Meet without a soul patch.

The week after Nationals and leading to the District Meet didn't go well. My training was sporadic, and my energy level was low. I don't even remember how well I ran at the District 16 indoor meet. I ran the Mile and placed, maybe second or third, but I'm not even sure. I think I ran the 880, but it could have been the 1000. What I do distinctly remember is warming up outside between races and wondering if my season, and college career, was over. I wasn't sure

I'd be able to compete outdoors with the injury, and I didn't think it would heal quickly enough if I took an extended time off to run the last couple of meets. And even if it did heal by May 1, I wouldn't be in shape. It was a warm day for late winter and the sun was bright, but I didn't feel like sunshine. I went back inside the fieldhouse and ran a poor race to end my indoor season.

I decided to take a few days off after indoor district to see if my tendon would improve, but it didn't. The first outdoor meet was a little more than a week after the end of the indoor season at Rolla, where I ran the 800. My tendon was sore, and my speed was quickly diminishing because of my lack of fitness, but mostly because the injury prevented me from being able to sprint fast. Nonetheless, I actually ran faster than I expected, but finishing well back of the winning time of 1:54 with my own 1:58. Now, 1:58 is dead slow, but I thought I just might be able to take a few seconds off as the season progressed if I could work through the pain. I knew my normal kick was lacking and it wouldn't suddenly reemerge unless my tendon healed, and that wouldn't happen as long as I kept running. But I still might be able to run 1:54 through memory and strength. That kind of time never materialized but I was also concerned about the 1500m. I could run a decent 800 through familiarity, but the 1500 took more fitness, at least for me. I just didn't know if I had a good 1500 in me at that point, and the reason for running the 800 early was because Coach understood that as well.

Because we had encountered cold, bad weather in the previous few years going north for early season track meets, Coach Oz decided to travel south into Arkansas for a late March meet. The meet was held at Ouachita Baptist University, and I was entered in the 800. There were two heats and for some reason I was in the slow race. Although I hadn't done anything to warrant fast heat consideration in 1985, my past performances indicated that I should have been in the second race. Coach must have entered an incorrect time for me. But it didn't matter. Because I was in the slower of the heats, I went out hard in an attempt to run a fast time and place high. Even by the end of the first lap, which I hit in 56 seconds, I was slowing and feeling the pace. I led through 700 meters but was passed coming off the curve for the last straight. My legs were dead. I ran as hard as I could down the stretch and finished in 2nd with another 1:58. I don't know if I placed or not. I do know the second heat was faster, maybe 1:53, so I doubt I finished in the top six.

During spring break, I stayed on campus and tried to work hard while at the same time not making the tendon injury worse. I just couldn't find that happy medium. I ran one long run in a heavy cold rainstorm, which didn't do the injury any favors. I should have never gone out on the run in the first place in those conditions, but to be truthful, the tendon wasn't any worse the next day, although that's not saying much. On a Saturday meet at Flo Valley around mid-season, Coach told me it was time to try the 1500. I wasn't optimistic about running well. After all, I'd only been able to muster 1:58 800s during the outdoor season and they were difficult. Missouri Baptist had a good 1500m runner, but I didn't know that going into the race. In fact, although I raced him in cross-country and during indoor track, I only recognized his face but didn't know how good he was. He might have even beaten me in the indoor district mile, but I couldn't remember. I believe his name was Quirk, but I can't be sure. I followed him throughout the race, and the pace seemed reasonable.

As we came off the final curve, I went wide to pass and to use my speed to sprint away for the win. Of course, my speed was gone, so the final stretch was a struggle, although I wasn't in distress, I just didn't have a good kick. At one point, right before the finish, I thought I had him. I knew I was a couple of inches ahead, but as we leaned for the tape, it was too close to call. But I knew I'd been beaten. We were both credited with the same time of 4:00, but he won. I wasn't that disappointed because I didn't think I could come within 8 seconds of 4:00. And I wasn't tired. I knew I could run faster, but not the last 100 meters. My splits needed to be faster. The

Missouri Baptist runner was grateful to get the competition, and he was a nice guy. I just needed to find a way to beat him!

Two days later we were at Lincoln University for their evening meet. The University of Missouri brought along some runners, which could make the 1500m interesting. The metric mile started out fair but not overly fast. I still couldn't figure out my real fitness, and if a fast pace was best, or a moderate one, but at Lincoln I was content to follow close to the front. I think we hit 2:06 at the 800, and I felt pretty good. A lap later, as we passed 1200 meters, I was still fairly strong, but not really comfortable. But no one took off at that point and I was in 4th or 5th. During my junior year I would have been ready to pounce and might have done so already, but not in 1985. Coming off the last curve, from a slower third lap, the race began, and I was left behind. I was right there with 110 meters to the finish, but I didn't have a kick. And, unlike the previous meet where I ran 4:00, my legs were dead. Somehow, I managed to finish 5th, but I was almost completely spent. My head was pounding, and I could hardly hear.

The winner ran 3:55 with an outstanding last 100, and my 5th place time was 3:58.0. I was beaten by slightly less than 3 seconds, but it felt like a mile, especially because of how competitive I was most of the race. For the first time in my career, I missed a race. I was in the bathroom incapacitated trying to recover. I thought I was going to vomit, but I didn't. Since the races were so close together in this meet, when I finally emerged from the restroom, the athletes were lined up for the 800m. I missed the half.

In such a difficult time of my track career, and the end of my career to boot, I thought about what I had achieved and what I hadn't, and what I knew would not happen in college. It was disappointing that Coach hadn't taken me, and others who were deserving, to the NAIA Outdoor Nationals. But at the same time, the positive side was that I ended up being so much better than I could have ever imagined when I was in high school in Kansas. I thought about some of the guys who were on the cross-country and/or track teams who didn't make it. Some guys I remembered their names because they were on the team for a year or so, and others who couldn't cut the tough training. Even now, 40 years later I can occasionally see a face but it's usually only fleeting – and names? Forget it, because at that time I had no empathy for them for not sticking it out, so I didn't waste my energy trying to know their names or their short time on the team. Much of the time, most of us didn't even know they had quit. Maybe you would see one on campus and remembered that you hadn't seen them on the team for a few weeks or months. But I think many just left school at some point. I was too busy training and competing with my dedicated teammates to give a damn. Now, I wish I hadn't been that way. I wish I'd have been more supportive when they first arrived, but I was young and competitive and if they couldn't cut it, it wasn't my problem. I had plenty of good friends on the team who always stayed. And I think they felt the same way I did about those who just vanished into forgotten memory.

So, it was more than halfway through my fifth year, and it wasn't going to finish as I had hoped, but even in my injured state, I was still much better than I could have dreamed five years before. That gave me comfort and I planned to do my best the last few weeks and let the chips fall where they may on a good small college career. And maybe I could help some of the young runners on the team succeed. I asked myself a question – could I have made it at the Division I level, in a good Division I program? And I answered "yes!" Absolutely, I would have been a nice runner at that level, especially in track. I was OK, which was good enough for me.

Coach devised a good way I could help some of the young middle-distance runners on the team, and more specifically, Kenny Nobles and Tony Pate. For some reason, neither one had distinguished themselves yet. Kenny ran a 1:59 in high school and Tony's best 800 in high school was 1:56. They should have been running much faster than they were by this time of the season. And Kenny was a sophomore and should have been acclimated to Coach's system. But they hadn't even come close to 2:00 in college for the 800m. Kenny was an outstanding athlete who could have played college football or basketball. I think Kenny was the best all-around athlete on campus, and with his good speed should have been running 1:52 or faster his second year.

Coach had us run a series of 660s on the track and placed me 20 yards behind Kenny and Tony and told me to catch them and told them not to let me beat them. So, I ran 680 yards, although Coach timed me for a 660. I remember telling my teammates not to let me catch them on the first one, and they obliged. I ran 1:26 on the first and almost caught them, but they were able to remain ahead, although my time was faster. But both finished under 1:30, which is what they needed. All my 660s during that workout were 1:28 or faster, and I never caught Kenny and Tony. We ran the workout a couple more times and I always finished in the 1:26 to 1:28 range and might have even run one in 1:25. I don't think I ever caught either one of them, so they were running well, but it still didn't show in their race results.

We competed at the Washington Invitational in St. Louis, and I not only wanted to win the 1500 but also help Kenny and Tony run well in the 800. The meet was held at Ladue High School because the new WU track wasn't finished. Their old track that I had never raced on but did look at a couple of times was three-laps to a mile. Some of my teammates when I first arrived at SofO had competed on the odd track, where they held the track and field competition in the 1904 Olympics. The high school track was very nice, although it had seams that were beginning to separate and fold upward. But as long as one avoided a couple of places, falling could be prevented. In the 1500m I decided to go out conservatively and then attempt to run the second half faster, or negative splits. I didn't think there was anyone in the race to challenge me or at least run a hard early pace. Although the meet was held in St. Louis, Missouri Baptist, an area college, was not there, and I didn't notice any other teams with fast 1500 guys.

I thought about the 1980 Olympic 1500 that I watched on TV when the East German, Jürgen Straub led early in a slow pace and took off with about 700 meters out to steal the race. He took silver behind Coe but ahead of Ovett. Of course, my pace would be much slower, and my acceleration would not be nearly as potent, but to the competition in my race, my plan was that it wouldn't make a difference to them. I would still run away from the other runners. My plan worked perfectly as no one was willing to take the lead from me as I plodded away for the first two laps. But that changed at 800m. I tried to push from there and found I didn't have anything, but my saving grace is that no one else seemed to have anything in the tank either, or they were content to stay where they were and outkick me down the stretch. However, I did accelerate to a small degree and my last lap was fairly good, although clearly, at least to me, not spectacular. I did run negative splits, and my winning time was a respectable 4:06. But it was tied for my second slowest 1500m during my three years of college meets at SofO, even counting the outdoor miles, replacing the 4:03 I ran in 1983 at Rolla. The only time I ran slower was in '83 in the cold and wind at Northwest Missouri.

I was still very happy with the race because I had won, although I was also never challenged. Nonetheless, a win was a win, and I didn't seem to have much energy during the race. There was plenty of time between my first race and the 800m, so I decided that I would be recovered enough to help Kenny and Tony with their races. I told both that there was no logical reason why I should beat them, especially after I ran the 1500 and they didn't. I told them that I would set a pace for them, about 58 seconds at the 400, so they could be in a position the break 2:00. I told them I would try and keep up that pace as long as I could beyond the first lap to help them, but by 300 to go they needed to get by me and race each other home. They agreed that this was a good approach, and we set our sights on making sure the plan worked.

I was fine with sacrificing my race to help my teammates and it didn't matter anyway, as far as I was concerned, because I knew I was only good for one race a meet. At the break I settled into a comfortable pace, one that felt like a 58. Kenny and Tony stayed close as one runner steadily pulled away. I crossed 400 in 58, just as planned, and I was in second or third place, so Kenny and Tony were in a competitive position to get 2nd and 3rd if they stayed with me through 500 meters. But they began to fall back, so I slowed in an attempt to get them back with me. At 500m they fell back further but I didn't pick up the pace, hoping that one or both would start to accelerate. It never happened. At 600m I was in second and felt strong, so I ran to remain in that position.

The leader was much too far ahead to catch, but I didn't lose ground to him during the final half lap. I finished 2nd in a slow 1:58, behind the winner who crossed the finish line in 1:53. I was amazed that I wasn't tired and wondered how fast I could have run that day. I know I would not have won, but I could have remained with the leader for 600, and I do believe I could have run 1:55, but we'll never know. It's possible that I would have run slower than 1:58 if I'd attempted to stay with the leader because I think he hit 54 at the 400, and that might have deadened my legs with the 1500 in them. Nonetheless, I was happy with the race, at least my race, but disappointed I was not able to help my teammates.

The last meet of the season, and as it turned out, the last track meet of my career was District 16 hosted by Park College. My parents drove to the meet from southeast Kansas to the north side of Kansas City to see me run my last meet. The track had a black all-weather surface but there were virtually no stands or bleachers. Luckily, my parents had time to leave and buy lawn chairs. Coach greeted my mom and dad enthusiastically and at some point, told them he wished he had others like me because I was dedicated and worked as hard as anyone he had ever had. I appreciated the complement, and I did work hard and was dedicated, but I know he coached others through the years who were the same – but I doubt there were many. Although Fresh didn't compete as a senior I saw the same dedication from him. And I think Steve Davis did the same, but of course that was implanted in us from our years in two outstanding high school programs in the Southeast Kansas League!!

It's amazing how I could go from a track athlete in junior high who hated practice, to one that loved working hard and tried to outwork everyone. But it's probably not that uncommon. That's why, as a youth coach today, I'm patent with kids who don't work hard before they are 14, even though some have tremendous talent, because I know there is a chance they will become dedicated. I try not to push too much with the youngsters because that can really turn them off. And for the young kids who love to practice hard, I still don't push because I want them to continue to love the sport. Now, if they are 16 and older, then I will get on them because it's time to learn to work hard.

Early in the District Meet a huge thunderstorm rolled through with heavy rain and hail, with strong winds, so everyone took cover. The meet was delayed for quite a while and when it resumed the track, which didn't drain well, was full of water, especially the first two lanes. Although the storm cooled the temperature, the humidity rose, and when the sun popped through, the temperature climbed. But I wasn't bothered by this during my warmup for the 1500m. My goal was to win, but I knew it would difficult. Park had a runner, David More, to whom I had never lost, but he made the finals in the indoor national 1000 when I didn't and made All-American, and he was running well. And Quirk was there, who I think had run 3:55 during the season, along with his teammate Anthony Leaks, who was an outstanding 800m runner as well as a 400m hurdler. The 1500 was a little beyond Leaks' comfort zone, I think, but I knew he could run a good one. So, it appeared to me that there were four of us who had a realistic chance to compete for the victory.

The pace at the beginning was moderate and steady. However, the cool water on the track splashed up and tightened my calves, which in turn made my injured tendon sore. In fact, it began to hurt. But I wasn't about to slow down. I don't recall any of my splits in the race. I had asked Coach Oz if he would take me to Nationals, which was held in Michigan. He told me if the meet had been much closer, he probably would, but I needed to run 3:51 in order go this year. I knew that was out of reach, although I did consider going for it before the race began. But the bigger goal was to win. If I'd thought I had a realistic shot at 3:51, then I would have gone for it.

As the field approached the last lap the four of us that I thought would be in the lead were the only ones in contention. More was clearly stronger than the rest of us and he began to slightly pull away. I tried to go with him but just couldn't do it. He had come a long way since I had first raced him. With 300 meters to go, Quirk, Leaks, and I were racing for second place, and it was close. No one seemed to gain an advantage over the others. In my attempt to go with the leader, I had not been able to separate, and it's possible the two Missouri Baptist runners also tried to follow the Park athlete. As we rounded the last curve, I sensed that the other two were a bit in distress so I tried to attack coming off the curve, but I couldn't shake either one. I don't know if Quirk had more speed than me, but I know Leaks did even without my injury. But his natural speed wasn't helping him here. I could see as we ran three abreast that his legs were heavy, although my legs were heavy too. It must have been a site to see the three of us running side-by-side-by-side coming down the stretch with no one gaining an advantage. With about 20 meters from the finish line, I thought I had second place because I think I was a couple of inches ahead. But as in the Flo Valley meet, when we leaned, I was sure I was in third or fourth. It was so close I couldn't be sure if I was second, third, or fourth. When it was sorted out, I was given 4th place, and the three of us were timed exactly the same to the tenth. We ran 4:01 although I don't remember the tenths. The winner ran 3:57. I knew my place was correct and I think Quirk took 2nd. Of course, I was disappointed especially because my parents didn't see me win, but my memory of that race is positive, and I was proud to have raced Quirk and Leaks to the wire – the three of us ran great! And Leaks' athleticism was evident as were his guts.

Despite not winning, or even taking third, at least my parents saw me give everything I had. But I still had the 800 to run. There was plenty of time to recover between races, but since my fitness level was down, I wasn't sure I could run a good half after the hard 1500. I felt tired but relaxed as the 800 was about to start. This would prove to be my last track race and my last competitive race. I got lucky in the 800. First, most of the water was gone from the track and second, the pace was slow. And I wasn't about to push because my best chance to finish well was for the pace to lag. But it was also a catch 22. If I pushed the pace, I could take the legs from my competitors, and they wouldn't have a kick. But I wasn't fit enough to pull that off and my legs would be dead as well. If I allowed the pace to remain slow, then I would probably get out kicked. But I knew there were other strategies and the one that might work was to surprise the field at some point and steal the race before they could respond. This was not likely to work but it was my best chance to win.

After a slow first lap in about 60 seconds or a little faster, no one took the reins. This bode well for me as I remained just off the lead. Into the back stretch the pace didn't pick up. This surprised me because I was sure that someone would spurt to the lead. But in my condition, it was too early for me to make a move. Finally, just before the final curve with 210 meters to go I burst to the lead with everything I had. Ideally, I would have waited a bit longer before taking the lead, but that was not practical here because I needed to use the curve to my advantage. If the guys with the best speed were boxed in when I made my move, they would have to work out of that situation and move around others on the curve while I pulled away. This way I might have just enough of a lead coming off the curve to hold on. It was a good plan, but it didn't work.

I did get into the lead and held it more than halfway through the curve, but then I was passed by a guy in a purple singlet from Tarkio College. I held on to second through the curve, but then the flood gates opened, and guys went around me like I was standing still including Kenny Nobles. I think I ended up in 6th. Kenny placed 5th and the winning time was 1:58 by the Tarkio runner. I ran 2:01. There's no doubt I could have run 1:57 or 1:58 that day off a faster pace, but I wouldn't have placed any higher. The race turned out to be the best it could have been to give me the best shot at winning, I just couldn't pull it off. As it turned out, even if the best couple of kickers would have been boxed, others would have passed me. Of that I'm confident. I might have finished in 4th and at best 3rd. But I gave everything I had.

So, my college running career was over in May 1985. I could have achieved more, which is true for many, but accomplished much more than I ever could have realized when I graduated from high school in 1980. Is there a lesson? Absolutely!! You don't have to be a world-class athlete to be successful, and you don't even have to win most of your races. Just be as good as you can at that moment and work hard. I loved Coach Osburn, but sometimes it was a love, but never hate relationship. Maybe the best way to describe it was a love/frustration relationship. I don't coach like Coach Oz, and many things I learned about how to coach was by not emulating him. But he made me a very good small college runner despite the limitations in the training philosophy and the inconsistencies from week to week. And to be honest, when I arrived at SofO, I think my philosophy was similar. But as time went by, I changed my mind on what I thought would make me a better runner. Coach's approach of high mileage and tons of repeats allowed me to make huge strides, but I could only improve to a certain point. Then I needed a new approach to reach 3:43 in the 1500 or faster, and even as fast as 1:48 in the 800, times I believe at my core I could have run. But in the end, the only workouts that really hurt me were the Hollister steps.

From the outdoor 1500m and mile races I can remember running at SofO, including the summer meets, I had 18 wins and 6 loses, which included a 10-1 record in 1983. Of the six loses, three were second place finishes, one was 4th, and I had two in 5th place. So, while I didn't set the world on fire on the national scene, I was a damn good middle-distance runner in the small area in which I raced. And until Kenny beat me in that last 800, I never lost to a School of the Ozarks teammate on the track in a college meet. Mike defeated me in a summer meet 2-mile, but that was it. In high school I didn't win a single individual race after my sophomore year, not one! During my one year in junior college, I won once. So compared to my career before SofO, my running career at SofO was pretty good, which included one school record and two in which I finished my career as the second fastest in school history. Not too shabby for a slow 2:01 high school 800m runner.

I think the secret to success is persistence, just like the time in the mid-1960s when I finally caught a trout in that Arizona cement pond. If I worked hard enough and kept running races, eventually I'd catch that trout – I'd win a race and then another and then another. I ended up catching a lot of trout. And maybe a few of those dam runs helped! In the end, a career, no matter what it's in, doesn't need to be great to be meaningful, even if it's only meaningful to you. And the races against really good guys are memorable to me, and I remember many of them even if I can't quite recall some names. And most of those guys were like me in many ways – they loved the competition and had very little narcissistic tendencies. Adulation and recognition are great, but achieving something through hard work, no matter who notices, is more important and significant on the individual level. And I can live with that.

I was insecure on several levels when I was in college. In fact, I still am. I'm actually very confident in my track/running coaching ability and in my training program, which is always evolving. But I do have issues when others don't recognize my ability or question my training program. This is difficult for me to admit. I feel, sometimes, that I must justify my coaching approach, or who I am, even though I believe at the core that my training program is excellent. And I continue to grow. I speak with other coaches and talk with competitive and former competitive runners such as my old college friend, Steve Davis. And I've gotten to know CPT, Chaplain Shawn Found, who was an All-American at the University of Colorado in the early '90s, and a 28:30 10,000m guy on the track. It's amazing how much we are on the same page, and how much we have learned from our mistakes. And his wife, fellow Kansan Jennifer Found, who was a fantastic runner at Kansas State University, is a good sounding board as well. She coaches at one of the Little Rock private schools.

In college, I didn't know if I put energy into running because of insecurities, and I still haven't figured that out. I had times when I was extremely lonely, especially after Chris Marcak and Mike Heuton left school. I was not happy with Chris for leaving me there on my own, but I also never held it against him. Chris made the hall-of-fame at the school he transferred to, which I'm sure wouldn't have happened at College of the Ozarks. There are not enough track athletes in CofO's hall-of-fame. For me, the loneliness didn't last long as I became great friends with Mark Bollinger (a long-time coach who I bounce off ideas), and later Mark Adkerson.

But I was still insecure. Not so much about my running, because as time went on, I became more confident in my ability even if I never realized my full potential. But more so intellectually. I just didn't think I made the grade. I was intimidated by intellectuals, whether they were students or faculty. It took me years to realize that I was as smart as most – I can hold my own. Those old insecurities still rise to pinch me on occasion. In the end, maybe I'm not much different than millions of people. There are things about college I would change. Not incidents such as egging the school on Halloween, that's just young stupidity that has no lasting consequences (unless we would have been caught!). But how I treated a few teammates, especially the younger ones. I liked most of them, but I just didn't want them to beat me!

I'm also a reflective man. And I think about those who suffered so much more than I can imagine. I have no reason to complain. One such person was an old friend, who I never got to know really well, Darcy Wakefield. I got to know Darcy in 1988, when I interned at the Washburn-Norlands Living History Center in Livermore, Maine. Darcy was the granddaughter of Billie Gammon, an extraordinary woman in her 70s who was the founder and director of the Norlands. Billie and I became fast friends and as I reached my early 30s, she dreamed of me becoming the director of the Norlands, but it was not to be. Darcy was a smart girl, who in 1988 graduated from high school. Darcy and I got our picture in a local newspaper taken at the Norlands standing next to a yoke of oxen. I never saw Darcy again after my internship ended in late June. But Billie always told me what Darcy was up to, and she made Darcy aware of what I was doing.

Darcy loved to run. But several years later, while on a run, she realized something wasn't right. She was diagnosed with ALS. Billie kept me abreast with Darcy's condition and life. I decided to write Darcy and received a most wonderful letter in return. Her letter was so optimistic, and I just couldn't imagine that I would be that way if I was in the same situation. With ALS, Darcy had a baby, but she didn't live long after that. Still, she is such an inspiration. Billie died a few years later, and I miss her. Despite my insecurities, and regardless of what life has thrown my way so far, including not reaching the level of running I wanted, I can't fathom dealing with what Darcy experienced, or her family. It puts life into perspective.

And I've had a great life, and great family, and I've met wonderful people. And even those who were not so wonderful are still mostly positive experiences. By the way, you can read about Darcy and living with ALS in her book *I Remember Running: The Year I Got Everything I Ever Wanted - and ALS*, 2006.

Sometimes, I wonder what led me to become a competitive runner. Was it insecurities? Maybe. Was it because I loved it? Well, yes, eventually. But I didn't start out that way, at least when it came to training. I had to learn to love that, which took a few years. So why did I stick with the sport during those uncommitted years? I really don't know unless it was competition and accomplishment. That must be it because I always loved the competition – I loved to win!

Chapter 18
Rumblings

Those of us that are true track fans and participants (athletes and coaches) keep talking about the lack of popularity of our sport in the United States. But what do we do about it? Well, we run college meets with 8 heats of the 800m, for example, and most people don't want to sit through all of that. We call these heats "preferred" and "invite" and other names and even I don't understand what they mean and why athletes are entered in the heats in which they compete. Then there's the example of the 2016 Prefontaine Classic. There were a pair of Mile races contested. Both had outstanding fields. But there were also two high school sub-4 milers in the races, Andrew Hunter, and Michael Slagowski, and the meet director failed to place them in the same race. Instead, we got two good mile races, but we get good (and sometimes great, such as 2023!) races every year at Pre. But their dual would have been special. True, I don't know the circumstances that placed the runners in different mile races, but it seems to me the meet director could have run the kids together. And both young men did their jobs well – Hunter ran 3:58 in the featured Bowerman Mile, and Slagowski ran 3:59 in the National Mile.

In the United States, the track has increasingly become a fourth-rate sport – not only because of how it's covered and the interest from Americans but also because of how the sport is run or not run. For example, at the end of May 2017, the Pre Classic in Eugene, Oregon, was held on the same weekend as the two NCAA Regional meets. What idiot, or idiots, screwed that up? Let's go ahead and shoot ourselves in the foot. And the sport, at least in America, is close to shooting itself in the head. Drug scandals, poor sportsmanship (not necessarily from the athletes), and atrocious management are killing the sport here. However, there are terrific young athletes who deserve more from the sport's governing body and meet organizers and the NCAA. But what do I know? I was only a good NAIA runner who never climbed to the national class level. Foolish fighting within the organization and trivial bickering and power struggles seem to be the norm, and the welfare of the athletes is forgotten in the melee. In my old races, the 1500 and 800, American athletes such as Cole Hocker, Yared Nuguse, Hobbs Kessler, and Bryce Hoppel, as well as distance runner Grant Fisher, and all-American track athletes deserve more.

And the youth track is uneven at best. In Arkansas, USAT&F is weak for youth, with few meets. This is in a state where one of the most celebrated college track programs hails. The AAU has a number of meets, so many youth athletes belong to clubs that are members of that organization. I've carried cards from both organizations for a few years, although only sporadically with USAT&F. USAT&F needs to do a better job of promoting youth track evenly throughout the country and provide high-quality meets. This is indeed a difficult task because the organization relies on volunteers out of necessity. And many, if not most, of the volunteers, are dedicated to the sport and do a fantastic job – but there are not enough of them. However, the organization, run by adults, needs to put the young athletes first instead of fighting over power and prestige.

*

Unfortunately, this country suffers from a ton of bad high school coaches. Some don't get it, or they don't care. Others know the sport extremely well and have tremendous results but work the kids so hard that they are constantly injured and/or burned out before they get to college. Only a few kids can handle 80 to 110-mile weeks month after month. It's too damn much for the bodies of a high majority of 16- to 18-year-old kids. I believe in hard work for high school athletes, but not excessive miles for the sake of doing miles – these are just wasted miles, and for what? Injuries! At the same time, I've seen high school coaches put their distance kids on the track four or five days a week during January and February, running intense speed work and repeats. If they had any strength from cross-country, these kids lose it with this approach, and injuries are common as well.

I have met and witnessed more bad high school coaches over the years than I can count. And they're in colleges as well, even at the biggest, most successful schools. Luckily, I've seen a few outstanding high school and college coaches, and some coached me. And there are some outstanding coaches in central Arkansas. I've never met nor spoken with the great American Miler Steve Scott. But I have read his comments about his training philosophy at the former NAIA and now NCAA Division II school Cal State San Marcos. From what I have read, Scott has it right – he's figured it out, and I bet his athletes loved running for him. Although now retired from coaching, Steve Scott has a lot to teach us about training.

I also find coaches who don't see the world around them. It is not unusual, in my experience, to find coaches who don't recognize athletes from other teams and their accomplishments or have not paid attention to athletes outside the parameters of their interests. A few years ago, while talking with one of the most respected high school distance coaches in the area, I mentioned a kid who had recently run a 47 400m. This coach didn't have a clue who I was talking about despite the race taking place at a meet his team attended! And they had competed against that sprinter's high school team at several meets that year. His blinders restricted him to the 800-, 1600-, and 3200-meter races – too narrow for a track coach.

Some club coaches are pitiful as well, although most of the coaches on the club with which I was affiliated are good and have the kids' best interests in mind. That's why we joined in the first place. But we did have a coach for a single season who missed the boat on compassion, knowledge, and tact. A few years ago, we had a young man, a quarter-miler, who had been working hard during the summer to improve and become good enough to qualify for the AAU Junior Olympic Games. His best time was about 52.0, which was far behind our best 400 runner, whose best time was 47.1 (the athlete mentioned in the previous paragraph). We also had two other outstanding short sprinters that year, one who had best times of 10.48 and 21.11, both FATs, who ran on our 3:14 4x400 the year before. So, it was easy for our 52 kids to get lost in the shuffle.

In the national qualifying meet, he ran with extreme heart, and at the finish, he leaned so far to get second that he fell hard. But he finished second behind his teammate in a breakthrough 49.4. He was elated. Later in the 4x400, he ran the third leg in 49.9 and handed off to our outstanding anchor in 2nd place, but well behind the leading team. Our "one-year coach" immediately began to berate and criticize our third leg for not being closer to the lead. He asked him several times, "why did you do [name of the fourth leg] that way?" This kid had just lowered his PR in the 400 by close to 3 seconds and followed it up with a sub-50 leg, and he was being beaten over the head with a severe scolding. One of our good sprinters, running the first leg, had a leg injury and could not run a fast leg, so the team was far behind when our new sub-50 kid got the baton. The second place for the relay was no one's fault; they ran well under the circumstances. My wife, son, and I took the kid to the meet and back home. When we stopped to eat on our return, I could tell he was distraught. He was a person who didn't say much, but he did open up about what the coach had done to him, which I had witnessed. I told the athlete not to worry about what that coach said, but he still hurt.

Un-invited: a few short years ago, a local, small, private 1A team was uninvited to a high school track meet because they didn't have enough athletes. They competed in the meet the year before but not in 2019. One of the kids in the school competed for my track club, and he had a great shot at winning the 1600m and possibly the 800. The winner ran 4:56, second place was over 5 minutes, and the runner who finished in 6th ran in the mid-5:20s. So, it was slow. What difference did it make if the kid came from a small school with few athletes? Our kid was good enough – he ran 4:43 that year. And even if he wasn't good enough to win, why not allow him to run? After all, some kids from the bigger schools barely broke 6 minutes. So, there wasn't a time requirement. I don't know how to respond to this other than to say it's bizarre and asinine. Why do we constantly kick ourselves in this sport? Nothing good came out of this decision. All it did was deny a few high school kids the opportunity to compete in a local meet. So, the school replaced that meet with one the next week, which was much further away.

At a 2021 meet with all large schools, a kid in my club, competing for his high school team, ran a terrific 800m. He was in 4th place with 300m left and then moved up, just as we discussed. He has good speed, and this was his first race of the year, but he ran like he was in top form. Coming off the last turn, he went wide to pass for the lead and was able to get maybe a yard between him and the runner in the second position. Then, the runner in the second made one final push. Thrillingly, as the two athletes hit the finish line, it was not clear who won. I couldn't tell from my position. About 5 minutes after the race, I asked our kid what place he got and if he knew the final time. He wasn't told. Later in the evening, long after the meet ended, I texted him, and he still didn't know his time or if he had won. Twenty-four hours later, we didn't know if he was first or second, and what time he ran – the results weren't posted! What are we doing when an athlete doesn't know if he won and doesn't know his time?

*

Cheating in track and field, especially doping, has become an epidemic in the sport. Some can deny it, but they have their heads in the sand. I remember Frank Shorter taking the silver medal in the 1976 Olympic Marathon. I don't remember his Munich win, but I knew he was the defending Olympic champion and favored to win in Montreal. Now, it's not unusual for elite runners to fade in races even when they are in top condition, and it's fairly common in the marathon, a race of 26 miles that can be extraordinarily fickle. But Shorter ran a great race. I thought something wasn't right at the time, even though I was only 14. I couldn't put my finger on it, but something was off. Over the years, Shorter has indicated that he thinks the East German Gold Medalist was blood doping. The man was an unknown and had just run away from Shorter with a few miles to go. And I don't think this is sour grapes on the part of Shorter. He won Olympic Gold in 1972 – taking Sliver in '76 doesn't tarnish his legacy one iota. And even though I possess no evidence, I believe Shorter is 100% correct. Anyway, it's my first understanding that performances could be improved in the laboratory. In high school, our track coach talked a couple of times about weight guys taking steroids while he was a track runner in college, but I wasn't quite sure what that meant other than it made them throw their implements further and shrink a certain part of their anatomy.

*

I have become increasingly dismayed by the lack of understanding of the sport by those who should know better. Sometimes, I'll hear criticism from coaches or others at youth meets who talk about how a race or the individuals in the race were somehow not worthy because the times were slow. And I'll sometimes admit that a race wasn't very fast, but I won't criticize the kids running the race because they didn't live up to some artificial standard. Sometimes, the criticism comes from someone fast and views races from their elite prism, but they were never a world record holder, so someone was still faster. Others criticize those who never tried training and competing, and if they did, they weren't very good, which means they were criticizing themselves. Either way, they don't credit the kids for their hard work. Not all kids have the potential to be great athletes, but they can still work hard and compete the best they can.

A few years ago, I was told by a current college coach that my fastest 1500 was a good time for a small college runner in its day, indicating that it wouldn't hold up today. Good for its day? I've looked up plenty of results for NAIA, as well as NCAA Division II and III competitors, and my 1500 would be pretty damn competitive today. And this coach didn't have a 1500 runner even close to my times! In an unsophisticated look at the 2017 NAIA and Division III conference meets, I found only two or three who ran faster than my best 1500. Of course, this does not mean they didn't run good times in the metric mile in other 2017 meets, but one can get a good indication of the quality of runners.

We didn't have a conference meet in track, but my best time in the district meet was 4:01, which I did twice – winning in 1982 and 4th in 1985. In '82, the objective was to win, just as many who won their races in 2017, and the time was irrelevant. In '85, I was just trying to keep up! So, times are slower in championship meets on many occasions. But I would have won most of the races in today's small college conferences. Were Jim Ryun's 3:51 miles in 1966 and 1967 only good for the day? No. These times are good today as well. Plus, his 3:51s and a 3:33 1500, all world record times, were run mostly on his own on cinder tracks. But there are those who dismiss his accomplishments as good races in a by-gone time. In my opinion, Ryun would have run at least 3:45 today in the mile and 3:27 in the 1500m. He would be one of the best today, and I doubt it would even be close (although Ingebrigtsen, Hocker, Kerr, and Nuguse probably have already made me eat my words!). Jim Ryun is one of the few Americans to win an Olympic medal in the 1500 when he took the silver in 1968, and it took 7,000 ft. altitude to beat him. And that's not to say he would have beaten Matthew Centrowitz in 2016, but it would have been a great race – although it was still a great race.

Let's look at Matthew Centrowitz. Although one can never argue that Centrowitz was as dominant as Jim Ryun, at least for a couple of years, he has been pretty darn good. I've heard some say he got lucky winning the 2016 Olympic gold medal in the 1500 because the pace was so slow, and he only ran 3:50.0 to win, which somehow cheapens the accomplishment. Lucky? You've got to be kidding me. It was an exciting race, and I think it would have been easier to win at a fast pace. The hardest type of race for him to win, probably for any of the competitors for that matter, was the pedestrian pace they ran. The pace might have been easy, but the race was not. Nonetheless, it makes many of us feel better about our competitive records.

Centrowitz was not some Johnny-come-lately. He barely missed a medal in the 2012 1500 at the London Olympics and medaled in the World Championships. He was a seasoned competitor when he toed the line of the Olympic 1500 in Rio and was primed to take a medal. The bottom line? Centrowitz ran a great race, leading from beginning to end, in one of the toughest types of races to win! There was nothing pedestrian about the last 500 meters. He earned it! Give him credit.

*

USA Track and Field needs to step up to the plate and do something in the best interest of the athletes and the fans. It reminds me of the old AAU when that organization managed track in this country as a dictatorship. Instead of looking out for the athletes, that organization looked out for itself or the leaders for themselves. And it seems that is what USAT&F is doing today. The organization needs to take the high road and bring in caring leaders. The organization circles the wagons and becomes defiant. Athletes need to rebel, and some have tried, but it won't get better unless the mass of them does it. It will take some high-profile athletes in high-profile events to protest, but most are treated better, so they don't seem interested in helping those below them and improving the sport. As long as they have it good, they won't reach out to help, and I can't blame them. And their shoe companies might drop them as well. But if they are one of the best, another shoe company should pick them up.

And what about the shoe companies and the shoe wars. If a shoe company based in the United States sells me a pair of shoes made in some far-away land and claims it's an American product, it's lying – it's a foreign shoe. If I want a foreign shoe made by a foreign company, then that's what I'll buy. I have a hard time believing that a shoe manufactured by an American company with cheap labor from Asia is going to be the same quality of that same shoe made in America. A company can slap its logo on a pile of dog shit and call it their new training shoe, but I know better, I can smell the stench.

Track athletes need a way to make a better living. It seems that there is a lot of potential in the country that is never fully realized because athletes can't make enough money to remain active in the sport. Only the top athletes can make enough money, and many of them don't either. A distance runner might take a few years to mature into a great runner on the international stage but without the support early in a career when the times and race results are not superb, that athlete may have to get out or turn exclusively to road racing, which can be a good option, but doesn't do much for track and field. For distance runners, it would be nice to see a cross-country series as well, with sponsorship and money. Unfortunately, track and field athletes in some events don't have opportunities to make a living in the sport no matter how good they are. Shot putters and hammer throwers, for example, don't have the same chance to succeed as sprinters and 1500m runners. It's not a level playing field, and I doubt it is between men and women either. In March 2024, eight runners, led by Grant Fisher and Nico Young, broke the 27:00 barrier in a 10,000 race at a track meet in the United States. That's phenomenal. And how many of those eight are making multi-millions from track and field?

One thing USAT&F has done is create coaching certification. I was mostly against this when it was first started, but it can be a very positive experience, and it can help the level of track coaching in the country. I went through the Level 1 course, and it was a very informative experience. I'd like to advance to Level II, but as a part-time coach, I can't afford to take the time off to travel across the country. There are very few Level II classes offered, and none in my area. It's as if USAT&F doesn't want coaches to take the Level II course. Since COVID, these courses have gone online, and that helps. But nothing beats being in the presence of good coaches who teach well and being around the coaches taking the course. I emailed USATF at one point to get information about the Level II course because my Level I expired during COVID, but I never received a response.

*

There's a certain air that has developed among young white American male distance runners. They see themselves as superior to those who don't do what they do, especially other track and field athletes and those who compete in other sports. The reason, as far as I can determine, is that they don't think others are worthy because they don't understand the distance running culture and they don't believe other athletes work as hard. But they also look down upon young distance runners who are slow. Although I can't confirm this outright, I don't think this attitude is prevalent among the world class American distance runners. It seems to be good high school and college distance runners, and it's embarrassing! It's possible that I'm wrong, but I don't remember this culture when I was a high school and college runner. There was most certainly a distance running culture, but it was not condescending, as I remember.

403

The culture that was developed by Frank Shorter, Bill Rodgers, and other distance runners of their generation seemed to be inclusive and encouraged others to run for fitness no matter how well they ran. As much as I love middle-distance and distance running, I'm not in love with the current culture. Interestingly, I don't feel this with women distance runners. But among the male of the species, especially the 1500m runners and up, it's not an endearing trait. When Kenny Moore wrote those great stories for *Sports Illustrated*, I never got the sense that he was writing exclusively for the distance running elite. No, he was writing for the general audience, and it worked – we were all in!

Several years ago, while I was teaching at Minot State University in northwest North Dakota, I attended the first cross-country race that year, which was a home meet. A couple of the athletes were in my classes, and I wanted to watch them and their teammates. Plus, I enjoy cross-country meets. When I arrived, it was pointed out to me that three or four young men working at the finish line area were former Minot State cross-country runners whose team had been outstanding. During the men's race I was out on the course and didn't see the finish, so as I made my way back to the finish line after the race, I asked a couple of people if they knew the winning time, which they didn't. As I passed by the finish line, I saw the former Minot State runners under a tent and decided to ask them the winning time since they worked the meet. When I approached and asked them my question, it's as if I entered a sacred zone and the smugness was thick. One, who was either sitting or leaning on a table with his arms folded, looked at me with a grin of distain and finally answered with a condescending tone. That's the attitude I'm speaking about. Thank goodness the rest of my experience as a visiting professor at MSU was great!

During the women's race I was close enough to the finish to see the winner cross the line. I think she was from the University of Mary. After she finished, she walked by me, and I told her she ran a great race. She said thanks and seemed generally happy someone she didn't know acknowledged her performance. A few years ago, I was working the long jump at an AAU youth meet in Arkansas. One of the competitors was Jarrion Lawson from Texarkana, Texas, who went on to the University of Arkansas and finished 4th in the Olympic long jump in 2016. On this particular day, he won easily in a horrible and dangerous pit. His winning jump was 23 feet and change, not one of his best days. After the competition was over, I told him he was the best high school long jumper I'd ever seen and that his 23-foot jump in this dangerous pit was great. He was very appreciative of my comment. And what do Lawson and the young lady from the University of Mary have in common? Neither are young white men who run distance.

Having said that, in the AAU youth track and field world, at least where I'm at, distance runners are treated as second-class citizens. Sprinting is king around here. In most of the meets, sprinting is good in all the age groups, but we only see a few good distance runners, and by the time the kids reach the 15-16 division the good distance runners quit AAU. If you look at the 17-18 Junior Olympic records from the national meet, they go back to 1980, my senior year, which is the first year the meet went to meters. The 800 records from 1980, was finally broken in 2012, and the 1500m from 1980 still stands. The 3000m record is from the early 1980s and it's not nearly as fast as the 8:46 two mile from 1979.

Conversely, the national high school records for the same distances are more recent, and the depth of high school times in these races are as good as they have ever been. I love the sprints too and think the 400 is one of the great races. I also enjoy the field events. But I want to see some emphases placed on the middle-distance and distance races as well. In this area, USAT&T Junior Olympic competition is not any better for the distances.

*

I think I'm showing my age. I've noticed that many of today's youth demonstrate a complete lack of respect for adults, and it's gotten worse over the years, at least as I see it. Of course, I see my generation as having a much better rapport with adults, although we were told by adults that our generation had gone to the dogs. My memory has probably faded. I suspect that plenty of kids from my era disrespected older folks, too. Having said that, I do think it has worsened. A few years ago, we took our cross-country kids to the track to run a time trial about 10 days before our first meet. When we began to line the team up, the cheerleaders ran onto the track to run a couple of laps. I asked them if they could run in the outside lanes because we were timing our kids. The lack of respect and disdain that was shown to me and the cross-country team was apprehensible. I asked them again, this time indicating that they should get out of lane one, but it didn't work. After four or five times, I finally had to yell at them; some still didn't leave the inside lanes, and one even yelled at me. They were determined to defy me. The football team was practicing on the field, and one of the coaches went over to them and said they needed to listen to me. When I later spoke with the coach, I indicated that sometimes my temper gets the best of me (not one of my good traits!). He said he completely understood and that because the cheerleaders were not familiar with me, they tended not to respect my authority. What a crock, although he is completely correct in his assessment. Nonetheless, it should not have made a difference. This was my third season as coach of the cross-country team, and those girls saw me out there with the team on a daily basis.

Even with my team, I see something that bothers me. I can't put my finger on it, and it's not necessarily a lack of respect because I think I have that, but there is a passiveness to my instructions. I have to get on them for not listening, and many have the attention span of a gnat. Less than two weeks before the first meet, I hadn't named a boy's captain because my juniors and seniors had not demonstrated much leadership. Kids show up for practice when they want and

406

don't when they don't want to be there. Some wonder why they don't perform well in races, and others don't understand that to get better, one must try to improve by practicing and not walking for most of the workout. Others just don't think about it. I created a team contract for every team member to sign, along with their parents, and I even signed it because I have obligations and the team should have certain expectations from me, but I'm not sure it's working. I love the kids and am trying to build a cross-country culture in the school district.

*

It's a natural inclination to move kids up to the next distance, such as making a 1500 kid a 3000m runner. But I don't think that's always for the best. Nonetheless, it's not always a bad idea, especially for those who run shorter distances. Almost all sprinters want to run the 100m, and my college teammate, Willie Williams, didn't even like running the 200m. But if a kid continually finishes back in the pack in the short sprints, maybe the 400 is the key. I don't find that most kids want anything to do with the 400m. But why finish 7th every week in the 100m when it's possible for a top three finish in the one-lapper? Some parents want their kid to be the fastest sprinter but won't accept that their daughter or son isn't quite fast enough. If that 14-year-old kid moves up to the 400 and, with work, becomes a good quarter-miler, then why not make the change? And that young athlete can continue to compete in the 100 and 200-meter races.

Sometimes, these kids become good short sprinters after competing in a long sprint for a couple of years. Some parents have the invalid impression that moving up in distance will somehow take speed away from their kids. In other words, they will become slower. Of course, this is a fallacy. We had a kid on our track club a few years ago who was not a fast sprinter in his youth. So, he moved to the 400 around the age of 11. By the time he was 16 years old, he ran a

47. The quarter gave him strength, and his high school 100 and 200m times were outstanding.

For kids who run distance, I believe it can be beneficial to start out with the 3000m and then let them move down as they get older. It's not uncommon for a male runner to move down to the 800 and be a good half-miler by 17 or 18 years of age after running longer races in the preceding years. A year or so after I graduated from college, a two-miler from my high school was moved down to the 800 during his senior year by my old coach, Riley Cartwright. If the kid broke 11:00 as a junior, then it was just barely. But as a senior, he ran a 1:59.0 800m and even qualified for the State Meet in the 400m. Obviously, Coach Cartwright noticed something in this kid, and after two years of finishing back in the pack over 8 laps, he became the best half-miler in the Southeast Kansas League. But I don't think those two seasons as a distance runner were a waste. Those years gave him the strength to run one and two laps well. I'm sure after a couple of years of racing eight times around the track, two laps seemed easy!

*

At the 1978 Kansas State Track and Field Meet, I watched several events, including the 2-mile run. In 1979, my teammate, Brad Burkes, qualified for State in the 2-mile, just as he did in '78. But when we arrived, we found out that he was competing in a race called the 3200 meters. What the hell was a 3200? Well, it was 8 laps on a 400-meter track, and we were told it was around three and a half seconds faster than a 2-mile race. And to top that off, Brad wasn't going to run in the *Mile*! Instead, he was racing in something they were calling the 1600 meters. What, no Mile? This was purely un-American. The powers that be who made the decision to do away with the mile and 2-mile would have been blacklisted in the early 1950s – it seemed like a communist plot! What I didn't know then was that this was a national trend as more tracks being built were going away from the imperial distance of 440 yards to the international distance of 400 meters. And this needed to happen, in my opinion. After all, the 400 meters and 800 meters are actual international and Olympic distances. But 1600 and 3200?

It didn't take me long to realize, and I have not changed my mind, that the conversion to 1600 and 3200 from the mile and 2-miles was caused by laziness. That's right, pure laziness. It was easier to run the traditional four and eight laps on 400-meter tracks from the same start and finish line. But it wouldn't have been hard to move the starting line 30 and a half feet behind the finish line, and you would have the actual mile. They were doing this in Europe all the time. And if there was an absolute need to go to meters, then why not the 1500 and 3000? These are real international events. I think the fear was that Americans wouldn't understand those races. So, let's just keep the traditional four and eight laps because they are familiar, even though they are not the real mile and 2-mile distances, but instead some bizarre "invented" races to make us feel good about ourselves. But it didn't really work, at least at first. Our hometown newspaper indicated that Brad took 3rd in the 1600m at 9:37. But to be honest, I could see why the sports editor got the 1600 and 3200 confused. He had never heard of these races either, and he did understand track.

Quit being lazy and go back to the damn mile and 2-mile!! We don't have to revert to the 880, 440, and 220. Keep the meter equivalents because those are real race distances. In 1979, the first year Kansas went to meters, I remember looking over the meet program and seeing the state meet record in the mile for the big schools. It was 3:58 by the great Jim Ryun in 1965. The winning time of the 1600m for class 6A in '79 was 4:15, a pretty good time. When I looked at the program at the 1980 Kansas State Track meet, I noticed that the meet record for the 6A 1600 was 4:15. What happened to Jim Ryun? Was he now irrelevant? What happened to Ryun's 3:58 mile? How do you erase his great race? As I continued to peruse the program, I found that Ryun and all others who held state meet records in the running events in all classes were relegated to the back pages – the records were retired – they no longer mattered. Since the length of the track didn't impact the field events, those records remained. That was fine if a time from 1979 legitimately broke a record. For example, the winning time in the 1A 1600 was 4:15 and clearly broke the old mile record, which I believe was 4:20.

*

A few years ago, there was a movement in Europe to erase all world records that still stand, which were set before 2005. Apparently, blood samples from that year forward have been kept so they can be re-tested as screening techniques become more sophisticated. I have no doubt that some of the records set in the late 20th century were done under the influence of performance-enhancing drugs, and I would love to see a clean sport. But I'm sure other records set before 2005 were clean performances. It's asinine to take away records by association – in this case, associated with a timeframe before 2005. Take the records before that year and accept them as is. Someday, they will all be gone through new performances. With this new proposal, would it mean that if an athlete set a world record before 2005, whether it still stands or not, that person would not be officially recognized as a former world record holder? Now, I see that they might go back to 1992 when out-of-competition testing began. Still asinine, though.

What do we tell Ron Clarke, or Evelyn Ashford, or Mac Wilkins, or Steve Ovett, or Jane Frederick, or Bob Beamon, or Walter Schmidt, or Anne Smith, or Henry Rono? Do we tell Ingrid Kristiansen, Colette Besson, Filbert Bayi, Peter Snell, Emma George, Fernando Mamede, and Rafer Johnson that they never actually set and held world records? And what do we say to Roger Bannister's family? We know we've been saying for 70 years that he was the first to break 4:00 in the mile, but we won't admit that anymore. That has been stricken from history; it never happened. Now, if 2005 is used, Elkanah

Angwenyi is the first sub-four miler. And sorry, John Walker, but the first sub-3:50 mile was accomplished by Daham Bashir.

And what about all those who won gold, silver, and bronze in the Olympics? Never happened. The first Olympiad of the modern world was held in 2008 in the city of Beijing. Beginning in 2004 and working back, all who won medals will have to return them and have the record wiped from the books. And don't worry about the medals; we'll just melt them down and use the material for new Olympic medals. What about national records? Will the US keep Mike Powell's long jump record, or does he lose it along with his world record? It all sounds absurd. Surely, no one will erase the World Championship and Olympic results. But I never thought there would be talk of washing away our history of the sport's world records. It has been a while since I've heard the conversation to remove records.

*

From the youth level, through high school and college track and field and running, and into the senior level, on the National and World track and field stage, the sport is suffering, and we only have ourselves to blame. We don't do much to foster a changing sport to make it nationally and internationally viable. At the Rio Olympics, there were so many empty seats for track that I thought they had forgotten to open the gates. I recently watched a track meet on TV, and I think 5 events were televised. It was the most boring meet I've ever seen. I know I complained about meets that are too long with multiple heats of 800s, 1500s, and even 100s, and I've attended youth meets that last more than 8 hour – much too long. But at the Diamond League meets, only a handful of events are contested. A full contingent of events, both men and women, are needed. The meets would not last very long, especially if there were only one heat for each event.

This sport has so much potential, and yet we continue to throw it under the bus and then run over it, over and over. I have thought the Kansas High School State Track Meet is too large, but the state must be doing something right. Look at a photo of the meet held at Cessna Stadium at Wichita State (although it's being replaced), and you'll find thousands of people in the stands, on both sides of the track. Sure, many are athletes, coaches, and parents, but there are tons of others there as well. I remember the first time I ran at the Kansas State Meet in 1979. Sure, I didn't run well, but the atmosphere was unbelievable. And in 1980, my second year, the crowd gave me a shot of adrenaline, and I ran great. What a feeling. I wish we could bottle and release that environment at all meets in this country and worldwide.

*

Let's end with something positive. At a USAT&F Level 1 coaching clinic, I met a kindred spirit in Tom Schexnayder. Tom, who coached high school track and cross-country at E.D. White Catholic High School in Thibodaux, Louisiana, was a track athlete at School of the Ozarks and ran for Coach Oz just as I did. He finished in 1977, and my last competitive year was 1985, so we were never teammates. But we both loved Coach Oz and separately, trying to get track and field restarted at our alma mater. In addition, we were both involved in getting the school records up-to-date and recognized. We didn't know the other was doing the same. Getting to know Tom has helped me revise my enthusiasm for the sport.

Postscript

John Johnson and I were very close and good friends and remained close for several years. I served as his best man at his wedding in 1985. In 1993, I moved to Des Moines, Iowa, and John visited me and Alice right before we moved. We stayed in contact for about a year, and then he must have moved because when I wrote, the letter was returned. Over the years, I attempted to find him, but locating a person with the name John Johnson is difficult. My sister thought she found him on Facebook a few years ago, but I could never connect with him. Then, in June 2017, while doing a casual check to see if I could again find him, I must have used the right combination of search words because I finally located John. Unfortunately, I found his obituary from October 2015. I was devastated. John was one of the best friends I ever had. I held out hope that someday I would be able to find him and renew our friendship. I have reconnected with his mother and found that he served in Iraq while in the Army. There was a time when John, Hando and I were inseparable. It has been 45 years since Brad Strathe, Hando, John, and I took 2nd at the State Meet in the 4x800, but that time is still the Parsons High School record. And John's 1:55.9 in the 800m also remains the school record. Hando's fastest 2-mile is the second fastest on the track in school history. My memories are good.

In the summer of 2019, Coach Barcus was diagnosed with pancreatic cancer. I found out in September. I immediately called him. Over the years, I called Coach many times and tried to visit him when I was at Parsons. In October, I returned to Parsons with my son, and Ryan and I visited Coach. He was in good spirits, and we had a great conversation. I never saw him again, but I still called Coach Barcus throughout the first half 2020. COVID-19 made it difficult during the spring because he couldn't have visitors, but I kept in touch. I last spoke with Coach in June, and a couple of weeks later, he passed away. Coach Barcus had a tremendous positive influence on my life, as he did for countless others. Two of them were Coaches Cartwright and Coach Billions. Coach Cartwright died in 2024, and Coach Billions passed away in '23. Coach Turner (Teach) passed away in 2024, as did my father. Coach Osburn died several years ago. I'm now in my 60s, and it's difficult to think about those mentors who are no longer here. But, at the same time, their positive influence remains with me today.

Photo Gallery

When I was a cowboy, 1963. Possibly at Griffith Park.

Another pitch over my head, 1973.

At the SMS Relays, 1982.

My first trophy, Fall 1980.

Winning the 800 at the Lawrence Open at the University of Kansas, July 1982.

The Outlook, November 17, 1982, page 4

: ix Bobcat Country runners recently qualified for the National meet, to be held in Wisconsin on Saturday. Several hundred runners will be competing in the event from across the nation. (Photo by Bruce McAtee)

Raymond Screws, former Parsons High School runner, was a member of the cross country team at the School of the Ozarks in Point Lookout, Mo. He qualified for the National Association of Intercollegiate Athletics championships, held in Kenosha, Wis.

NATIONALS 1982

AROUND 210 OF 440
                    RUNNERS

Southwestern Runner Takes 1st in NAIA Race

11-20-82

Associated Press

KENOSHA, Wis. — Steve Delano of Southwestern College won the men's 8,000-meter race in 25 minutes and one second Saturday at the National Association of Intercollegiate Athletics cross country championship meet at Wisconsin-Parkside.

Delano, a native of Winfield, was pushed by Southwestern teammate Mike Lambing, who finished third in 25:23.

Canada's Simon Frazier University, with three runners finishing among the top 10, won the team championship. Simon Frazier outscored Saginaw Valley, Mich., 49-167. Placing in the top 10 for Simon Frazier were Mike Maraum, fourth, 25:25; Bill Britten, fifth, 25:25; and Roth Chilton, ninth, 25:33.

Katie Webb won the women's 5,000-meter race in 17 41 to lead Marquette to the women's team title. Marquette beat runner-up Wisconsin-Eau Claire, 48-109, for the championship. Wisconsin-Eau Claire was paced by Deanna Marchello, who finished second in 17:53.

Men's 8,000—1, **Steve Delano,** Southwestern, **25:01.** 2. Don Stearns, stern Oregon State 25:07 **3, Mike Lambing, Southwestern, 25:23.** 4. consin-Eau Claire, 17:53 3. Carolyn Shield Mike Maraum. Simon Frazier 25:25. 5. Bill ten, Simon Frazier 25:25. 6. Ben San- sal. New Mexico Highlands 25:38 7 nnie Parks, Central State Oklahoma 25:32 8 Dave Wolff Wisconsin-Stout 25:33 9 Roth Chilton, Simon Frazier 25:33 10 Steve Guymon, Oklahoma Chris- tian. 25:35.

Men's team scoring—Simon Frazier 49 Saginaw Valley Michigan 167. Wisconsin- La Crosse 169. New Mexico Highlands 181 Willamette 211. Malone 222. Moore- head State 231. Wisconsin-Stout 252. Ad ams State (defending champion) 254. 261 Western Washington 324

Women's 5,000—1 Katie Webb. Mar- quette 17 41 2. Deanna Marchello. Wis- Wisconsin-Eau Claire 17:56. 4. Kriss Durdy. Pacific Lutheran 18:02. 5. Diane Held. Marquette, 18:22. 6. Karen Rudd, Si- mon Frazier, 18:24 7 Kathy Keller. Port- land 18:25. 8. Lesha Wood Emporia State 18:28. 9. Terry Mathinson. Portland, 18:32 10 Denise Falzone. Adams State, 18:32.

Women's team scoring—Marquette 48. Wisconsin-Eau Claire 109 Simon Frazier 128 Adams State (defending champion) 131. Pacific Lutheran 134 Portland 141 Moorehead State 164. Wisconsin-Parkside 239, Midland Lutheran 242. Jamestown 291

Runners win spots at Nationals

Six members of the S of O Cross Country team will be going to the National meet at the University of Wisconsin at Parkside on November 20. Cheryl Smith, Linda Roberts, Terrie Camden, Chris Mar- cak, Ray Screws, and Mike Heuton had to compete in the District meet in order to make it to the National meet.

Cross Country Coach Robert Osburn stated, "They've worked very hard and certainly deserved it." Osburn explained that the team had to train hard in order to make it to the National meet. On regular work hours the students ran 10-12 miles a day and also did more running on their own. There will be an estimated 400 participants in the men's race and 300 par- ticipants in the women's race. The first 25 runners at the National meet will be named "All-American."

Cheryl Smith said "I run because I really like to run and to glorify God," she added "I feel great about qualifying for Nationals and I hope I am able to glorify God whether I win or not." Smith also said that she ap- preciated her coach and learned a lot from him. Ter- rie Camden stated, "I've been running Cross Country for three years and this is

Nationals and I've been look- ing forward to it." Linda Roberts remarked, "I felt I accomplished something over all in running the races and I'm really looking for- ward to going to Nationals."

The three men were very glad to be going to Na- tionals also. Mike Heuton said, "I dreamed about going and it finally come true." Ray Screws stated, "When I was running the District in the last mile I was hurting but I thought about the Na- tionals and that kept me go- ing since I was in good posi- tion to be in the Nationals." Chris Marcak came in first place in the District meet. Marcak said that the com- mon goal for the team was to make it to Nationals and he

417

1On a run in 1981, Acacia Club Road. L to R: Darren Wickliff, Steve Davis, me, Chris Marcak

School of the Ozarks Track Team, 1983. I'm third from left, back row.

With Mike Heuton, March 1983. Set School Mile Record, 4:18:3.

My Cross Country picture, 1982.

4-4-79

FIRST AT THE FINISH — Raymond Screws of Parsons breaks the tape to complete a winning effort in the Class 5-A two-mile relay by the host team in Wednesday's invitational meet here. At left, in the center of the track is Jeff Norris of Labette County of Altamont, the third-place finisher. Parsons runners who carried the baton before Screws were Buster Fuentez, Louis Greaves and Mike Butler.

Winning the 2-mile relay at the Parsons Invitational, 1979.

Summary

Team scores — Southern Arkansas 146, Arkansas Tech 118, Central Arkansas 85, Harding 51, College of the Ozarks 51, School of the Ozarks 39

400 Relay — Southern Arkansas, 41.19 (new meet record); Arkansas Tech; School of the Ozarks.

1,500 — Screws, SofO, 3:57.96; Dietz, ATU; Tate, CofO

110 HH — Franklin, ATU, 14.55 (new meet record); Roberts, UCA; Linn, ATU

High jump — George, SAU, 6-10 (ties meet record); Crott, CofO; Douglas, CofO

Long jump — Epps, SAU, 20-0 ½; Hensen, UCA; Hagen, ATU

400 — Hagen, ATU, 48.28 (new meet record); Glass, SAU; Bland, SAU

Discus — Force, SAU, 151-6; Card, SAU;

Please see TECH on Page 2B.

TECH

Continued from Page 1B.

Teague, Harding

Triple jump — George, SAU, 45-0; Epps, SAU; Hensen, UCA

100 — Williams, CofO, 10.53; Woodbury, SAU; McCoy, Harding

800 — Sittin, unattached, 1:53.85; Nelson, UCA; Westover, Harding

800 Relay — Arkansas Tech, 1:28.50 (new meet record); UCA; SAU

Shot put — Force, SAU, 52-10 ½; Fleming, UCA; Brown, UCA

200 — Williams, CofO, 21.44 (new meet record); Woodbury, SAU; McCoy, Harding

Pole vault — Chilton, ATU, 13-6 (ties meet record); VanDerkaaij, Harding; Hicks, SofO

400 IH — Franklin, ATU, 53.09 (ties meet record); White, UCA; Calvin, ATU

5,000 — O'Connor, Harding, 15:53.16; McCohn, Harding; Dietz, AU

1,600 Relay — SAU, 3:14.03; UCA; ATU

High individual scorer was Sammy Epps of SAU with 30 ½ points.

NAIA DISTRICT 18
in Liberty 1983

Men

6-MILE RUN: 1. Barth Winkler, Westminster 30:46.40; 2. Rick Blount, Park 31:51.9; 3. Phil Hoffman, Park 32:23.21.

SHOT PUT: 1. Don Brown, William Jewell 45-½; 2. Neil Sudbrock, Tarkio 44-5½; 3. Calvin Pritchard, School of Ozarks 44.

MILE: 1. Roy Gomez, School of Ozarks 4:24.53; 2. David Mare, Park 4:29.13; 3. Jonathan Vest, Park 4:35.78.

440: 1. Mark Gregory, Park :51.30; 2. Nate Lampkins, School of Ozarks 51:33.3; 3. Jeff Todd, Missouri Valley :52.47.

440 RELAY: 1. Missouri Valley (Bob Fitzpatrick, Paul Johnson, Ewell Gordon, Jeff Todd) 44.04; 2. School of Ozarks, 44.98; 3. Tarkio, 45.54.

POLE VAULT: 1. Sean Fister, Park 15-0; 2. Rick Tucker, Park 14-6.

LONG JUMP: 1. Regie Coulter, William Jewell 21-9¾; 2. Benny Straghorne, School of Ozarks 21-2; 3. Mike Hendricks, Park 20-7.

100: 1. Mike Bedsmie, William Jewell 10.45; 2. Paul Johnson, Missouri Valley 10.46; 3. Trenton Branson, School of Ozarks 10.76.

120 HIGH HURDLES: 1. James Neptune, Park :15.80; 2. Brad Lewis, William Jewell 16:00; 3. Kenny Holstein, School of Ozarks 16:33.

JAVELIN: 1. Steve Spencer, Park 195-2; 2. Ryan Sharkey, Missouri Valley 181-2; 3. Sean Fister, Park 174-3.

880: 1. Ron Chilton, Park 1:59.53; 2. Roy Screws, School of Ozarks 1:59.59; 3. Todd Maier, Park 2:00.52.

220: 1. Mike Bedsmie, William Jewell :22.22; 2. Paul Johnson, Missouri Valley :22.50; 3. David Johnson, Tarkio :22.86.

440 HIGH HURDLES: 1. Brad Lewis, William Jewell :57.15; 2. Doug Schmiel, Tarkio; 3. Bob Granger, Westminster 58.18.

TRIPLE JUMP: 1. Mike Gent, Rockhurst 45-4; 2. Regie Coulter, William Jewell 43-1; 3. Nate Lampkin, School of Ozarks 41-7.

HIGH JUMP: 1. Regie Coulter, William Jewell 6-4; 2. Pat Keller, William Jewell 6-2; 3. Kent Smith, William Jewell 6-0.

3-MILE RUN: 1. Barth Winkler, Westminster 15:09.47; 2. Rick Blount, School of Ozarks 15:22.50; 3. Jonathan Vest, Park 15:24.70.

MILE RELAY: 1. Park (Eddie Hicks, Jim Nelson, Mark Gregory, Ron Chilton); 2. Tarkio 3:31.25; 3. School of Ozarks 3:31.84.

Screws of School of the Ozarks hung on to edge Tech's Tom Dietz (left) down the stretch of the 1,500-meter run.

Winning a hotly contested 1500m on a cold, windy day at Arkansas Tech in 3:57, 1983.

itlook, April 13, 1983, page 4

Continuing to finish strong in the meet, the 'Cats picked up five second-places. Wilbert Daniels ran a 50.7 in the 400 m. dash, behind teammate Burton, and also grabbed second in the 200 m. dash (22.5). Also getting second were the 400 m. relay team of Burton, Benny Strayhorn, Daniels, and anchorman Trenton Brinson (44.2); Mark Hargett in the 400 intermediate hurdles (60.2), and Paul Taylor in the 10,000 m. run (33.23).

n run at St. Louis

e S of O men's and s track team made a it. Louis for the meet irday at Flo Valley. n scores were kept. r teams participated f O fared well.

e men came away : firsts; Reggie Burton ain in the 400 meter 0.2), Kenny Holstine 110 m. high hurdles double winner Ray-icrews, in both the and 1500 m. runs and (4:06.8), respec-ind Calvin Pritchard, field events, the shot cus (44'5" and 125'9" ively.]

The Bobcats showed their depth as they also picked up five third-places; Brinson in the 100 m. dash (11.25), Hargett in the 110 m. high hurdles, Taylor in the 5,000 m. run (16.20), Keith Rogers in the long jump (20'9"), and Rogers again in the triple jump (42'4").

The Bobcats took fourth place three times; Strayhorn in the 100 m. dash (11.8), Mark Bollinger in the 1500 m. run (4:17), and Ed Heuton in the 5,000 m. run (17:32).

The men finished up with two fifths; Bollinger in the 800 m. (2:06) and Holstine in the long jump, and one sixth; Holstine in the triple jump.

On Monday, the 4th, S o O held a home meet in which Loras (of Iowa) and Tulsa University joined the 'Cats in a tri-meet. S of O won with a 99-point total. Loras was next, with 62 points, and Tulsa picked up 15.

The 'Cats had eleven firsts, seven seconds, nine third-places, and four fourth-place finishes.

The men are scheduled to run at Lioncoln University in Jefferson City for their next meet.

Winning a mile race in 4:18 when I was sick, 1983. I was about to vomit here, but never did.

423

Running a 5-mile Cross Country race with the flu in Rolla, MO, 1984. My teammate, Randy Gray has his jacket around is elbows.

Our outstanding School of the Ozarks Track Team, 1982.

Racing Tom Becker in the mile, 1983. I won in a school record.

My first track meet for the School of the Ozarks. I won the 880 at Pittsburg State University, 1982.

Track

College

Triangular at Rolla
Southwest Missouri State 89, Missouri-Rolla 68, School of the Ozarks 30.

400-meter relay — 1, School of the Ozarks. 43.6 seconds.

Shot put — 1, Larry Peuker, SMS, 49 feet 2½ inches; 2, Gorham, Rolla; 3, Gaillard, Rolla; 4, Brad Reynolds, SMS.

3000-meter steeplechase — 1, Mark Branaman, SMS, 9:31.4 minutes; 2, Bullard, Rolla; 3, Bob White, SMS; 4, Hanze, Rolla.

1500-meter run — 1, Raymond Screws, S of O, 4:03.63 minutes; 2, Tom Becker, SMS; 3, Saver, Rolla; 4, Scott Mantooth, SMS.

110-meter high hurdles — 1, Rick Welish, Rolla, :15.45 seconds; 2, Dave Buchert, SMS; 3, Holstein, S of O.

400-meter dash — 1, Mark Snyder, SMS, :49.22 seconds; 2, Burton, S of O; 3, Schoencker, Rolla; 4, Ike, Rolla.

100-meter dash — 1, Troy McClain, SMS, :10.92 seconds; 2, Brinson, S of O; 3, Brian Van Fosson, SMS; 4, Richard Harmon, SMS.

800-meter run — 1, Rod Pixler, SMS, 1:56.7 minutes; 2, Birthwick, Rolla; 3, Terry Schwabe, SMS; 4, Branton White, SMS.

Discus — 1, John Kenneson, SMS, 152 feet 7¾ inches; 2, Gorham, Rolla; 3, Gaillard, Rolla; 4, Peuker, SMS.

Pole vault — 1, Dave Hicks, S of O, 14 feet; 2, Henry, Rolla.

400-meter intermediate hurdles — 1, Rick Welish, Rolla, :56.25; 2, Taylor, Rolla; 3, Doug Adams, SMS; 4, Furtune, Rolla.

Long jump — 1, Troy McClain, SMS, 21 feet 7 inches; 2, Proctor, Rolla; 3, Jim Lockey, SMS; 4, Rogers, S of O.

200-meter run — 1, Mark Snyder, SMS, :22.3 seconds; 2, Troy McClain, SMS; 3, Brian Van Fosson, SMS; 4,

3-22-83

425

Raymond Screws, Senior year, Parsons (Kansas) High School Football, 1979.

Racing the Pepsi Challenge 10K in Springfield, MO, April 1983.

Rozier, Ravens earn awards Arkansas meet

3-81

Mike Rozier, a 1980 Junior College All-American running back, used a toss of 204 feet, 11 inches to win the junior college javelin title at the 1981 Arkansas Relays in Little Rock, Ark.

Rozier, who will transfer to Nebraska next fall, also anchored the 400-meter relay to a third-place finish with a time of 42.8 seconds.

After racing in the mile at Allen Fieldhouse, University of Kansas, 1981.

Joining Rozier on the relay squad was Tim Wilson, freshman running back Melvin Gray and Kenny Mitchell.

Carl Brown was fifth in the mile run with a time of 3:27.3 and Ray Screws was fifth in the 1,500 meter run with a 4:11.0 pace.

Reco Hawkins placed fourth in the 110 low hurdles with a 15.07 while Wilson finished fourth in the long jump with a leap of 23 feet, four inches.

Special to the Journal

DODGE CITY — Hutchinson Community College rolled up 242 team points while running away with the Jayhawk Conference Eastern Division track championship here Wednesday.

Barton County finished in the runner-up spot with 93 points compared to a Coffeyville squad that compiled 40 points and fifth-place status.

Dodge City (68) and Butler County (61) claimed third- and fourth-place honors while Pratt (17) and Neosho County (6) rounded out the team standings.

Coffeyville's Tim Wilson used a leap of 21 feet, 5 inches for second in the long jump and Mel Grey took a pair of third-place medals with an 11.2-second pace in the 100-meter dash and a 22.6 in the 220. Grey also anchored the 400-meter relay team to third place with a 43.3.

Three fifth-place finishes were awarded to Ray Screws (4:09) in the 1500-meter run, Jerome Phillips (52.0) in the 400 and the Red Ravens' 1600-meter relay team, which found Phillipps, Screws, Karl Brown, and Verl McGaughy running a 3:35.

Racing in the 800M at University of Kansas, July 1981.

Me running in the 880 with a bad foot and a farmer's tan, Kansas State University, June 1979.

Here I'm running the third leg of the 4x800 relay at the State Meet at Wichita State University, May 1980.

Showing off one of my medals, 1981.

18 Years Old, 1980.

With my cousin Phillip Mercado, Thanksgiving, 1982.

Ready for a run with John Johnson in Pittsburg, Kansas, Summer 1981.

The School of the Ozarks Cross Country Team, 1981. I'm on the back row next to Coach Osburn.

Parsons Viking seniors, 1979.

Dixon-Williams take top honors

APRIL - 82

Roy Dixon and Willie Williams came out on top Saturday, April 24, at the Southwest State University Relays. Dixon and Williams scored the most individual points to become the first and second most outstanding performers in the relays Saturday.

Dixon is still undefeated in the long jump. Saturday was no different, Dixon took first with a jump of 22'7¼". Teammate Williams joined Dixon in placing the event, taking fourth with a 21'5¼" jump.

Dixon took top honors in his special event, the triple jump, taking first with 45'3".

A member of the 400 m. relay, Dixon again, along with Williams, contributed their talents to take first. Along with Williams and Dixon, Wilbert Daniels, and Trenton Brinson made up the four man team. The team ran an excellent time of 42.26 seconds.

Brinson, Daniels, Williams, and Jerry Goodrich got together and again using their speed and talent took first in the 800 relay. Running the relay in impressive time, the last team member crossed the finish line in 1 minute and 30 seconds.

The men had a long and productive day because once

again Williams, Daniels, Goodrich, along with Nate Lampkin took top honors in the mile relay also. Time for the run was 3 minutes and 25 seconds.

Williams showed his speed by breaking the tape in the 100 m. in 10.6 seconds. Brinson followed close behind for third place in 10.8 seconds.

In the long distances, S of O had three members placing. Ray Screws ran the 1500 m. in 4 minutes .015 seconds to take first.

Paul Taylor showed his strength and endurance by coming in second in the 10,000 m. run. Taylor's time was .33 minutes and 14 seconds.

Running the 5000 m. in good time, was Chris Marcak. Taking third in the event, he ran it in 15 minutes and 30 seconds.

In the remaining field events, Mark Hicks took third in the pole vault. Hick's successful attempt carried him over the bar at 14'6".

Tommy Sanders threw the javelin a 164'4", good enough to place fourth.

Coach Robert Osburn was very pleased with the team's performance. He felt the team had a great day and good team effort.

I'm second from the right in the SMS Relays 1500, April 1982. I won in 4:01.

www.ingramcontent.com/pod-product-compliance
Lightning Source LLC
Chambersburg PA
CBHW070859120626
46546CB00001B/60